Süleymanname

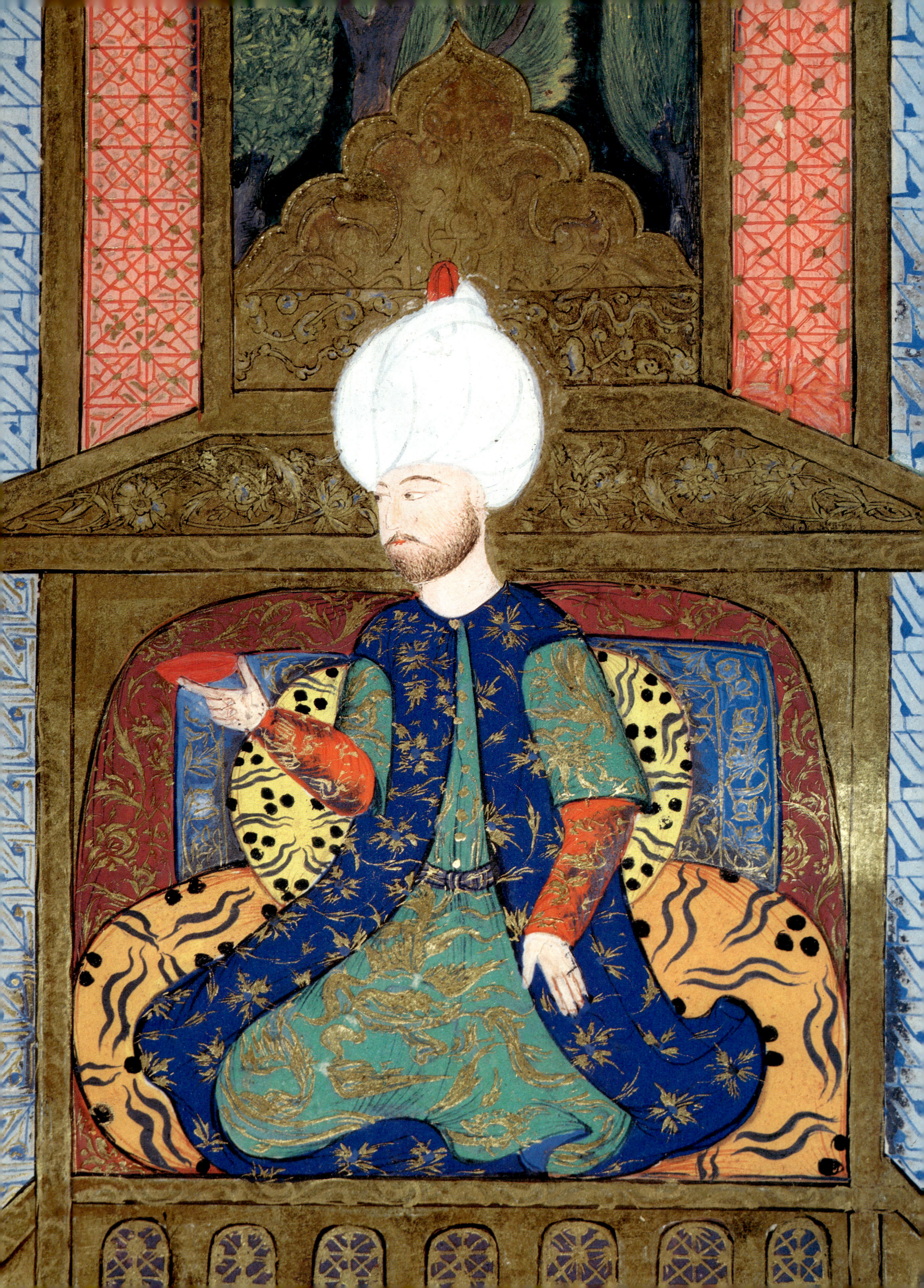

Süleymanname

The Illustrated History
of Süleyman the Magnificent

Esin Atıl

National Gallery of Art, Washington
Harry N. Abrams, Inc., Publishers, New York

Copyright © 1986 Board of Trustees, National Gallery of Art, Washington. All rights reserved. No part of this publication may be reproduced without written permission of the National Gallery of Art, Washington, D.C. 20565.

This book was produced by the Editors Office, National Gallery of Art, Washington.

Color photographs taken by Reha Günay
Edited by Anne Summerscale
Designed by Melanie B. Ness

The clothbound edition is published by Harry N. Abrams, Inc., New York
Printed and bound in Italy by Amilcare Pizzi S.p.A., Milan

Cover: Reception of Barbaros Hayreddin Paşa (detail of illustration on page 168).

Frontispiece: Süleyman Presented with the Ruby Cup (detail of illustration on page 216).

Library of Congress Cataloging-in-Publication Data
Atıl, Esin.
Süleymanname: the illustrated history of Süleyman the Magnificent.
Bibliography: p.
Includes index.
1. Arif Çelebi, d. 1561. Sulaymānnāmah—Illustrations. 2. Turkey—History—Suleiman I, 1520-1555—Pictorial works. 3. Topkapı Sarayı Müzesi. Kütüphane. Manuscript. 160—Illustrations. 4. Illumination of books and manuscripts, Turkish. 5. Topkapı Sarayı Müzesi. Kütüphane. I. Arif Çelebi, d. 1561. Sulaymānnāmah. II. Title.
ND3399.A72A85 1986   745.6'7'09561   85-29676
ISBN 0-89468-088-9 (paper)
ISBN 0-8109-1505-7 (cloth)

Contents

Foreword   7

Acknowledgments   9

Note on Transliteration   10

The Age of Süleyman   11

   Süleyman, the Sultan   15

      Ottoman Society and Institutions   23

      Artistic Production of the Age   31

The Şahnameci and His Works   55

   Şahname-i Al-i Osman   57

     Süleymanname   61

The Plates   79

Appendices   235

   Chronology   235

   Genealogy   238

   Contents of the Süleymanname   239

   Cast of Characters   245

   Location of Events   252

   Payroll Registers of 1557-1558   255

Shortened References   257

Select Bibliography   261

Glossary   265

Index   269

Foreword

THIS PUBLICATION on the *Süleymanname* introduces to a wide public not only one of the masterpieces of sixteenth-century art from Turkey but is itself a twin celebration of the greatest period in Ottoman history and of its greatest sultan, Süleyman the Magnificent. He ruled over a vast and well-governed empire and his glorious achievements were unmatched by those of his contemporaries Charles V, Francis I, Henry VIII and Elizabeth I of England. A treasure carefully preserved in the library of the Topkapı Palace Museum in İstanbul, the *Süleymanname* attests to the perfection and sophistication of the highly refined art of the book, an art form that had been cultivated in the Islamic world since its beginnings.

The publication of this edition together with Dr. Esin Atıl's historical and critical commentary should lead to a new appreciation of this great era and artistic tradition. Dr. Atıl, Guest Curator at the National Gallery of Art for the exhibition *The Age of Sultan Süleyman the Magnificent*, shows how the courtly art of illustrated manuscripts was extended under Süleyman's enlightened patronage to include what she describes as a new mode of documentary realism. For the first time, events in a sultan's life were recorded in the paintings accompanying the text in what became a visual documentary record. Although in some respects the art of manuscript illustration remained conservative, respecting long-established conventions, nevertheless many of the paintings mark an original turn toward accuracy of observation— an art in which the painter becomes more literally a witness.

It is indeed fortunate that the illustrations in the *Süleymanname* are reproduced in facsimile, since the fragility and the uniqueness of the original manuscript have made it almost inaccessible for study. We are grateful to the Koç Group of Turkey, long known for their support of the arts in that country, for the generosity which made possible the design and production of this truly magnificent edition. Their wish to mark their sixtieth anniversary with the publication of this book has given the National Gallery a chance to participate in a scholarly project that will deepen our knowledge and enjoyment of Ottoman art. It presents a welcome opportunity to preview the exhibition, which is devoted to all the arts from Süleyman's reign.

J. CARTER BROWN
Director, National Gallery of Art

Acknowledgments

THIS BOOK IS devoted to the study of the illustrations in Arifi's *Süleymanname*, which recreate many of the events, settings, and personages of Sultan Süleyman's reign. In attempting to provide the political and social background for the paintings, I relied on a number of historical sources, which are listed in the bibliography. Arifi's text was consulted to identify the subjects of the scenes and to determine their chronological sequence. His account requires detailed analysis by scholars who specialize in the historical and literary genres of the period. It is hoped that the publication of this book will prompt a proper study of Arifi's contribution to Ottoman historiography.

I have always been fascinated by the tradition of illustrated Turkish histories. The artists who worked on these texts created a corpus of paintings that not only document the lives and times of their patrons but also combine accuracy with originality, a highly refined aesthetic awareness, and technical virtuosity. All the illustrated histories I studied led me back to the *Süleymanname*, where this courtly tradition originated. It is to the anonymous artists of the *Süleymanname* that this book should be dedicated.

I owe a debt of gratitude to my friends and colleagues Filiz Çağman and Zeren Tanındı, chief curator and assistant curator of the Library of the Topkapı Palace Museum, where I spent many productive and enjoyable months working on illustrated Ottoman manuscripts. They shared their extensive knowledge of the field with me, graciously provided references, and offered constructive criticism. This study on the *Süleymanname* could not have been accomplished without their encouragement and assistance.

I would like to thank Nurettin Yardımcı, General Director of Antiquities in the Ministry of Culture and Tourism of the Republic of Turkey, for kindly granting permission to publish the illustrations in the *Süleymanname*. I would also like to thank Sabahattin Türkoğlu, the Director of the Topkapı Palace Museum; Nazan Tapan-Ölçer, the Director of the Turkish and Islamic Arts Museum; and Erol Pakin, the Director of the İstanbul University Library, for their generosity in making accessible their collections for both research and photography. In addition, I would like to acknowledge the assistance of Reha Günay, Professor of Architecture at Yıldız University, İstanbul, who provided the color transparencies and most of the reference photographs used in the book.

The staff of the National Gallery of Art has been extremely supportive and has enthusiastically participated in the production of the book. I owe special thanks to Melanie B. Ness, the designer; Anne Summerscale, the editor; and Maryrose Smyth, my assistant.

But above all I would like to acknowledge Rahmi Koç, whose corporation sponsored the publication. This book not only commemorates the patronage of Sultan Süleyman the Magnificent but also that of Koç Holding which upholds the tradition of supporting the arts.

E.A.

Note on Transliteration

All Turkish names, places, and titles are spelled according to official modern Turkish orthography. Modern Turkish transliteration is also used for Arabic and Persian words when used within the Turkish context. Non-Turkish names of individuals and cities or regions outside the boundaries of the Republic of Turkey follow English spelling.

The following is a guide to the pronunciation of Turkish words:

c	pronounced "j" as in "John"
ç	pronounced "ch" as in "chair"
ğ	soft guttural, lengthens vowel preceding it
ı	pronounced somewhat like "e" as in open
j	pronounced like the French "j" in "Jacques"
ö	pronounced like the French "eu" as in "peu"
ş	pronounced "sh" as in "shall"
ü	pronounced like the French "u" as in "lune"

When a Turkish term appears for the first time in the text, it is italicized and followed by a translation or an explanation. These terms are also listed in the Glossary.

The following abbreviations are used for collections frequently cited in the notes:

BL	London, The British Library
CB	Dublin, The Chester Beatty Library
DK	Cairo, Dar al-Kuttub
İÜ	İstanbul, İstanbul Üniversite Kütüphanesi
NB	Vienna, Nationalbibliothek
TİEM	İstanbul, Türk ve İslam Eserleri Müzesi
TSM	İstanbul, Topkapı Sarayı Müzesi

The Age of Süleyman

THE TURKS, whose original homeland was in Central Asia, began their infiltration of the central Islamic lands in the second half of the eighth century, entering the service of the caliphs of Baghdad. In the following centuries wave after wave of Turkish tribes moved westward, converted to Islam, and settled in Turkestan, Afghanistan, eastern Iran, and northern India. One of these tribes, the Seljuks, migrated in the eleventh century and established sovereignty over Iran, Iraq, Syria, and Anatolia. The Seljuk state of Anatolia lasted until the beginning of the fourteenth century, when its authority disintegrated and the region became divided among a number of rival Turkish emirates.

The northwestern corner of Anatolia, comprising the ancient province of Bithynia, was claimed by Osman (1299?-1324?) after the collapse of the Seljuk state. Osman founded the Osmanlı, or Ottoman, dynasty in which the rule passed from father to son (or to the eldest male in the family) for over six hundred years; in 1923 this dynasty was replaced by the Republic of Turkey. During the formative years of the Ottoman Empire Osman's descendants took Bursa, which became the first capital; then they moved into İznik (Nicea) and İzmit (Nicodemia), crossed the Dardanelles into Thrace, and entered Edirne (Adrianople), which was chosen as the second capital. The Ottomans soon extended their rule into central, northeastern, and southwestern Anatolia as well as into Macedonia, Bulgaria, and Rumania.

It was during the reign of Mehmed II (1451-1480) that the emirate of Osman became a world power. In 1453 Mehmed, known as the Conqueror, captured Constantinople, the capital of the Byzantine Empire, moved his court there, and founded the Topkapı Palace, which became the administrative seat of the state and symbol of Ottoman power. He then undertook systematic campaigns to expand his realm and to form a protective ring around his new capital, now called İstanbul. In the west his armies swept through Greece, Albania, and Yugoslavia, occupying the Balkans as far as Belgrade. His navy overpowered the Venetians, captured several islands in the Aegean, and landed at Otranto, at the tip of the Italian peninsula. In Anatolia he put an end to the Greek rule in Trabzon (Trebizond), wiped out the remaining Turkish emirates in the south, and inflicted serious defeats upon the Mamluk sultans, who were ruling Syria and Egypt. The Crimea was annexed together with regions bordering the Sea of Azov. The Ottomans were now the rulers of Anatolia and the eastern Balkans, controlling these lands from their court in İstanbul.

After a brief period of consolidation under Bayezid II (1480-1512) the expansion of the Ottoman frontiers continued under subsequent sultans. Selim I (1512-1520) campaigned in the south and southeast; he cap-

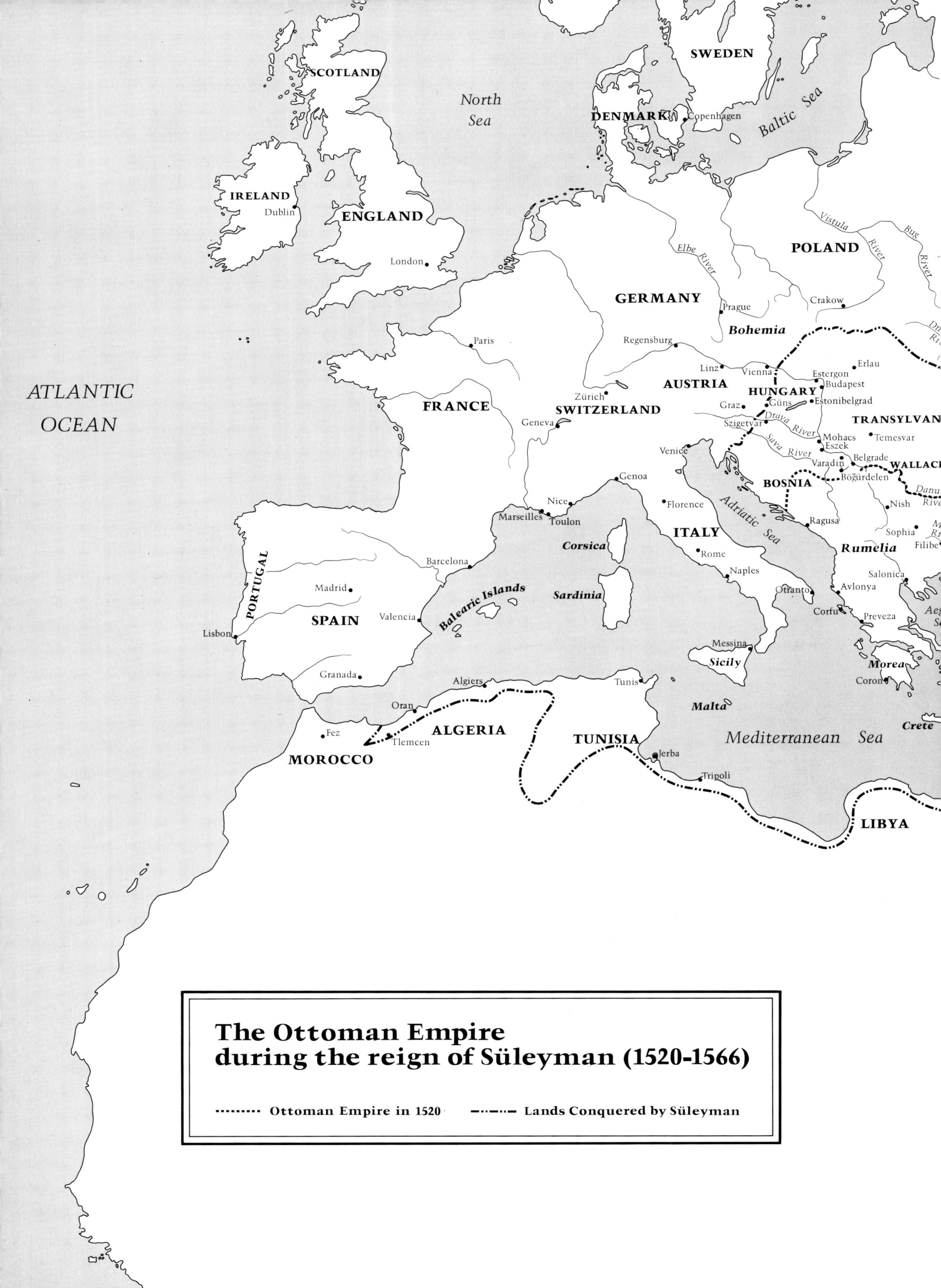

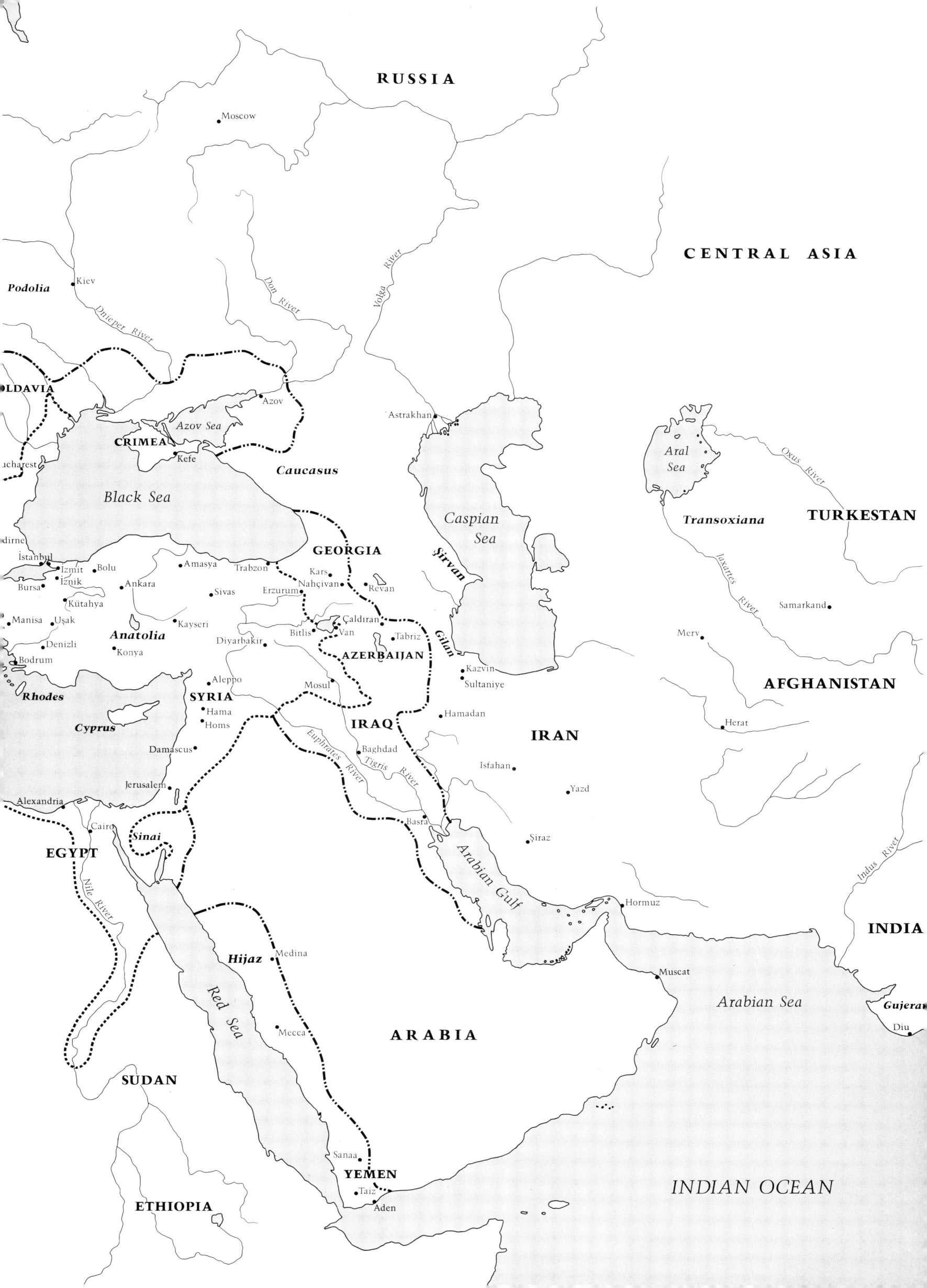

tured Azerbaijan and the Safavid capital of Tabriz, and then defeated the Mamluks at Marj Dabiq and Cairo, incorporating into his empire Syria, Palestine, and Egypt as well as the Hijaz. The Ottoman sultan was now the caliph of Islam and the guardian of Mecca, Medina, and Jerusalem, the three holy cities of the Islamic world, and possessed the great cultural centers of Tabriz, Damascus, and Cairo. The Ottomans were firmly established in the strategic lands linking three continents—Asia, Africa, and Europe—and dominated the surrounding seas.

This powerful and vast empire was Selim's legacy to Süleyman (1520-1566), the tenth ruler of the house of Osman, who was destined to change the course of world history. He was the Ottoman sultan with the longest rule—forty-six years—and the one who more than doubled the boundaries of his realm. At his death the Ottoman Empire extended over 3,364,210 square kilometers (1,227,800 square miles).[1] In the west it embraced Greece, Albania, Bulgaria, Yugoslavia, Rumania, Hungary, and parts of Czechoslovakia, reaching as far as Vienna, the capital of Austria; in the north it controlled the Crimea and the provinces between the Don and the Dnieper rivers; in the east and southeast it extended to the Caspian Sea and included Georgia, Azerbaijan, western Iran, central Islamic lands, and the regions along the Arabian Gulf and the Red Sea; in the south it claimed Egypt, Sudan, Somalia, Ethiopia, and the northern African countries, including Libya, Tunisia, Algeria, and parts of Morocco, extending below the equator. The Black Sea, Arabian Gulf, Red Sea, and the Mediterranean were controlled by the Ottoman navy.

Süleyman, a brilliant military strategist, statesman, and administrator, is known in Turkish as Kanuni (Lawgiver) because of his remarkable activities as a lawmaker. In Europe he is known as Süleyman the Great or the Magnificent due to his truly magnificent political, social, administrative, and cultural achievements.

Süleyman had been superbly trained for the sultanate having been in charge of the *sancaks* (provinces) of Bolu, Kefe (Kaffa), and Manisa since he was fifteen. It was the Ottoman practice to send its princes, accompanied by tutors, at an early age to serve as governors in provinces in order to gain experience in administrative and military affairs.

During his sultanate, Süleyman fought on both the western and eastern fronts, personally leading thirteen campaigns against the Habsburgs, who controlled most of Europe, and the Safavids, who ruled in Iran. Süleyman was the first to take the city of Belgrade, which had resisted a number of Ottoman attacks, and put an end to the crusading Knights of Saint John at Rhodes. He annexed Hungary and besieged Vienna; recaptured Tabriz and took Baghdad, adding Iraq and western Iran to his empire. His fleet, led by the celebrated Barbaros Hayreddin Paşa and other daring admirals, inflicted serious damage on the combined forces of Europe, raiding lands as far as the Indian coast on the Arabian Sea.

Süleyman was born in an age of kings, powerful and influential men destined to shape the world. His military victories, inherited and acquired wealth, and patronage of art and architecture surpassed those of his allies and adversaries. Süleyman's rivals were such great figures as Charles V, the king of Spain (1516-1550) and the emperor of the Holy Roman Empire (1521-1557); Ferdinand, the archduke of Austria who replaced his brother Charles V as emperor (1558-1564); and Louis II, the king of Hungary (1516-1526), who was related to Charles V and Ferdinand by marriage. Another adversary was Şah Tahmasp (1524-1576), the second ruler of the Safavid dynasty of Iran. Among Süleyman's allies were Francis I (1515-1547) and Henry II (1547-1559), the kings of France; John Zapolya (died 1540), the voyvoda of Transylvania, later crowned king of Hungary by the sultan; the kings of Poland; and the hans of the Crimea. It was also the age of great seafarers, including Barbaros Hayreddin Paşa, Seydi Ali Reis, Piri Reis, and Andrea Doria.

Europe in the sixteenth century, despite its energetic leaders, was torn by constant conflict between the Habsburgs, headed by Charles V, and the French, led by Francis I, who had been a contender for the crown of the Holy Roman Empire. England, ruled by Henry VIII, as well as the papacy and the Italian states of Venice, Genoa, and Florence were constantly changing sides. Europe was not only split between the forces of Charles V and Francis I but also divided between the followers of Martin Luther and the pope with Protestantism gradually gaining recognition and power over Catholicism. Süleyman not only allied himself with the French but also supported and protected the Lutherans and Calvinists against the Catholics. By his relentless pressure on the Habsburgs and the papacy he succeeded in perpetuating the state of political disunity in Europe and helped to bring about the official recognition of Protestantism. Hungary, an Ottoman province, became a stronghold of Calvinism, and both Lutherans and Calvinists obtained concessions in France.

Süleyman, the Sultan

Süleyman was born in Trabzon on 6 November 1494[2] while his father Selim was serving there as governor. His mother was Hafsa, thought to be the daughter of the Crimean ruler Mengili Giray Han.[3] The prince lived in Trabzon until 1509, when he was given the sancak of Bolu in northwestern Anatolia; a few months later he was sent to Kefe in the Crimea, where he held the same post for three years. After his father, Selim I, ascended the Ottoman throne in 1512, he was asked to reside in İstanbul while Selim was busy fighting in Anatolia. The following year he was appointed governor of Manisa, where he wrote his earliest work on the administration of justice, the *Siyasetname* (Book of Politics).

During Selim's campaign against the Safavids and Mamluks in 1514 and 1516-1517, Süleyman was asked to serve as regent and move to Edirne to protect the western flanks of the empire. Süleyman was back in Manisa by the time Selim died on 22 September 1520. The crown prince arrived in İstanbul on 30 September and his accession ceremonies took place the following day.[4] Since he did not have any surviving brothers at the time, he was the only heir to the throne.[5]

International politics are a crucial part of the history of Süleyman's era. The sultan was soon to become a central protagonist in European affairs. Shortly before his accession Charles V, the Habsburg king of Spain, and Francis I, the Valois king of France, were contending for the crown of the Holy Roman Empire. When Charles V was elected Holy Roman Emperor in 1521, war broke out between the two rivals and Europe became divided. Süleyman took advantage of the situation and launched the first of his thirteen *sefer-i hümayuns* (imperial campaigns), nine of which were directed against the Habsburgs, most of them against Ferdinand, who repeatedly invaded Hungary and Transylvania, attempting to extend his rule into these regions.

Süleyman's first official acts after becoming sultan were to release the confiscated goods of Iranian merchants and free some 600 prisoners taken during his father's campaign to Tabriz. He then started preparations for his first imperial campaign. Before he could embark on this mission the sultan had to settle an internal problem involving Canberdi Gazali, the former Mamluk commander appointed *beylerbeyi* (governor-general) of Syria, who had misjudged the youthfulness and presumed inexperience of the new ruler by rebelling and capturing towns in Syria and Palestine. Hayırbay, the beylerbeyi of Egypt, remained loyal to the sultan and was instrumental in preventing the spread of Gazali's revolt. Ferhad Paşa, dispatched from İstanbul to put an end to the Gazali rebellion, succeeded in killing the rebel outside of Damascus in the winter of 1521.

The murder of the Ottoman ambassador to the Hungarian court by Louis II provided Süleyman with the pretext to march into Hungary. Riding at the head of his army, Süleyman entered Belgrade on 29 August 1521, securing the Ottoman frontier along the southern reaches of the Danube.

His second imperial campaign was directed against Rhodes, which was controlled by the Knights of Saint John, who had settled there in 1308 after their expulsion from Palestine. The formidable fortress of Rhodes fell on 21 December 1522 after a long and fierce battle involving both the Ottoman army headed by Süleyman and the navy commanded first by Mustafa Paşa, then by Ahmed Paşa. In defeating the last Christian stronghold in the Islamic world, Süleyman gained control in the Aegean. The knights reestablished themselves in the west by building an equally strong fortress on the island of Malta, given to them by Charles V, and continued their attacks against the Ottomans.

Süleyman's spectacular victories over Belgrade and Rhodes within the first two years of his reign sent shock waves throughout Europe. Both fortresses had withstood previous attacks by his predecessors, including Mehmed II. The young sultan had proved to be an even more able commander, moving swiftly to remove obstacles in his quest for complete control of eastern Europe and the Mediterranean.

In the following year the sultan had to contend with an uprising in Egypt. Süleyman had by-passed the second vezir Ahmed Paşa to appoint his old and trusted friend İbrahim as the grand vezir, giving the province of Egypt to Ahmed Paşa. Ahmed Paşa felt slighted and rebelled. İbrahim Paşa quickly put down the uprising and restored Ottoman control over this important province.

Before long the sultan was drawn back into European affairs. He formed an alliance with the French, which was the first in a series of political, commercial, and cultural relations between the two powers. Francis I, who had been defeated and imprisoned by Charles V, sent an envoy to İstanbul in 1525 with letters from him and his mother, Louise of Savoy, asking Süleyman for help in preventing Charles V from controlling Europe. Süleyman's celebrated answer is indicative of his awareness of his destiny and the pride he felt in his empire and the achievements of his forefathers:

> I, the sultan of sultans, the leader of the lords, the crown of the sovereigns of the earth, the shadow of God in the two worlds [that is, the caliph of Islam], the sultan and padişah [chief among şahs] of the Mediterranean, Black Sea, Rumelia, Anatolia, Karaman, Dulkadır, Diyarbakır, Azerbaijan, Iran, Syria, Egypt, Mecca, Medina, all the Arab lands—which were conquered by myself—[I] am Sultan Süleyman, the son of Selim Han, the son of Bayezid Han.

> And you Francis, the king of the province of France, have sent a letter to my court with your able man Frajan[6] together with verbal communications informing that the enemy has entered your country and imprisoned you, asking for my grace and support, hoping for your freedom. Whatever you have said has been relayed to me. Now, it is not befitting for rulers to cower and to be imprisoned. Keep your spirits high, do not be heartbroken. Our glorious ancestors have never refrained from expelling the enemy and conquering lands. I also follow in their footsteps, conquering nations and mighty fortresses with my horse saddled and my sword girthed night and day. May God bestow charity to you. You will learn our decision from your man.[7]

These words were not spoken in vain, for in the spring of the next year Süleyman, leading his third imperial campaign, marched into Hungary, which was allied with the Habsburgs. Louis II's forces were annihilated within two hours during the Battle of Mohacs on 29 August 1526. Süleyman entered Budapest, where he received John Zapolya, the voyvoda of Transylvania, who had joined the Ottoman army. Zapolya was now rewarded by being installed as the king of Hungary.

In the next two years the sultan was to be occupied with yet another internal revolt, which spread to eastern Anatolia. The rebellion led by Kalender included shiites and was supported by Şah Tahmasp of Iran, himself a shiite. Once again the grand vezir İbrahim Paşa was dispatched to confront the insurgents and succeeded in quelling the rebellion.

Meanwhile on the western front Ferdinand claimed himself the rightful heir to the throne of Hungary, captured Budapest, and expelled Zapolya. Conflict over Hungary would continue until the death of Ferdinand, who would attack and seize major fortresses as soon as the Ottomans withdrew or were involved with eastern campaigns.

Süleyman gathered his forces, marched into Hungary, and reinstalled Zapolya in Budapest. He then continued on to Vienna, the capital of Austria, besieging the city for two weeks between 26 September and 16 October 1529. This advance presented perhaps the most serious threat the Habsburgs had ever faced. The Ottomans had been able to move straight into the heart of Europe without any opposition. Charles V and Ferdinand refused to be drawn into battle and pulled back. Since winter was approaching and Süleyman had left his heavy artillery in Belgrade, Mohacs, and Budapest, he lifted the siege and headed home. He had made his point clear: there was no force strong enough to face the sultan and Hungary belonged to the Ottomans. During the siege of Vienna, the *akıncıs* (raiders) swept through Austria and Bohemia without any opposition from the Habsburgs.

The conflict over Hungary was resumed when Ferdinand and Süleyman failed to resolve their differences through diplomatic channels, and the Austrians besieged Budapest again. During his fifth campaign to the west in 1532, Süleyman's most notable conquest was the capture of Güns. The following year the two rulers signed a treaty, which provided a brief halt in Habsburg-Ottoman hostilities.

Now the sultan was free to attend to the problems in the Mediterranean and in the east. While Süleyman was campaigning in Austria, Andrea Doria, a Genoese admiral who shifted his allegiance from Francis I to Charles V, had attacked several Ottoman ports in Algeria and Greece. To the great embarrassment of the Turks he had captured the fortress of Coron in the Morea. Upon returning to İstanbul, the sultan summoned to the capital Barbaros Hayreddin Paşa, a formidable Turkish seaman and conqueror of Algeria. Barbaros Hayreddin Paşa was asked to take over the naval forces and made *kaptan-ı derya* (grand admiral). Under his leadership, the Ottoman navy sailed from victory to victory, converting the Mediterranean into a Turkish lake. His first accomplishment was to capture Coron and Tunis; then he undertook systematic raids on the coastal towns of Italy and Spain.

Assured that the Mediterranean was in good hands, Süleyman now turned to the east. The Ottoman governor of Bitlis had joined the Safavids, a cause of serious concern in the court. Süleyman embarked on his sixth campaign (1534-1536) accompanied by İbrahim Paşa, who had recently been given the title of *serasker* (commander in chief of the army), the prerogative until now of only the sultan. The Ottomans entered Tabriz and then Baghdad, annexing Azerbaijan and Iraq. Several Iranian governors had joined the Ottomans, including the rulers of Gilan and Şirvan as well as Sam Mirza, one of the brothers of Şah Tahmasp. Although İbrahim Paşa was successful in supporting the imperial forces, he was accused of abusing his privileged position and undermining the authority of the sultan. After returning to İstanbul, Süleyman took the advice of his ministers and had İbrahim executed for treason.

Meanwhile the sultan concluded a treaty with the French to join forces in attacking the Habsburgs in the Mediterranean. In the spring of 1537 Süleyman moved into Albania and Greece, and besieged the fortress on the island of Corfu as a prelude to the invasion of Italy. The fortress held out and Süleyman was forced to lift the siege.

The following year the sultan embarked on his eighth campaign, which resulted in the annexation of southern Moldavia. While the sultan was occupied with this campaign, the greatest Ottoman victory at sea took place. On 28 September 1538, Barbaros Hayreddin Paşa confronted at Preveza the joint forces of the Holy Roman Empire, the papacy, and the Italian states of Venice, Genoa, and Florence in addition to ships supplied by Portugal and the Knights of Malta. The spectacular 600-piece armada carrying 60,000 men was commanded by Andrea Doria. Within five hours Barbaros Hayreddin Paşa emerged as the victor, inflicting such a devastating blow on the Europeans that they did not recover for four decades. This ended any hope of containing Ottoman power in the Mediterranean. The Ottoman victory initiated the great age of Turkish supremacy at sea; daring captains and commanders claimed Mediterranean ports, sailed uncontested in the Indian Ocean, and landed in Gujerat in 1538. The period between 1520 and 1540 was one of continuous victories for Süleyman, who had proven that he was indeed the Grand Turk and the Magnificent.

The contest for supremacy in Hungary resumed when John Zapolya died in 1540 leaving an infant son on the throne. Ferdinand, quick to take advantage of the situation, moved in and besieged Budapest. Süleyman was compelled to recapture the city and formally annex Hungary, which in 1541 became a province controlled by an Ottoman beylerbeyi.

Yet another siege of Budapest by the Austrians forced the sultan to embark on his tenth campaign in 1543. Meanwhile Barbaros Hayreddin Paşa, sent to aid the French in Marseilles, was attacking Nice and other ports on the Mediterranean. Süleyman secured his sovereignty over Budapest and went on to conquer Pecs, Estergon (Esztergom), and Estonibelgrad (Székesfehérvár). Upon returning to İstanbul he appointed Rüstem Paşa as the new grand vezir.

In 1547 Süleyman signed a five-year peace treaty with the Habsburgs in which Ferdinand was allowed to keep a portion of Hungary, paying in return a yearly tribute. In the same year the Franco-Ottoman alliance was renewed by Henry II, who had succeeded Francis I and was convinced that his monarchy would survive against Charles V only with the sultan's support.

Süleyman was now free to confront the problem posed by the Safavids, who had taken Tabriz and were ravaging Georgia. In the same year Elkas Mirza, a brother of Tahmasp, arrived in the Ottoman court after an unsuccessful insurrection against the şah and offered his services to the sultan. When Süleyman embarked on his eleventh campaign (1548-1549), Elkas was sent with an army to fight against the şah's forces. He advanced into Hamadan and Isfahan while Süleyman recaptured Tabriz, Van, and most of Georgia.

As soon as Süleyman withdrew his forces and returned to İstanbul, Tahmasp began attacking Erzurum and Van, compelling the sultan to launch his twelfth campaign (1553-1555), the third against the Safavids. The war with Iran resulted in the conquest of Nahçivan (Nakhichevan) and Revan (Erivan). Süleyman decided to spend the winter of 1555 in Amasya, where peace treaties with the Habsburgs and Safavids were signed. The Habsburg delegation, headed by Ogier Ghiselin de Busbecq,[8] obtained a six-month cease-fire; and the Safavids reached an agreement on their boundaries.

During the 1550s Süleyman was faced with family problems and lost two of his sons. Şehzade (Prince) Mustafa, his eldest son, was extremely popular with the soldiers and was accused of plotting to usurp him. Mustafa was killed by the royal executioners when he came to see his father at Aktepe, near Konya, on 6 October 1553. Cihangir, Süleyman's ailing youngest son, was so distressed at the execution of his brother that he fell ill and died the following month. Shortly after, a man in Salonica claimed Mustafa's identity, gathered a force, and started an uprising against the sultan. Süleyman dispatched one of his vezirs, Mehmed Paşa, who caught the pretender and brought him to İstanbul to be tried.

Although there was sporadic fighting on the western front in subsequent years, the Habsburgs ceased to be a major threat after the death of Charles V in 1558 and Süleyman did not lead an imperial campaign for some ten years. He was desolated by the loss of his beloved wife Hürrem, who died in 1558, and torn by the feud between his sons, Bayezid and Selim, which developed into a civil war by the spring of 1559. The battle at Konya resulted in the defeat of Bayezid, who fled with his four sons to the court of Tahmasp. Tahmasp held them for ransom and eventually sold them to the Ottomans for a substantial sum. In 1561 Bayezid and his sons were delivered to an Ottoman delegation in Kazvin and promptly executed.

In 1565 the Ottoman navy attempted and failed to capture Malta, the domain of the Knights of Saint John since their expulsion from Rhodes. The attack was commanded by Turgud Reis, who lost his life in the battle.

In the same year problems developed on the Ottoman-Austrian frontier and Süleyman embarked on his thirteenth sefer-i hümayun, leaving İstanbul in May 1566. This was his seventh campaign to bring Hungary fully within his control, an ambition he had been seeking to realize since the first year of his sultanate. The army arrived at Szigetvar on 6 August and besieged the fortress for a month. He died shortly after midnight on 7 September, a few hours before the fall of Szigetvar. His death was kept a secret from the army by the grand vezir, Sokollu Mehmed Paşa, until the crown prince Selim arrived from Anatolia to claim the sultanate and took command of the Ottoman forces outside Belgrade. Süleyman's body was taken to İstanbul and buried behind the Süleymaniye Mosque.

Although a number of regions were annexed by his descendants, extending Ottoman rule into Poland in the west and the Caucasus in the east, the lands conquered by Süleyman formed the core of the Ottoman Empire for centuries to come. The only impediments to the great expansion that took place during his long reign were Hormuz, Malta, and Vienna, which formed the outermost boundaries of his great empire.

Süleyman was considered to have been born under the most auspicious circumstances and was associated with two lucky numbers, ten and twelve. He was the tenth direct descendant of the house of Osman and reigned in the tenth century of the Hijra; he was also the twelfth ruler as there were two other Ottomans, Emir Süleyman and Emir Musa, who occupied the throne during the interregnum of 1402 to 1413. In addition he was associated with Solomon, the Old Testament patriarch, after whom he was named, Süleyman being the Turkish version of Solomon. According to tradition, his name was chosen when the Koran was opened at random and exposed the verse beginning with "It is from Solomon" (XXVII: 30). It was believed that Süleyman was the second Solomon, matching him in fame, wealth, wisdom, and justice.

Süleyman is described in contemporary sources as being a handsome, tall, slender, and well-built man with an oval face, hazel eyes, and straight nose. His bearing was imposing, regal, and self-confident; he enjoyed scholarly discourse and was an articulate conversationalist.[9]

Baron Busbecq, the Austrian ambassador to the court who met Süleyman in 1555 in Amasya when the sultan was over sixty, describes him as follows:

> ... his expression, as I have said, is anything but smiling, and has a sternness, which, though sad, is full of majesty ... he is beginning to feel the weight of the years, but his dignity of demeanour and his general physical appearance are worthy of the ruler of so vast an empire.[10]

Historians agree that Süleyman was the epitome of physical and moral virtues. He won the love and respect of his officials and subjects; he was a righteous ruler, always thinking of the welfare of the state, even to the extent of sacrificing his sons and favorite grand vezirs. He chose the best men available to fill the posts in the administration, ranking experience and competence above all.

The sultan was very fond of hunting and would take time off to engage in this sport during campaigns. He often visited his favorite hunting grounds outside Edirne and Aleppo and asked his sons to join him on these excursions.

Süleyman was by training a goldsmith, following the tradition of the Ottoman house that every ruler had to have a practical trade. He was well versed in Arabic, Persian, and Çağatay (Eastern Turkish) and was an accomplished poet, writing in Persian and Turkish under the pseudonym Muhibbi (meaning "beloved friend"). In addition he was a great builder and patron of the arts, which during his long and dynamic reign reached innovative and productive levels unmatched before and after.

But above all he was a legislator and determined the administrative and fiscal laws that regulated the state and its subjects. Although the *şeriat* (Islamic law) was the law of the empire, the Ottoman sultans asserted the right to issue *fermans* (decrees) on matters not covered in Islamic traditions. These fermans became the *kanuns* (sultanic laws) of the empire. Collected and codified under *Kanunname-i Al-i Osman* (Laws of the House of Osman), they formed the basis of much modern constitutional law. Süleyman's formulations of hundreds of legislative acts earned him the title Kanuni. His laws covered every subject from landrights, taxation, concessions given to foreign merchants, and war treaties to endowments of social and charitable institutions.[11]

Shortly after his accession Süleyman married Hürrem[12] whose devotion to him and her children was unfailing. She is thought to have been of Ukrainian or Slavic descent, born to an impoverished priest around 1500 or 1504 in the town of Rogatino in Galicia, then a province of Poland. Known as Roxelane or La Rossa by the Europeans, who thought she was of Russian origin, the girl must have been enslaved during one of the Ottoman raids in Galicia and the Ukraine and sold to the court. She was given the name Hürrem (meaning "happy and smiling") since she had a radiant and joyous personality. She must have met Süleyman while he was in Kefe. Süleyman adored his wife and remained devoted to her throughout his life. Their legendary love is known through the letters exchanged while he was away on campaigns[13] and through the lyrical poems he composed in praise of her, which are included in his *Divan*.[14]

Before meeting Hürrem, Süleyman's *haseki* (favorite) was Gülbahar, who had given birth to Mustafa in 1515. The sultan appears to have had another haseki by the name of Gülfem. Hürrem, however, felt threatened only by Gülbahar, the mother of Süleyman's first son and the heir apparent to the throne. Their bitter rivalry was controlled by the efforts of Hafsa Sultan, the queen mother. After her death in 1534, Hürrem was free to dispose of Gülbahar; she convinced the sultan to send her away to join her son Mustafa, then the governor of Manisa. Gülbahar died in 1581, outliving Hürrem by some two decades.

Hürrem set a precedent in Ottoman history by insisting on residing in the Topkapı Palace to be near her husband. Up to that time the women lived in the Old Palace in the Bayezid district of İstanbul, and the Topkapı Palace, known then as the New Palace, was reserved for the administrative and educational activities of the empire. Hürrem's move to the Topkapı Palace around 1550 led to the development of the institution of the Harem, the residents of which exerted tremendous influence on the affairs of the state by their proximity to the sultans in subsequent years.

The marriage of Süleyman and Hürrem was also an unusual event in Ottoman history. With the exception of a few earlier sultans, who married for political reasons the daughters of neighboring states, this practice had been abandoned since the end of the fourteenth century.[15] The sultans were free to bestow their attentions on whom they desired among the women in the Harem; the first to give birth to a son rose in the ranks to become a haseki, her position second only to the *valide sultan* (queen mother) in the hierarchy. However, it is highly possible that Selim I married Hafsa,[16] who was not a slave but the daughter of the han of the Crimea.

After their marriage Hürrem gave birth to five sons and a daughter: Mehmed, the sultan's favorite and his chosen heir apparent; Abdullah who died at the age of four; Mihrimah, his only daughter, who married in

1539 the grand vezir Rüstem Paşa; Selim, who succeeded to the throne in 1566 being the only living son at the time of Süleyman's death; Bayezid, accused of inciting a civil war and executed with his sons after fleeing to the Safavid court; and Cihangir, a crippled and sensitive child. Very little is known about the sultan's other offspring. Historians mention Mahmud and Murad in addition to two unknown daughters whose mothers were not recorded.

As was customary in the Ottoman dynasty, the princes were sent at a very early age to serve as governors in the provinces; this gave them first-hand experience and training in military and administrative affairs. Süleyman assigned several sancaks to his sons, who were also given military commands during campaigns and appointed as regents in İstanbul or Edirne while he was engaged in battles along the frontiers. Mustafa was first sent to Manisa, then transferred to Amasya, and served as regent in İstanbul; Mehmed served in Manisa and took part in the Danubian campaign of 1537; Selim was the governor of Manisa, Konya, and Kütahya, served as regent in İstanbul, and accompanied his father in many campaigns; Bayezid was sent to Konya, Kütahya, and Amasya, joined his father during the 1541 conquest of Budapest, and was regent in İstanbul and Edirne; and Cihangir served in Aleppo, the sultan's favorite provincial outpost, and was with Süleyman during the 1553 Nahçivan campaign.

Historians agree that Hürrem had a strong influence on the sultan. She eliminated those who threatened her status in the court. She is said to have been instrumental in the execution of İbrahim Paşa, a confidant and trusted friend of the sultan since their teenage years and the husband of his sister Hadice; she schemed the expulsion of the grand vezir Hadım Süleyman Paşa in favor of her son-in-law Rüstem Paşa; and she instigated the elimination of another grand vezir, Kara Ahmed Paşa, in order to reinstate Rüstem Paşa in the position. Hürrem was thought to have also persuaded the sultan to execute his eldest son, Mustafa, on the ground of treason.

Throughout her life Hürrem strove with great determination to preserve her position in the palace and to secure the sultanate for her own sons.[17] She was not only shrewd and scheming, but also highly intelligent and personable, retaining the unfaltering devotion of her husband. She must have been educated to participate in the life of the court and she composed easily and fluently in Turkish, as is evident in her letters to the sultan.[18]

Hürrem appears to have been unwell when she spent the winter of 1557-1558 with Süleyman in Edirne. She died on 15 April 1558 upon their return to İstanbul and was buried behind the Süleymaniye Mosque. Süleyman was deeply affected by her death and soon began to suffer from ill health, the nature of which is not clearly known.

Süleyman was seriously ill when he embarked on his last campaign in 1566 and could barely sit on a horse.[19] He rode most of the time in a carriage but insisted on mounting his horse to ride at the head of his army and encourage his soldiers when they passed through towns and arrived at Szigetvar.

During the siege of the fortress Süleyman lay sick in his tent, worried about the long battle and its effect on his men. When he died on the eve of the fall of Szigetvar on 7 September, the grand vezir Sokollu Mehmed Paşa felt that the announcement of his death would demoralize the army or, worse still, start an uprising until the new sultan was present.

He sent word to the crown prince Selim, who was serving in Kütahya, requesting him to come to Belgrade to meet the army. Sokollu Mehmed Paşa had a Bosnian by the name of Hasan Ağa, who resembled Süleyman, impersonate the sultan until Selim arrived. Süleyman's last rites were performed in secret, his entrails buried near his tent, his body embalmed and placed in a coffin kept hidden from the army. Hasan Ağa, dressed in Süleyman's clothes, rode in a carriage, pretending to be the ailing sultan. Another official, Cafer Ağa, whose handwriting was similar to that of Süleyman, issued the sultan's written orders. Sokollu Mehmed Paşa delayed the army for over forty days in Szigetvar, moving out only when he was assured that Selim had arrived in Belgrade.

When Selim received news of Süleyman's death, he departed immediately, stopping briefly in İstanbul, where he formally took over the sultanate on 30 September. Then, riding at great speed, he crossed the Balkans in fifteen days and arrived in Belgrade.

Sokollu Mehmed Paşa announced the death of Süleyman when the army was four marching days from Belgrade. Renowned for their absolute discipline, the Ottoman soldiers went wild; they shouted, cried, and mourned the loss of their great leader who had led them from one victory to another for almost half a century. Order was resumed by sunrise and the soldiers solemnly fell back into their ranks. They marched quietly into Belgrade bearing in their midst the coffin of their beloved sultan. When they entered the city on 26 October they were met by Selim II, who led the prayers for the deceased.[20]

A few days later the soldiers moved out of Belgrade, proceeding toward İstanbul. The grieving residents of cities, towns, and villages lined the roads as the cortege passed by, paying their respects to their great sultan. When the army arrived in the capital on 28 November, Süleyman's body was finally laid to rest. He was buried behind the Süleymaniye Mosque,[21] next to the mausoleum of Hürrem, with the last religious rites led by Ebussuud Efendi, the *şeyhülislam* (chief enforcer of the Islamic law).[22]

Süleyman must have known that Szigetvar was his last campaign. He was seventy-two years old at the time, seriously ill, and had not led the army for over ten years; but he insisted that he himself command the Ottoman forces. If his wish had been to die on the field as a true *gazi* (warrior of the faith), his wish was fulfilled.

Ottoman Society and Institutions

When Süleyman ascended the Ottoman throne at the age of twenty-six in 1520 he inherited a phenomenal military and administrative machinery which, with the continued availability of able grand vezirs and commanders, enabled him to take advantage of the disunity among the European powers and to realize his territorial ambitions. The sultan's dynamism coupled with an impeccable system of centralized administration established by his predecessors brought Ottoman power to its highest point and provided the basis for a cultural explosion.

The Ottoman state was governed by a highly structured administration, at the head of which was the sultan. The grand vezir was the representative of the sultan's executive authority and thus held the highest attainable post among the administrators. The şeyhülislam, who represented the sultan's religious authority, headed the *ulema* (learned men) who were in charge of judicial and educational affairs.

The recruitment and training of administrative and military personnel were uniquely Ottoman in practice although by no means original in concept, having been employed to a certain extent by a number of earlier Islamic states. Some members of the central administration were themselves the children of administrators but the majority were recruited through the *devşirme* system in which non-Muslim boys were taken from impoverished rural areas in the Christian provinces and trained to serve the state. The largest group was absorbed into the army and the Janissary Corps while others were sent either to the provincial courts or to the palace to receive a superb education that enabled them to fill the highest positions in the empire. They became important officers in the palace, military commanders, governors, and even rose to the rank of grand vezir.

Almost all the grand vezirs of the empire had risen from the devşirme ranks and many married royal princesses. Among them were the celebrated grand vezirs İbrahim, who married Süleyman's sister Hadice; Rüstem, who married Mihrimah, the sultan's only daughter; and Sokollu Mehmed, who married the sultan's granddaughter Esmahan and remained grand vezir under Selim II and Murad III.

This system enabled the sultan to have a fresh supply of highly trained and totally dedicated administrators and military personnel whose loyalty to the sovereign was unquestioning. They had no allegiance to race or creed and their existence was devoted to serving the state.

The Palace

The palace not only functioned as the administrative center of the state but also served as the institution in which the elite was educated. Its organizational structure was mirrored in the provincial courts, which also combined administrative and educational responsibilities. The institution of the palace was divided into the Birun (Outer Service), Enderun (Inner Service), and Harem. Its organizational structure is clearly reflected in the plan of the Topkapı Palace.[23] Founded in 1459 by Mehmed II with new courtyards, buildings, terraces, and gardens added by subsequent sultans, it was the seat of the government until the mid-nineteenth century.[24]

figure 1

The vast palace occupied the northern tip of the peninsula overlooking the Golden Horn, Bosphorus, and Marmara Sea. To those in the palace it provided a magnificent view of İstanbul; to the world it proclaimed Ottoman power and dominance over the city that had been chosen as the capital by all its previous rulers. The palace is thought to have had a staff of up to 20,000 of which some 4,000 or 5,000 lived on the premises. Originally called the New Palace, it later came to be known as the Topkapı (Cannon Gate) Palace after one of its gates. It was conceived from the beginning as the educational and administrative heart of the empire and designed as a fortified structure with high walls and massive gates leading into three consecutive courtyards. A fourth courtyard and a major portion of the Harem were added in the next century.

The first courtyard, entered through the Bab-ı Hümayun (Imperial Gate), was open to the public. It functioned as a service area with facili-

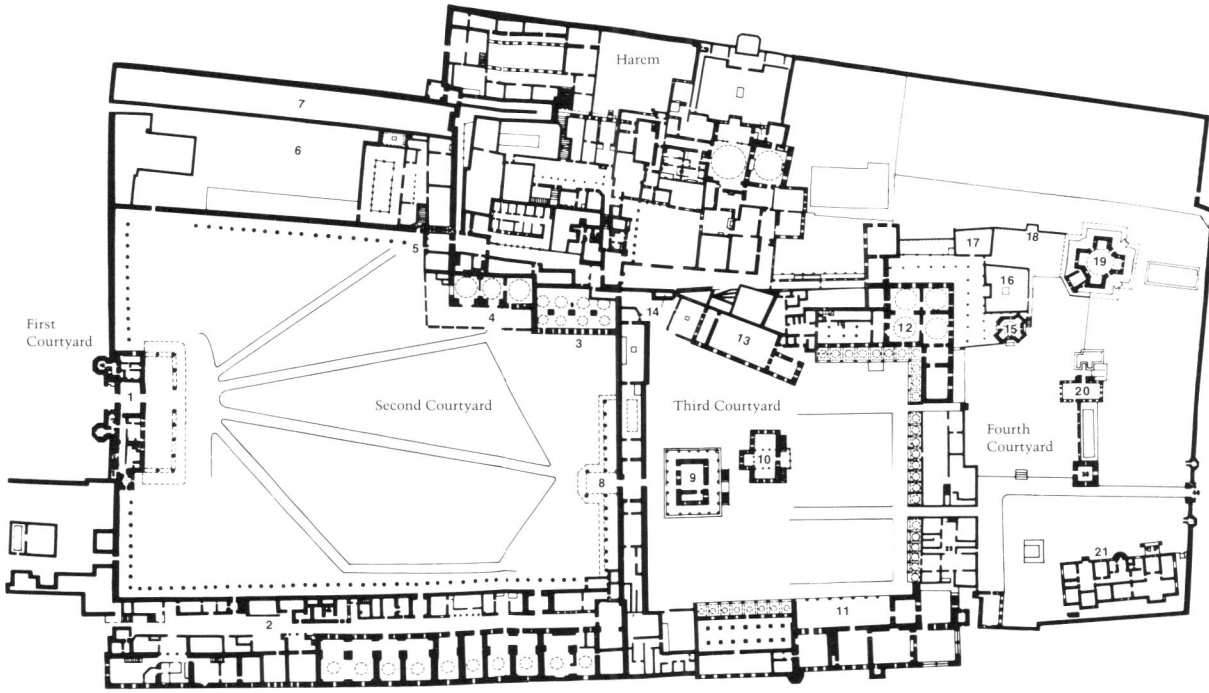

1. Babüsselam (Gate of Salutations)
2. Imperial Kitchens
3. İç Hazine (Inner Treasury)
4. Kubbealtı (Chamber of the Divan-ı Hümayun)
5. Araba Kapısı (Carriage Door)
6. Has Ahır (Imperial Stables)
7. Raht Hazinesi (Harness Treasury)
8. Babüssaade (Gate of Felicity)
9. Arz Odası (Reception Room)
10. Library of Ahmed III
11. Hazine (Imperial Treasury)
12. Has Oda (Privy Chamber)
13. Ağalar Camii (Mosque of the Ağas)
14. Kuşhane Kapısı (Birdcage Door)
15. Revan Köşkü (Revan Pavilion)
16. Pool
17. Sünnet Odası (Circumcision Room)
18. İftariye (Domed Baldachin)
19. Bağdat Köşkü (Baghdad Pavilion)
20. Sofa Köşkü (Pavilion of Ahmed III)
21. Mecidiye Köşkü (Pavilion of Abdülmecid)

1. Topkapı Palace: plan (above) and general view (below).

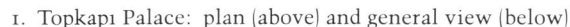

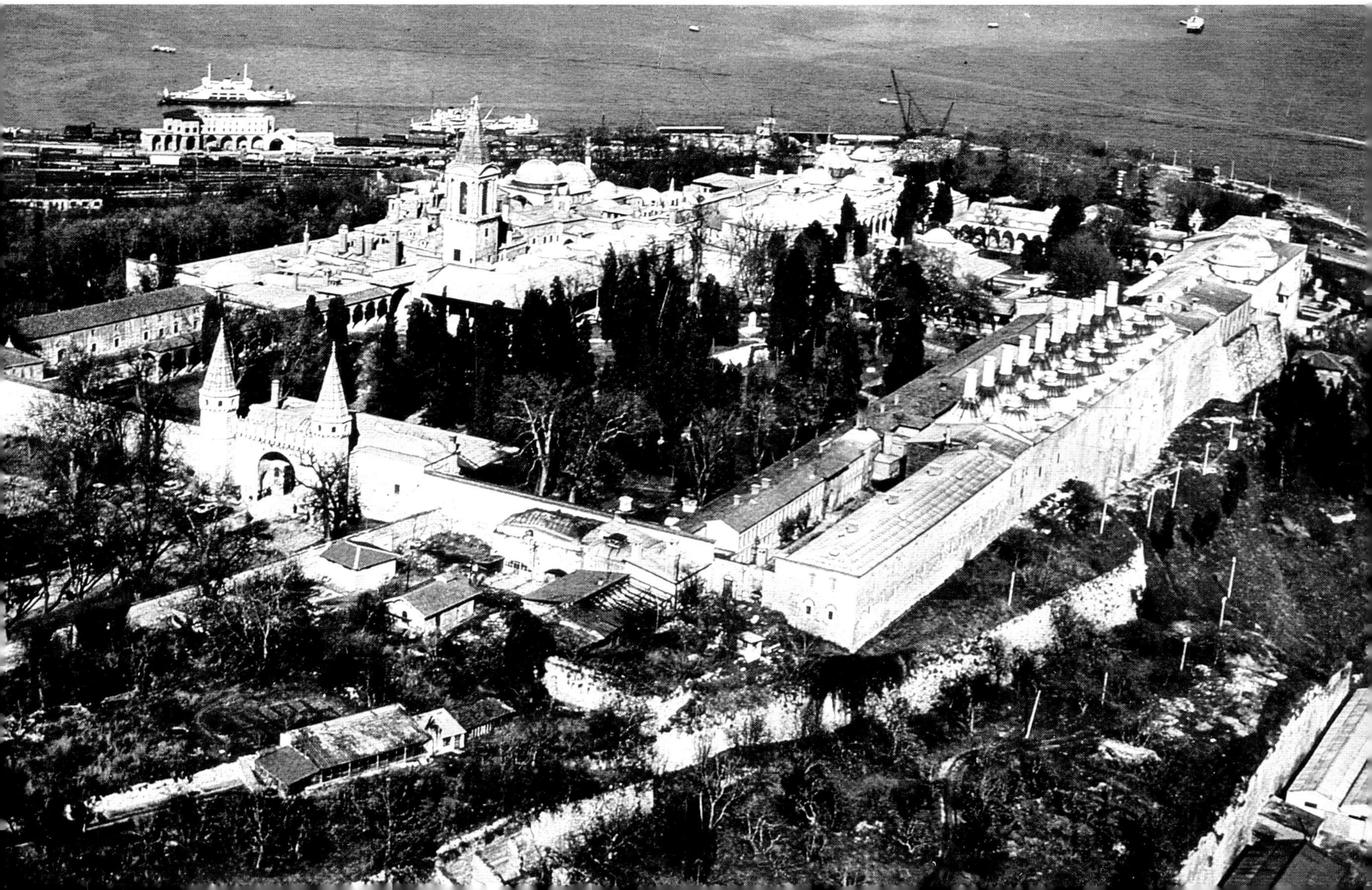

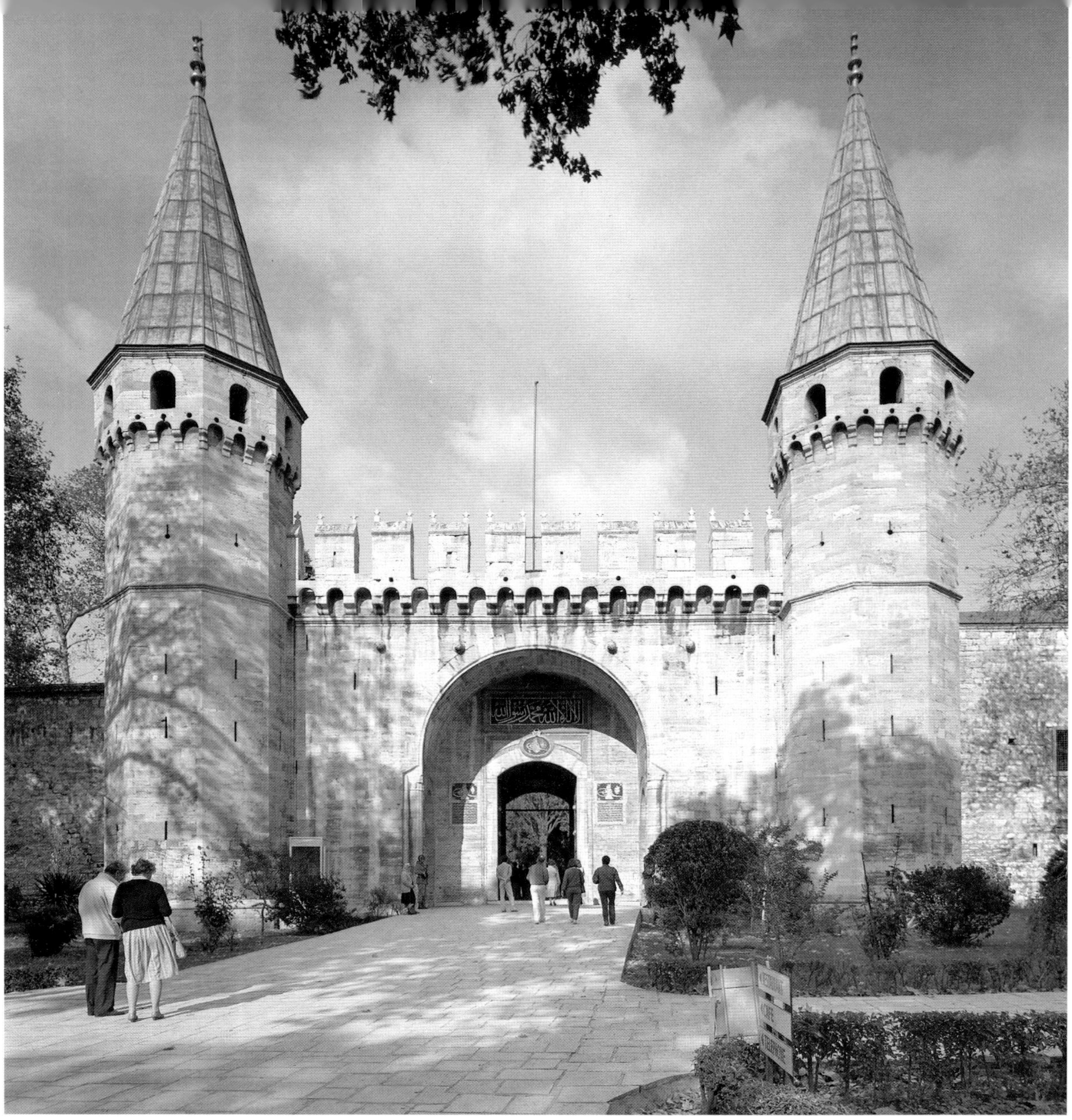

2. (above) Babüsselam, the second gate of the Topkapı Palace.

3. (below) Babüssaade, the third gate of the Topkapı Palace.

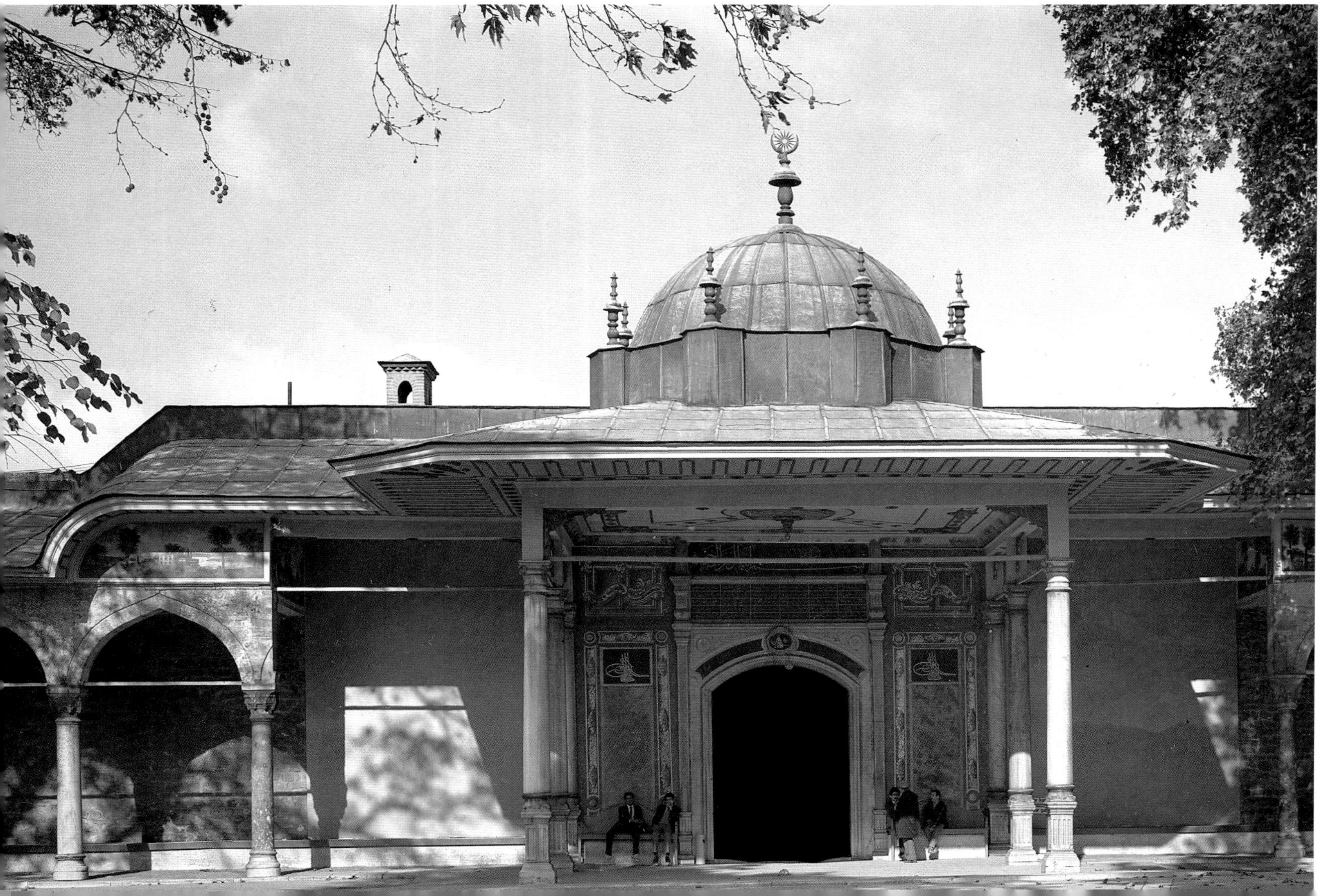

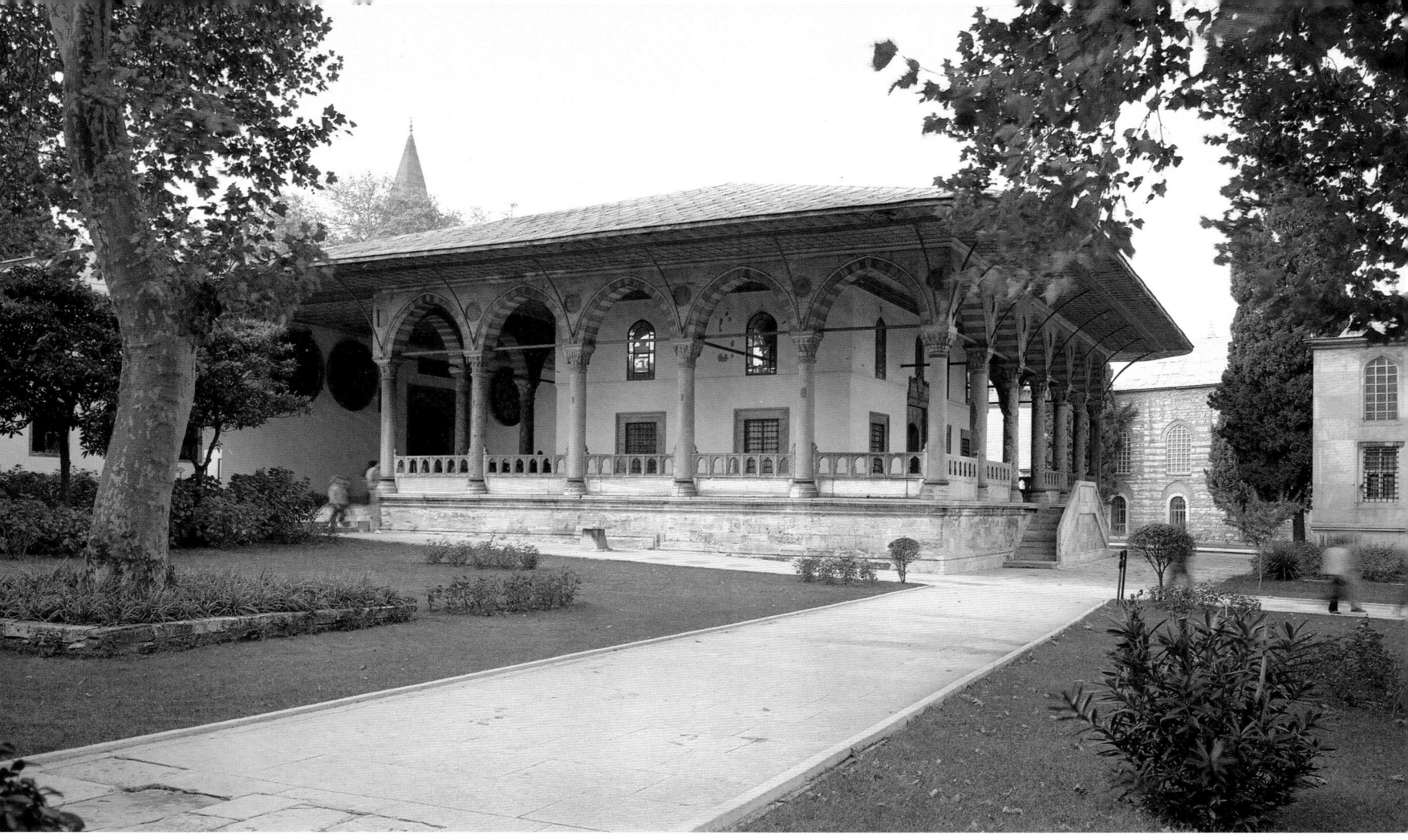

4. Arz Odası, the Reception Room in the third courtyard of the Topkapı Palace.

ties for the Birun staff, which included tutors for the sultans and princes; physicians and astrologers; officers in charge of building and maintaining the palace; chief architects of the state; supervisors of the mint, arsenal, and kitchens; those responsible for procurement of supplies and in charge of the stables; imperial standard bearers, gatekeepers, messengers, gardeners, sultans' personal guards, and artisans.

At the end of the first courtyard was the Babüsselam (Gate of Salutations), also called Orta Kapı (Central Gate), flanked by two massive towers leading into the second courtyard. Only the sultan could pass through this gate on horseback; all others were obliged to dismount and enter on foot. The second courtyard was open to those who had official business in the palace and contained chambers for the Divan-ı Hümayun (Imperial Council of Ministers), the grand vezir, and his staff. Leading from the second courtyard were the imperial kitchens consisting of ten units, each serving a different group in the palace, and the imperial stables.

figure 2

The Babüssaade (Gate of Felicity) was the entrance into the third courtyard, which was open only to the highest ranking officials and special ambassadors. During accession ceremonies and religious holidays the throne of the sultan would be placed in front of this gate. This was the setting in which the sultan received homage from his subjects. The third courtyard was the inner sanctum of the palace and housed the staff of the Enderun School, whose primary role was to train novices recruited from the devşirme ranks.

figure 3

The Enderun School was headed by the *ağa* (chief) of the Babüssaade, who was chosen from the white eunuchs in the palace and ranked immediately below the grand vezir and the şeyhülislam. He was also the guardian of the third gate, and thus was known as the *kapı ağası*. Novices were subjected to a rigid education and advanced according to their capabilities and competence. After graduating they were assigned as *iç oğlans* (pages) to various chambers, the most important of which were the Hazine (Treasury), Kiler (Larder), Seferli Oda (Campaign Chamber), and the Has Oda (Privy Chamber). In time the pages were promoted to the ranks of the Enderun ağas. The ultimate achievement was to serve in the Has Oda, which was headed by the Has Oda başı (head of the Privy Chamber) and included the *silahdar ağa* (imperial swordbearer), *çuhadar ağa* (imperial valet), *rikapdar ağa* (imperial stirrupholder), *dübend oğlanı* (keeper of the linen), and *sır katibi* (confidential secretary). These officials had direct access to the sultan and were thus in a privileged position. After serving in the palace, some of the ağas were sent to the Birun, others were given commissions in the provinces or the military forces.[25]

figure 4

The buildings in the third courtyard included the Arz Odası (Reception Chamber), the Has Oda, the Hazine, and various facilities for the Enderun School such as meeting rooms, dormitories, baths, and mosques. The Arz Odası served as the formal reception room for dignitaries and foreign envoys; the Hazine housed the sultan's private collection of rare and precious objects; and the Has Oda, besides its other functions, was the repository of the *mukaddes emanetler* (sacred trusts), which included the mantle, bow, and standard of the Prophet Muhammed, the swords of the first four caliphs, and the earliest Koran attributed to the third orthodox caliph, Osman. These sacred objects had been brought back from Egypt by Selim I when he assumed the caliphate and became the spiritual leader of Islam.

The Harem (meaning "sacred place") was the private domain of the sultan and the area where members of his family resided. Originally women and children were housed in the Old Palace and not allowed into the Topkapı Palace. It was after the 1550s that they began to reside in the Topkapı Palace. Hürrem had insisted on living close to the sultan, and was assigned quarters for herself and her retinue in the Harem section, which abutted the second and third courtyards of the palace. After the late sixteenth century this section grew to include over 360 chambers with suites for the valide sultan, hasekis, şehzades, eunuchs, tutors, and a large number of attendants and servants. Built on several levels, it consisted of bedrooms, reception areas, libraries, dining rooms, baths, and infirmaries placed around courtyards and gardens.

Although the Harem was not a formal part of the Ottoman administrative system, it had the same rigid hierarchy along with flexibility of upward movement as the Enderun School. At the top was the valide sultan, whose son was the reigning sultan. She was by far the most powerful woman at the court and frequently advised the sultan on domestic and foreign affairs.

The Harem, often referred to as a court within a court, housed a large number of women. They were guarded by the black eunuchs, whose chief was called the *darüssaade* or *kızlar ağası* (chief of the realm of felicity or of the women). The lowest ranking members of the Harem were the servants and attendants of the women. When a girl's relationship with the sultan became permanent and produced a son, she became a haseki or *has odalık* (favorite).[26] There were normally four hasekis, who could be rotating, the mother of the eldest son ranking as the *baş haseki* (head favorite). The day of triumph came if and when her son ascended the Ottoman throne and she was elevated to the exalted position of valide sultan.

The women in the Harem were of slave origin who had been captured, purchased, or given as gifts; they were trained either in the İstanbul palace or in the provincial courts and presented to the sultan. In many ways their lives resembled those of the devşirme children. They received an excellent education and could advance in rank. Many were married off to vezirs and commanders; they could divorce their husbands, return to the palace, or be married to other officials, if they so desired. Some of the enterprising ones established their own charitable institutions and sponsored the building of architectural complexes. Hürrem and Mihrimah were among the most energetic patrons. Although marriages were performed during the early years of the empire in order to form alliances with neighboring states, this practice had been abandoned by the fifteenth century. Süleyman was one of the very few sultans who officially took a wife.[27]

The fourth courtyard of the Topkapı Palace, which was expanded in later centuries, did not have a formal entrance. During Süleyman's reign this area was a part of the imperial gardens extending to the waterfront, with pleasure pavilions and boathouses lining the shore.

Central Administration

The political, judicial, and financial affairs of the state were administered by the Divan-ı Hümayun, which was headed by the sultan, the supreme ruler of the empire, the commander in chief of the armed forces, and the protector of Islam. His executive representative was the *sadrazam*, also called *vezir-i azam* (grand vezir), who frequently substituted for the sultan.[28]

The Divan consisted of four groups: vezirs, *kazaskers, defterdars,* and the *nişancı.* The vezirs, who had the title *paşa,* were responsible for political affairs and included the three highest officials in charge of major provinces and the beylerbeyis of Rumelia and Anatolia; the kazaskers of Rumelia and Anatolia were the representatives of the ulema and oversaw judicial affairs; the defterdars accounted for the finances of the state and divided their workload between Rumelia and Anatolia; and the nişancı served as a chancellor, authenticating the sultan's fermans by affixing the imperial *tuğra* (monogram). Also included in the Divan was the *reisülküttab* (chief of clerks in charge of correspondence and records), and a number of additional staff members, such as the *çavuşbaşı* (head usher), *kapıcıbaşı* (head gatekeeper) together with secretaries, translators, and the master of petitions. Membership in the Divan varied according to the number of vezirs and beylerbeyis.[29] The council met in the Kubbealtı (domed chamber in the second courtyard of the palace) four days a week for at least seven to eight hours a day.

The sultan's primary responsibility was the enforcement of justice and the Divan functioned basically as a supreme court and executive council where complaints and grievances from the subjects were reviewed, national and international affairs discussed, and administrative policies formulated. Rising above the Kubbealtı was the Adalet Kulesi (Tower of Justice), which symbolized the sultan's preeminence as the enforcer of justice.

The empire was divided into *beylerbeyliks* or *eyalets* (major provinces), under which were sancaks, whose governors held the title of *bey* and supervised the *timars* (fiefs), in which specific lands were assigned to individuals who collected revenues in return for supplying the state with armies when needed. The administrative structure of the residencies of the beylerbeyis and sancakbeyis followed the system employed in the palace institution.

The armed forces of the empire were made up of the Kapıkulu (Slaves of the Porte) Army drawn from the devşirme ranks and the Provincial Army supplied basically by the timar holders. The Kapıkulu Army included the fearsome Janissary Corps, the infantry also responsible for guarding the sultan, keeping order in the capital, and protecting the fortresses when not campaigning. Numbering about 12,000 men during Şüleyman's reign, they were highly disciplined and well trained, ready for battle at all times. Since the janissaries were not allowed to marry and have families, they could devote their lives to serving the sultan. Other corps in the Kapıkulu Army included the artillery, who manned the cannons and guns using gunpowder; the miners, who dug mines and trenches during sieges; and mortarmen, who provided the mortars, mines, grenades, and bombs for assaults on enemy strongholds. This section also had its cavalry of some 6,000 men, which supplemented that of the Provincial Army.

The Provincial Army was the largest of all Ottoman forces and consisted of about 40,000 *timarlı sipahis* (cavalry of the timar holders) who joined the sultan when requested, kept order in the provinces, and provided the garrisons along the frontiers. Belonging to the Provincial Army were other units, such as guards of the fortresses; the akıncıs and the *delils*, who functioned as forward attack forces and raided the countryside.

The organization of the Ottoman naval forces became developed under Barbaros Hayreddin Paşa, who was appointed kaptan-ı derya by Süleyman in 1534. The navy was made up of a number of ships built in the imperial dockyards, each commanded by a *reis* (captain).

Learned Institution

The ulema, who used the title *efendi,* were responsible for enforcing and interpreting the şeriat; administering the kanuns; providing educational institutions with professors and teachers; and supervising curriculum in schools and *medreses* (universities). The institution was headed by the şeyhülislam; under him were the kazaskers, *müftis* (jurisconsults), *kadıs* (judges), and *müderris* (professors).

The müftis studied and interpreted the Islamic law, coordinating with the kadıs, who were in charge of the district courts. The function of the müderris was to oversee hundreds of schools which taught a variety of subjects, including languages, poetry, logic, philosophy, theology, ethics, physical sciences, religion, law, and jurisprudence in addition to the analysis of the Koran and the Hadis (Traditions of the Prophet). With the establishment of the four medreses in the Süleymaniye Complex in the 1550s, greater emphasis was given to advanced studies in sciences, particularly to medicine and mathematics. The members of the ulema were themselves highly acclaimed as scholars and many produced significant works in literature, poetry, and history.

Subjects of the Sultan

The sultan was viewed as the protector, or shepherd, of the population of his empire (the Turkish word for population, *reaya*, means "flock"). The people either lived in cities, towns, and villages or were nomadic. The urban and rural dwellers were exempt from military service but the nomadic tribes were called to serve in the army.

The population consisted of *millets* (nations). After the conquest of the central Islamic lands the Muslims constituted the largest millet. Since the şeriat was applicable only to Muslims, non-Muslim millets —including those of Orthodox Greeks, Jews, and Armenians—had their own patriarchs or grand rabbis who dealt with the Ottoman authorities and administered their own individual systems of law. They had the freedom to follow their own faiths, rituals, and traditions.

In addition to the millets were a number of sufi or mystic sects, such as the Bektaşis and the Mevlevis, both founded in the thirteenth century. The Bektaşi order, considered heterodox by orthodox Islam, had a following among the janissaries and was therefore officially sanctioned by the sultan. The existence of this order, as well as the other sufi sects, was tolerated and their members were free to practice their beliefs as long as they did not conflict with the affairs of the state.

The rural population cultivated the land and raised animals, and was taxed in return for the protection guaranteed by the state. The urban population engaged in industrial and commercial activities, profits of which were also taxed. The craftsmen belonged to a highly structured system of *esnaf* (guilds), each of which had its own *şeyh* (spiritual or moral leader), *kethüda* (lieutenant), board of elders, masters, and apprentices, and adhered to a rigid system of membership and advancement. The guilds had members of various religious faiths and could be called upon to participate in campaigns by providing the armed forces with the required goods and services.

The merchants were by far the richest of the urban dwellers and could accumulate great wealth due to the free enterprise system supported by the state. They paid limited taxes and traded internationally in the great centers of İstanbul, Bursa, Edirne, Salonica, and Cairo.

Artistic Production of the Age

The reign of Süleyman was not only the high point of political and economic development but also the golden age of Ottoman culture. Artistic production flourished under the sultan's demanding and generous patronage. The members of the administration themselves practiced the arts and many excelled in poetry, painting, literature, and history. The imperial studios employed hundreds of men from all parts of the empire, their origins as varied as the lands ruled by the sultan. This period saw the synthesis of European, Islamic, and Turkish traditions and the creation of an artistic vocabulary that was unique to the Ottoman world.

It was the age of giants among architects and artists. Some of the most famous were Sinan, the great architect; Nigari, the portraitist; Matrakcı, the illustrator of histories; Şahkulu, the creator of the *saz* style; Kara Memi, the innovator of the naturalistic genre; Mehmed, the master bookbinder; and Karahisari, the celebrated calligrapher.

This period was renowned for the construction of monumental architecture, with the sultan, members of his family, and high court officials commissioning one spectacular building after another. Artists of great talent were employed in the production of manuscripts. Their bookbindings, calligraphy, illuminations, and illustrations were works of rare sophistication and aesthetic perfection. Such achievements were matched by the works of goldsmiths, jewelers, arms and armor makers, woodworkers, clothmakers, embroiderers, rug weavers, and potters.

Literature and Poetry

The age of Süleyman was remarkable for its literary and historical productivity. The greatest intellects belonged to the ulema. Its most renowned member was Ebussuud (1490-1575), who served as şeyhülislam for close to three decades. He issued thousands of *fetvas* and sanctioned the opening of the first Turkish coffeehouses and performances of the Karagöz (Shadow Theater). Other ulema scholars included Kemalpaşazade (1468-1533), known as İbni Kemal, şeyhülislam, poet, translator, and historian; Taşköprülüzade Ahmed (1495-1553), kadı and historian, famous for his biographies of learned men; Aşık Çelebi (1520-1572), kadı, historian, poet, and biographer; and Hoca Sâdeddin (1536-1599), şeyhülislam, poet, and historian.

The central administration also produced famous scholars, the most outstanding of whom were: Aşıkpaşazade (1393-1481), soldier and historian of tremendous influence; Matrakcı Nasuh (d. 1564?), an officer in the Enderun, who was a mathematician, swordsman, inventor of athletic games, and the illustrator of his own historical works; Ahmed Feridun (d. 1583), commander, governor, nişancı, reisülküttab, and defterdar, known for his histories, one of which was illustrated; (Gelibolulu) Mustafa Ali (1541-1599), defterdar and historian who wrote an account of the artists; and İbrahim Peçevi (1574-1650), commander, defterdar, and governor, whose history covers in detail the events between 1520 and 1641. A number of grand vezirs, including Lütfi (1488-1553) and Rüstem (1500-1561) also wrote histories.

In addition there were geographical and maritime studies by such naval commanders as Piri Reis (1465?-1554), who wrote the *Kitab-ı Bahriye*, a guide to the Mediterranean; and Seydi Ali Reis (1498-1562), the author of the geography of the Indian Ocean and of autobiographical accounts of his famous travels in India, Transoxiana, and Iran.

Poetry was by far the most popular of the court arts, and was encouraged by the sultan, his grand vezirs (İbrahim and Rüstem in particular), and the members of the court. Süleyman was himself a poet, writing in Persian and Turkish under the pseudonym Muhibbi. The sultan's *gazels* (odes) collected in his *Divan* combine lyricism and mysticism with humility and sincerity.[30]

Süleyman belongs to a long list of poet sultans, including Murad II, Mehmed II, Bayezid II, and Selim I. Five of his sons are known to have practiced the art of poetry as did his grandson, Murad III, and great-grandson, Mehmed III.

This was the age of Fuzuli (d. 1563?), the immortal poet from Baghdad, who wrote in Azeri-Turkish, best known for his *Divan* and romance, *Leyla ve Mecnun*; and Baki (1526-1600), the great lyric poet of İstanbul and the sultan's favorite, famous for his elegy on Süleyman. Other well-known poets were Fazlı (d. 1563?), who was in the service of Şehzades Mehmed and Mustafa before joining the court of Selim II; Yahya Bey, a former devşirme child whose elegy for Şehzade Mustafa nearly cost him his life; and Latifi (d. 1585?), who wrote a biography of the poets.

Architecture and the Arts

Süleyman's passion for poetry was matched only by his enthusiastic patronage of art and architecture. During his reign İstanbul became the busiest and the largest city in the empire with merchants and artisans arriving daily in large numbers to reap its riches. The allure of the city became even greater with the construction of various public buildings commissioned by the court. The master who designed and built these was a genius named Sinan (1490?-1588),[31] under whom Ottoman architecture found its most perfect expression and monumentality of form.

Sinan, an engineer and architect, is thought to have been born around 1490 in Kayseri. He was recruited into the Janissary Corps in 1512 and accompanied the sultan on many campaigns, building bridges and roads. Appointed the royal architect by Süleyman, he was responsible for over 300 monuments scattered throughout the empire. He continued to work for subsequent sultans, achieving his ambition of building the largest and highest dome in history with the Selimiye Mosque in Edirne, constructed in 1575.

Sinan's most spectacular complex was built for Süleyman between 1550 and 1557. Called the Süleymaniye, it consisted of over a dozen buildings arranged around a mosque and included four universities, a college of medicine, elementary and secondary schools, a hospital, hospice, soup kitchen, bath, shopping center, cemetery, and mausoleums for Süleyman and Hürrem, together with residences for students, staff, and caretakers. The mosque is a most impressive structure, its central dome hovering over some 400 smaller domes that cascade to the ground. The edifice was decorated with tiles, carved stonework, inlaid woodwork, stained glass, pile rugs, and thousands of glass lamps.[32]

figure 5

Süleyman also commissioned Sinan to build a medrese in memory of his father, Selim I, as well as mosques and attached buildings commemorating his sons, Şehzades Mehmed and Cihangir. His daughter Mihrimah employed Sinan to build her mosques and charitable institutions as did his wife Hürrem, who was in fact the first to hire him. In 1538/1539 Sinan constructed for her a complex that included a mosque, school, university, hospital, and soup kitchen in the Aksaray district; and in 1556/1557 he completed the largest and most remarkable bath with separate units for men and women, facing the At Meydanı. He was also given major commissions for complexes by such dignitaries as İbrahim, Rüstem, and Sokollu Mehmed Paşas.

Süleyman sponsored a number of other building activities, including waterworks in İstanbul and bridges over the Büyük Çekmeçe, Danube, Sava, and Meriç rivers. He built and restored Baghdad's holy sites, notably the tomb of Ebu Hanife, the originator of the Hanefi sect of Islam to which the Ottomans belonged; and that of Abdülkadir el-Gilani, the founder of the Kadiriye dervishes. He also restored Celaleddin Rumi's mausoleum in Konya, adding a number of new structures. In addition the sultan built monasteries for the Bektaşi dervishes in Seyyid Battal Gazi; constructed a complex in Damascus; restored the

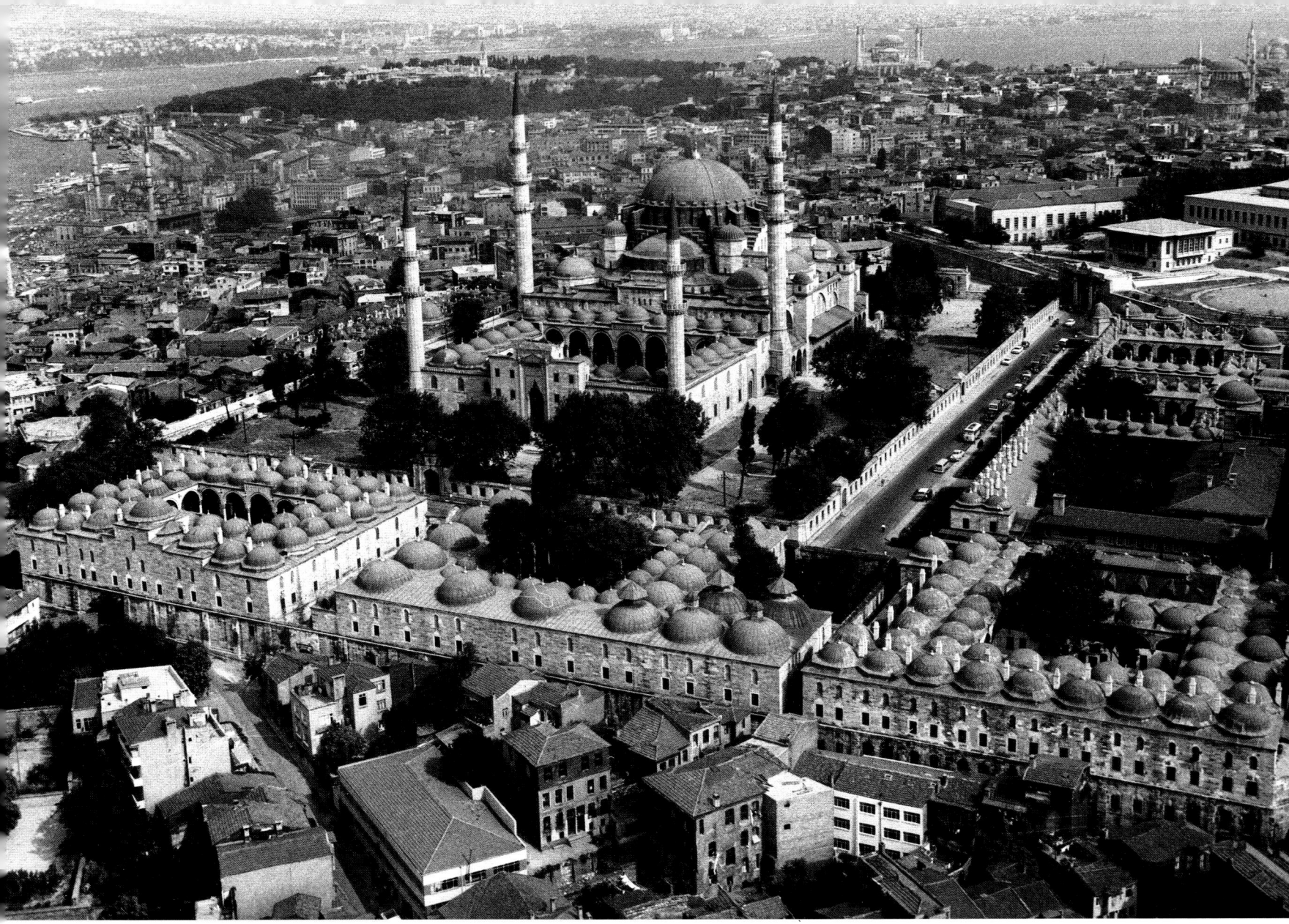

5. General view of the Süleymaniye Complex.

Dome of the Rock in Jerusalem; and renovated and redecorated the Kaaba in Mecca, building four medreses for the four sects of orthodox Islam (Hanefi, Şafii, Maliki, and Hanbeli).

These religious, charitable, and educational establishments were supported by *vakıfs* (endowments) in which certain lands and real estate together with their income were assigned to the foundations to cover their maintenance expenses and staff salaries. The Ottoman vakıfs, in existence since the beginning of the empire, enabled these foundations to be independent and self-sufficient. The sultan, members of his family, grand vezirs, and a number of other individuals established vakıfs to support their architectural complexes.

Süleyman himself endowed several religious and charitable institutions in Hürrem's name, including soup kitchens in Mecca and Medina; and a caravansaray, mosque, soup kitchen, and fountain on the Meriç River outside Edirne. He assigned the income from several towns and villages to maintain these endowments. The terms of individual deeds or trusts were recorded in a *Vakfiye* (Book of Endowments), which included the tuğra of the sultan and was beautifully transcribed and illuminated by court artists.

All the arts from architectural decoration to manuscript illumination had an unprecedented flowering under Süleyman. The sultan took a great interest in education and art despite his great commitment to the administrative, judicial, military, and diplomatic tasks of the state. He personally supervised the curricula in the universities. Anticipating the need for future engineers and physicians, he expanded the facilities for studying mathematics and medicine. He would scrutinize the new works of writers and artists, judging them by the highest standards. He rewarded painters, bookbinders, and calligraphers with cash bonuses and gifts during religious holidays. He is said to have read in one night Ali Çelebi's lengthy *Hümayunname*, the Turkish translation of *Kalila va Dimna*, the classical Arabic book on princely behavior. He carefully went over some 30,000 verses of his own biography, the *Süleymanname*, which was written in Persian.

The bustling artistic activities in İstanbul created a need for competent artists and craftsmen, and they came from all corners of the empire to seek employment in its famed capital. Some joined the artisans' guilds in the city while others were admitted into the Ehl-i Hiref (Community of the Talented) to serve the sultan. The Ehl-i Hiref, which was formally attached to the Birun, included men of all trades, from calligraphers to cobblers.

The Ehl-i Hiref was tightly structured and was administered in the same manner as the other branches of the state. Its members constituted an elite which had a dominant influence on Ottoman culture although a large number of other artists and craftsmen also worked in the capital.[33] Artists also resided in provincial centers, some of which specialized in the production of particular wares. For instance, Bursa was a major center for the manufacture of textiles; İznik met most of the state's need for ceramics and tiles; and Uşak was the center of rug weaving. No doubt artisans were employed in all the major cities of the empire to meet local demands.[34]

The decorative vocabulary of Ottoman art was highly centralized and the designs created for the court were soon employed by all the arts. The impact of court designs on brocaded silks, velvets, and rugs as well as on ceramics and tiles is evident. Kaftans made of expensive fabrics had a special significance in the Ottoman world and would be presented as *hilats* (robes of honor) to deserving officials and visiting dignitaries. Those worn by the sultans were carefully preserved in the Hazine. Although the most sumptuous examples were commissioned for the court, brocaded silks and velvets were also manufactured for local consumption and for export to foreign markets. Turkish textiles and rugs were particularly favored by the Europeans and were greatly appreciated in ecclesiastic and aristocratic circles.

Tiles were in great demand as a result of the construction of new buildings. After the 1550s, they began to include a thick, rich red that came to characterize Ottoman ceramics. The decoration of these tiles, as well as of ceramic vessels, relied on both stylized and naturalistic motifs, the origin of which can be found in the manuscript illuminations produced in the *nakkaşhane* (imperial painting studio).

Nakkaşhane and Its Artists

One of the units in the Ehl-i Hiref, the Cemaat-i Nakkaşan (Society of Painters), was composed of artists whose duty was to decorate the manuscripts commissioned for the imperial libraries. The men were paid daily wages, which were recorded in the payroll registers drawn every three months. Special projects required independent funding, which was also dutifully recorded in the palace archives. The imperial society of painters was at times supplemented by individuals working outside the court. In addition, there were several members of the administration who practiced the art of painting or participated in the production of imperial manuscripts.[35]

The term nakkaşhane appears to denote an institution rather than an actual building, although there was a nakkaşhane building outside the palace, on the main road used during official parades near the Alay Köşkü where the sultan viewed the processions.[36] Since the membership in the nakkaşhane at times reached well over one hundred men, this building must have been used more as a meeting center or a gathering place where the artists had access to reference books, where new projects were discussed and distributed, and where finished folios were compiled into the final volumes. It is likely that some painters worked at home or shared studios with fellow artists in the city, while others resided in the nakkaşhane building itself.

The earliest records on the nakkaşhane date from the reign of Süleyman and include six payroll registers drawn between 1526 and 1566. Belonging to his reign are several other records that list the gifts exchanged between the sultan and the artists during religious holidays.[37]

In 1526 the nakkaşhane comprised forty-one members headed by Şahkulu.[38] The group included ten artists who either came from Iran or were the sons of Iranian masters in addition to a pair of Circassians, an Albanian, and a Moldavian. Nine of the men had registered during the reign of Bayezid II, and thirteen had arrived during the reign of Selim I.

The next register drawn in 1545 shows that an internal division took place, separating the fifty-nine member nakkaşhane into two corps, the Rumiyan and the Aceman.[39] The former, once again headed by Şahkulu, had forty-four men and included four Bosnians, three Austrians, two Circassians, and one each from Albania, Moldavia, and Rumelia. The latter contained fifteen artists, ten of whom were from Tabriz and one from Isfahan. It appears that the Aceman corps was exclusively made up of artists from Iran while the Rumiyan included all the others.

The same division into the Rumiyan and Aceman corps appears in 1557-1558. Of the two documents bearing these dates, one appears to be incomplete and lists only the Rumiyan group,[40] which has thirty-four members, headed by Mehmed Şah, who was recorded earlier as having come from Tabriz. His corps includes several Albanians, Bosnians, and Hungarians as well as one man each from Austria, Circassia, Georgia, and Moldavia.

The second document with the same date[41] lists thirty-nine members: twenty-six are in the Rumiyan group, now headed by Kara Memi, and thirteen are in the Aceman group. The former includes several Bosnians and one man each from Albania, Georgia, and Moldavia; the latter is made up primarily of artists from Tabriz, but contains individuals from Hungary and Isfahan together with a man of undetermined European origin.

The document of 1566[42] once again shows the same two divisions and includes thirty-seven men. The thirty-one-member Rumiyan group is headed by Mehmed Sinan and contains the same mixture of men. The Aceman corps is composed of one European and five artists from Tabriz; among them is Mehmed Şah, who was the head of the Rumiyan corps in 1557-1558.

The next two registers, dated 1596,⁴³ show a totally different structure: there are 124 to 129 members equally divided into masters and apprentices within a single corps. The director is now called the *sernakkaşan* (head of the painters) and is followed by the kethüda and *serbölük* (head of the corps). Almost all the members appear to be native artists, with the exception of single men whose names indicate they were originally from Albania, Bosnia, Europe, and Georgia.

Information compiled from all available sources indicates that the first recorded head of the nakkaşhane was Hasan b. Abdülcelil, also known as Hasan Çelebi,⁴⁴ who was listed as the *nakkaşbaşı* or sernakkaşan in 1510 and held this position through the 1540s. Şahkulu, listed as number one in 1526, became the serbölük of the Rumiyan corps in 1545. In 1557-1558 a new man, Mehmed Şah, emerged as the serbölük of the same corps; the nakkaşbaşı during these years was Kara Memi.

Hasan b. Abdülcelil was the son of an Iranian master and joined the nakkaşhane during the reign of Bayezid II, probably around 1500. His salary after the 1510s rose to twenty-five to thirty-five *akçes* (silver coins) a day, the highest for those years. He was, however, making less than Şahkulu in 1526. Although not mentioned in the 1545 register, he exchanged gifts with the sultan until c. 1555.

Şahkulu, also called Şahkulu-ı Bağdadi, must have been born in Baghdad. He is recorded as having been exiled from Tabriz, most likely around 1501 when Şah Ismail took over. He first lived in Amasya, then came to İstanbul and joined the imperial society of painters at some time between December 1520 and January 1521. He held the highest rank in 1526, was the serbölük in 1545, and is mentioned in a document dated 1555/1556 as having died before he could receive gifts from the sultan.

Şahkulu has left hardly any signed works although he is credited with the development of the Ottoman saz style.⁴⁵ This style, applied to designs composed of *hatayis* (composite blossoms) and twisting serrate leaves, originated with drawings in which masterful brushstrokes created a fantastic world inhabited by dragons, *chilins* (four-legged imaginary creatures), lions, and *peris* (fairies). Many drawings in the saz style show either animals in combat, single peris, or are studies of hatayis and leaves. One example, that of a flying peri, bears the attribution "the work of Şahkulu," which is thought to be authentic;⁴⁶ another, that of a dragon, contains his seal and a notation by a later artist stating "this dragon is the work of Master Şahkulu-i Rumi."⁴⁷ He is also recorded in a document dated c. 1545 as having given a representation of a peri on paper to the sultan. In (Gelibolulu) Mustafa Ali's biography of artists, Şahkulu is said to have been trained in Tabriz by a master named Aka Mirak,⁴⁸ and to have had a rather unpleasant disposition that caused him to feud with fellow artists.

figures 6-8

More information is available on the next nakkaşbaşı, Kara Memi. Mustafa Ali states that he was the greatest student of Şahkulu and the master of Süleyman's nakkaşhane, calling him a *müzehhib* (illuminator). Kara Memi, also identified as Mehmed-i Siyah or Mehmed Çelebi Siyah, is first listed in the 1545 register, which gives the names of two of his apprentices, Mustafa b. Yusuf and Hamza of Austria. In the register of 1557-1558 he is recorded as the nakkaşbaşı and has an apprentice by the name of Nebi.

Among the artists recorded in the documents dating from Süleyman's reign Kara Memi is one of the very few whose style can be traced

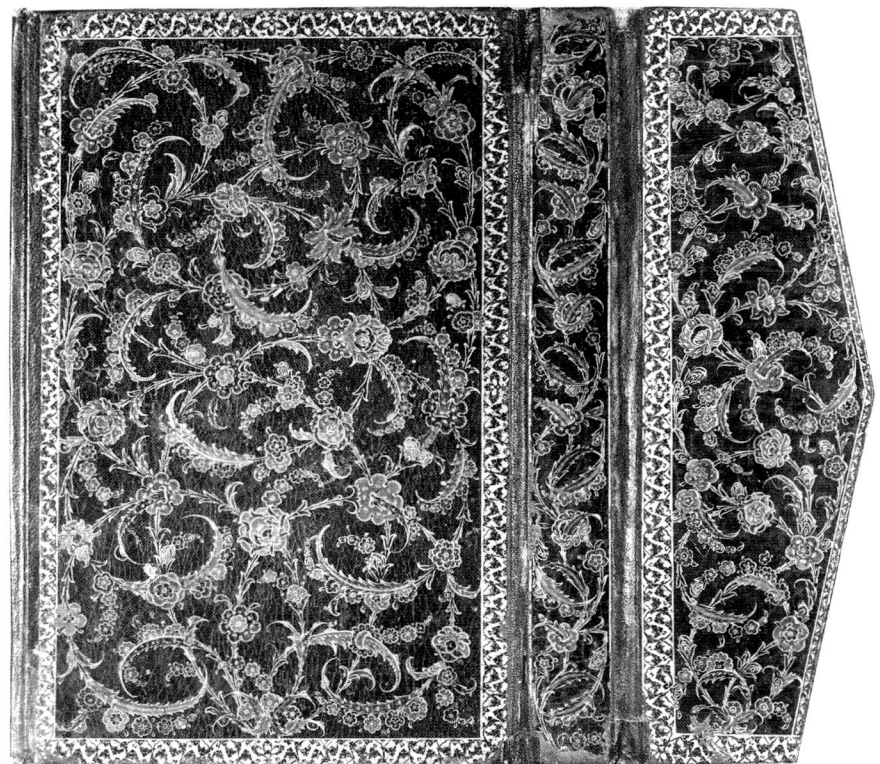
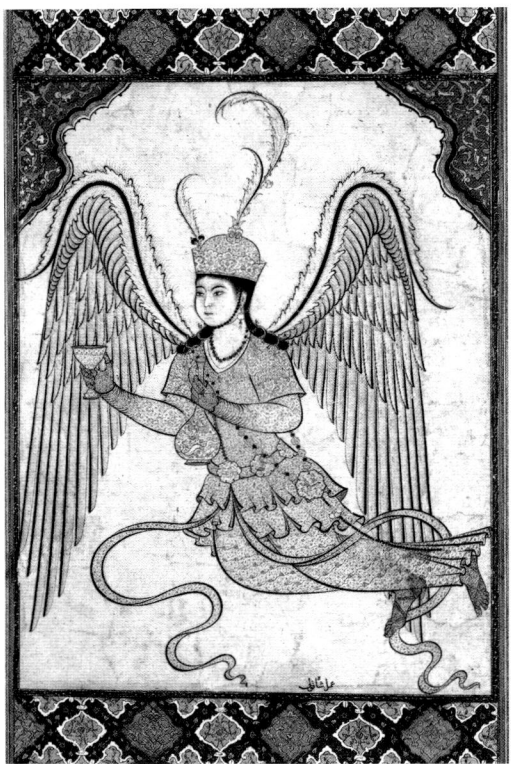

6. (above left) Exterior of lacquer bookbinding, from the *Hamse* of Nevai, transcribed by Pir Ahmed b. İskender in 1530/1531 (İstanbul, Topkapı Sarayı Müzesi, H. 802).

7. (above right) Flying Peri, attributed to Şahkulu, c. 1550 (Washington, D.C., Freer Gallery of Art, 37.7).

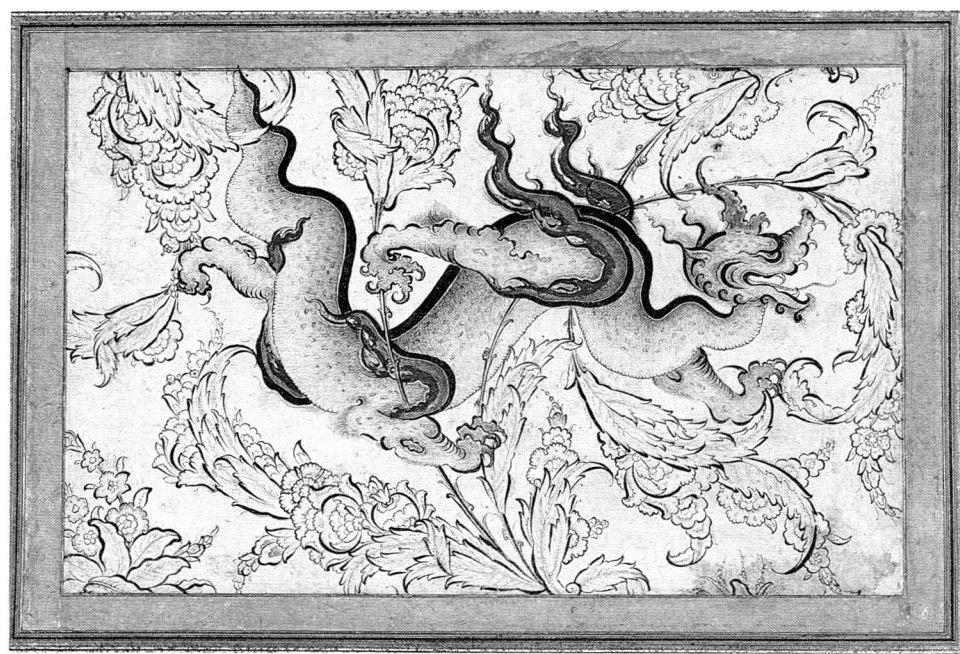

8. (right) Dragon, c. 1560 (İstanbul, Üniversite Kütüphanesi, F 1426, fol. 47b).

from existing manuscripts. A notation in a Koran originally copied in 1344/1345 by Abdullah Sayrafi, and decorated and rebound in Süleyman's court, states that the illuminations were made in 1554 by Kara Memi and that the book was bound in 1555 by Mehmed Çelebi.[49] A second manuscript, the *Divan-i Muhibbi*, was transcribed in 1565/1566 by Mehmed Şerif and illuminated by Kara Memi according to the colophon.[50] The illuminations of these manuscripts are exquisite. They reveal an unusual interest in naturalistic flora with sprays of spring flowers and blossoming trees. Kara Memi's distinctive style also appears in manuscripts dated between the 1540s and 1560s.[51]

Another painter mentioned in the registers who can be identified with an actual work is Bayram b. Derviş, the illuminator of a Koran

figure 9

figure 10

figure 11

38

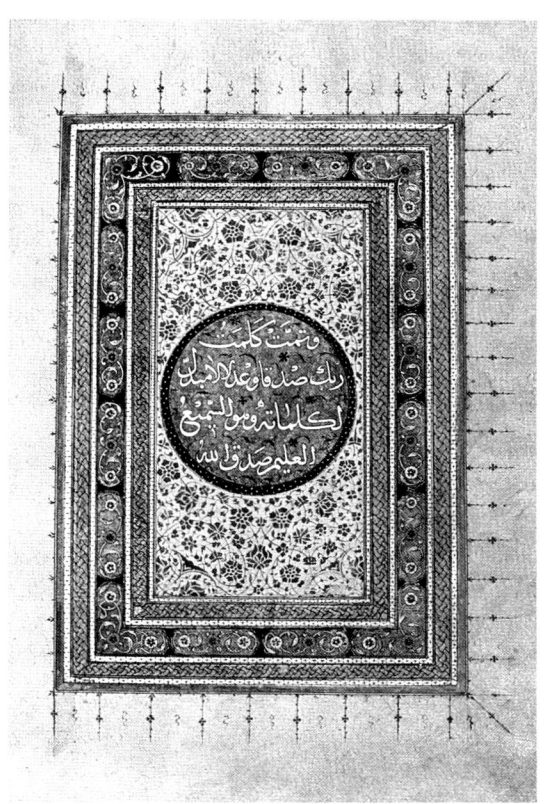
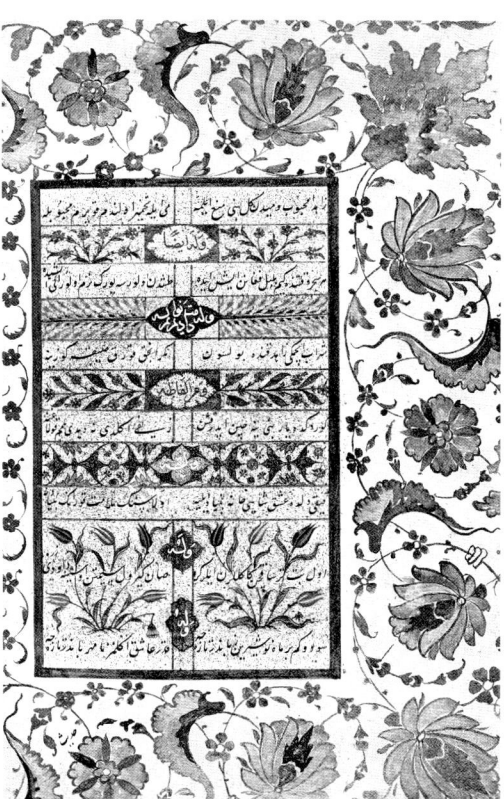

9. Illuminated folio by Kara Memi, dated 1554, from a Koran transcribed by Abdullah Sayrafi in 1344/1345 (İstanbul, Topkapı Sarayı Müzesi, E.H. 49, fol. 1a).

10. Illuminated folio by Kara Memi, from the *Divan-ı Muhibbi* transcribed by Mehmed Şerif in 1565/1566 (İstanbul, Üniversite Kütüphanesi, T. 5467, fol. 360b).

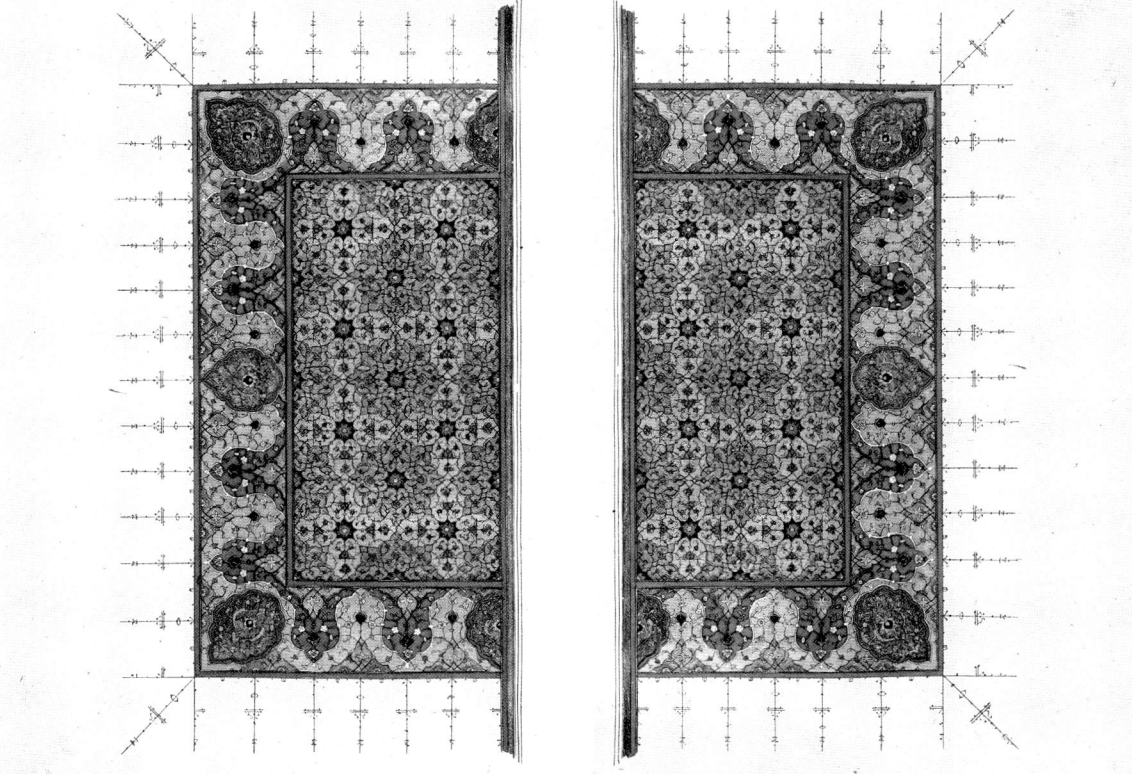

11. Illuminated frontispiece by Bayram b. Derviş, from a Koran transcribed by Abdullah b. İlyas in 1523/1524 (İstanbul, Topkapı Sarayı Müzesi, E.H. 58, fols. 1b-2a).

transcribed in 1523/1524 by Abdullah b. İlyas and dedicated to Süleyman.[52] Bayram was recorded in 1526 as having joined the studio during the reign of Bayezid II. The register of 1557-1558 gives his date of death as 5 November 1558. His son, Mehmed b. Bayram, registered in the studio in 1499, is mentioned in the document of 1526; the name of another son, Ali, appears in the 1526 and 1545 registers.

The documents listed above suggest that the nakkaşhane was already established during the reign of Bayezid II and that it was supplemented by artists from Tabriz brought back by Selim I. Around the 1540s it was divided into two groups: the first, called Rumiyan, included men mostly from Anatolia and the western provinces of the empire; the second, named Aceman, was primarily made up of Iranians. This separation, which continued through the 1560s, was by no means absolute since some westerners could work in the Aceman group and certain Tabrizi artists, namely Mehmed Şah, could be assigned to the Rumiyan corps. The exact purpose of the two divisions is yet to be properly understood and must have served an unknown administrative function.

The hierarchy within the nakkaşhane as well as the daily wages fluctuated; for instance, Şahkulu's salary in 1526 was lower than that of Melek Ahmed, who ranked below him, but higher than that of the nakkaşbaşı, Hasan b. Abdülcelil. It is possible that other registers were drawn for individual projects for which the artists were assigned specific duties that required different wages.[53]

The duties of the artists also varied and a nakkaş could engage in the art of illumination, as did Kara Memi and Bayram b. Derviş. The training in the nakkaşhane obviously prepared the men to undertake different projects and they were given the opportunity to practice more than one form of art.

Membership was drawn from all corners of the empire although from the 1520s to the 1560s it appears to have drawn heavily either on masters from Tabriz or on their trainees. The Tabrizi artists either emigrated to the Ottoman capital or came as a part of Selim I's booty after the 1514 conquest of Tabriz. Although it is thought that Selim transported to the capital some 1,000 artists, craftsmen, scholars, and poets, the registers record only thirteen men who entered the painting studio during his reign. A related document lists sixteen painters and adds a note stating that there were twenty-three others just as talented.[54] Of these sixteen names eleven are mentioned in various documents and payroll registers. It is possible that the others entered different corps of the Ehl-i Hiref or joined the local guilds.

It should be noted that Selim must have also brought Syrian and Egyptian artists to İstanbul after the defeat of the Mamluks in 1517. The Mamluk court in Cairo had begun to sponsor major illustrated manuscripts, which appear to have been produced by artists trained in Tabriz and Şiraz.[55]

The payroll registers and other documents pertaining to the Ehl-i Hiref also list the bookbinders of the age, who belonged to the Cemaat-i Mücellidan (Society of Bookbinders).[56] For over a century, this society was dominated by a remarkable family headed by the patriarch Ahmed, who was recorded as being an imperial master bookbinder at the time of his death in 1518.[57] Ahmed's four sons, Mustafa, Hasan, Hüseyin, and Mehmed, are listed in the registers dated between 1526 and 1566; Mehmed was the head of the society in 1545 and 1566 while his son, Süleyman, replaced him in 1596. His descendants continued the tradition well into the second quarter of the seventeenth century.

Another master bookbinder, Hürrem-i Rum, was employed between 1545 and 1596; his son, Mehmed, also worked in the imperial society. A third master, Ahmed Kamil, active 1545-1558, was also followed by sons.

Among the bookbinders listed in the registers only one artist, Mehmed b. Ahmed, can be identified with extant works. Listed as the serbölük in 1566, he is mentioned as Mehmed Çelebi, who in 1555 bound the Koran by Abdullah Sayrafi, working with Kara Memi.[58] Unfortunately, the binding of this manuscript was later removed and is now lost.

The esteemed calligraphers of the age, Şeyh Hamdullah (1429?-1520) and Ahmed Karahisari (1469?-1556), who transcribed many Korans illuminated by the nakkaşhane artists, were not a part of the Ehl-i Hiref.[59] Highly respected for their art as well as for their transcriptions of the Holy Book of Islam, they must have enjoyed a very special status in the court. Whether they received regular salaries is doubtful since copying the Koran was considered a pious act that could not be compensated by money. They were, however, amply rewarded for their contributions.

Şeyh Hamdullah, son of Mustafa Dede, a şeyh from Bukhara, was born in Amasya. He tutored Bayezid II while the latter was the governor of that city and came with the sultan to İstanbul. A revered master who produced close to fifty Korans in addition to a number of collections of prayers and albums of calligraphic samples, Şeyh Hamdullah was also a renowned athlete, who excelled in archery, hunting, and swimming. He is known to have refused commissions from Süleyman, stating that he was too old. In fact, he died two months after the sultan's accession to the throne.

Ahmed Karahisari, the great calligrapher of the age, produced many Korans, albums, and other volumes, and worked on architectural inscriptions. An innovative artist, he excelled in both majestic and minuscule scripts, writing in all forms of angular and cursive styles. His monumental Koran, started in 1540 and completed in 1593 by his follower and adopted son Hasan (died 1594?), is a masterpiece of the art of calligraphy and illumination, each page inventively composed and brilliantly executed.[60]

figure 35

It was the creations of the nakkaşhane artists that had the strongest impact on the decorative vocabulary of the age. Both the saz style attributed to Şahkulu and the naturalistic genre developed by Kara Memi were employed on bookbindings, illuminations, metalwork, woodwork, textiles, rugs, ceramics, tiles, and a variety of other arts. The saz style, characterized by hatayi blossoms and serrate leaves, continued to be practiced well into the 1900s, having an exuberant revival in the early eighteenth century. The naturalistic style—with its blossoming fruit trees, tulips, carnations, roses, hyacinths, and other spring flowers—was the distinctive theme of the age, leaving its mark on art up through the nineteenth century.

Illustrated Manuscripts

The manuscript illustrations produced during Süleyman's reign reflect the eclecticism of the nakkaşhane in contrast to the homogeneous style found in works dating from the last quarter of the sixteenth century. Close to sixty illustrated volumes are known to have been produced in the İstanbul studio; three-fourths of these are devoted to classical literature and poetry; the rest describe contemporary events and establish the tradition of illustrated historiography, which is unique to the Ottoman world. In addition, there are dozens of imperial albums incorporating hundreds of paintings, drawings, illuminations, and calligraphic samples dating from these years.

The literary manuscripts illustrated in the court consist of both Persian classics, including the works of Jami, Nizami, Sadi, Arifi, Hafiz, and Firdausi, and Turkish texts, such as those written by Ali Şir Nevai, Şeyhi, Ulvi Çelebi, Hamdi Çelebi, Musa Abdi, and Fuzuli. The collection of the Persian poems of Selim I, entitled the *Divan-ı Selimi*, was also illustrated in the court as were Turkish translations of the Firdausi's *Şahname*.

The styles of these illustrations reveal a mixture of traditions, combining the features associated with the schools of Herat, Tabriz, Şiraz, İstanbul, and possibly even of Cairo. As was the case with the painters listed in the payroll registers, it was the artists trained in Tabriz, or coming from Herat via Tabriz,[61] who had the strongest impact on the manuscripts produced between the 1520s and the 1540s. It should be mentioned that by the first quarter of the sixteenth century, the tradition of Herat had been absorbed into that of Tabriz and it is often difficult to determine which school had the strongest direct impact on the nakkaşhane.

The style of Herat appears in such works as the *Divans* of Jami and Ali Şir Nevai,[62] while that of Tabriz is seen in a number of manuscripts, including the *Şahname* of Firdausi[63] and the *Hamse* of Nizami.[64] In several manuscripts these influences are blended with the styles of native artists, who use Ottoman garments and headdresses on the figures and attempt to create local settings. This combination is particularly noticeable in the paintings of the *Hamse* of Ali Şir Nevai, copied in 1530/1531;[65] and in the *Tercüme-i Şahname*, dated around 1530.[66]

The next strong impact on the nakkaşhane came from Şiraz, showing both the Akkoyunlu and Safavid styles of the late fifteenth and early sixteenth centuries. The appearance of this tradition predates the reign of Süleyman and can be found in the paintings produced in Edirne

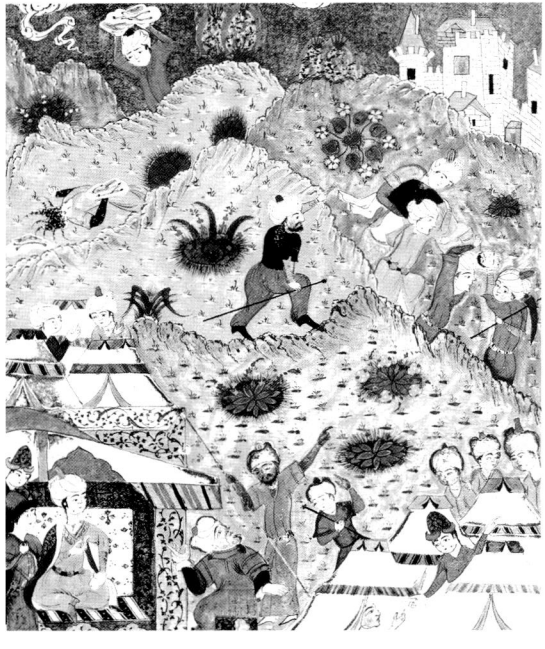

12. (left) Capture of Ferhad by Hüsrev, from the *Hamse* of Nevai transcribed by Pir Ahmed b. İskender in 1530/1531 (İstanbul, Topkapı Sarayı Müzesi, H. 802, fol. 99a).

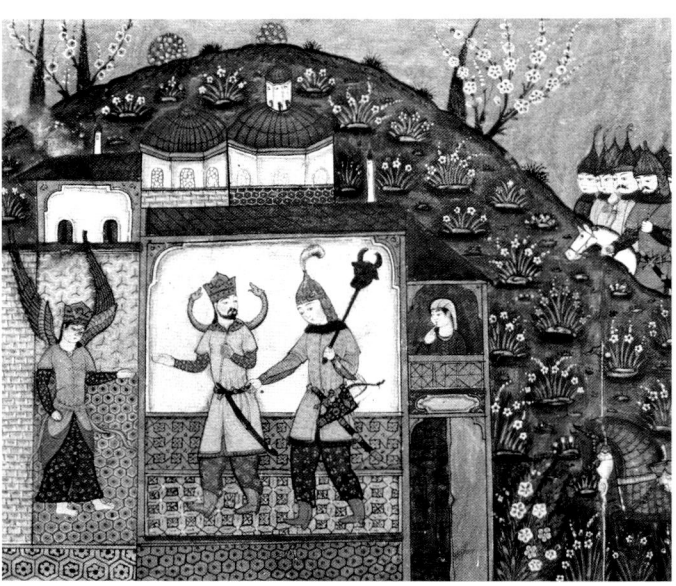

13. (right) Zahhak and Feridun, from the *Tercüme-i Şahname*, c. 1530 (İstanbul, Topkapı Sarayı Müzesi, H. 1116, fol. 14b).

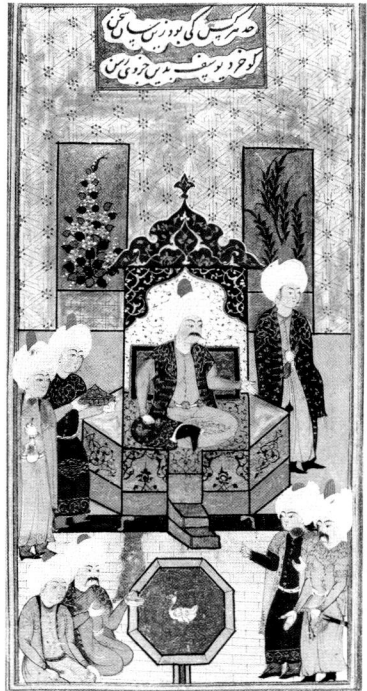
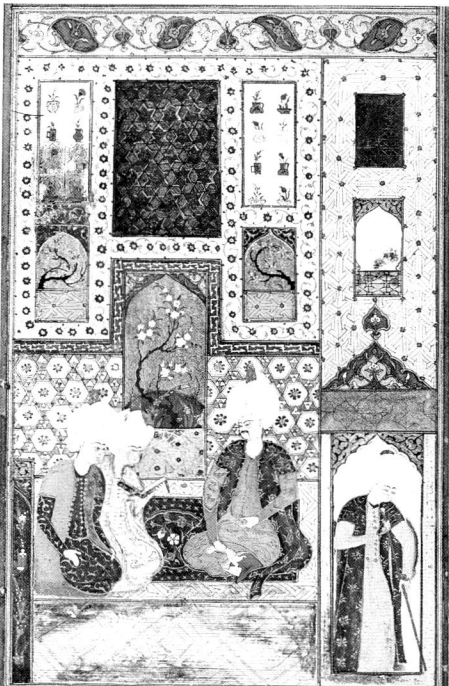
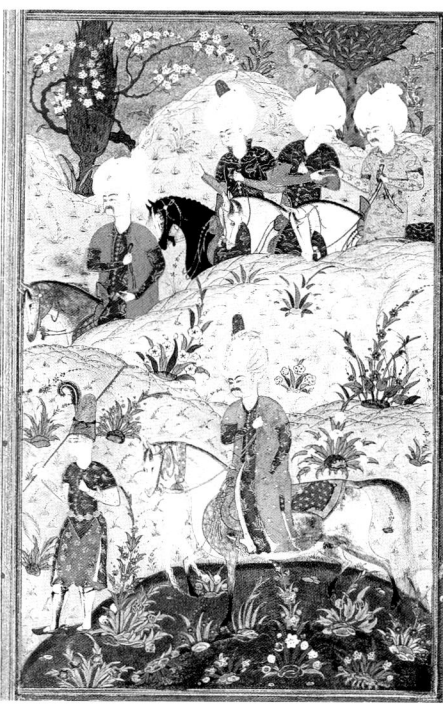
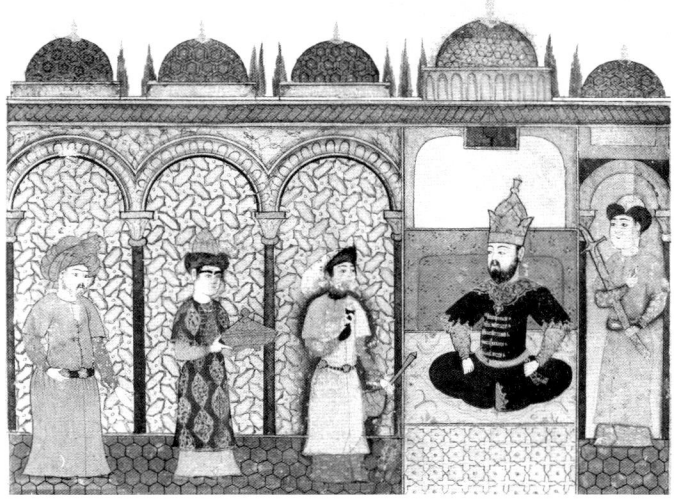

14. (above left) Enthronement of a Prince, from the *Mantık at-Tayr* of Attar, dated 1515 (İstanbul, Topkapı Sarayı Müzesi, E.H. 1512, fol. 84a).

15. (above right) Sultan Selim I in His Library (left) and Riding with His Court (right), from the *Divan-ı Selimi* transcribed by Şahsuvar Selimi, c. 1520 (İstanbul, Üniversite Kütüphanesi, F. 1330, fols. 27b-28a).

16. (left) Enthronement of a King, from the *Tercüme-i Şahname*, c. 1560-1570 (İstanbul, Topkapı Sarayı Müzesi, H. 1522, fol. 494b).

and İstanbul around the beginning of the sixteenth century. Its continuation in this period is observed in two copies of the *Hamse* of Nizami[67] and in a copy of the *Şahname* produced in Şiraz in 1495, its frontispiece added in İstanbul around 1550.[68]

The problem of determining the influence of Cairo has yet to be resolved. The artists employed in the last Mamluk court had been practicing the traditions established in Tabriz and Şiraz[69] and blended their styles with those of their colleagues when they joined the Ottoman studio.

Two rather distinct styles began to evolve in the nakkaşhane around the 1520s. The first is highly decorative with a limited repertoire of scenes depicting either hunts or enthronements with formulaic landscapes or architectural settings. The figures have long drooping mustaches and wear voluminous turbans wrapped around tall batons. This style, which shows the influence of Herat, dominated Ottoman painting between 1520 and 1560. Making its initial appearance in the *Mantık at-Tayr* of Attar dated 1515,[70] it is seen in a large number of other literary works, including the *Divan-ı Selimi*,[71] as well as in the historical works

figures 14 and 15

of Arifi, which will be discussed in detail later.

The second style, less coherent but nevertheless original, is found in the paintings of native artists, who worked on contemporary or almost contemporary Turkish texts that had not been previously illustrated. These isolated attempts include Musa Abdi's *Camaspname* of 1527,[72] Fuzuli's *Hadikat üs-Sueda* of c. 1550.[73] and Şeyhi's *Hüsrev ve Şirin* of about the same date.[74] Included in this group is a copy of the *Tercüme-i Şahname* datable to the 1560s,[75] which incorporates local features into the representation of Iranian epic history.

figure 16

Illustrated Histories

It is with the historical genre that the classical Ottoman style was firmly established. Illustrated volumes devoted to general histories of the Ottoman dynasty, biographies of individual sultans, or descriptions of specific festive events or campaigns became the preoccupation of the nakkaşhane after the 1560s. Written and illustrated by men who witnessed the events, these volumes are like documentary filmstrips. They recreate the personages and the settings of the Ottoman Empire as well as its various institutions and ceremonies.

Although the tradition of illustrated histories is not unique to the Ottomans, the extraordinary productivity of Ottoman illustrators over the course of some four centuries is unmatched by that of any other civilization. Earlier or contemporary attempts in other Islamic countries were either isolated or sporadic undertakings and included universal histories by Tabari and Reşideddin (Rashid al-Din) and biographies of individual rulers such as Timur, Babur, and Akbar. The glorification of the dynasty and its rulers was primarily an Ottoman tradition in which the best talents of the empire were employed. The volumes, which were subjected to close inspection by the sultan and high court officials from their initial conception to their completion, were cared for and preserved in the imperial libraries. They were produced for private use, for the enjoyment of the members of the dynasty. One wonders whether they did not also serve as guides for future sultans, who were expected to revere and benefit from the glorious achievements of their predecessors. The sultans' consciousness of their role in history, their pride in their ancestry, and their claim to the right to rule over a vast and expanding empire are evident in these magnificently produced volumes.

Ottoman historiography dates back to the early years of the empire.[76] General histories of the dynasty, usually entitled *Tarih-i Al-i Osman* (History of the House of Osman), were written by a number of authors in the fourteenth and fifteenth centuries, including Ahmedi (died 1412) and Aşıkpaşazade. Historiography flourished during Süleyman's long reign, when a number of chronicles and histories were composed by such renowned scholars as Kemalpaşazade, Taşköprülüzade Ahmed, Aşık Çelebi, Hoca Sadeddin, Ahmed Feridun, (Gelibolulu) Mustafa Ali, and Lütfi. Included in this renowned group of historians is Nasuh al-Silahi al-Matraki, known as Matrakcı Nasuh, who will be discussed later.

Illustrated histories began to make their appearance around 1500, starting with the *Şahname* of Melik Ümmü, an unknown historian who wrote about the reign of Bayezid II.[77] The next volume is the *Selimname* of Şükrü Bitlisi, written in Turkish verse and presented to Süley-

17. (above) View of İstanbul, from the *Beyan-ı Menazil-i Sefer-i Irakeyn* written, transcribed, and illustrated by Matrakcı, c. 1537 (İstanbul, Üniversite Kütüphanesi, T. 5964, fols. 8b-9a).

18. (below) View of Genoa, from the *Tarih-i Feth-i Siklos, Estergon, ve Estonibelgrad* written, transcribed and illustrated by Matrakcı, c. 1545 (İstanbul, Topkapı Sarayı Müzesi, H. 1608, fols. 32b-33a.

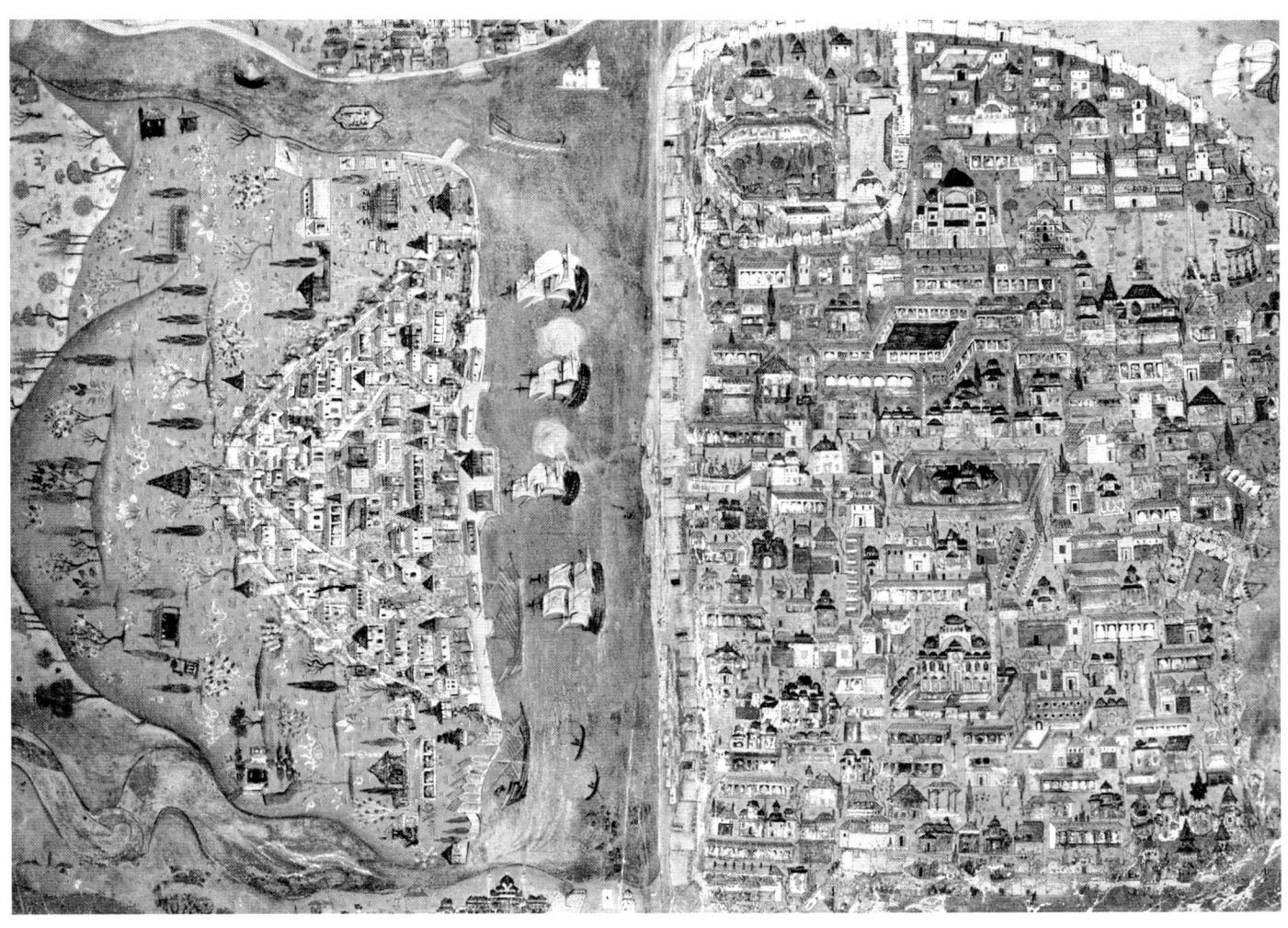

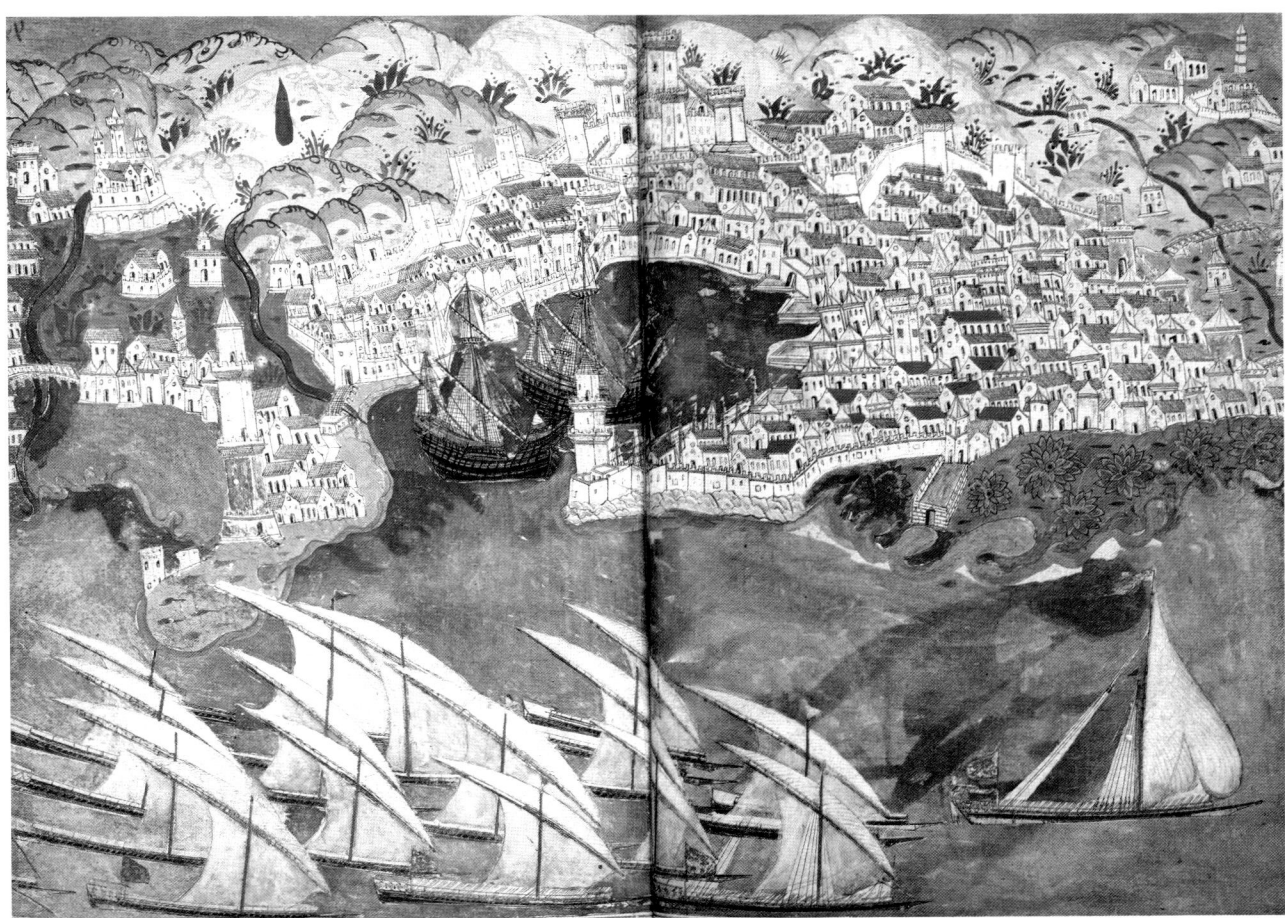

man around 1525.[78] The *Selimname,* illustrated with twenty-four paintings, includes a frontispiece representing the author together with the calligrapher and painter, neither of whom is named. Revealing stylistic influences from Herat, the paintings represent the first attempt at documenting historic figures and events.

The subsequent group of manuscripts composed in Turkish prose was revolutionary. Matrakcı Nasuh, their author as well as illustrator, depicts the cities and ports conquered by the Ottomans with a keen eye for detail. Since the paintings lack figures, they fall within the topographic or portulan genres. The earliest appears to be the *Beyan-ı Menazil-i Sefer-i Irakeyn,*[79] which describes Süleyman's campaign of 1534-1536 to Iraq and Iran. Completed around 1537, it is illustrated with 128 paintings that depict the cities and regions in which the army halted. Nasuh's unique conception, original style, and insistence on accuracy had an enduring impact on the painters of the nakkaşhane.

figure 17

Nasuh also wrote and illustrated two other volumes. One of these is the *Tarih-i Sultan Bayezid,* c. 1540-1545,[80] which narrates the events involving Bayezid II and his brother Cem in the 1480s and 1490s, and contains ten paintings showing a number of fortresses and ports. The other is entitled the *Tarih-i Feth-i Siklos, Estergon, ve Estonibelgrad* (also called *Süleymanname*), c. 1545-1550,[81] which describes Süleyman's Hungarian campaign of 1543 as well as Barbaros Hayreddin Paşa's naval activities on the French coast of the Mediterranean of the same year; it contains thirty-two scenes depicting both land and sea fortresses and towns.

figure 18

Nasuh, a man of exceptional talent, appears to have been born in Bosnia, possibly in the town of Visoka.[82] Educated in the Enderun, he was appointed as one of its ağas by Bayezid II and retained this position until his death, which is thought to have occurred in 1564. Nasuh wrote extensively on history, mathematics, and swordsmanship; he was, in addition,

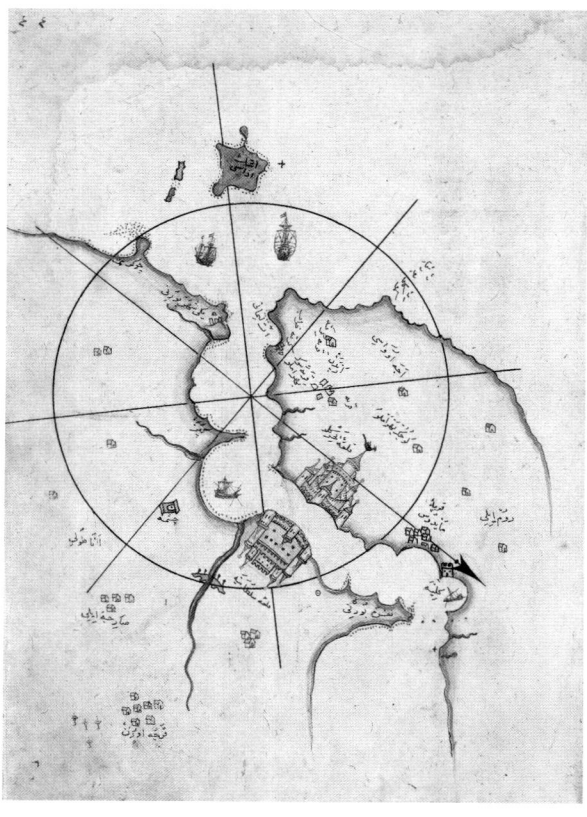
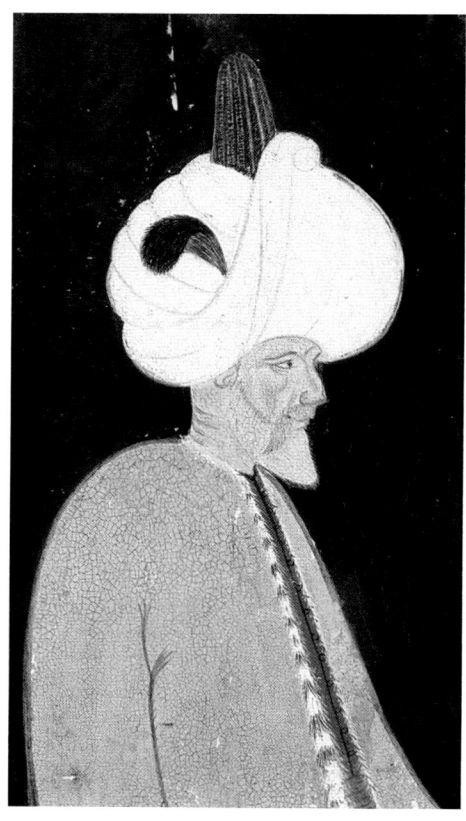

19. (left) View of Çanakkale, from the *Kitab-ı Bahriye* written, transcribed, and illustrated by Piri Reis in 1525/1526 (İstanbul, Topkapı Sarayı Müzesi, H. 642, fol. 44a).

20. (right) Portrait of Sultan Süleyman (detail) by Nigari, c. 1560 (İstanbul, Topkapı Sarayı Müzesi, H. 2134/8).

an accomplished calligrapher and painter. He came to be called Matrakçı after inventing the game of *matrak* (played by throwing sticks) to celebrate the 1530 circumcision festival for Şehzades Mustafa, Mehmed, and Selim. Nasuh is far better known for his historical works written in Turkish. They range from the translation of Tabari's universal history and biographies of Bayezid II and Selim I to detailed eyewitness accounts of the reign of Süleyman covering the years from 1520 to the 1560s. Since he had joined the sultan on many campaigns, he was able to recreate the events with great accuracy.

An artist whose painting style and educational background resemble those of Nasuh was Piri Reis, a famous captain in the imperial navy. Known for his celebrated map of the Americas[83] presented to Selim I in 1513, he also wrote in 1521 the *Kitab-ı Bahriye*, a book on maritime arts and a guide to Mediterranean ports, which he revised in 1525. The earliest illustrated manuscript among some thirty existing copies of the revised version is dated 1525/1526.[84] Presented to Süleyman, it contains 215 maps and representations of ports executed by the writer. Piri Reis, born around 1465, was the nephew of the famous captain Kemal and served with him in the Mediterranean. After an unsuccessful confrontation with the Portuguese in the Arabian Gulf, he was accused of taking bribes to lift the siege of Hormuz, which resulted in his execution in 1554.

A colleague of Piri Reis was Haydar Reis, a naval commander who used the pseudonym Nigari when signing his paintings.[85] Like Nasuh and Piri Reis, Nigari was not employed in the Ehl-i Hiref but belonged to the central administration. Rendered on single sheets, his representations of Süleyman, Selim II, and Barbaros Hayreddin Paşa were painted from life. Nigari was influential in promoting the genre of portraiture which, together with the topographic and portulan styles initiated by Nasuh and Piri Reis, had a strong impact on the development of Ottoman illustrated histories. A highly learned man, Nigari was a poet and historian as well as a painter. His home in the Galata district of İstanbul was the gathering place of scholars and writers. He is thought to have died at the age of eighty in 1572, having served both Süleyman and his son Selim II.

In addition to encouraging the work of biographers, chroniclers, and historians of the empire, the Ottoman sultans created the post of the *şahnameci* (writer of a *şahname*, book of kings) to compose imperial biographies.[86] This post, founded by Mehmed II, was first occupied by Şehdi, whose *Tarih-i Al-i Osman* was never illustrated. The next şahnameci was Fethullah Arif Çelebi, known as Arifi, the court historiographer during Süleyman's reign.

Arifi, who arrived in İstanbul from Şirvan in 1547, wrote the five-volume *Şahname-i Al-i Osman*, which is discussed in detail in the following section. The fifth book in this series was the *Süleymanname*, covering the events from 1520 to 1555. Arifi was the first official şahnameci of the sultans whose works were illustrated. When he died in 1561/1562, he was replaced by Eflatun, a colleague from Şirvan who is not known to have produced any histories. When Eflatun died in 1569, the post was given to Lokman, the most prolific of all the şahnamecis. Lokman's successor was Talikizade, who held the position between 1596/1597 to 1599/1600 and continued the tradition. The last of the official court biographers was Nadiri, working in the first half of the seventeenth century.

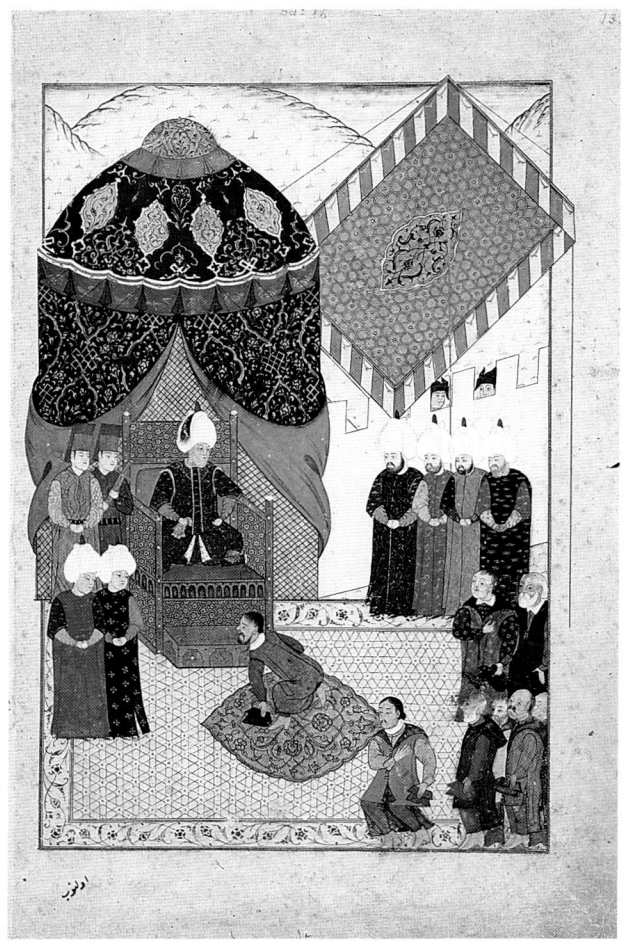

21. Sultan Süleyman Receiving Stephen Zapolya, from the *Nüzhet el-Esrar el-Ahbar der Sefer-i Sigetvar* of Ahmed Feridun Paşa, dated 1568/1569 (İstanbul, Topkapı Sarayı Müzesi, H. 1339, fol. 16b).

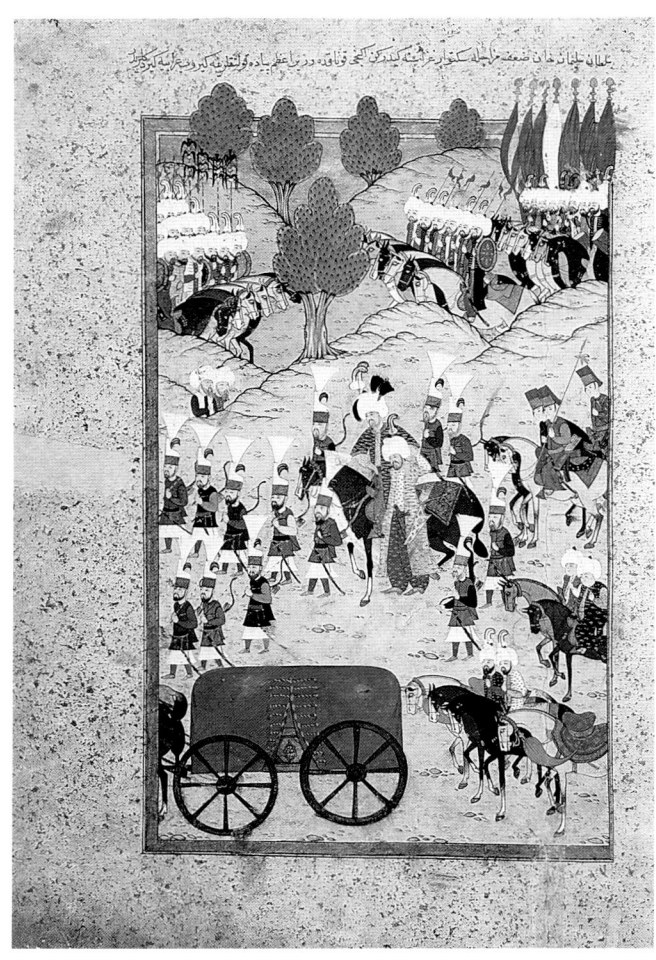

22. Sultan Süleyman Marching Toward Szigetvar, from the *Hünername* of Lokman, volume II, dated 1588 (İstanbul, Topkapı Sarayı Müzesi, H. 1524, fol. 276a).

The legacy of Süleyman continued well beyond his reign. Later şahnamecis and historians praised his magnificent achievements, which were duly illustrated by court painters. Süleyman's last campaign to Szigetvar is described in Ahmed Feridun Paşa's *Nüzhet el-Esrar el-Ahbar der Sefer-i Sigetvar*.[87] Completed in 1568/1569, this Turkish work was illustrated by Osman, whose style was first seen around 1560 and continued to dominate illustrated imperial histories well into the early decades of the seventeenth century.

Osman and his associates worked primarily with Lokman, who held the post of the şahnameci for twenty-five years. Their first cooperative effort was the *Tarih-i Sultan Süleyman*,[88] copied in 1579 by Kasım al-Hüseyni el-Aridi il-Kazvini. It was conceived as the final chapter of the *Süleymanname* and narrated the events of the last years of Süleyman's life, concluding with his death in 1566. The volume is illustrated with thirty-two paintings, which reveal the full development of the classical style of Ottoman painting.

Lokman also wrote the biographies of the ensuing sultans: the *Şahname-i Selim Han* on Selim II, of which two illustrated copies exist, dated c. 1575 and 1581,[89] and the two-volume *Şahinşahname* on Murad III, completed in 1581 and 1592-1597.[90] His two-volume *Hünername* covers the history of the Ottomans in the first part, which is dated 1584/1585, and the life of Süleyman in the second part, completed in

1588.[91] This extraordinary şahnameci composed both in Persian and Turkish verse and also produced a genealogy of the Ottoman dynasty, entitled *Kıyafet el-İnsaniye fi Şemail-i Osmaniye* in 1579, of which several illustrated copies were made.[92] In addition, he wrote a universal history, the *Zübdet üt-Tevarih*, of which three illustrated versions exist,[93] and a voluminous work narrating the 1582 circumcision festival for the son of Murad III, entitled the *Surname*.[94] The paintings in these histories constitute the corpus of the classical style.

Osman and the other painters in the nakkaşhane owed much to the figure type, landscapes, and architectural settings created by the master of the *Süleymanname* whose compositions of specific activities—accession ceremonies, receptions of dignitaries, parades of the armies, battles, and sieges of fortresses—not only served the painters of the classical period as prototypes but were used as models until as late as the nineteenth century.

The *Süleymanname* is a majestic work of art, its impeccable workmanship, innovative style, and refinement befitting the fame of its subject. Together with Sinan's Süleymaniye complex completed in 1557, which reflects in monumental form the grandeur of the sultan's achievement, the book commemorates Süleyman as ruler and conqueror of a vast empire, documenting in detail the magnificence of his reign.

NOTES

1. The extent of the lands under direct control of the Ottomans at the death of Süleyman is generally accepted as being 877,800 square miles, which included 462,700 square miles in Asia, 224,100 square miles in Europe, and 191,000 square miles in Africa. In addition, the Ottomans controlled the tributary states of Moldavia, Wallachia, and Crimea, which had a total of some 350,000 square miles (Pitcher 1972, 134-135).

2. Some historical sources give 27 April 1495 as the date of birth of Süleyman. The earlier date used here is accepted by such scholars as M. Tayyip Gökbilgin, 1964, while the later one is given in Danişmend 1971, vol. 1, 400. Lokman, the court historian, also uses the earlier date in his *Kıyafet el-İnsaniye fi Şemail-i Osmaniye*, a biography of the sultans written in 1579 (TSM, H. 1563, transcribed c. 1579-1580, fol. 55b).

3. There seems to be some confusion about Hafsa's origin. Some historians state that it was Ayşe, another wife of Selim I, who was the daughter of Mengili Giray Han; they give as Hafsa's father a man named Abdülmümin or Abdülhay, an unknown personage, suggesting that she was of slave origin.

4. Some sources give as his accession date 30 September 1520, the day he arrived in İstanbul; others mention that the actual accession ceremonies took place the following day, 1 October, which seems more likely.

5. Sources give the names of three brothers—Abdullah, Mahmud, and Murad—who appear to have died before Süleyman's accession. It is thought that they were killed by Selim I in 1514 after he ascended the throne. Selim I, who forced his own father to abdicate, must have wanted Süleyman to be his sole heir.

6. This envoy must be Jean Frangipani (Rouillard 1938, 106).

7. Rendered in English from Irmak and Çağlar 1973, 392.

8. The letters of Busbecq, who was in the Ottoman court between 1554 and 1562, vividly describe his impressions of İstanbul, cities and towns on the way to Amasya, and the meeting with the sultan. They are translated into English in Forster 1968. Busbecq was accompanied by Melchior Lorichs, an artist who executed various vistas of the capital and studies of Ottoman figures, including portraits of Süleyman. See Fischer 1962 and Eyice 1970 for a study of his works. The drawings and engravings of Lorichs were published several times. Most of his works appear in Oberhummer 1902.

9. Lokman, *Kıyafet el-İnsaniye fi Şemail-i Osmaniye*, transcribed c. 1579-1580, TSM, H. 1563, fols. 55b-61b. For Süleyman's portrait in this work see Atasoy 1972, 12.

10. Forster 1968, 59 and 65.

11. For a study of Süleyman's legislation see İnalcık 1969.

12. The exact date of the wedding is not known. It is thought to have taken place after Süleyman arrived in İstanbul and ascended the throne.

13. Some of the letters written by Hürrem to Süleyman are published in Uluçay 1956, 80-84. Also published there are letters to the sultan from his daughter, Mihrimah, and granddaughter, Hümaşah (Uluçay 1956, 84-95). See also İnalcık 1973, 87.

14. There is yet to be a critical study of Süleyman's poetry. A few of his gazels are translated into English in Gibb 1904, vol. 3, 9-10. For a modern Turkish transcription of the *Divan-ı Muhibbi* see Çabuk 1980.

15. Only two other official marriages are known to have taken place after Süleyman's: in 1622 Osman II married the daughter of the şeyhülislam and in 1647 İbrahim married a former slave girl (Alderson 1982, 95-96).

16. See note 3.

17. Hürrem obviously feared most the Ottoman law of fratricide in which the sultan upon his accession to the throne would execute all his brothers, thus preventing any possible opposition and civil war. Her endeavor to eliminate Mustafa was also an act of self-preservation since she was then guaranteed to become the queen mother.

18. See note 13. Acting like a true empress, Hürrem also sent a letter in 1548 to Sigismund, king of Poland, congratulating him on his accession to the throne. It is difficult to determine whether she actually wrote the letters to Süleyman; the letter to the king of Poland, however, shows a different style of writing and must have been transcribed by a scribe (Abrahamowicz 1959, 103).

19. His lack of strength is clearly visible in one of the illustrations in Lokman's 1579 *Tarih-i Sultan Süleyman,* where he is supported by his grand vezir when riding a horse (CB, MS 413, fol. 46a; Ünver 1970, fig. 2). The same episode is represented in Lokman's *Hünername,* volume II, dated 1588 in TSM, H. 1524, fol. 276a (Fehér 1976, pl. XXXVIII; and Çağman nd, pl. 9).

20. Selim appears to have held a second accession ceremony in Belgrade where he must have needed the support of the army. It is his second accession ceremony that is illustrated in historical manuscripts. They appear in Ahmed Feridun Paşa's *Nüzhet el-Esrar el-Ahbar der Sefer-i Sigetvar* of 1568/1569 in TSM, H. 1339, fols. 110b-111a (Atıl 1980, pl. 22). They also appear in the two copies of Lokman's *Şahname-i Selim Han,* one dated c. 1575, in BL, or. 7043, fol. 14a (Frankfurt 1985, vol. 2, no. 1/16a) and the second dated 1581. One half of the latter scene is in Boston Museum of Fine Arts, 14.694; the other is in TSM, A. 3595, fol. 26b (Atasoy and Çağman 1974, pl. 14).

21. It appears that although space for the mausoleums of Süleyman and Hürrem was reserved behind the Süleymaniye Mosque, the structures themselves were not built until after their deaths. A painting in Lokman's 1579 *Tarih-i Sultan Süleyman* (CB, MS. 413, fol. 115b; Ünver 1970, fig. 5) shows Süleyman's coffin being carried to the mosque while figures dig a grave under a tent in the courtyard, next to the mausoleum of Hürrem, who died eight years earlier. His tomb is not depicted and therefore was not yet built. It may have been considered bad taste or ominous to construct a mausoleum before the intended actually died. Süleyman's body must have been first buried under the tent; then the mausoleum, which was already designed, was erected over it.

22. The same painting mentioned above shows a large chest carried in front of Süleyman's coffin. It was rumored that Süleyman wished to be buried with this chest, contrary to Islamic practice. It was, however, traditional for the sultans' possessions, such as kaftans and other personal belongings, to be laid on top of their coffins or stored in the mausoleums. The story goes that as the ulema were discussing the proper way to comply with Süleyman's wishes during his funeral, the chest fell down and its contents spilled out. It contained small pieces of paper, the fetvas issued by the şeyhülislam. This anecdote indicates the importance Süleyman gave to conforming his kanuns with the şeriat (Ünver 1970, 306).

23. For an architectural study of the palace see Eldem and Akozan 1982.

24. In the 1850s the sultans moved to the recently built Dolmabahçe Palace on the western shores of the Bosphorus. The Topkapı Palace was used by the retired and elderly members of the court until it was converted into a museum in the 1920s.

25. See İnalcık 1973, 82-83, tables 1 and 2, for the advancement of the ağas and their numbers.

26. The world "odalisque" is derived from odalık. In nineteenth-century European paintings it was used to identify sensual females bathing or reclining in what were then thought to be Harem chambers.

27. See note 15.

28. The sultan observed the sessions from a chamber built into the Adalet Kulesi which was connected to the Harem. It overlooked the Kubbealtı and was hidden by a window

with a grille. Since the Divan members never knew if or when he was actually listening in, they behaved as if he were always present. This procedure was begun during the reign of Süleyman, who often asked his grand vezir İbrahim Paşa to substitute for him at meetings of the Divan.

29. Originally there were only two beylerbeyis: one for Anatolia, the Asian provinces, and another for Rumelia, the European provinces. As the empire expanded a number of new beylerbeyliks were created. During Süleyman's reign they increased to about two dozen. See Pitcher 1972, 124-129; and İnalcık 1973, 106, table 3. The janissary ağası, the kaptan-ı derya, and the darülsaade ağası later became members of the Divan.

30. A rare manuscript in İstanbul (TSM, H. 1132) contains the *Divan-ı Muhibbi* written by Süleyman himself. There exist several versions of the *Divan* produced during his lifetime, the most beautifully illuminated ones being the two copies transcribed by Mehmed Şerif in 1565/1566 (TSM, R. 738 mük.; İÜ, T. 5467). See note 15 on page 76.

31. For the works of Sinan see Goodwin 1971, 196-284; Sözen 1975; Kuran 1978; and Bates 1980, 102-123.

32. The list of artists and the expenses of the Süleymaniye complex are published in Barkan 1972-1979. See also Rogers 1982. The endowment is studied in Kürkçüoğlu 1962.

33. Evliya Çelebi, writing in the first quarter of the seventeenth century, lists hundreds of artisans and craftsmen working in the city. See Danışman 1969-1971, vol. 2, 207-334.

34. Among the most important centers were the sancaks of the crown princes. Published documents from Süleyman's courts in Kefe and Manisa indicate a large staff and include a number of Ehl-i Hiref artists, such as hatmakers, furriers, halberd makers, bowmakers, goldsmiths, boothmakers, saddlers, and musicians (Uluçay 1970, 237-249). Another active sancak was Amasya, where the earliest illustrated Ottoman manuscripts were produced (Kappert 1976; and Atıl 1980, 154-155).

35. Among these were Matrakcı Nasuh, Piri Reis, and Haydar Reis, whose works are discussed in the following section. Other Enderun members included Hasan Paşa, a kapıcıbaşı, janissary ağa, and beylerbeyi, who illustrated several official histories in 1570-1610 (Akalay 1979; and Atıl 1980, 198 and 203-206, ills. 97-101). A later dignitary was Ahmed Nakşi, an astrologer and the official timekeeper of the Süleymaniye Mosque, who worked on both literary and historical manuscripts during the first quarter of the seventeenth century (Atıl 1978; and Atıl 1980, 212-215, ill. 110 and pls. 30-31).

36. This structure is illustrated in the *Surname-i Vehbi* of c. 1720 (Atıl 1980, 221-222 and ill. 120).

37. These are listed in Meriç 1963.

38. An undated register drawn before 1526 lists forty-one members of the Cemaat-i Nakkaşan and nine members of the Cemaat-i Mücellidan, society of bookbinders (TSM, Archives D. 9613-2; Meriç 1953 and 1954, no. I). Another document dated Rebiülahir 932 (15 January–12 February 1526) lists the same forty-one nakkaşan and eight of the mücellidan, giving information on their backgrounds and dates of entry into the society (TSM, Archives D. 9613-1; Meriç 1953 and 1954, no. II).

39. This register, dated Muharrem, Safer, and Rebiülevvel 952 (15 March–11 June 1545), includes fifty-nine nakkaşan and twelve mücellidan (TSM, Archives D. 9613-3; Meriç 1953 and 1954, no. III).

40. The document, dated Rebiülevvel, Rebiülahir, and Cumadeyn 965 (22 December 1557–20 March 1558), lists thirty-four nakkaşan and ten mücellidan (TSM, Archives D. 6500; Meriç 1953 and 1954, no. IV). See pages 255 and 256.

41. The register, drawn between Muharrem 965 and Muharrem 966 (24 October 1557–14 October 1558), includes thirty-nine nakkaşan and ten mücellidan (TSM, Archives D. 9612; Meriç 1953 and 1954, no. V).

42. This unpublished document drawn in Muharrem, Safer, and Rebiülevvel 974 (19 July–15 October 1566), lists thirty-eight nakkaşan and ten mücellidan (İstanbul, Başvekalet Arşivi, D. 6196).

43. One of these is dated Receb, Şaban, and Ramazan 1005 (2 March–29 May 1596) and lists 124 nakkaşan equally divided into sixty-two masters and sixty-two apprentices; and thirty-eight mücellidan, of which twenty-three are masters (TSM, Archives D. 9613-13; Meriç 1953 and 1954, no. VI). The second register, dated Muharrem, Safer, Rebiülevvel 1005 (26 August–22 November 1596) has 129 nakkaşan and thirty-nine mücellidan (TSM, Archives D. 9613-15; Meriç 1953 and 1954, no. VII). These two registers contain the largest number of salaried painters and bookbinders in the history of the Ehl-i Hiref. Membership in the society shows a decrease in subsequent years. See Atıl 1980, 234, note 3.

44. The registers list several Hasans, three of them called Çelebi, an honorific title, which makes the identification of the nakkaşbaşı difficult. One Hasan Çelebi was the father of an artist named Hüseyin and died during the reign of Selim I; another was Büyük (Elder) Hasan Çelebi, presumably Hasan b. Mehmed; a third was Küçük (Younger) Hasan Çelebi, that is, Hasan b. Abdülcelil.

45. For a study of the saz style and its originators see Denny 1983.

46. Atıl 1973, no. 4; Atıl 1980, ill. 89; and Denny 1983, pl. 6.

47. This drawing is in the so-called Behram Mirza Album in TSM, H. 2154, fol. 2a (Dickson and Welch 1981, 54).

48. For this artist see Dickson and Welch 1981, 95-117.

49. This manuscript is in TSM, E.H. 49; the notation appears on fol. 1a (Karatay 1962-1969, vol. 1, no. 141).

50. İÜ, T. 5467 (İstanbul 1983, E 62).

51. For other works attributed to Kara Memi see pages 64 and 65.

52. This manuscript is in TSM, E.H. 58; Bayram's name appears in the colophon on fol. 477b; İstanbul 1983, E 57.

53. The payroll registers record only the daily retainers given to the artists, who must have received additional payments when assigned to specific projects. Qualified artists were generously rewarded by gifts and cash bonuses during religious holidays and upon the completion of their tasks. Unfortunately the registers from the reign of Süleyman are incomplete and documents related to the expenses involved with special projects are missing.

54. This document is partially published in Meriç 1953, no. LXXIV. In addition to the painters there were four men listed under "musicians" and eighteen men listed under "müteferrika," which included calligraphers, goldsmiths, metalworkers, tilemakers, and glassmakers.

55. See Atıl 1984.

56. See notes 37-43.

57. The society of the nakkaşan was also family oriented with several sons and fathers working in the studio. Their genealogies, however, are not as clear as those of the mücellidan since not only were there many more members in the studio but several had the same name.

58. See note 49.

59. Calligraphers of the reign of Süleyman are discussed in Derman 1970. Many manuscripts, however, were not signed and the scribes' actual works are unknown.

60. The expenses of this spectacular manuscript, which is in TSM, H.S. 5, are well documented in Meriç 1953, no. CXV. See also İstanbul 1983, E 192.

61. Artists listed as "Tebrizi" in the registers must have included Herati painters who had been exiled to Tabriz after the fall of the Timurid Empire. Celalzade Koca Nişancı Mustafa (died 1558) in his *Selimname* mentions that on 13 September 1514 Bedi üz-Zaman, the last Timurid sultan of Herat exiled to Tabriz, came to İstanbul with his entire court of scholars and artists (TSM, H. 1415, fol. 107a; Karatay 1961b, no. 635). The painters in Bedi üz-Zaman's retinue must have been responsible for the strong impact of Herat found in Ottoman paintings. This influence is described in Çağman 1978.

62. For the *Divan* of Jami (TSM, H. 987) and collected poems of Nevai (TSM, H. 983 and R. 806; and DK, MS. 3) see Stchoukine 1966, nos. 11 and 23; Çağman 1978, 237-238 and fig. 21; Atıl 1980, ill. 73.

63. TSM, H. 1499 (Stchoukine 1966, no. 20; Atıl 1980, pl. 18).

64. TSM, B. 145 transcribed in 1498 with paintings added c. 1540 (Karatay 1961a, no. 429).

65. TSM, H. 802 (Stchoukine 1966, no. 10; Atıl 1980, ill. 74).

66. TSM, H. 1116 (Atıl 1980, ill. 75).

67. TSM, H. 753 and H. 764 (Karatay 1961a, nos. 470 and 465 respectively). The former is published in Stchoukine 1972 and Akalay 1973.

68. TSM, R. 1542 (Karatay 1961a, no. 344).

69. See note 55.

70. TSM, E.H. 1512 (Çağman 1978, figs. 18 and 19; Atıl 1980, pl. 17; Çağman 1980, pl. 160; and İstanbul 1983, E 55). This manuscript was the first to be produced after the conquest of Tabriz in 1514 and proves that artists from Herat came to the studio at that time. See also note 61.

71. İÜ, F. 1330 (Atıl 1980, pl. 19; İstanbul 1983, E 56).

72. BL, Add. 24962 (Stchoukine 1966, no. 9; and Titley 1981, no. 1).

73. Binney 1979, no. 9. This manuscript appears to be one of the oldest known illustrated copies of Fuzuli's work.

74. TİEM, 1960 (Çığ 1959, no. 5).

75. TSM, H. 1522 (Atıl 1980, ill. 76).

76. See İnalcık 1964.

77. TSM, H. 1123 (Atıl 1980, 164). This work was transcribed and illuminated by Derviş Mahmud b. Abdullah and contains seven illustrations.

78. TSM, H. 1597-1598 (Stchoukine 1966, no. 8; Çağman 1978, fig. 20; Atıl 1980, ill. 77).

79. İÜ, T. 5964. Facsimile published in Yurdaydın 1976; see also İstanbul 1983, E 74.

80. TSM, R. 1272 (Akalay 1969).

81. TSM, R. 1608 (Akalay 1969; Fehér 1976, figs. 1-9 and pls. XXIII-XXVI; Atıl 1980, ill. 79; and Çağman 1980, pl. 161).

82. For his life and works see Yurdaydın 1976, 1-30, and 115-173 in English.

83. TSM, R. 1633 mük. (İstanbul 1983, E 73).

84. TSM, H. 642. For a study of the work see İnan 1954 and Soucek 1973.

85. For an early study of his paintings see Ünver 1946. See also Binney 1979, nos. 11 and 12; Atıl 1980, ills. 85-87; Welch and Welch 1982, no. 6; and İstanbul 1983, E 69.

86. For a study of this important post see Woodhead 1983.

87. TSM, H. 1339 (Stchoukine 1966, no. 29; Fehér 1976, pls. XXXVII, XL-XLII, and XLIV-XLVII; Atıl 1980, ill. 84 and pl. 22; and İstanbul 1983, E 172 with additional bibliography). See also note 20.

88. CB, MS. 413 (Minorsky 1958, no. 413; Stchoukine 1966, no. 33; Atasoy and Çağman 1974, pls. 12 and 13; and Rogers 1983, nos. 76-78). See also note 19.

89. BL, Or. 7043; TSM, A. 3595. The former is published in Meredith-Owens 1962 and Titley 1981, no. 49. The latter is published in Çağman 1973. See also note 20.

90. Volume I of the work is in İÜ, F. 1404; volume II is in TSM, B. 200 (Stchoukine 1966, no. 45; and İstanbul 1983, E. 173 and 187 with full bibliography).

91. Both volumes are in TSM, H. 1523 and H. 1524. Volume I is published in Anafarta 1969; for complete references see İstanbul 1983, E. 184. See also note 19.

92. Some of these contain portraits of the first twelve sultans up to Murad III while others were appended in later years and include the subsequent rulers. The earlier ones are in İÜ, T. 6087 (dated 1579) and T. 6088 (c. 1580); TSM, H. 1563 (c. 1579-1580), R. 1264 (dated 1587), and R. 1265 (dated 1588/1589); and BL, Add. 7880 (dated 1588/1589). See Atasoy 1972; Titley 1981, no. 46. See also notes 2 and 9.

93. These are in TİEM, 1973 (dated 1583); CB, MS. 414 (dated 1583); and TSM, H. 1321 (dated 1588). See Minorsky 1958, no. 414; Renda 1973 and 1976; Atıl 1980, ill. 103; and İstanbul 1983, E 180. This work is also called the *Silsilename* (Book of Genealogy).

94. TSM, H. 1344 (Atıl 1980, pl. 25; İstanbul 1983, E 174 and 175 with full bibliography).

The Şahnameci and His Works

THE *Şahname-i Al-i Osman*, composed in Persian verse by Fethullah Arif Çelebi, known as Arifi, is the first illustrated official history of the Ottoman dynasty. The author was the son of Derviş Mehmed of Abadan and the grandson of a respected Egyptian seyh, İbrahim Gülşeni.[1] Arifi had joined the court of Elkas Mirza, the brother of the Şah Tahmasp and the governor of Şirvan, as a secretary. When Elkas sought the protection of the Ottomans after his unsuccessful rebellion against the şah and escaped to İstanbul in 1547, he brought members of his court with him, including Derviş Mehmed and two poets, Arifi and Eflatun. Derviş Mehmed later served as an envoy between the sultan and Elkas while both Arifi and Eflatun became employed as official historians.

Arifi's first activities in the Ottoman court must have pleased the sultan, who appointed him şahnameci with a daily stipend of twenty-five akçes and commissioned him to compose a history of the Ottoman dynasty, using Firdausi's *Şahname* as a model. Süleyman appears to have been satisfied with the poet's work since the şahnameci's salary was gradually increased to seventy akçes a day. When some twenty or thirty thousand verses were completed, the sultan was so impressed with the text that he requested that a special group of calligraphers and painters be assigned to the project. A new building was constructed in the Topkapı Palace to house the şahnameci and his staff.[2]

Arifi's popularity with the sultan and the success of his works awakened the jealousy of his colleagues, particularly of Eflatun, a fellow poet, and Şahkulu, the celebrated chief painter of the nakkaşhane. Although Eflatun became the şahnameci after Arifi's death, he is not known to have produced any works during his seven- or eight-year tenure at that post. Şahkulu, who died in 1555/1556, did not have the opportunity to work on the *Şahname-i Al-i Osman*; he was either excluded from the group of painters chosen to illustrate the text, or died before such a decision could have been made. Nevertheless, the two anonymous master painters Arifi presumably selected to illustrate his work, identified here as Painters A and B, were indeed remarkable men; one was the doyen of the studio, whose style had dominated literary manuscripts for almost half a century, and the other was a revolutionary artist, who changed the course of Ottoman painting.

Arifi conceived the *Şahname-i Al-i Osman* as a five-volume set. The first volume began with the creation of man and included the early patriarchs; the second most likely described the rise of Islam; the third must have contained an account of the early Turkish empires and the Seljuks; the fourth was devoted to the foundation of the Ottoman Empire; and the fifth commemorated the life and achievements of his patron, Süleyman, the greatest of all rulers. The second and third volumes of the work were either never finished or are now lost. What remains are the following books:

VOLUME I: *Anbiyaname*; transcription completed in 12 Jumada I 965 (2 March 1558) by Yusuf el-Heravi; 48 folios with 19 lines of *nastalik* in 4 columns; 10 paintings by a single artist; text: from creation of Adam to birth of Gog and Magog; size (trimmed): 31.0 x 19.5 cm. (12³⁄₁₆ x 7¹¹⁄₁₆ in.); now in a private collection.[3]

VOLUME II: missing; a painting depicting Prophet Muhammed (?) with three disciples in a mosque by the same hand as the painter of volume I appears to belong to this book; mounted on an album page; size: 33.8 x 21.0 cm. (13¼ x 8⁵⁄₁₆ in.), original folio (trimmed): 19.1 x 10.1 cm. (7 x 4 in.); now in Los Angeles County Museum of Art, M. 73.5.446.[4]

VOLUME III: missing.

VOLUME IV: undated; colophon and final chapters missing; existing section transcribed by Mirza Huy-i Şirazi; 205 folios with 19 lines of nastalik in 4 columns; 34 paintings by a single artist; text: from the founding of the house of Osman to the year 1402; size: 36.5 x 24.5 cm. (14⅜ x 9⅝ in.); formerly in New York, Kraus Collection.[5]

VOLUME V: *Süleymanname*; transcription completed in mid-Ramazan 965 (late June-early July 1558) by Ali b. Emir Bey Şirvani; 617 folios with 15 lines of nastalik in 4 columns; 69 paintings (4 spread to double folios) attributed to five different artists; text: from 1520 to 1555; size: 37.0 x 25.4 cm. (14½ x 10 in.); İstanbul, Topkapı Palace Museum, H. 1517.[6]

The *Süleymanname*, which has the longest text and the largest number of paintings, was the most important volume since its subject was the sultan himself. Of the five artists employed to illustrate this book, one, Painter A, was solely responsible for the scenes in the *Anbiyaname* and the single folio attributed to the second volume; another, Painter B, executed the entire set in the fourth volume; other works of the remaining three artists have not yet been identified. More will be said on the stylistic features of these painters later in this chapter.

Arifi must have worked with phenomenal speed in writing and supervising the production of this voluminous history. Even if he started working immediately after his arrival in İstanbul, the work was transcribed, illustrated, and bound within just a decade.[7] The colophons of volumes I and V state that their transcriptions were completed in the same year, suggesting that after Arifi finished the text, it was quickly distributed to the calligraphers, illuminators, and painters, who worked simultaneously on the various volumes.

Volume IV, which bears the name of the calligrapher who transcribed the extant section but not the date, must have been distributed to two copyists: Mirza Huy-i Şirazi was assigned the first half that extended to the year 1402 while another artist was given the remaining chapters. Either the second calligrapher did not finish his section or that portion is now lost.

The *Şahname-i Al-i Osman* was not Arifi's only work for Süleyman. Although the poet's name is not given in the text, he must have composed the *Futuhat-ı Cemile*,[8] devoted to the 1551-1552 campaigns of vezirs Mehmed and Ahmed Paşas against the fortresses of Temesvar, Pecs, Lipva, and Erlau in Hungary and Transylvania. The work, transcribed in 1557/1558 by Abu Turab el-Hasani el-Hüseyni, is illustrated with seven paintings (one spread to double folios) that show the hand of the same master, Painter A, who worked on the *Anbiyaname* and many of the scenes in the *Süleymanname*. Since the paintings are rather crude in comparison to those in the other two books, either this manuscript was the artist's first commission, or he was too busy with the *Şahname-i Al-i Osman* volumes and relied on an assistant. The same artist executed the three paintings in Arifi's only illustrated literary text, the *Ravzat al-Uşak*,[9] which must have been completed around 1560.

Arifi is thought to have also written a *Divan* and other historical texts, including an account of the campaigns of Hadım Süleyman Paşa, one of Süleyman's grand vezirs. He also wrote a description of the conflicts between Selim I and his father, Bayezid II, and brother, Ahmed.[10]

Arifi set a precedent for future şahnamecis of the Ottoman Empire: he worked with a particular group of artists and appears to have had a say in the choice of painters.

Şahname-i Al-i Osman

Arifi's ambitious history of the Ottoman dynasty was conceived as a matching set of five volumes, each following the same size and layout with four columns to a page. The text was copied in nastalik with the headings rendered in *nesih*. Dedicatory folios, title pages, and section headings were illuminated as were the triangular units inserted around a select group of diagonally placed lines. The gold-speckled and polished paper was of the finest quality. Of the remaining three volumes, only two have their original bindings; the other appears to have been restored a few generations later.

Volume I, called the *Anbiyaname*, has been trimmed some six centimeters on all sides and rebound in the last two decades of the sixteenth century, when the illuminated opening folios were added (fols. 1b-2a). A few folios contain triangular units inserted into the text that are illuminated with either stylized blossoms, cloudbands, rumis, and hatayis, or naturalistic flowers and trees. The headings, rendered in blue or red nesih, are framed by gold bands and adorned with blossoms. The text begins with praises to the sultan and includes the history of the world from the creation of Adam to the birth of Gog and Magog. The colophon (fol. 48b) states that the work was written at the request of Sultan Süleyman and transcribed by Yusuf el-Heravi on 12 Jumada I 965 (2 March 1558), giving the day and year in digits. The calligrapher, originating from Herat, is otherwise unrecorded. The author of the work is not mentioned in the volume.

The ten illustrations, executed by one of the anonymous masters of the *Süleymanname* identified as Painter A, are quite remarkable and fall into two groups. The first group consists of seven paintings and has the traditional rectangular format with a few lines of text inserted above and below the scenes. Two of these represent heavenly settings: the Miraj (Night Journey of the Prophet Muhammed) and Adam with angels. Two others are set within a landscape: the sacrifice of Cain and Abel, and the battle of Seth and Cain. The remaining three scenes take place in front of architectural structures: Adam and Eve in the Garden of Eden, İdris

figure 23

23-26. Illustrations from the *Şahname-i Al-i Osman* of Arifi, volume I, transcribed by Yusuf el-Heravi in 1558 (Private Collection).

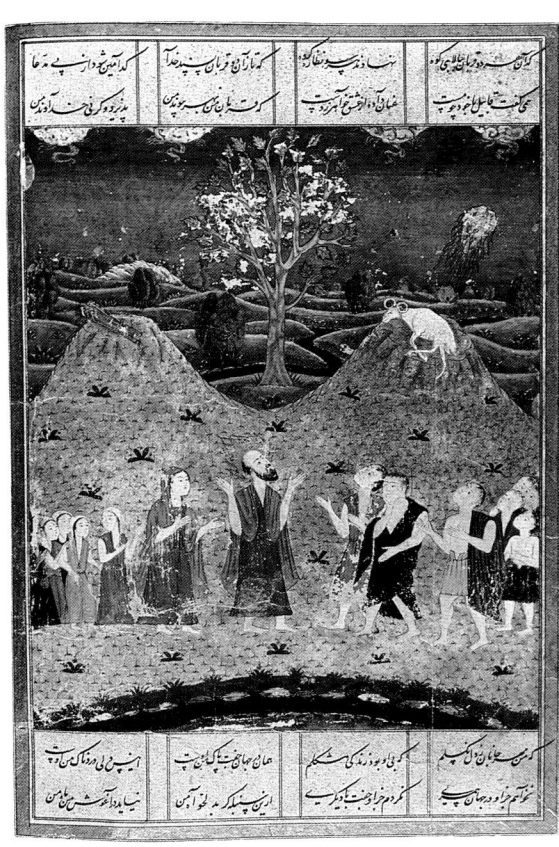

23. Sacrifice of Cain and Abel (fol. 24b).

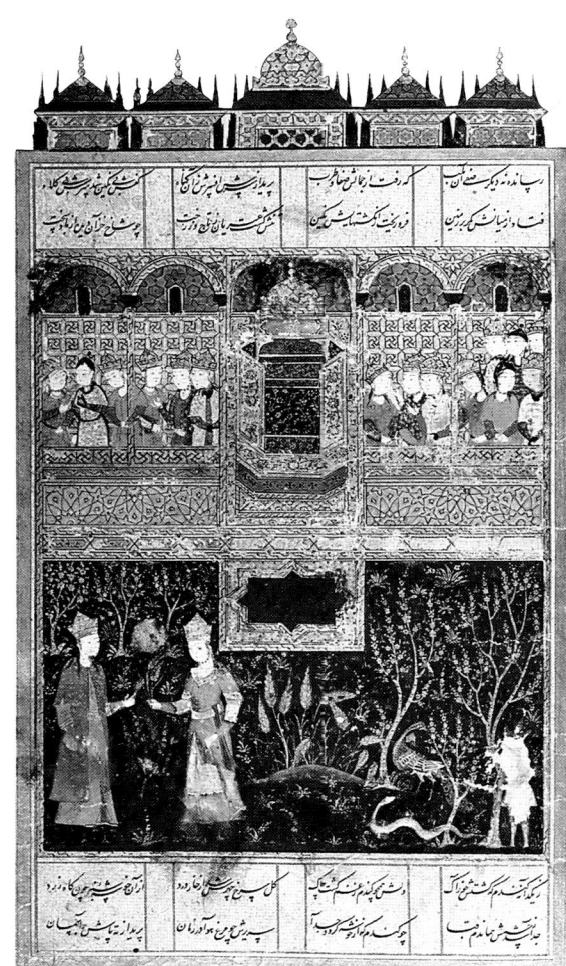

24. Eve Giving Adam the Grain of Paradise (fol. 20a).

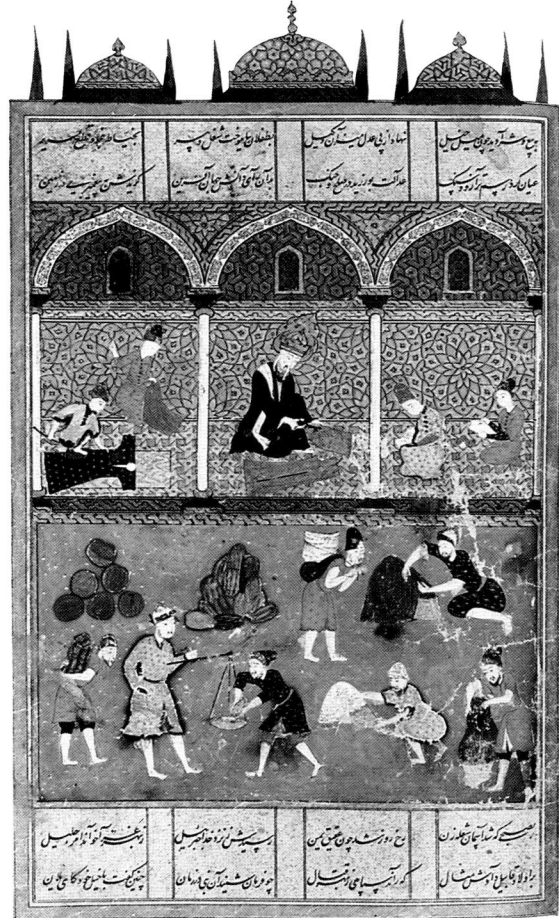

25. İdris Teaching Tailoring and Use of Weights (fol. 28a).

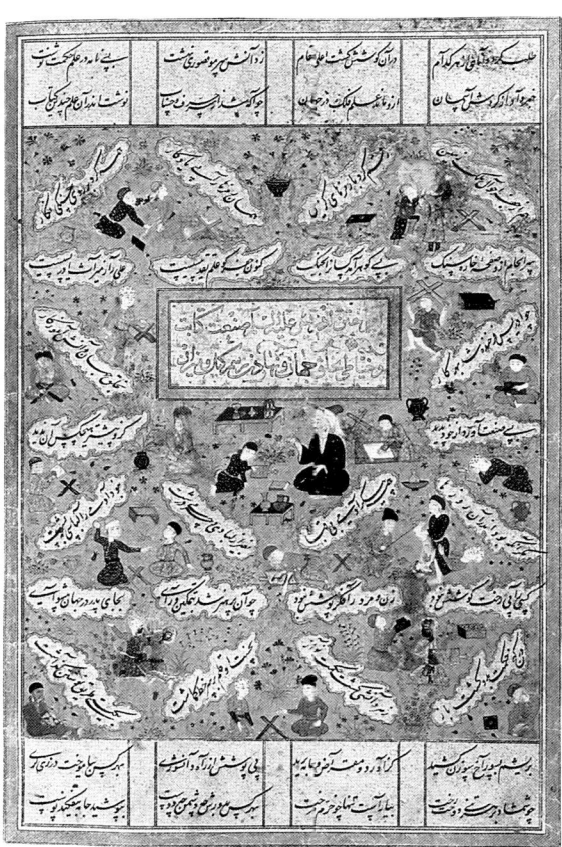

26. İdris Teaching Writing and Tailoring (fol. 38b).

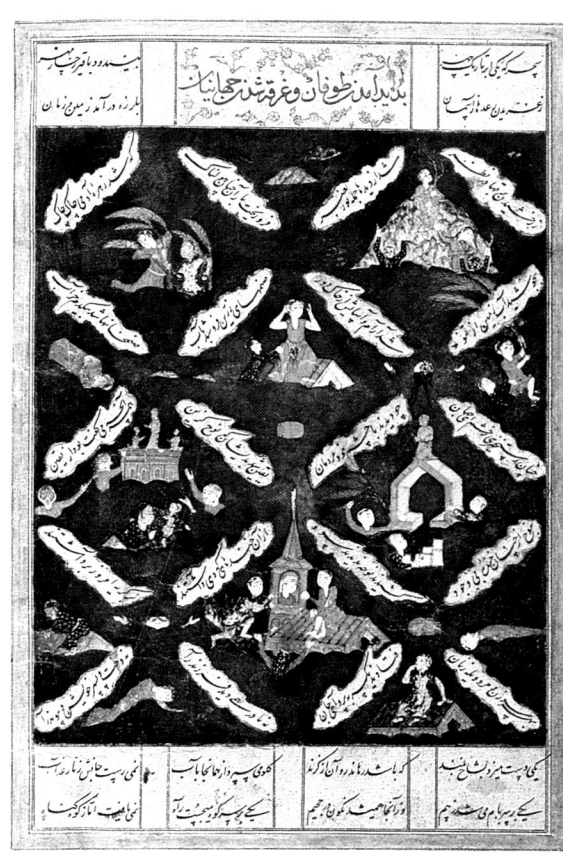
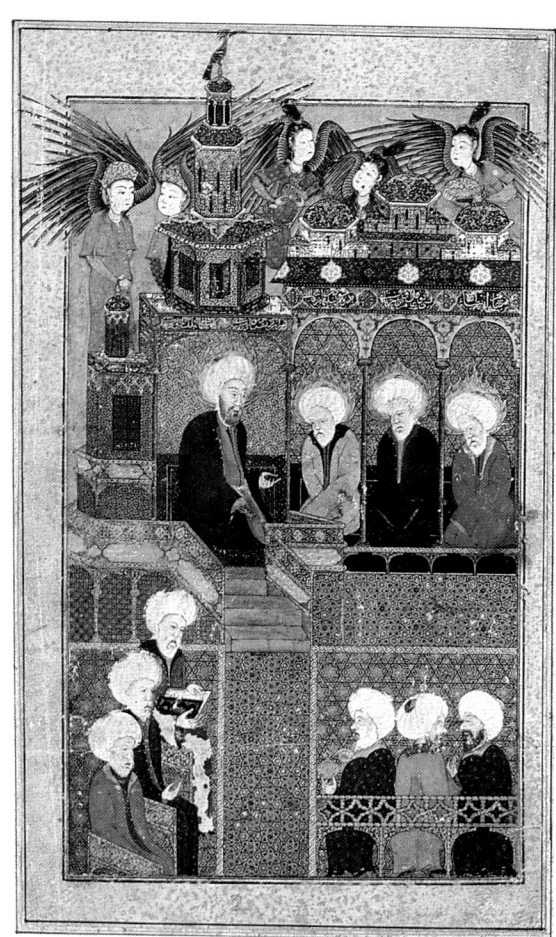

27. The Deluge, from the *Şahname-i Al-i Osman* of Arifi, volume I, transcribed by Yusuf el-Heravi in 1558 (Private Collection, fol. 45b).

28. Prophet Muhammed with His Companions in a Mosque, c. 1558 (Los Angeles, Los Angeles County Museum of Art, M. 73.5.446).

teaching tailoring and measuring, and Zahhak ordering the execution of Cemşid (Jamshid). The architectural settings and landscapes employing perspective and containing naturalistic elements are similar to the scenes found in the *Süleymanname*.

figures 24 and 25

The second group of three paintings is revolutionary. It is conceived as a series of vignettes separated by diagonal lines of text which create diamond-shaped and triangular units within the rectangular picture frame. The scenes designed in this diagrammatic manner represent: İdris teaching calligraphy, an outdoor school setting with boys writing, reading, and misbehaving; Cemşid teaching husbandry, a rural landscape with farm houses, animals, and figures; and the Deluge with figures climbing trees, roofs, and mountains to escape the flood.

figures 26 and 27

Volumes II and III, which are missing, were either never finished or left the palace, their present whereabouts unknown. A single painting in the Los Angeles County Museum of Art executed in the style of Painter A appears to have been removed from volume II, which, following the sequence of other Ottoman histories, must have been devoted to the rise of Islam. This painting, cropped and mounted on an album page, represents a scene in the mosque with a bearded figure lecturing to three elderly disciples, while angels hover above the towers and domes of the structure. The haloed figures may represent the Prophet Muhammed and three of his immediate followers, Ebu Bekir, Ömer, and Osman. Volume III must have continued with the early Turkish dynasties and included the history of the Seljuks.

figure 28

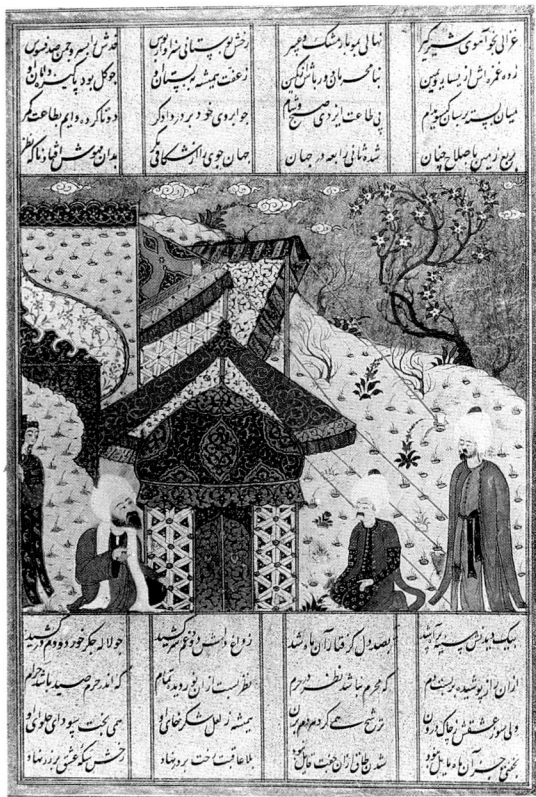

29. Sultan Osman I with Şeyh Edebalı, from the *Şahname-i Al-i Osman* of Arifi, volume IV, transcribed by Mirza Huy-i Şirazi, c. 1558 (Private Collection, fol. 9a).

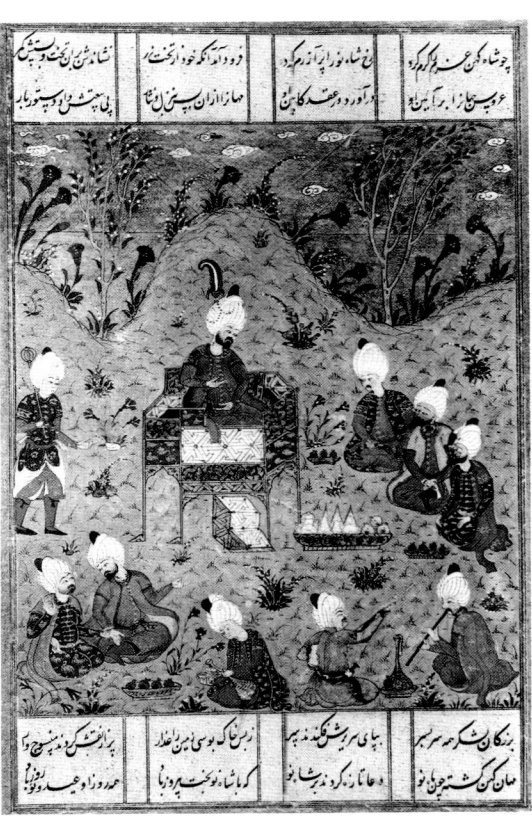

30. Enthronement of Sultan Osman I, from the *Şahname-i Al-i Osman* of Arifi, volume IV, transcribed by Mirza Huy-i Şirazi, c. 1558 (Private Collection, fol. 56b).

Volume IV, which is undated, begins with the reign of Osman I and concludes with that of Bayezid I and the Battle of Ankara of 1402. It has also been trimmed a centimeter or more and rebound, using the original covers. The first folio has a dedicatory medallion giving the name of Sultan Süleyman on one side and the opening verses on the other, both of which are illuminated. The format and decorative elements in the text follow those seen in the first volume. The manuscript mentions the name of the author, Arifi, as well as that of the copyist, Mirza Huy-i Şirazi, who is otherwise unknown. It appears that the second half of the text, covering the period from 1403 to 1520, is missing. The text's thirty-four illustrations, executed by the artist identified as Painter B of the *Süleymanname*, are all on single folios; they are either bordered at the top and bottom with several lines of text, or individual verses are inserted into scenes in the upper and bottom portions.

figures 29-32

The exterior scenes, of which there are twenty-six, show high rounded hills, often with trees or figures behind them. The landscape serves as a backdrop for battles and sieges, receptions in tents, enthronements, and courtly gatherings. Some of the scenes involving sieges are very similar to those in the *Süleymanname*.

The interior scenes, numbering only eight, have schematic compositions with the same arched structures in the background and courtyards in the foreground. One of these represents the court of the Byzantine emperor, Cantacuzene, while the others show that of the Ottoman sultans: Osman, Orhan, Murad I, and Bayezid I.

Landscapes and architectural structures are embellished with schematically rendered flora and geometric patterns. Their highly decora-

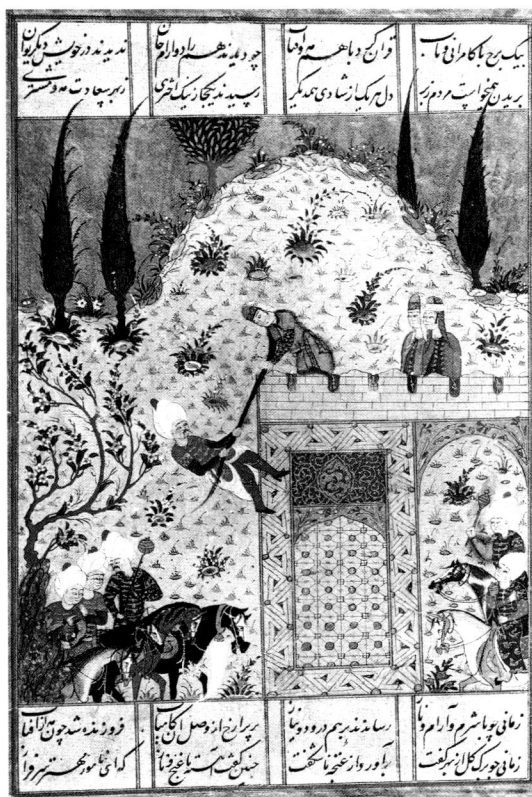

31. Abdürrahman Gazi Climbing the Fortress of Ados, from the *Şahname-i Al-i Osman* of Arifi, volume IV, transcribed by Mirza Huy-i Şirazi, c. 1558 (Private Collection, fol. 70b).

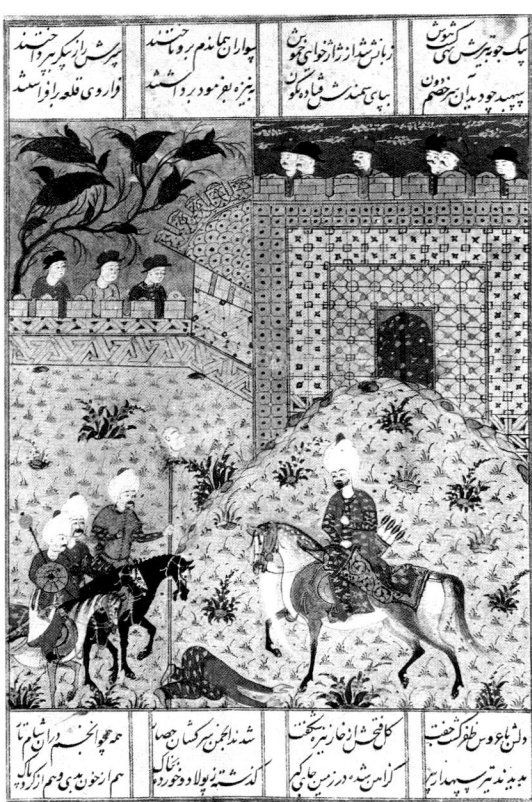

32. Sultan Orhan and the Executed Byzantine Prince after the Battle of Koyunhisar, from the *Şahname-i Al-i Osman* of Arifi, volume IV, transcribed by Mirza Huy-i Şirazi, c. 1558 (Private Collection, fol. 76a).

tive effect is identical to that of the artist's paintings in the *Süleymanname*. His male figures are distinguished by their long mustaches and large white turbans wrapped around thick red batons. This volume is one of the rare works of the period that also depicts the ladies of the court. They are attired in long-sleeved robes worn under short-sleeved kaftans similar to those used by the men, but instead of turbans wear caps wrapped with kerchiefs. A number of the scenes recall the illustrations in early sixteenth-century copies of Firdausi's and Nizami's works produced in Tabriz and Şiraz. They include battles, outdoor entertainment scenes, and meetings of kings and queens.

It is impossible to determine when volumes I and IV (or, for that matter, volumes I to IV) left the imperial libraries. The seals and librarian's notes on the *Anbiyaname* have been erased with the only legible one reading "Hüseyin 1101 (1738)." The fourth volume has on the dedicatory page a rubbed seal which cannot be read.

Süleymanname

The *Süleymanname*, the only intact volume carefully preserved in its original library, is registered in the Hazine collection of the Topkapı Palace. It has the most extensive text (617 folios) and the largest number of illustrations (sixty-five scenes) to have been created by a staff of painters.

The manuscript contains a magnificent gold-stamped leather binding and opens with two illuminated folios that have lobed medallions

see plates on pages 147 and 151

bearing the title and dedication (fols. 1b-2a), followed by another pair of illuminated folios that contain Koranic verses and the first fourteen lines of the text (fols. 2b-3a). The text, written on fine gold-speckled polished paper, is divided into four columns by thin gold bands outlined in black and enclosed by a thick gold frame. In contrast to the extant volumes, which contain nineteen lines to a page, each folio of this work has fifteen lines. The headings are rendered in red, blue, and gold nesih and illuminated with contrasting red, blue, and gold blossoms. A number of lines are written diagonally, creating triangular units that are filled with a variety of naturalistic and stylized motifs.

The text begins with the accession ceremonies of the sultan in 1520 and ends with the events of 1555. Its colophon (fol. 617b) states that the transcription of the work was concluded in mid-Ramazan 965 (late June-early July 1558) by el-Muzaffer Ali b. Emir Bey Şirvani, who perhaps came to the court from Şirvan together with Arifi as a member of Elkas Mirza's retinue in 1547.

The work not only has 30,000 verses, the same number thought to be used in Firdausi's *Şahname*, but it is also written in the *mesnevi* genre and employs the *mütekarib* meter.[11] At the time Arifi was composing the work, Firdausi's epic was being copied and illustrated in the court, which must have provided an additional stimulus for the creation of the history. Dating from these years are illustrated Persian copies as well as Turkish translations of the *Şahname*.[12]

The *Süleymanname* is in excellent condition having been cherished by its owners over the centuries and preserved with meticulous care. The joints between the covers, spine, fore-edge flap,[13] and flap were repaired at a later date, as were the edges of some of the folios; two blank sheets were added to the beginning and the end at that time.

Some of the illustrations show dark stains caused by the pigments used by the painters. These stains are particularly noticeable in the faces of several figures executed by Painter A and in some of the landscape elements in scenes attributed to both Painter A and Painter B. They are most likely the result of the lead carbonate and lead oxide used in the whites and pinks that have changed to sulphides over time.

Arifi's text follows the chronological sequence of the events fairly closely, and is divided into a number of sections and subsections. The illustrations almost always appear at the end of the section that describes the event, with the exception of one or two scenes that represent an earlier episode.

The ratio between text and illustration averages four to eight folios of text between each painting. In only three or four instances two, three, or fifteen folios of text appear between the scenes, and in one or two exceptional instances there is a long span of text, ranging from nine to twenty-two folios, before an event is illustrated.

The text narrates the thirty-five-year period between 1520 and 1555. The illustrations omit the events of nine of these years (1523, 1528, 1531, 1536, 1540, 1542, 1545-1546, and 1550) but represent each of the remaining years with an average of one painting; in some cases two to four paintings are devoted to a year. The most frequently illustrated years are 1521, 1526, and 1553. One episode, the siege of Rhodes in 1522, is exceptional in that it is illustrated by three consecutive paintings.

Bookbinding

The beautifully crafted and sumptuous binding of the *Süleymanname* was designed to harmonize with the book's imperial subject matter. The exterior is covered in blackish-brown leather and decorated with a gold-stamped oval central medallion with pendants on its vertical axis, and is enclosed by a wide frame. The interior, covered with reddish-brown leather, has a similar central medallion with pendants and corner quadrants, but since it omits the wide border, the composition has a spacious feeling due to more of the field being shown. The spine and the fore-edge flap both contain a row of five medallions while the design of the covers is echoed on the flap with the same decorative scheme used throughout the exterior and the interior.

see plates on pages 81 and 82

The layout of the exterior and interior covers and the harmonious combination of diverse motifs (such as cloudbands, hatayis, and serrate leaves) indicate that the classical Ottoman style of bookbinding and the saz genre of decoration were firmly established by the 1550s. The binding is obviously the work of a master at the height of his career.

The payroll registers of the society of imperial bookbinders state that Mehmed b. Ahmed, who entered the studio during the reign of Selim I, was the chief of the group between 1545 and 1566. Although it was not customary to record the names of the bookbinders in the manuscripts, Mehmed, called Mehmed Çelebi, is mentioned in a copy of a Koran originally transcribed in 1344/1345 as having bound the work in 1555.[14] The same artist must have been commissioned to create the spectacular binding of the *Süleymanname* as well as the covers for other imperial manuscripts, including those of the *Divan-ı Muhibbi*.[15]

33. (left) Exterior of stamped and gilded leather bookbinding from the *Divan-ı Muhibbi*, c. 1560 (İstanbul, Türk ve İslam Eserleri Müzesi, 1962).

34. (right) Exterior of stamped and gilded leather bookbinding, from the *Divan-ı Muhibbi*, transcribed by Mehmed Şerif in 1565/1566 (İstanbul, Topkapı Sarayı Müzesi, R. 738 mük.).

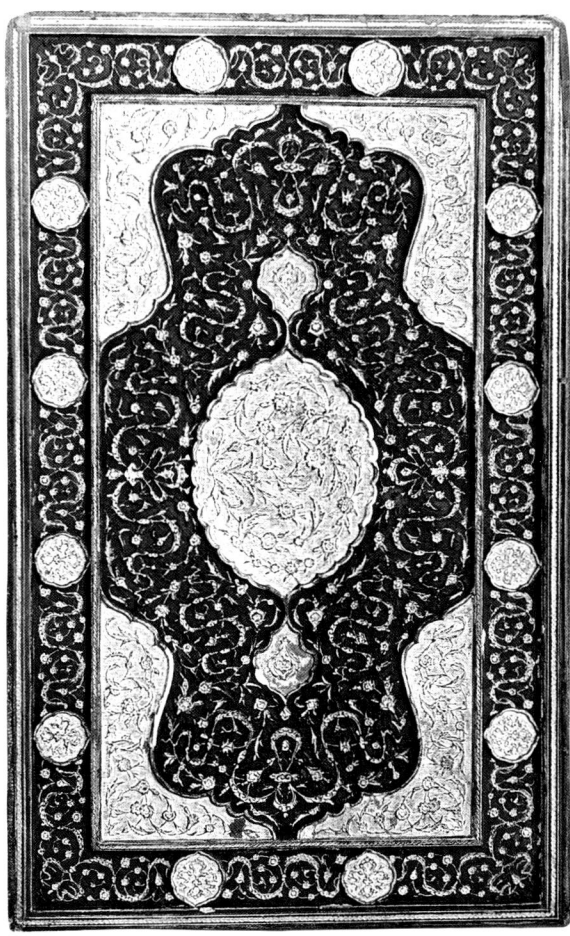
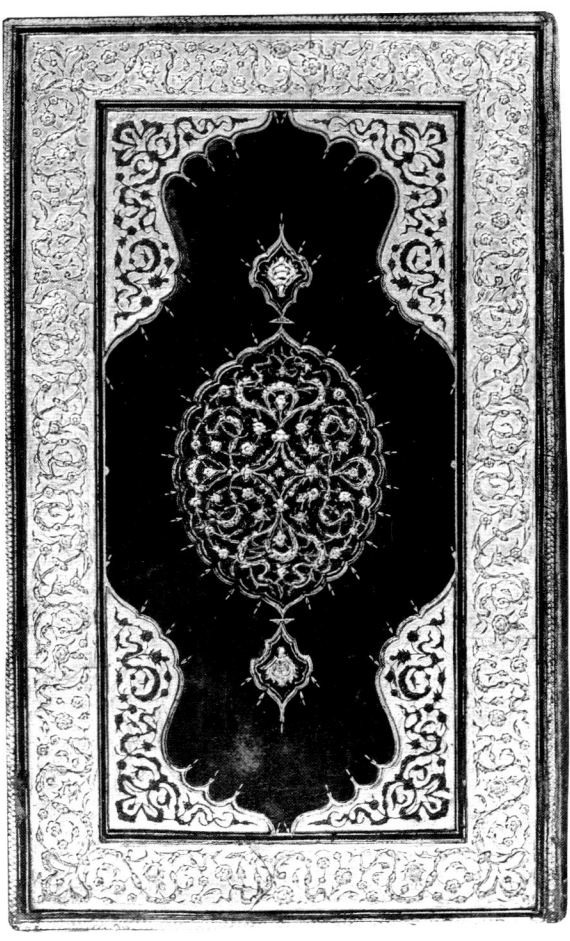

Illuminations

The illuminations of the *Süleymanname* were the work of an outstanding artist who employed both traditional and innovative designs. The dedicatory medallions on the first folios (1b-2a) are placed on a field covered with two superimposed concentric scrolls, one bearing composite leaves and hatayis, the other stencillike flowers. These concentric scrolls came to be identified with the artistic vocabulary of the age and were widely used on the sultan's tuğras as well as on ceramics[16] after the second quarter of the sixteenth century.

see plates on pages 84 and 85

The decoration of the double folios at the beginning (fols. 2b-3a) shows extraordinary finesse and incorporates a variety of motifs. Filling the rectangular compartments around the text are cloudbands, naturalistic flowers, and sprays of blossoming branches; the wide frame enclosing both folios contains reciprocal arches with *rumis* (elongated leaves), hatayis, and other blossoms; the outer band, composed of flamelike leaves, extends into the margins with a series of floral finials. The same motifs were used in the illuminated headings and decorative units inserted into the text, each one of which shows a different composition.

see plates on pages 88 and 89

The layout of these folios is identical to that of the pair found in the beginning of a Koran transcribed by Ahmed Karahisari in 1546[17] and presented to Süleyman. The most striking theme in both examples is the sprays of blossoming branches in the pair of blue panels flanking the text. This design also appears on other imperial manuscripts, including a *Vakfiye* dated 1540,[18] and was frequently used on ceramics, tiles, textiles, and rugs produced for the court.[19]

figure 35

The illuminator also employs naturalistic blossoms and trees in the decoration of the headings, following the style that first appeared in the 1540 *Vakfiye* mentioned above and in the beautiful doublures of the lacquer binding of the Persian translations of the Hadis[20] presented to Şehzade Mehmed around the same date. Here the artist presents a glorious garden, luxuriant in its display of blossoming fruit trees and spring flowers, including tulips, carnations, roses, hyacinths, irises, violets, and narcissus. These elements were reemployed in the decoration of an imperial album compiled around the 1560s.[21] The volume is bound with a unique tortoiseshell cover and contains verses written by such celebrated Iranian calligraphers as Şah Mahmud, drawings of dragons and hatayis, and three-dimensional *kaatı* (découpage) gardens made of minuscule pieces of paper.

figure 36

Several manuscripts written by the great calligraphers of the past (redecorated and rebound in Süleyman's court) show the same elements. The most notable among these volumes is the Koran by Abdullah Sayrafi which was decorated in 1554 by Kara Memi.[22] The artist also worked on the most magnificent copy of the *Divan-ı Muhibbi*,[23] transcribed by Mehmed Şerif in 1565/1566. Each of the 367 folios in this volume, including the double dedication at the beginning, is embellished with a profusion of decorative themes, ranging from traditional rumis and floral scrolls to an incredible variety of naturalistic flora. The illuminator's name is given in two places, an indication of the significance of his contribution. Although Kara Memi is not mentioned in an equally sumptuous version of the same work, copied by the same calligrapher in 1565/1566,[24] his characteristic style is clearly apparent in these illuminations.

figures 9 and 10

As a student of Şahkulu, Kara Memi must have practiced the saz

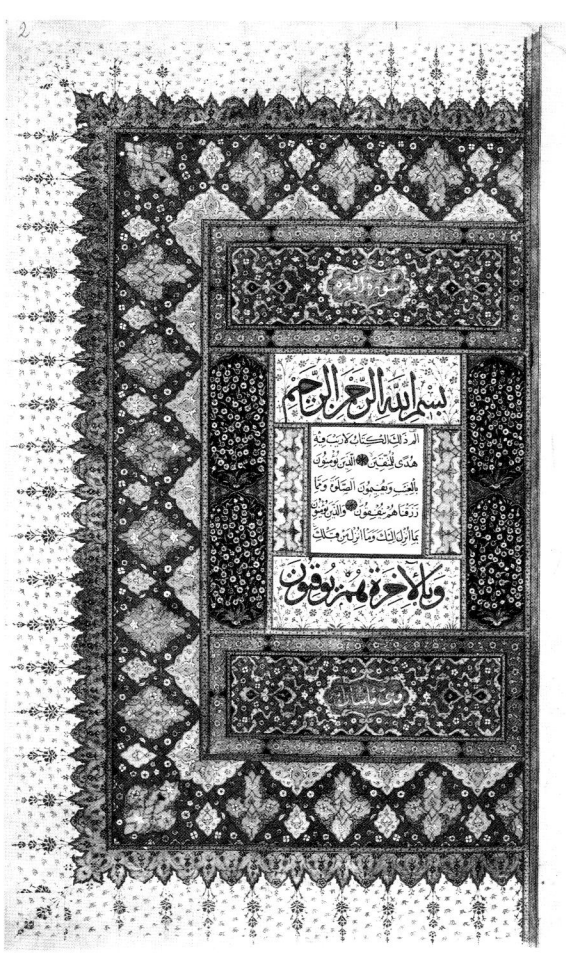

35. Illuminated frontispiece (left half), from a Koran transcribed by Ahmed Karahisari in 1546 (İstanbul, Topkapı Sarayı Müzesi Y.Y. 999, fol. 2a).

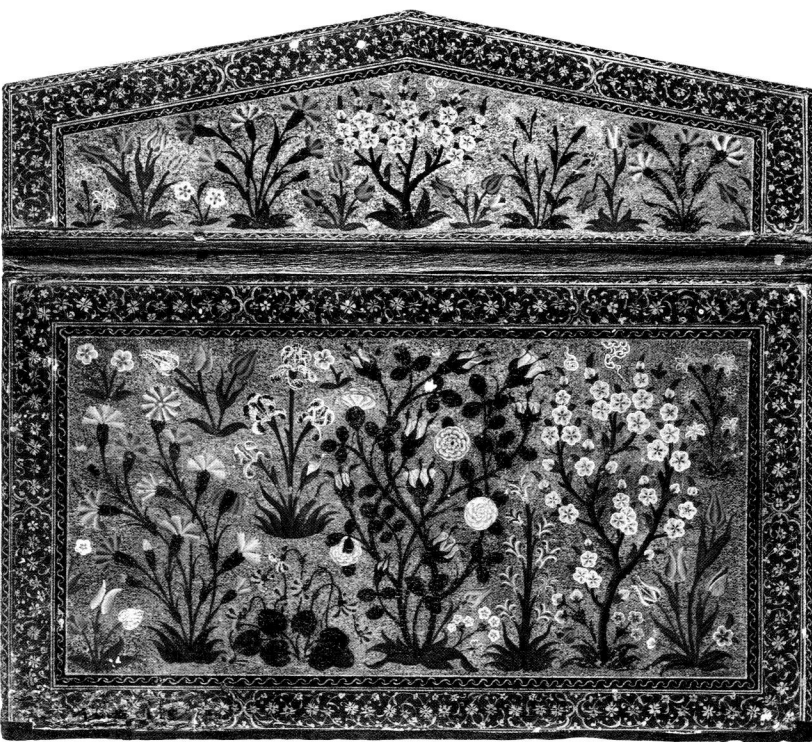

36. Interior of lacquer bookbinding, from a Hadis transcribed by Ali, c. 1540 (İstanbul, Topkapı Sarayı Müzesi, E.H. 2851).

style and executed drawings of dragons and angels in imperial albums. One drawing of an angel with a fully colored naturalistic tree and floral spray in the foreground[25] could be by his hand.

The illuminations in the *Süleymanname* can be attributed to Kara Memi, who headed the Rumiyan corps in 1558-1559 and must have been assigned to work on the sultan's history due to his reputation as a müzehhib. It is also very possible that the landscape elements with blossoming branches, thickly foliated trees, and clusters of flowers in the illustrations were also by his hand.

Illustrations

The sixty-nine paintings (or sixty-five scenes since four are spread to double folios) reveal the hands of two major and three minor artists, who must have been chosen for their expertise, familiarity with the subjects represented, and tenure in the nakkaşhane. Unfortunately, their names are not given in the manuscript and they cannot be identified through archival sources, such as payroll registers and other lists of artists.

The paintings in the *Süleymanname* are almost full page with the exception of a verse or two either placed at the top and bottom, or inserted at the upper and/or lower corners. Only two scenes are devoid of text panels (3 and 29).[26] A few verses, however, appear on the architecture itself (29 and 64) as do honorific titles referring to the sultan (31 and 64).

see plates on pages 90-232

In several instances the paintings extend into the margin and architectural components, banners, and trees project from the top.

The master of the *Süleymanname*, Painter A, was responsible for forty-one scenes including the four on double folios. He is by far the most innovative of the painters; his figures and compositions are rendered with a documentary realism that became the standard for later illustrated histories. He appears to have worked with an Iranian artist (Painter D) as well as with a man familiar with eastern European settings (Painter E), who may also have assisted him in the *Anbiyaname*.

The second largest group of paintings, twenty-two scenes, reveals the hand of Painter B, the same artist who worked on the illustrations in the fourth volume of the *Şahname-i Al-i Osman*. An artist trained in Iran, Painter C, produced two of the illustrations while Painters D and E assisted Painter A in the representation of certain episodes.

Painter A, who recreates the historic personages and the actual settings of the events, was a man of great talent and creativity who broke free of traditional and formulaic figure types and compositions. His interest in portraiture is immediately apparent; the characters in his scenes—members of the court, Europeans, or natives of other regions—have distinguishable features. The authenticity of the settings indicates that he either had a firsthand knowledge of these sites (especially the units of the Topkapı Palace) or obtained information and assistance from other sources. His acute observation and realistic depiction consistently appear in such details as garments and furnishings, structural and decorative elements in architecture, ceremonial and military protocol. He represents with great clarity the hierarchy of the court in which each man's attire and position were rigidly controlled and differentiated.

Painter A was the Ottoman artist who established the standard compositions for accession ceremonies, receptions both in the field and in the palace, and military campaigns involving sieges of fortresses. These include a number of original scenes depicting specific episodes. They also include generalized themes where he either relied on earlier models or repeated himself once he determined the layout. Since many ceremonial episodes of the court followed a rigid protocol and took place in the same place, his repetitiveness probably represents the consistency in the procedures and settings.

His exterior scenes fall into six general types, which range from repetitive to unique. The most frequently encountered scenes involve receptions or other events that take place in or around the *otak-ı hümayun* (imperial tent), pitched on the skirts of a hill. A naturalistic tree often rises above the hill, with groups of riders, some of whom are in armor, emerging from behind. At times a river flows in the foreground or a central tree grows out of a body of water. Officials and other dignitaries line up in horizontal registers in the foreground with a group of attendants flanking the sultan, who sits on a throne in front of his tent under a canopy that resembles a large rectangular umbrellalike structure. These scenes show receptions of commanders (17), the French delegation (33), Iranians (63), John Zapolya (28), and the infant Stephen Zapolya with his mother (43). They include such rare events as the visit of Şehzade Bayezid (58), performances of the archers (61), and the execution of a prisoner by an elephant (8).

Belonging to the tent-in-the-field series is a unique representation of the camp of Louis II in which Louis is surrounded in the foreground by a ring of kings and commanders, while his army stands massed in the background (18). The work shows the hand of two painters, Painter A and Painter E. Painter E, whose specialty was eastern European themes, must have been asked to depict the protagonists in this scene showing the camp of the Hungarians. In three other outdoor receptions involving the Safavids, Tahmasp (37 and 56) and Elkas Mirza (51), Painter D was called upon. He must have been familiar with Iranian figure types, which he incorporated in the illustrations.

A second type of exterior scene is devoted to battles, the most spectacular of which is the double-folio Battle of Mohacs with the two armies facing each other on opposite pages (20). Other battles either show the armies converging towards the center (41), a pair of combatting warriors flanked by members of their units (19), or a fleeing commander turning back to shoot at the enemy (54). A related episode is the death on the battlefield with figures framing the fatally wounded (21). In these scenes the soldiers, whether Habsburg or Ottoman, are attired in their characteristic garments. The various Ottoman regiments—the janissaries, akıncıs, delils, sipahis, and *mehter* (military band)—as well as their commanders and officers can be clearly identified by their costumes.

The third type incorporates certain features from the first two groups in its depictions of fortresses under siege. The magnificent double folio showing the siege of Belgrade (9) employs the theme of the sultan sitting in his tent, surrounded by his advisors and attendants on the left while the city of Belgrade is on the right, complete with its distinctive architecture and figure types. Eastern European cities are also seen in the background of other siege scenes with the action taking place in the foreground, as in the battle of Güns (24) and Temesvar (55).

A related painting with European setting and figures is the unique representation of the registering of the devşirme (2), which reveals the collaboration of Painter E. The combination of a fortress in the background and a reception in a tent in the foreground is found in the meeting that takes place outside Tabriz (37), one of the two illustrations of Painter A depicting Iranian-type structures. Here he also relies on Painter D for his figures.

The fourth type of exterior scene includes specific activities in the field or outside the cities, with or without architectural settings. Painter A's second eastern-type building appears in the scene of the arrival of the sultan at Kasr-ı Şirin (36). An architectural setting, this time one of local origin, is incorporated into the departure of the princes from İstanbul (44). Armies marching to war or parading fall into the same category, as seen in the sultan being greeted by his officers (7) and in the meeting of Şehzade Selim and the commanders of the Anatolian forces (60), which is almost a mirror image of the former with a figure kissing the boot of the mounted prince. Finally, the army on the move with identifiable regiments appears in the scene of the gathering of the Rumelian forces (62).

The fifth type of exterior scene depicts the sultan hunting alone or with the princes. One of these (38) shows two princes hunting in the foreground with Süleyman, attended by his retinue, riding in the background. The layout of the scene recalls the march-of-the-army series. The other hunts show the sultan either as a spectator (59) or as the solo participant, placed on a dazzling gold hill (16).

Most of these exterior scenes are set against high hills with naturalistic trees; at times a large single tree grows from a pond (a favorite device of the artist), and rivers flow in the foreground or encircle the fortresses. In a few cases a delicately drawn blossoming tree appears together with a type of tree that has lush green foliage. The landscape is sprinkled with clusters of leaves and flowers and with minute tufts of grass. Some of the hills have fantastic craggy formations; in two cases the rocks are animated with human heads (33 and 54).

The vezirs, commanders, special regiments, and imperial attendants participating in these exterior scenes are carefully identified. The sultan is frequently accompanied by his vezirs, Has Oda ağas, and iç oğlans when enthroned; his *peyks* and *solaks* (personal guards) and Has Oda ağas attend him when he rides, true to Ottoman tradition and court protocol.

The majority of the interior scenes take place in the Topkapı Palace. Its first and second courtyards are described explicitly in the accession of the sultan (1) and spread across double folios. Painter A was the first Ottoman artist to represent the palace realistically and to identify the actual location of the episodes. The circular arrangement of the figures waiting to be received by the sultan, who is enthroned in front of the Babüssaade, established a prototype for centuries to come. A second double folio shows the northern arcade of the second courtyard with the Kubbealtı (3). A single folio most likely portrays a section of the third courtyard, creating a less formal setting for the meeting of the sultan and Barbaros Hayreddin Paşa (35). Another identifiable location is the palace of the beylerbeyi in Cairo (4) with palm trees and native population.

The remaining interior scenes represent beautifully decorated pavilions with the sultan attended by his Has Oda ağas, iç oğlans, and vezirs. In three of the paintings he is either entertained by musicians and dancers (6), presented gifts during a circumcision festival (40), or receives a rare bowl from one of his officials (57). The first takes place in the Edirne Palace according to the text; the other two probably represent the Has Oda in the Topkapı with a built-in throne in the background and a marble fountain in the foreground.

Two of the receptions also take place in the Topkapı Palace, presumably in the Arz Odası, immediately opposite the entrance. Here the sultan is receiving either the Safavid ambassador (31), who brings gifts carried by janissaries, or his cousin Devlet Giray, han of the Crimean Tatars (53). In these two scenes the Babüssaade, guarded by its *kapıcıs* (gatekeepers), appears in the foreground. Two other scenes, which take place in Aleppo and Amasya (50 and 64), have similar settings, indicating that the design of the provincial palaces reflected the architectural features of the Topkapı Palace. In a fifth illustration the sultan receives his grand vezir İbrahim Paşa in a pavilion looking out into a garden with a fountain (24), its location thought to be somewhere in the third courtyard of the Topkapı Palace.

Architectural structures extend their domes and turrets beyond the upper frame of the paintings. Their facades are broken into various compartments adorned with geometric motifs, at times blending horizontal floors with vertical walls. The two scenes depicting the Has Oda (40 and 57) are exceptionally detailed, showing a complicated series of doorways, passages, multiple stories, and arched openings.

Finely executed and highly detailed architectural components, landscape elements, garments, and furnishings reveal the hand of an artist trained in the art of illumination. Some otak and pavilion scenes combine such a rich diversity of patterns that their effect is not unlike that of the abstract compositions found in the frontispieces of imperial manuscripts.

Many of the designs used on the garments and furnishings must have been taken from existing textiles since they represent ogival, vertical-stem, and *çintemani* (double wavy lines and triple balls) patterns as well as rumi and hatayi motifs frequently encountered in the brocades and velvets of the period.

The artist uses bright and contrasting colors. His landscapes often have cobalt-blue and hot-pink hills against a gold sky. For local architecture he uses blue, green, and pink units outlined with darker hues, simulating tiled surfaces, while his European buildings tend to be plain beige or white with red or brown roofs. For garments and furnishings he frequently employs oranges, pinks, pale or deep blues, golden and mustard yellows, and bright apple-greens. He also paints various tones of gold on gold, creating shimmering and rich textures. One of his outstanding achievements is the painterly use of pigments and the use of shading. This is particularly noticeable in the luxuriantly foliated green trees and delicately modeled faces.

Painter A's figures are carefully drawn and painted. Courtly types and military personnel are attired in appropriate garments and show a consistency of proportions. Occasionally he inserts foreign types, such as Arabs (4 and 50) and Africans (4 and 8), uses a Madonna-and-Child theme (43), or depicts a caricaturelike entertainer (40).

Painter A, an artist of great originality, was above all an impeccable draftsman and colorist. He was also able to create illusionistic backgrounds with receding planes and elements that decrease in scale and to suggest volume through modeling and drapery while at the same time employing intricate patterns to produce a kaleidoscopic effect in architectural settings. His style shows certain Herati and Tabrizi elements and he definitely relies on older models for the basic structure of some of his repetitive compositions, such as receptions in tents and pavilions, battles, and hunts. But by incorporating contemporary features—costumes and specific vignettes—he transforms them into distinct and precisely identified scenes.

The artist appears to have worked with Painter D on three scenes involving the Iranians (37, 51, and 56), possibly because the latter was more familiar with Safavid figures and settings. He also relied on a man closely acquainted with European types of figures and architecture, Painter E, who may have assisted the master in a number of illustrations (2, 7-9, 18-20, 28, 33, 34, 41, 43, 54, and 55). Painter E's most prominent contributions are the scenes devoted to the recruiting of the devşirme children (2) and the Hungarians in the camp of Louis II (18).

Painter A's work appears in three other manuscripts written either by Arifi or attributed to him. The earliest is the 1557/1558 *Futuhat-ı Cemile* mentioned above.[27] Two of its seven paintings, one spread to double folios, are definitely by his hand;[28] the others appear to be the work of an unidentified assistant who followed the master's style.

figures 37 and 38

His next commission was the ten paintings in the *Anbiyaname*,[29] which show the same stylistic features as those in the *Süleymanname*. An assistant seems to have worked with him on one of the scenes.[30] The architectural settings employed in this work resemble those representing the Topkapı Palace with arcades around courtyards and domes extending beyond the upper frame. Landscapes also recall the *Süleymanname* in their delicate blossoming fruit trees and lushly foliated trees as

figures 23-27

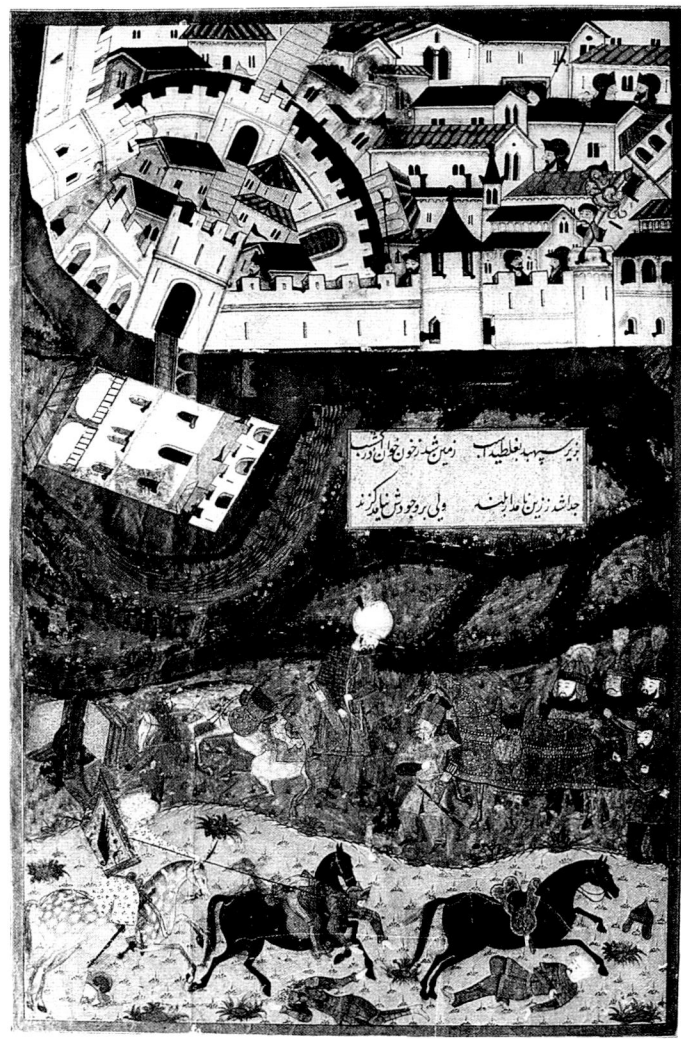
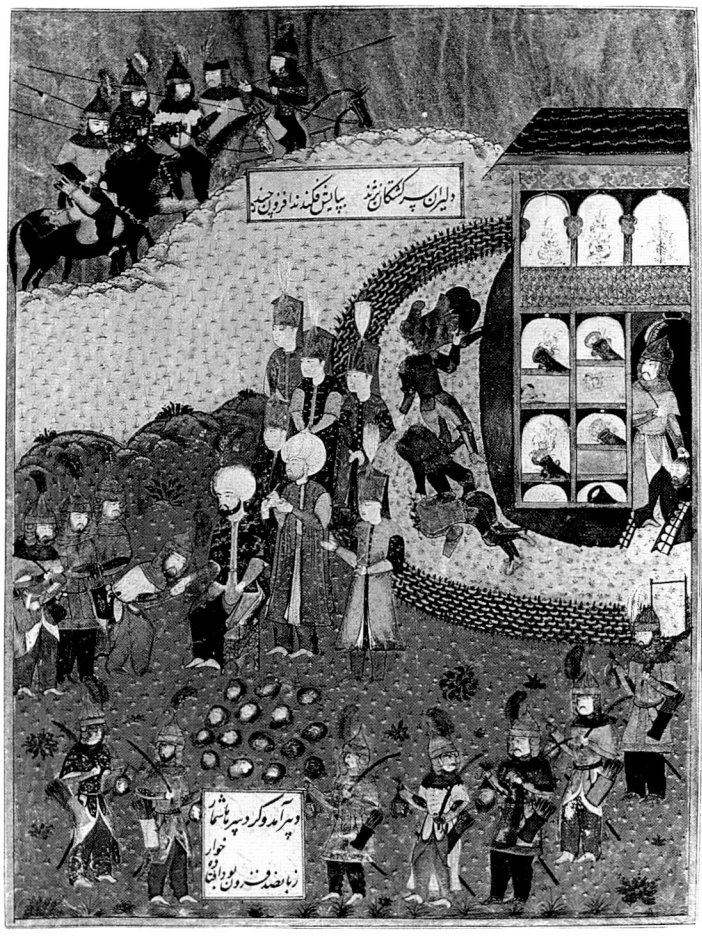

figure 28

figures 39-41

37. (left) Siege of Temesvar by Ahmed Paşa (left half), from the *Futuhat-ı Cemile* attributed to Arifi, transcribed by Abu Turab el-Hasani el-Hüseyni in 1557/1558 (İstanbul, Topkapı Sarayı Müzesi, H. 1592, fol. 19a).

38. (right) Mehmed Paşa Inspecting Prisoners, from the *Futuhat-ı Cemile* attributed to Arifi, transcribed by Abu Turab el-Hasani el-Hüseyni in 1557/1558 (İstanbul, Topkapı Sarayı Müzesi, H. 1592, fol. 25a).

well as in their illusionistic backgrounds with receding planes. Painter A most likely also executed the detached scene in a mosque, attributed to the second volume of Arifi's history.[31]

His last activities appear in Arifi's *Ravzat al-Uşak*,[32] a poetic work with three remarkable paintings representing a princely couple in a palace with the lady gazing at her reflection in the pool; a purely genre scene showing a butcher's shop; and the fable of the fox with the animal dressed as a dervish walking in a landscape, its background showing a pastoral scene of a shepherd and farmer and a distant European town. One wonders whether Painter A worked with his European colleague on the last scene or had already mastered this type of architecture by the 1560s.

Several manuscripts produced in the nakkaşhane in the 1530s show traces of the style perfected by Painter A. The 1530/1531 *Hamse* of Ali Şir Nevai[33] contains sixteen paintings that attempt to recreate local architectural settings. One of the illustrations has a combination of a fortress in the background and tents in the foreground that anticipates the siege scenes employed in the *Süleymanname*. Local features are also prominent in the six paintings in the earliest illustrated Turkish translation of Firdausi's *Şahname*,[34] made around the same date. This interest in local structures and figures predates the age of Süleyman, making its first appearance in a group of manuscripts dating 1490-1500.[35]

Painter A, whose style appeared in the late 1550s, had a profound im-

70

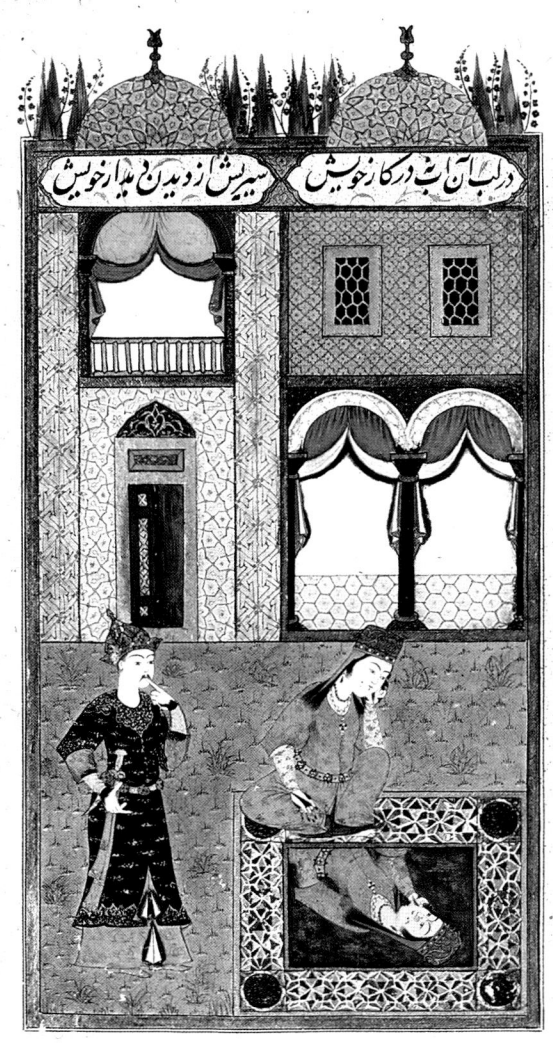

39. Royal Couple in a Courtyard (fol. 23a).

39-41. Illustrations from the *Ravzat al-Uşak* of Arifi, c. 1560 (San Diego, Edwin Binney, 3rd Collection).

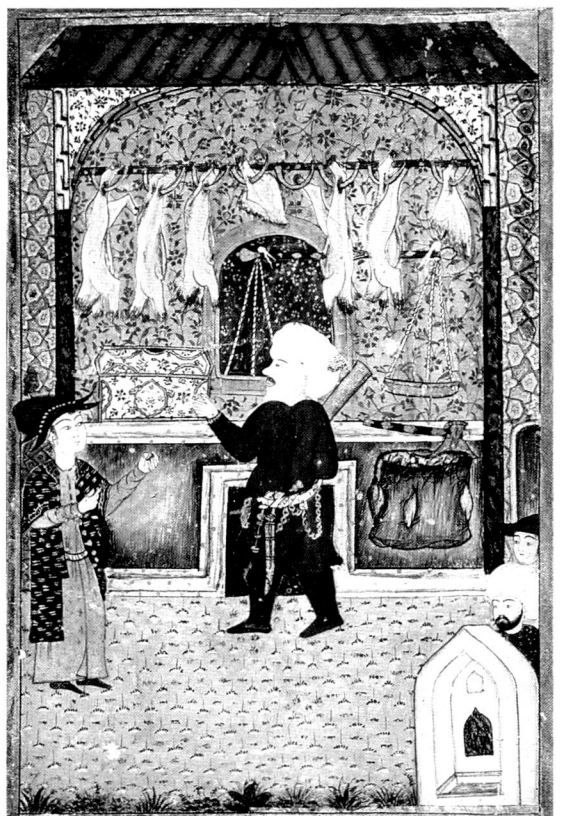

40. Butcher's Shop (fol. 29b).

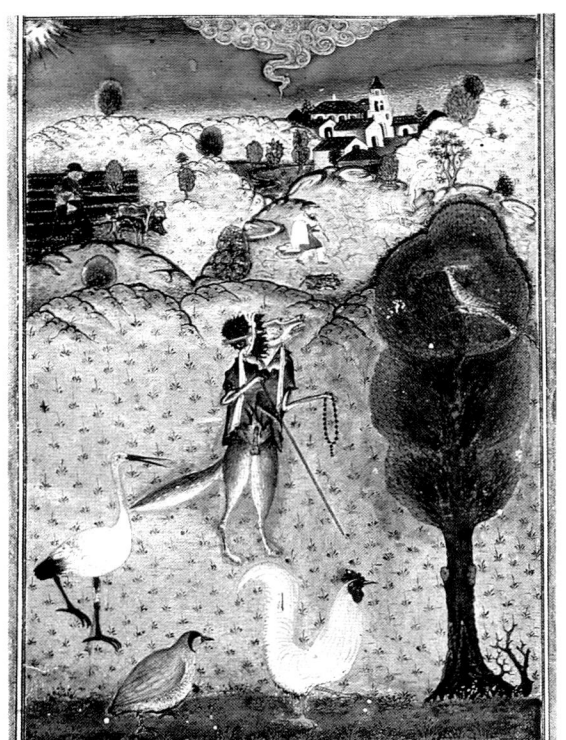

41. Fable of the Fox (fol. 41b).

pact on the future illustrators of şahnames and most likely trained Osman, the giant among the nakkaşhane artists. Osman's first work seems to be the *Tercüme-i Şahname*, c. 1560-1570,[36] followed by the *Nüzhet el-Esrar el-Ahbar der Sefer-i Sigetvar*, 1568/1569,[37] of Ahmed Feridun Paşa. Osman, who was employed in the nakkaşhane until the end of the sixteenth century, worked exclusively with the şahnameci Lokman, producing hundreds of illustrations.[38] His self-portrait, accompanied by Ali, a fellow artist who was also his brother-in-law, appears in the two copies of the *Şahname-i Selim Han*, a rare honor for a nakkaşhane member.[39]

figures 16 and 21

Painter B's style, in contrast, dominated the production of illustrated manuscripts during the reign of Süleyman, coming to an end with the *Süleymanname*. The works of this artist first appear in the 1515 copy of the *Mantık at-Tayr*,[40] one of the few illustrated manuscripts dating from the reign of Selim I. The same style is found in over a dozen literary works and anthologies, and in a rare lacquer bookbinding.[41] His only historical paintings appear in the fourth and fifth volumes of Arifi's *Şahname-i Al-i Osman*.

figures 14 and 15

Painter B was responsible for twenty-two scenes in the *Süleymanname*, his last work. Similar to the illustrations in volume IV of the *Şahname-i Al-i Osman*, the majority of the seventeen paintings that take place outdoors either depict sieges of fortresses, such as those of Rhodes (12-14), Budapest (26), and Estonibelgrad (45), or show battles within an architectural setting (22 and 52).

figures 29-32

The next group concentrates on battles with one or more pairs of figures in combat. It includes the fight between the Ottomans and Habsburgs during the İstabur campaign (42); the killing of rebel leaders Canberdi Gazali (5) and Kalender (23); and scenes showing such insurgents as Ahmed Paşa (15) and contender Mustafa (65).

A third group portrays imperial hunts with the sultan pursuing wild animals, either alone (10 and 11) or with two of his sons (46). Other exterior scenes show the imperial otak with the enthroned sultan inspecting prisoners (27) or soldiers climbing trees to escape the torrential rains (25).

Three of his interior scenes take place in the Topkapı Palace: one portrays the sultan conversing with Elkas Mirza in the Arz Odası (47); another shows him receiving the Austrian ambassador (32); and the third presumably takes place in the Kubbealtı, where the members of the Divan discuss the letter from Ferdinand presented by his envoys (30). The composition of the latter is reemployed in the scene representing the arrival of Elkas Mirza's gifts in Aleppo (49). An unusual illustration depicts a pavilion overlooking a garden in Kayseri (48).

Both the exterior and interior scenes follow the decorative style identified with the master. They are formulaic, especially when compared with the innovative realism of Painter A. Several of the scenes are exquisitely rendered, in particular those depicting the sultan arriving at Rhodes (12), hunting (10, 11, and 46), or conversing with Elkas Mirza in the palace (47). The scene showing the sultan in a pavilion in Kayseri (48) is remarkable for its composition and pensive atmosphere. The other paintings were either rapidly executed or made by an assistant since they show less care. One depicting soldiers climbing trees (25) has an unusual layout while the remaining ones follow the schemes employed in the fourth volume of Arifi's history.

Painter B is an artist who has great technical proficiency as well as a sense of humor. He is truly a *nakkaş*—an illuminator-painter who embellishes surfaces. He is basically a colorist and decorator with little or no interest in historical accuracy and documentation. His settings are generalized, lacking the specific features that help to identify the location of the events. They are also often ambiguous. A number of scenes occurring in structures behind gardens show contradictory spatial developments and obscurely defined relationships between interior and exterior components (see, for instance, 30, 32, and 49).

Painter B's figures are as generalized as his settings and the main protagonists can be identified only through their placement in the scenes and characteristic garments. On the other hand, he seems to be able to create deep emotions, as seen in the figure of the sultan in a few instances (see 14 and 48). He shows a wry humor in the depiction of captured enemy soldiers, who fall down in exaggerated postures (see 26 and 52), and in casual interactions between secondary figures (see, for instance, 23 and 65). His battle scenes and hunts are particularly lively and full of movement. His facility in the representation of such themes is also a strong feature of his literary works dating from the 1530s and the 1540s.

Painter B's choice of colors lies more in the pale and pastel range, particularly when compared with the colors of Painter A. The hills in the landscape are often dark green, pale blue, or turquoise; and architectural structures are generally painted pink, pale blue, and turquoise. In addition, he shows a preference for oranges, lilacs, dark-blues, golden-yellows, and olive-greens.

Painters C, D, and E, the other artists of the *Süleymanname*, contributed relatively few scenes. Painter C executed two illustrations, which are extremely traditional and follow the compositions used in literary works: the sultan entertained in a pavilion (29) or the sultan hunting (39). Obviously trained in the late Tabriz or Kazvin schools, he represents thin tall personages. His scenes contain a few static figures, derivative landscape elements, and delicately patterned architectural components.

Painter D, another artist trained in Tabriz, worked with Painter A on three scenes that narrate episodes involving the Safavids: Elkas Mirza receiving the envoy sent by the sultan (51) and Tahmasp with the Ottoman ambassadors (37 and 56).

Painter E also worked with Painter A and did not produce independent scenes. His expertise was in the knowledge of eastern European figure types, as can be seen in the scenes of the recruitment of the devşirme children (2) and the camp of Louis II (18). His figures are strangely proportioned and are awkwardly placed within the composition. He may have drawn on several different sources and lifted the figures from these illustrations.

The contribution of Painter E in other illustrations is difficult to determine; he may have worked on certain vignettes involving western elements, but the style of his master, Painter A, predominates in these scenes (see 7-9, 19, 20, 28, 33, 34, 41, 43, 54, and 55). It should be mentioned that western figures, identified by their costumes, were also used by Painter B (see 12-14, 26, 27, 30, 32, 42, and 45), which indicates that the nakkaşhane artists had access to suitable models.[42]

Although there are two payroll registers whose dates coincide with the year in which the *Süleymanname* was completed, the artists listed in these documents cannot be identified with the existing works. The only exceptions are Kara Memi and Bayram b. Derviş, both called nakkaş but known through their illuminations.

Study of such documents involves the problem of defining the duties of the men employed in the nakkaşhane and the meaning of the terms used to classify them. The term nakkaş obviously applied to painters as well as illuminators, to the men who decorated the manuscripts. Müzehhib, a term rarely used in the registers, seems to have identified the men who specialized only in illuminations; *ressam* and *musavvir*, equally rare in usage and found only in documents dating from the 1520s, seem to have meant painters and illustrators.

It is perhaps not surprising that the rigorous training of the nakkaşhane stressed competence in the art of illumination and held it above all other forms of book decoration. Many manuscript illustrations relied more on the artist's training as an illuminator than on his expertise as a painter. This leaning is evident in the overall decorative approach found in traditional manuscript illustrations, whose primary purpose was to embellish the book and enhance the text by providing visual commentaries. The paintings did not narrate the stories on their own and one has to rely on the text for the proper understanding of their meaning.

The distinction that exists in modern terminology between illuminator and painter was not present in the mid-sixteenth century and the term nakkaş was aptly applied to the decorators of these books. A member of the nakkaşhane was expected to work on the illuminations as well as on the illustrations of the texts. Since the art of illumination was applied to the Korans, it was far more prestigious and required greater training than did painting. This accounts for the practice of recording the names of accomplished illuminators in the manuscripts. The illustrations, on the other hand, were often collaborative efforts with other painters, were restricted by the requirements of the text, and were possibly controlled by the authors and nakkaşbaşıs, who may have had a say in the selection of themes to be illustrated and in their final production. The names of these artists, therefore, did not need to be recorded.

The situation changed drastically after the creation of the *Süleymanname*. Future artists of illustrated histories, such as Osman, Hasan, and Ahmed Nakşi, were not only mentioned in archival documents and praised in the texts of the works they illustrated but were also represented in these manuscripts by their self-portraits.[43]

The proper identification of the names of *Süleymanname*'s two major contributors, Painters A and B, is not possible with the existing documentation. Painter A burst into the scene in the late 1550s, his style already perfected. His work coincides with the activities of Kara Memi, who flourished between the 1540s and 1560s. It is very tempting to identify Painter A with Kara Memi, both of whom created original styles and themes that changed the course of Turkish art.

Painter B must have been one of the oldest members of the nakkaşhane working in the period from 1515 to 1558. One likely candidate listed in the payroll registers is Bayram b. Derviş, who came to the studio during the reign of Bayezid II and is recorded as having died on 5 November 1558, a few months after the completion of the *Süleymanname*. Bayram is known as the illuminator of the Koran transcribed in

1523/1524.[44] His son, Mehmed b. Bayram, was registered in 1499, suggesting that Bayram died at a fairly advanced age.

Schedule of Production

The schedule for the production of the *Süleymanname* must have been carefully planned, considering that volumes I and IV (possibly all five volumes) as well as Arifi's two other books *(Futuhat-ı Cemile* and *Ravzat al-Uşak)* were under way at the same time. The date in the colophon indicates when the transcription of the manuscript was completed and the volume was ready to be bound, the painters and illuminators having finished their assignments. The calligrapher collaborated with the others, leaving space for the illuminations and illustrations, and going back to add the headings and the verses inserted into the paintings. The entire production must have been designed and orchestrated with extreme precision, each man knowing his specific task and schedule.

The production of the paintings in the *Süleymanname* does not fall into an identifiable pattern: the painters either contributed single scenes or worked on groups of consecutive illustrations, all of which were assembled in a mixed order. The largest group, that of twelve consecutive scenes towards the end of the book (53-64), was executed by Painter A, who also produced sequels of sixes (16-21 and 33-38), fours (1-4 and 6-9), twos (40-41, 43-44, and 50-51), and made three single paintings (24, 28, and 31).

Painter B was responsible for a group of six consecutive illustrations (10-15) as well as sequels of five (45-49), three (25-27), and two (22-23). His remaining six scenes (5, 30, 32, 42, 52, and 65), together with Painter C's two illustrations (29 and 39), were mixed in with those of Painter A.

This scheme suggests that, in contrast to volumes I and IV (each of which contains the work of a single artist), the scenes were distributed to the painters individually or in groups, then reassembled into the manuscript prior to binding.

Where the painters actually worked on the folios is a matter of speculation. They must have gathered periodically in the nakkaşhane to check references, consult the nakkaşbaşı, and hand their finished work back to the calligrapher. They or the nakkaşbaşı most likely met with the other artists and the şahnameci in the nakkaşhane building. Since more than one man combined efforts in a number of scenes, it is likely that Painter A shared a studio with Painters D and E. The others, Painters B and C, most probably worked alone in their own ateliers, as did presumably the calligrapher and the bookbinder.

NOTES

1. For a study of Arifi see Sohrweide 1971; see also Woodhead 1983. Arifi himself mentions in the text of the *Süleymanname* that his father was Derviş Mehmed (fol. 504b) and that his home was Abadan (fol. 505a).
2. Woodhead 1983, 159-161 and 179 quoting from Aşık Çelebi. This is the earliest reference to an actual building housing the artists. It must have been on the same site as the one illustrated in the *Surname-i Vehbi*. See note 36 on page 51.
3. The work was sold in London in 1976 (Christie's 1976, lot 24).
4. Los Angeles 1973, no. 260.

5. Grube n.d., nos. 185-218. This study does not indicate where the calligrapher's name appears. Since the manuscript was inaccessible, its location could not be checked.

6. The paintings of this remarkable manuscript have been published in a number of studies, including Stchoukine 1966, no. 21; Akalay 1970; Atasoy 1970; Atasoy and Çağman 1974, pls. 7-9; Fehér 1976; Akalay 1978; Atıl 1980, ills. 80-83, pls. 20 and 21; and İstanbul 1983, E 70 and 71 with other references.

7. Judging from the extent of the existing volumes the *Şahname-i Al-i Osman* must have included some 90,000 verses. In addition, Arifi wrote several other works during these years.

8. TSM, H. 1592 (Fehér 1976). It appears to be an extended version of thirty-one folios devoted to the same campaign described in the *Süleymanname* (fols. 524a-542a). The protagonists are the vezirs Mehmed and Ahmed Paşas and not the sultan, who did not participate in this campaign. Hence the work is a *gazavatname*, or a book of a specific campaign, and not a şahname, which is a biographical account of a sultan's whole career. Matrakcı's three works as well as Ahmed Feridun Paşa's account of the Szigetvar campaign also fall within the genre of gazavatname since they describe individual campaigns or events.

9. Binney 1979, no. 13.

10. TSM, R. 1540 mük. (Karatay 1961a, no. 157); the manuscript is not illustrated.

11. Woodhead 1983, 164. Mesnevi contains rhymed couplets with each couplet having a different rhyme but following the same meter. The mütekarib meter was exclusively used in epics and has trisyllabic feet.

12. Among the Persian versions is a work produced c. 1535 that clearly reflects the style of Tabriz: TSM, H. 1499 (Atıl 1980, pl. 18). Turkish translations, in contrast, show the emergence of local styles, as seen in the c. 1530 copy in TSM, H. 1116; Atıl 1980, ill. 75. Another Turkish translation, executed c. 1560-1570 in TSM, H. 1522, reveals the hand of Osman and the characteristically Ottoman court style (Atıl 1980, ill. 76). It should be noted that the earliest illustrated Turkish version of Firdausi's *Şahname* was undertaken in the Mamluk court TSM, H. 1519, dated 1511. This manuscript, which contains local figures and settings, was brought back from Cairo by Selim I (Atıl 1984, 163-169 and pls. 8-13).

13. This term is used for the strip between the backcover and the flap. The strip, which is the same size as the spine, protects the exposed edges of the folios when the flap is tucked under the front cover, creating a boxlike effect.

14. See note 49 on page 52.

15. The most exquisite binding was made for an undated copy in TİEM, 1962 (Çığ 1971, pls. X and XI; Atıl 1980, ill. 92).

16. See, for example, the tuğra in TİEM, 2238 (Lowry 1982, pl. 185); a bottle in London, British Museum, 78 12-30 519; and a large bowl in London, Victoria and Albert Museum, 243-1876 (both published in İstanbul 1983, E 41 and 49).

17. TSM, Y.Y. 999 (Atıl 1980, ill. 91).

18. TİEM, 2191. This document is devoted to Hürrem's endowment in Aksaray. For the bookbinding see Çığ 1971, pl. VII.

19. See, for instance, the tile panels in the Mosque of Rüstem Paşa built in 1561 (Denny 1980, ill. 161) and a late sixteenth-century court rug in Vienna, Österreichisches Museum für Angewandte Kunst, T 8327 (Mackie 1980, pl. 55).

20. TSM, E. 2851 (İstanbul 1983, E 61).

21. İU, F. 1426, (İstanbul 1983 E 63 and 64).

22. See note 49 on page 52. A section in Arifi's *Süleymanname* (fol. 498a) lists the gifts sent to Süleyman from Elkas Mirza during the 1548-1549 campaign to Iran. Included in the group were Korans transcribed by Yakut and Abdullah Sayrafi. It is possible that the latter work is this example, which was refurbished several years later.

23. See note 50 on page 52.

24. TSM, R. 738 mük. (Karatay 1961b, vol. 2, no. 2330).

25. TSM, H. 2163, fol. 9a (unpublished).

26. Numbers used in parenthesis identify the illustrations reproduced on pages 90-232.

27. See note 8.

28. These two paintings are on fols. 18b-19a and 25a (Fehér 1976, pls. XXXIV and XXXVI). The former depicts the same episode of Ahmed Paşa's siege of Temesvar found in the *Süleymanname* (55) but is spread to double folios. It is possible that Painter A condensed this scene when working on the sultan's history.

29. See note 3.

30. The painting (fol. 6a) showing the Miraj reveals the hand of another artist.

31. See note 4.

32. See note 9.
33. See note 65 on page 52.
34. See note 66 on page 52.
35. See, for instance, Stchoukine 1966, pl. IV; and Atıl 1980, ills. 70 and 71.
36. See note 75 on page 53.
37. See notes 20 and 87 on pages 50 and 53.
38. Osman, mentioned in the payroll registers dated between 1566 and 1596, is praised in the texts of Lokman. He worked with this şahnameci on the following manuscripts: *Tarih-i Sultan Süleyman, Şahname-i Selim Han, Şahınşahname, Hünername, Kıyafet el-İnsaniye fi Şemail-i Osmaniye, Zübdet üt-Tevarih,* and *Surname.* For references to these works see notes 88-94 on page 53.
39. Osman and Ali are shown in the company of the author, Lokman, and the calligrapher, İlyas, while discussing the work with one of the leading scholars of the court, Şemseddin Ahmed Karabağı. The scene appears both in the c. 1575 London copy (fol. 7b) and in the 1581 version in İstanbul (fol. 9a). See Atıl 1980, ill. 93 for the painting in İstanbul; and Titley 1981, pl. 37 for the scene in London. See also notes 20 and 89 on pages 50 and 53.
40. See note 70 on page 52.
41. They appear in the following manuscripts:
    1. *Anthology* of c. 1520; CB, MS. 424 (Minorsky 1958, no. 424).
    2. *Divan* of Şahi dated 1528; TSM, B. 140 (Karatay 1961a, no. 668).
    3. *Divan* of Şahi c. 1530; NB, Cod. Mixt. 399 (Duda 1978-1979; and Duda 1983, Mixt. 399).
    4. *Divan* of Nevai dated 1533/1534; TSM, R. 806 (Stchoukine 1966, no. 12).
    5. *Divan* of Nevai of c. 1535; TSM, R. 804. (Stchoukine 1966, no. 13; and İstanbul 1983, E 58).
    6. *Guy ve Çevgan* of Arifi dated 1539/1540; TSM, H. 845 (Stchoukine 1966, no. 15; and İstanbul 1983, E 59).
    7. *Divan-ı Selimi* of c. 1530-1540; İÜ, F. 1330 (see note 71 on page 52).
    8. *Tuhfet el-Ahrar* of Jami of c. 1530-1540; TSM, R. 914 (Atasoy and Çağman 1974, pl. 5).
    9. *Tercüme-i Şahname* dated 1545/1546; TSM, H. 1520 (Stchoukine 1966, no. 18).

    The lacquer bookbinding of the *Divan* of Şahi of c. 1530 in Vienna (see no. 3 above) is exceptional for the period and shows the same finesse as the paintings in the book and in such imperial manuscripts as the *Divan-ı Selimi.*
42. Fifteenth- and sixteenth-century European prints are found in a number of albums compiled for the sultans and could have served as models to the painters. In addition, artists listed in the payroll registers as being from eastern Europe most likely practiced their own traditions. Campaigns to such capitals as Belgrade and Budapest must have enriched the court with illustrative material. It is mentioned that the library of Mathias Corvin was brought back from Budapest by Süleyman in 1526, but its contents were not recorded. Four manuscripts given in 1869 by Sultan Abdülaziz to Austria and thirty-five sent in 1877 by Sultan Abdülhamid to the University of Budapest appear to have belonged to this group (Atasoy 1970, 195). In addition to the library of Mathias Corvin, Süleyman brought back from Budapest two large bronze candlesticks, statues of Hercules, Apollo, and Diana, and a number of cannonballs. Two of the cannonballs were thought to have been left there during the 1456 siege of Budapest by Mehmed II. See Danişmend 1971, vol. 2, 118.
43. Osman's self-portrait, together with the representation of his colleague Ali, appears as the first painting in the *Şahname-i Selim Han.* See note 39. Hasan, an Enderun graduate who worked with Talikizade, the şahnameci who replaced Lokman in 1596/1597, executed his portrait together with those of the author and calligrapher in *Şahname-i Mehmed III* of c. 1596 in TSM, H. 1609, fol. 74a (Akalay 1979, fig. 1; and Atıl 1980, ill. 99). Ahmed Nakşi, another member of the administration, depicted himself in the presence of his patrons, Osman II and the grand vezir, in Taşköprülüzade's history of learned men, the *Şekayik-i Numaniye* of c. 1619, in TSM, H. 1263, fol. 259b (Atıl 1978 and 1980, pl. 30). See also note 35 on page 51. The earliest appearance of a self-portrait of an artist is found in the frontispiece of Şükrü Bitlisi's *Selimname* of c. 1525. See note 78 on page 53.
44. See note 52 on page 52.

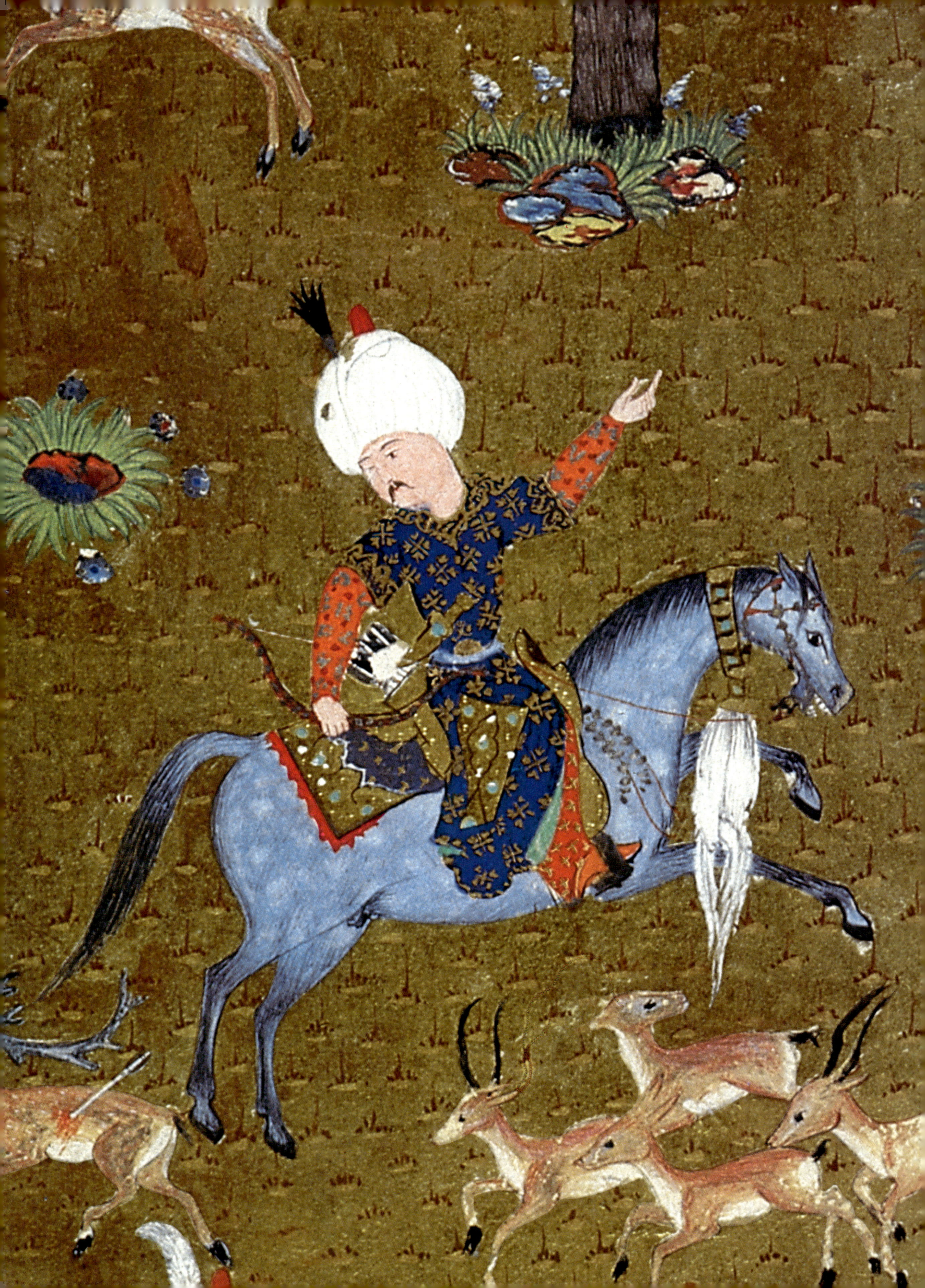

The Plates

detail of illustration on page 126

Bookbinding: exterior

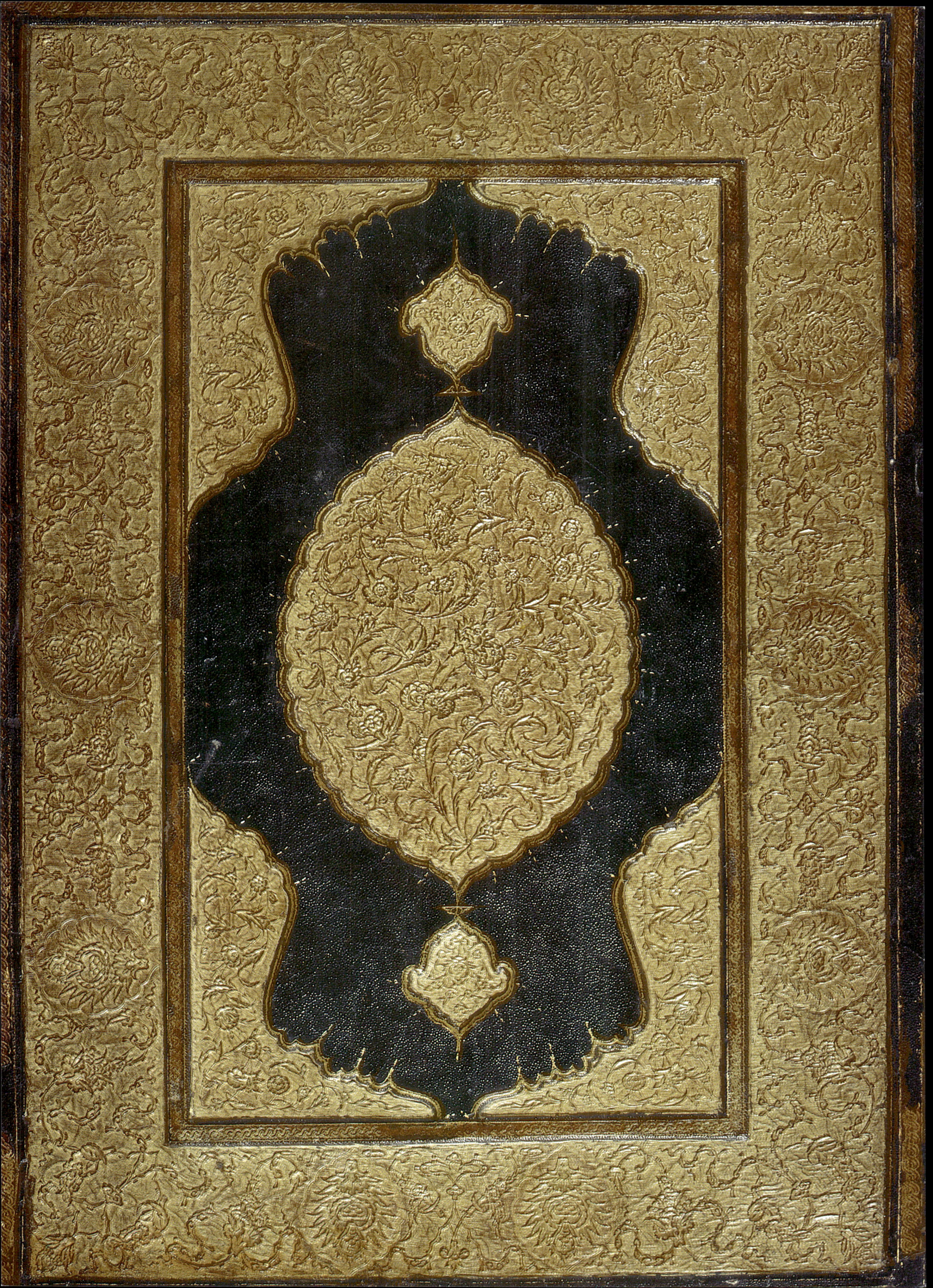

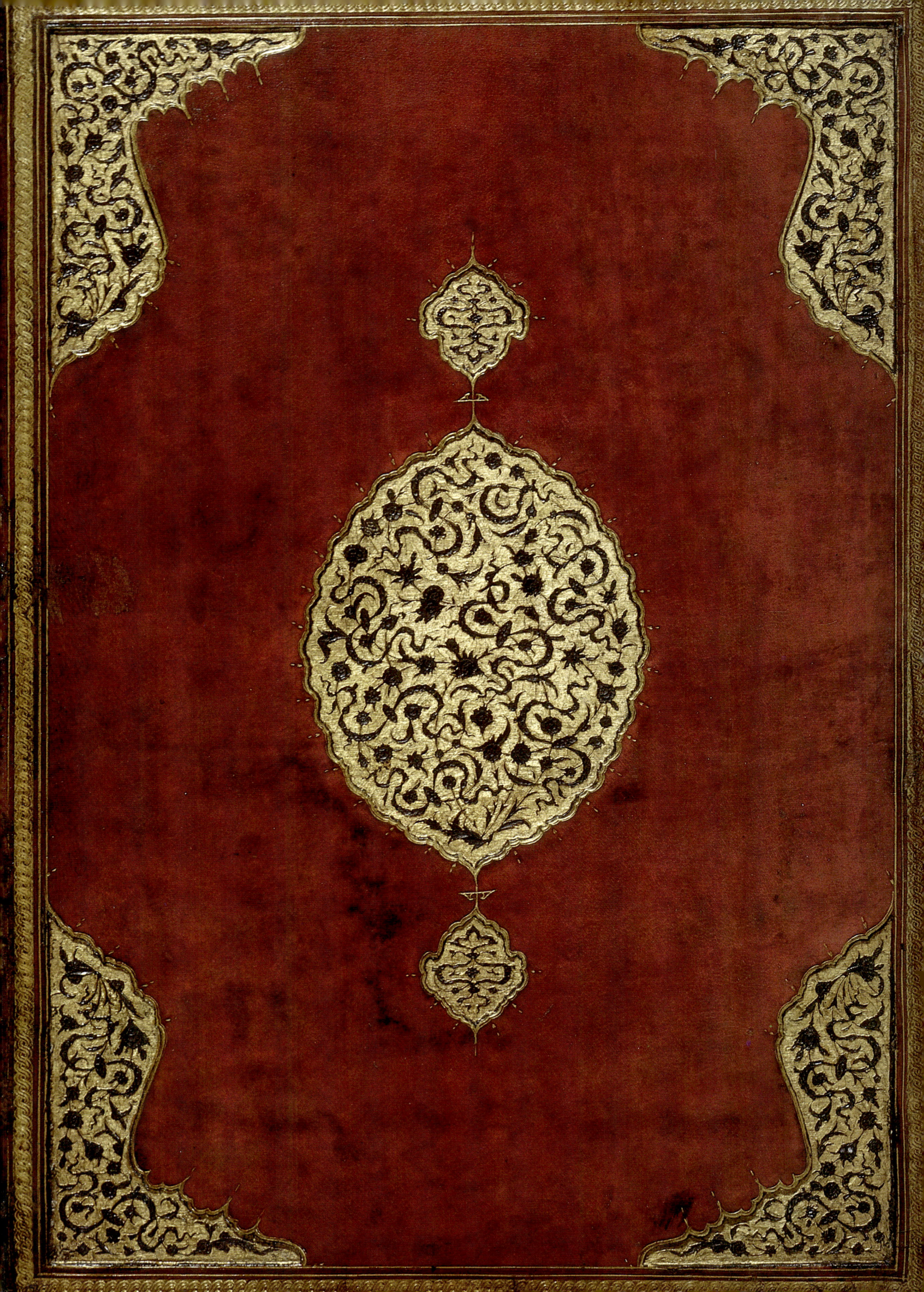

Bookbinding

THE BINDING OF the *Süleymanname* is one of the most sumptuous examples dating from this period. The layout of the exterior and interior surfaces, the proportions of the structural components, the juxtaposition of decorative motifs, and the execution indicate that a highly competent artist was employed for the creation of the covers of the illustrated history of the sultan and that no expenses were spared. It is the highest achievement of the art of bookbinding both aesthetically and technically.

The pasteboard core is covered with blackish-brown leather on the exterior and reddish-brown leather on the interior. The exterior has a thick gold-stamped outer band framed on both sides by thin braided strips; in the center is a large gold-stamped oval medallion with pendants on its vertical axis, enclosed by four lobed corner quadrants. Delicate scrolls composed of hatayi blossoms, serrate leaves, and overlapping floral elements fill these units. Additional cloudbands appear on the outer band, which is further enhanced by a series of lobed ovals rendered in high relief. The ovals, placed in threes and twos, are composed of a central hatayi surmounted by a pomegranate and flanked by two serrate leaves that create a flamelike border.

The striking majesty of the exterior provides a dramatic contrast to the quiet delicacy of the interior, which reveals a lighter and more airy composition. The central oval with pendants and the corner quadrants are spaciously placed and expose a larger field; a thin braid frames the covers. In contrast to the rich exterior, which displays a bold use of gold as the main surface decoration, the interior employs the gold in the background of the units. Hatayi scrolls and cloudbands filling the medallions and the quadrants are painted black and executed in relief.

The decorative elements are exquisitely rendered and extremely intricate. The delicate intertwining and rhythmical arrangement of cloudbands and hatayi scrolls reveal the highest level of refinement. The design of the bookbinding exemplifies the saz style of imperial Ottoman decorative arts. Scrolls composed of twisting and intersecting serrate leaves, and composite blossoms and buds depicted both frontally and in profile create a dense and yet harmonious interplay of movement and form.

Although the name of the maker is not mentioned in the manuscript, this spectacular bookbinding must be the work of the greatest master working in the court. It is attributed to Mehmed b. Ahmed, who is recorded as being the head of the imperial society of bookbinders between 1545 and 1566.

Bookbinding: interior

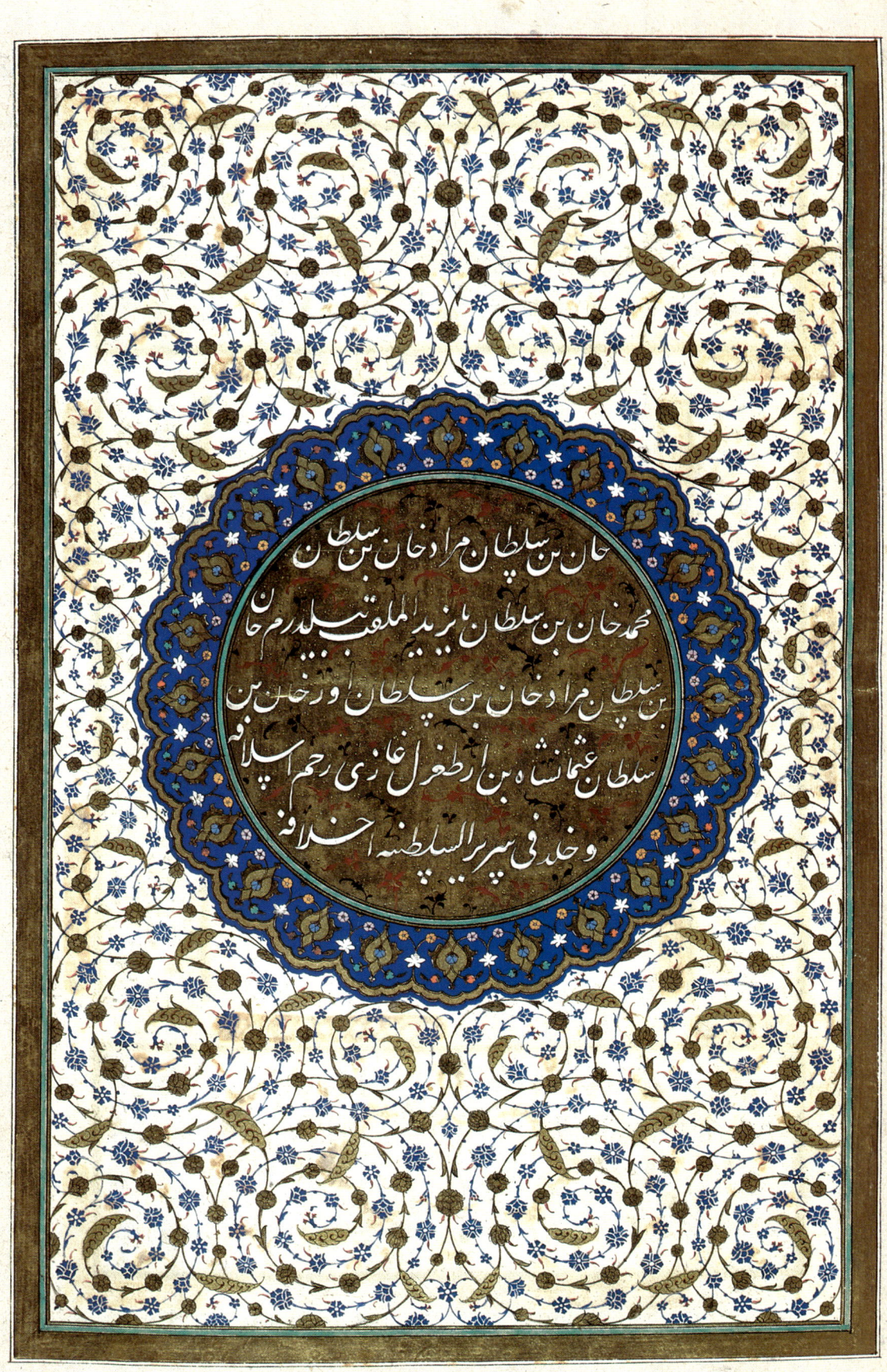

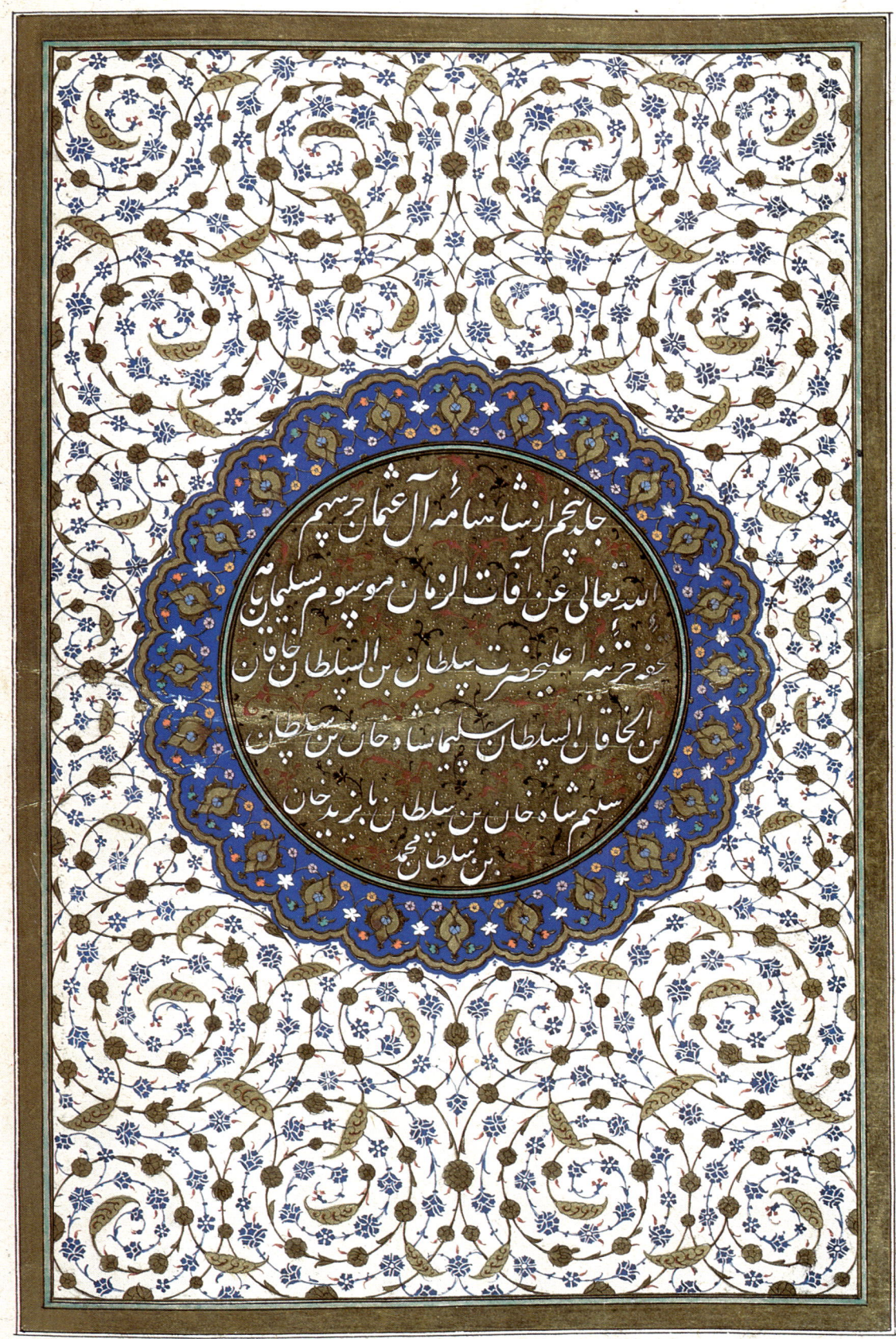

Zahriye (Dedication)

(folios 1b-2a)

THE DOUBLE FOLIOS containing the dedication and title placed at the beginning of the volume, called *zahriye*, are identical in design. Each folio has a gold central medallion enclosed by a lobed blue frame; the field is covered with two different types of blue and gold superimposed scrolls. The central medallions contain the title of the work and name of the patron, rendered in white nastalik script with white triple-balls and red and black floral sprays filling the interstices. The encircling frame, adorned with gold cartouches composed of split rumis and polychrome hatayis and other blossoms, is outlined by a scalloped band.

One of the superimposed scrolls in the field consists of a blue branch bearing stencillike hatayis and five- or six-petaled blossoms. The other has a gold vine with large composite leaves and hatayis. The scrolls create a series of concentric formations, recalling the design found on the tuğra of the sultan as well as on a particular group of ceramics painted in blue and turquoise. This concentric scroll became one of the elements that characterized the decorative vocabulary of the age.

The title of the book appears in the medallion on the right folio. The inscription states that the work, entitled the *Süleymanname*, is the fifth volume of the *Şahname-i Al-i Osman*. It is followed by the name of the patron and those of his forefathers: "*muhteşem* [magnificent] sultan, son of the sultan, hakan, son of the hakan, Sultan Süleyman Şah Han, son of Sultan Selim Şah Han, son of Sultan Bayezid Han, son of Sultan Mehmed."

The genealogy of the patron is continued in the medallion on the left folio: "Han, son of Sultan Murad Han, son of Sultan Mehmed Han, son of Sultan Bayezid called Yıldırım Han, son of Sultan Murad, son of Sultan Orhan, son of Sultan Osman Şah, son of Ertuğrul Gazi. May God have mercy and compassion for his ancestors and may the throne of the sultanate of his descendants be an eternal paradise. [The manuscript is] dedicated to his library."

It is interesting to note that not only all ten of Süleyman's illustrious ancestors are listed but also Ertuğrul, who was traditionally accepted as the predecessor of Osman, the founder of the Osmanlı, or Ottoman, dynasty. Ertuğrul was not considered to be the first Ottoman ruler and is hence called gazi, a champion warrior of the faith, and not a sultan.

Münacat (Prayers)

(folios 2b-3a)

THE *Süleymanname* opens with a spectacular double folio. Each folio has a text panel in the center with seven lines of black nastalik written in two columns and placed on a concentric blue hatayi scroll. Flanking the text are two pairs of lobed ovals enclosing branches with naturalistic blossoms growing from a cluster of leaves, placed on a deep blue ground. Above and below are rectangular panels with a profusion of polychrome flowers and gold cloudbands on the same blue ground; in the center of each is a gold cartouche with a verse written in white script. These units are framed by braided strips and floral bands broken into ovals and painted in two tones of gold. Enclosing them at the top, bottom, and outer sides is a wide border composed of reciprocal lobed arches, filled with polychrome blossoms on a blue ground and gold composite rumis and hatayis on a lighter gold ground. At the outer edge is another band with a most unusual design consisting of a series of flamelike gold leaves with polychrome blossoms on a blue ground. This band is outlined in red, which enhances the flamelike effect, and finished with blue finials containing stencillike hatayis and red blossoms.

The combination of blue and gold grounds, the application of two tones of gold, and the polychrome accents produce an incredibly rich and radiant effect. The use of both stylized and naturalistic motifs is a characteristic of mid-sixteenth-century decorative arts, as is the theme of branches with blossoms on a blue ground used in the oval panels flanking the text.

Meticulous attention to design, harmonious juxtaposition of decorative elements, and refined technique are also found in the works of an exceptional artist named Kara Memi, who headed the Rumiyan Corps of the nakkaşhane in 1557-1558 and illuminated a number of imperial manuscripts produced between the 1540s and 1560s. This artist must have also executed the dedicatory pages, the opening folios, and the decorative headings and subheadings of the *Süleymanname*.

Arifi begins the *Süleymanname* with a selection of verses from the Koran chosen specifically for the sultan. They appear in the gold cartouches above and below the text panels and read first across the top of both folios and then across the bottom: "It is from Solomon and is : In the name of God, the Merciful, the Compassionate (XXVII: 30). God commands justice, the doings of good, and liberality to kith and (XVI: 90) God loveth those who do good (II: 195)."

These verses stress the qualities of justice, generosity, and tolerance, and include a reference to Solomon, with whom the sultan shares his name as well as his reputation for judicial reform. The association of Süleyman with Solomon and references to the sultan's legal achievements frequently appear in historical and literary texts as well as in inscriptions on his architectural complexes and personal objects.

→

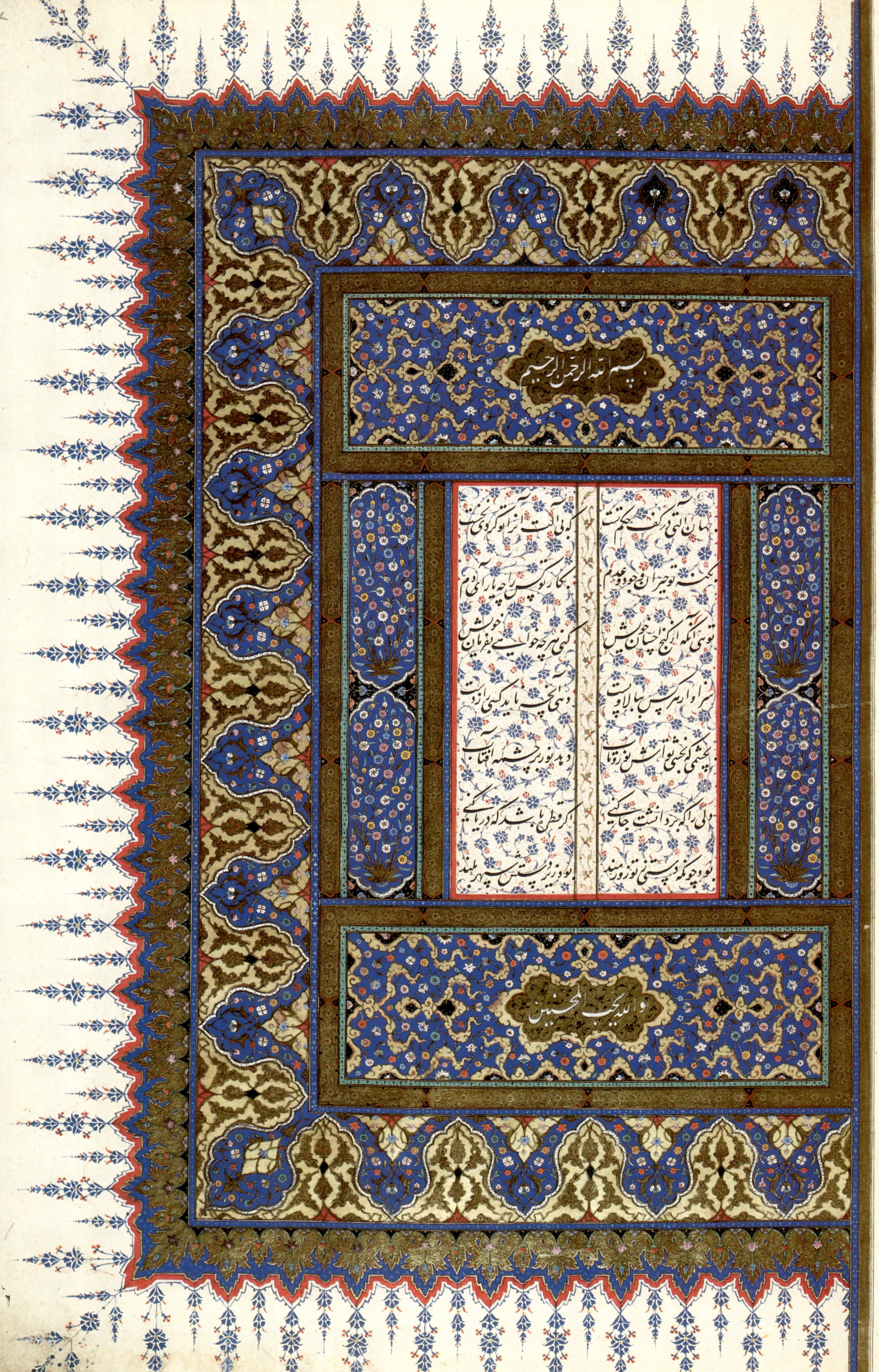

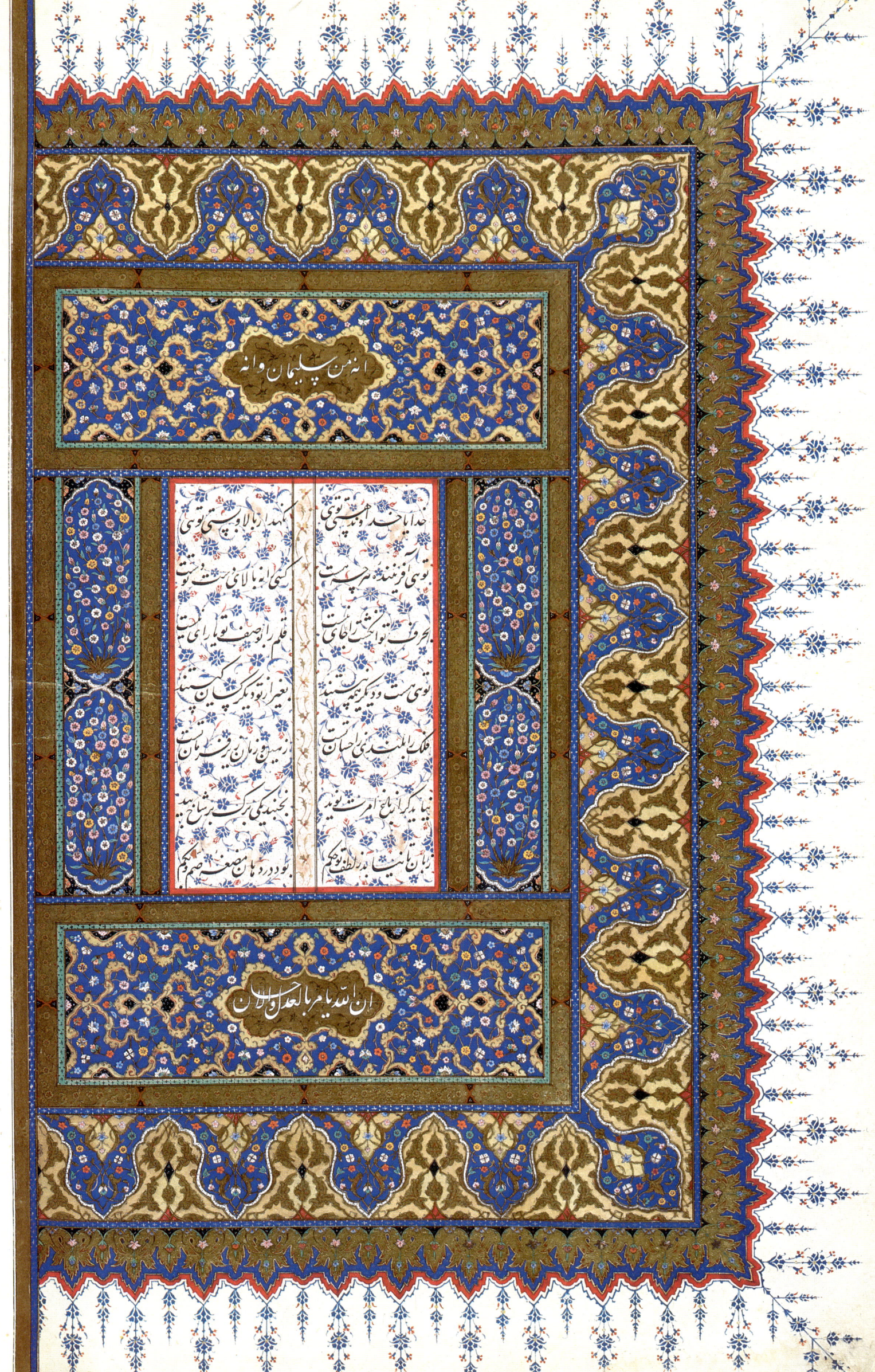

1. Accession Ceremonies

(folios 17b-18a)   Painter A

SÜLEYMAN WAS serving as the governor of Manisa when his father, Selim I, died on 22 September 1520 in Edirne while en route to a campaign. The crown prince, who was the only heir, immediately departed for the capital and arrived at the Topkapı Palace on 30 September. His accession ceremonies took place the following day.

Present during the ceremonies were the grand vezir Piri Mehmed Paşa, the second vezir Mustafa Paşa, and the third vezir Ferhad Paşa, all of whom had held the same posts under Selim I. Ferhad Paşa was also Selim I's brother-in-law, having married his sister Selçuk. Süleyman had appointed a fourth vezir, Kasım Paşa, who was his tutor in Manisa. This was the first time in Ottoman history that the Divan-ı Hümayun contained four vezirs. Also participating in the ceremony was the elderly şeyhülislam Zenbilli Ali Efendi, who had served the state for two decades. This distinguished theologian and scholar was the uncle of the grand vezir and had participated in some of Selim I's campaigns.

Süleyman, who ascended the Ottoman throne at the age of twenty-six, was superbly trained for the sultanate, having served as governor in such provinces as Bolu, Kefe, and Manisa since his adolescent years. He was deeply involved in legislation and issued hundreds of fermans, which became the kanuns of the Ottoman Empire, earning him the title Kanuni.

Süleyman is thought to have officially married his consort, Hürrem, shortly after arriving in İstanbul. He was extremely devoted to his wife and remained faithful to her throughout his life. Before meeting her, his hasekis were Gülfem and Gülbahar, who had given birth to sons. It was, however, one of Hürrem's sons who was destined to succeed him.

> The accession ceremonies of Ottoman sultans took place in the second courtyard of the Topkapı Palace, in front of the Babüssaade. This painting, spread to double folios, is the earliest representation of the ceremony in its proper setting. Conceived as two consecutive scenes, the left half represents the Bab-ı Hümayun in the foreground, the first courtyard in the center, and the Babüsselam in the background. Depicted on the right half is the second courtyard with the sultan enthroned in front of the arcade at the back. The Babüssaade, which was reconstructed in the nineteenth century with a large overhanging roof, is not portrayed behind the throne. It appears that during the sixteenth century the gate was less conspicuous and was thus omitted in the painting.
>
> The Bab-ı Hümayun represented here is a two-story structure with a series of windows in the second level and thin, tall chimneys on the roof. The entrance is guarded by a pair of kapıcıs while a group of men and boys approach the gate on horseback and on foot. In the first courtyard are additional riders and pedestrians who line up on either side of the path leading to the Babüsselam, an impressive gate flanked by two massive towers. A hexagonal fountain with a conical roof appears on the left while a large tree is seen through the opening of the gate. Janissaries, kapıcıs, and a solitary peyk mingle with the visitors and maintain order and security.
>
> The figures arriving at the palace and those already gathered in the first courtyard are attired in their ceremonial garments. They wear a variety of headgear, including turbans, tall felt or fur caps, and split-brimmed hats, indicating diverse groups among the civilian and military classes.
>
> The groups in the second courtyard contain high-ranking officers, commanders, and administrators, attended by staff-bearing kapıcıs. On the upper left is the sultan, who is seated on a gold throne and receives the homage of a kneeling dignitary. The grand vezir, Piri Mehmed Paşa, stands to his right with the three highest ranking vezirs—Mustafa, Ferhad, and Kasım Paşas—next to him. Below them are the white-bearded şeyhülislam Zenbilli Ali Efendi together with the kazaskers of Rumelia and Anatolia, wearing large flat turbans and fur-lined coats. Four clean-shaven iç oğlans, their hands clasped in respect like the vezirs,

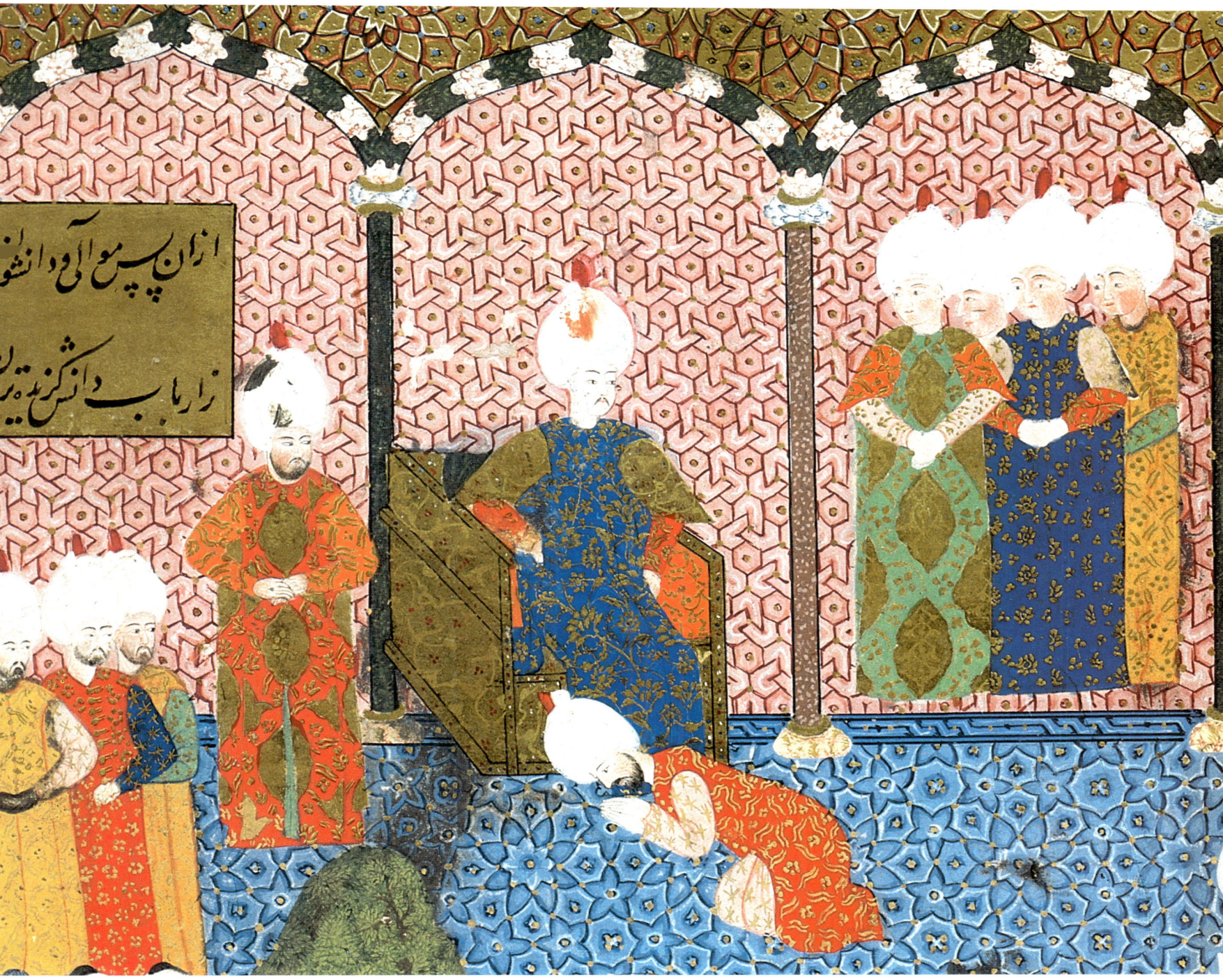

stand to the left of the sultan. The officials waiting to be received create a semicircular formation in front of the sultan, in the center of which are a pair of ushers or protocol officers.

Süleyman, attired in a blue ceremonial outer kaftan and a gold inner kaftan with long red sleeves, is portrayed as a youthful monarch with a thin mustache. His vezirs have short dark beards, indicating middle age, while the şeyhülislam and the kazaskers have long beards, suitable for their status and advanced age.

Two large, richly foliated trees grow in the courtyard, which is covered with tufts of grass and occasional bunches of flowers. Every surface—arches, walls, and pavement—is decorated with stylized stone or tile patterns. Above the marble columns of the arcade, two pairs of domes and cypress trees project into the upper margin as do the towers of the Bab-ı Hümayun on the left folio.

The atmosphere of the scene created by Painter A, the master of the *Süleymanname*, is at once ceremonial and casual. The static groups around the sultan reflect the rigid protocol of the state while the conversing and agitated visitors create a sense of excitement and movement that contrasts with the hierarchic stillness surrounding the main protagonists.

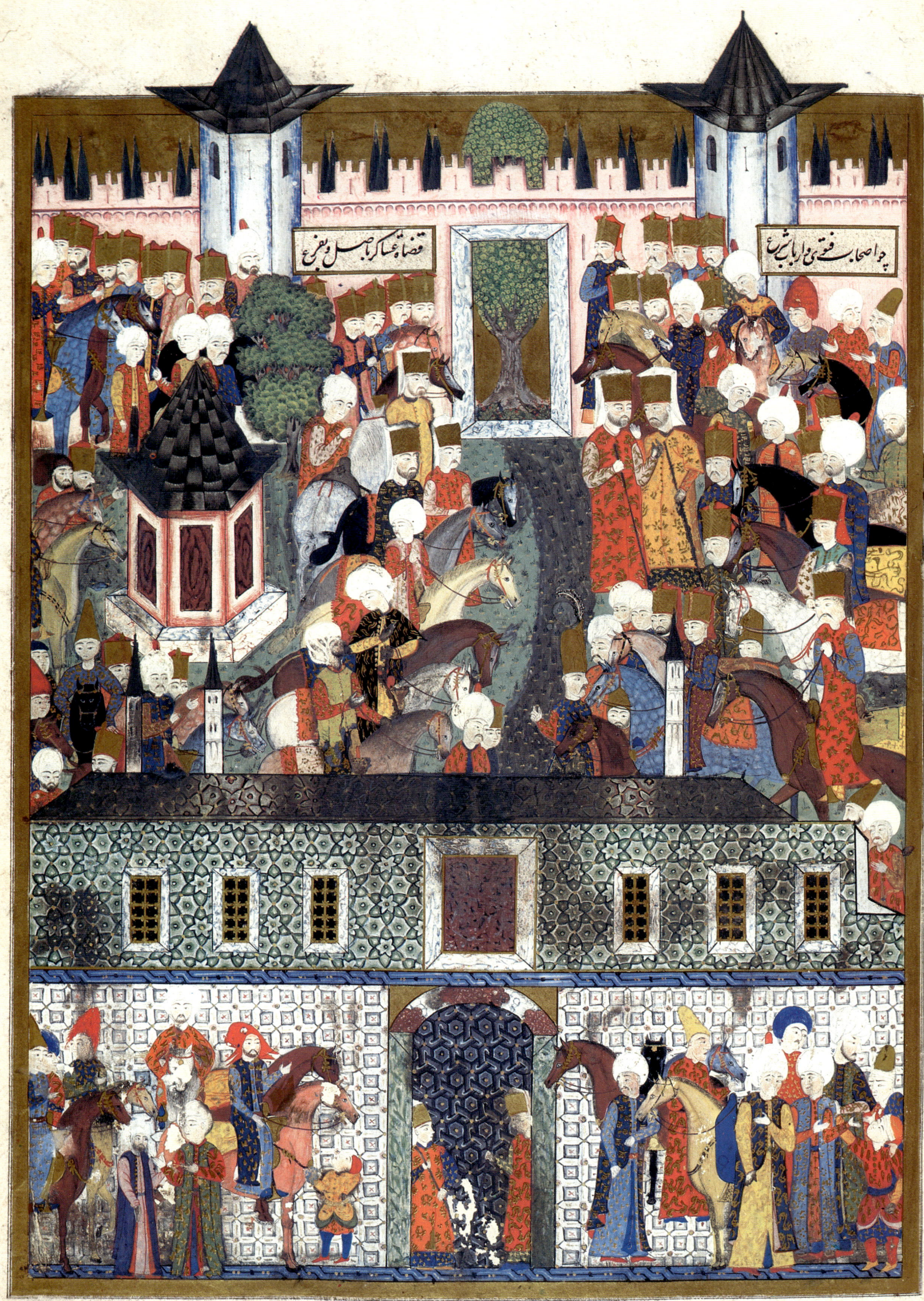

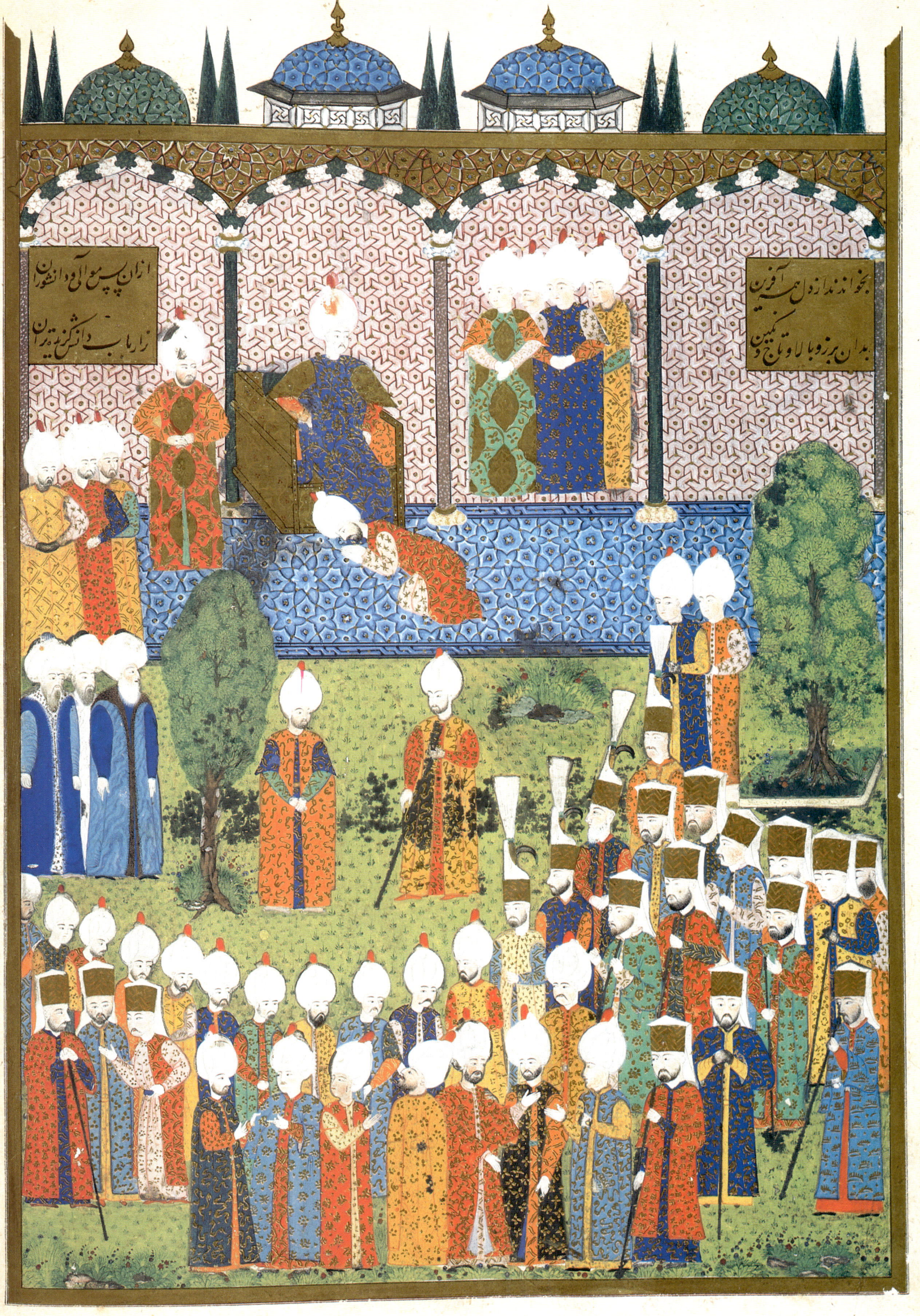

2. Recruitment of Tribute Children

(folio 31b) Painters A and E

AN IMPORTANT FUNCTION of Ottoman administration was the recruitment and training of personnel to serve the state. The majority of the administrators were the product of the devşirme system in which non-Muslim boys were taken by the state and educated according to their abilities. Some joined the Enderun School in the palace, some were sent to provincial courts, while others entered the Janissary Corps, the elite regiment of the army. The youths were given a rigid academic and military training, which enabled them to hold key positions in the empire. Upon completing their formal education they were assigned to civil or military services, advancing to become officers, commanders, governors, and vezirs. All the grand vezirs of the empire had been recruited through the devşirme and many married royal princesses.

The tribute children, having no inherited allegiance to race or creed, became the most loyal servants of the state. The devşirme system not only provided a continual fresh supply of well-trained soldiers and statemen, but also prohibited the creation of a hereditary aristocracy. Advancement was based on merit and competence, and any official could be ousted if he failed to perform his duties. The only person who could inherit his father's titles and possessions was the sultan, the supreme ruler.

This unique scene illustrating the recruiting of the devşirme children takes place in a Christian town in one of the western provinces. The *devşirme emini* (officer in charge of recruitment) wears a tall hat topped by a plume and sits on a red rug spread on a brick platform. He is counting the money given to the recruits as travel expenses from their hometown to the capital. His assistant records the town, province, parents, and birthdates of the children in a ledger; a copy of the record, which was required by the state, is on the rug. In the foreground, guarded by an officer, are six of the recruits, attired in their new red garments and caps, carrying bags that hold their only earthly possessions.

The men, women, and children of the town gather in front of an elaborate architectural setting with arches and high sloping roofs that represent non-Ottoman structures. A mother, most likely asking questions about her son's welfare, confronts a janissary, himself once a devşirme child. Next to her is a priest or monk wearing a dark robe and hat, equally apprehensive. Another woman, standing behind to the right of the devşirme emini, appears quite despondent, her young daughter clinging to her for comfort.

The representations of architecture and local figures indicate the hand of an artist who was familiar with the setting and residents of Christian communities in the Balkans. This style, identified as that of Painter E, appears whenever eastern European subjects are illustrated in the *Süleymanname*.

کسی را که با شد دو فرزند زیبا	پیشیو داراز یکی بی نیاز	کنون شاه را در سر مهر پیال	چنین گفت قابوس فرخنده فال
که سازد به حظ از دیار	روانی کی کند صاحب وقار	کند مهر او فرزند یکی	زبدبوزارش پی پنبه یک

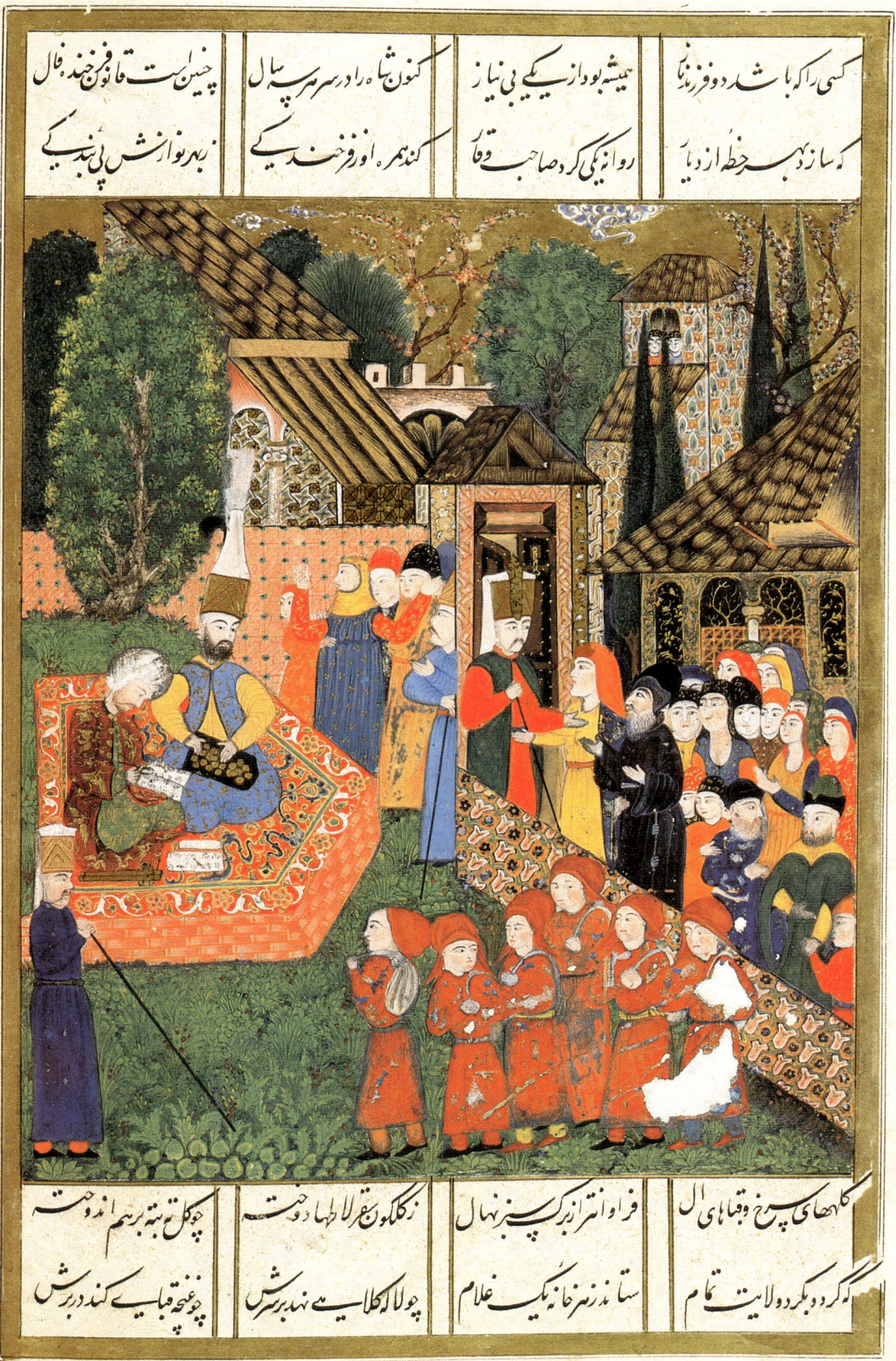

گاهمای سرخ وقباهای ال	فراوان تر از برگ سبز نهال	چوکلو نه برسم اندوخت	
اگر دو که دو لایت تمام	ستاده زمر خانه نیک غلام	چولا کلائی نهد برسرش	چو غنچه قبائی کند در برش

3. Meeting of the Divan

(folios 37b-38a)   Painter A

THE HIGHEST ADMINISTRATIVE organ of the state was the Divan-ı Hümayun, which consisted of ministers representing various branches of the state. The Divan met in the Kubbealtı, the domed chamber in the second courtyard of the palace, four days a week, their normal daily sessions lasting seven or eight hours with short recesses for meals and prayers.

Membership in the council varied in the course of the history of the Ottoman Empire. During Süleyman's reign it consisted of the grand vezir; three of the highest ranking vezirs, who were also the beylerbeyis of major provinces or high commanders; two kazaskers in charge of the judicial affairs in Rumelia and Antolia; two defterdars, who also divided their workload between Rumelia and Anatolia; the nişancı, who authenticated the fermans by affixing the imperial tuğra; and the reisülküttab, who was in charge of correspondence, records, and secretaries. The Divan also included other officials, such as the çavuşbaşı, kapıcıbaşı, and a number of recording secretaries, translators, and officers in charge of petitions.

The head of the Divan was the sultan—the supreme ruler, the commander in chief of the armed forces, and the protector of Islam. His executive assistant was the grand vezir, who represented the sultan during the meetings.

> The representation of the structures and activities in the second courtyard of the palace is based on acute observation. The accuracy of detail suggests that the artist must have had a first-hand knowledge of state proceedings. Spread on double folios, the painting describes a session of the Divan-ı Hümayun in the Kubbealtı.
>
> The left of the scene depicts the courtyard, framed at the top and left by the arcades with the Babüsselam on the far left. Groups of officials sit under the arches and hold animated discussions. On the upper right are four figures observing a pair of scribes working on scrolls with two *divits* (pencases) next to them. In the center are solaks, janissaries, kapıcıs, and other officers walking around the paradisiac courtyard filled with lushly foliated trees, wandering gazelles, and a large marble fountain. The bearded figure below the fountain, attired in a large turban and a fur-lined coat, appears to be arriving late for the meeting.
>
> The right half shows the Kubbealtı jutting into the courtyard and occupying two-thirds of the folio, with a portion of the courtyard shown in the foreground. Behind the arcaded facade of the Kubbealtı is a bird's-eye view of the Divan chamber. Seated on a "divan" covered with a red spread are the three highest ranking vezirs, the grand vezir, and the two kazaskers. On the far left is the nişancı, busy affixing the sultan's tuğra on a document. Opposite are the reisülküttab with the two defterdars; behind them are other officials, including scribes and possibly translators and the master of petitions. The çavuşbaşı and kapıcıbaşı stand in the center.
>
> Outside the Kubbealtı are several groups. On the far right a man weighs gold coins on a scale while another heats wax on a brazier, (the wax presumably was used when sealing the bags or chests with the recorded coins). Nearby four other figures take inventory. Opposite are more court officials, engaged in a heated conversation. The Adalet Kulesi and the four domes of the Kubbealtı appear in the background.
>
> By removing the roof of the Divan chamber the artist was able to show both the session of the ministers inside the Kubbealtı and the activities outside. Although the setting is static with emphasis given to repetitive architectural components, the animated gestures of the figures and the naturalistic poses of the working staff create a lively composition: Painter A has transformed a general description of the meeting of the Divan into a specific session during which the sultan's first edicts are issued and their contents speculated about by the figures in the courtyard. In addition, the state is taking inventory of the gold in the treasury to finance the forthcoming campaigns.

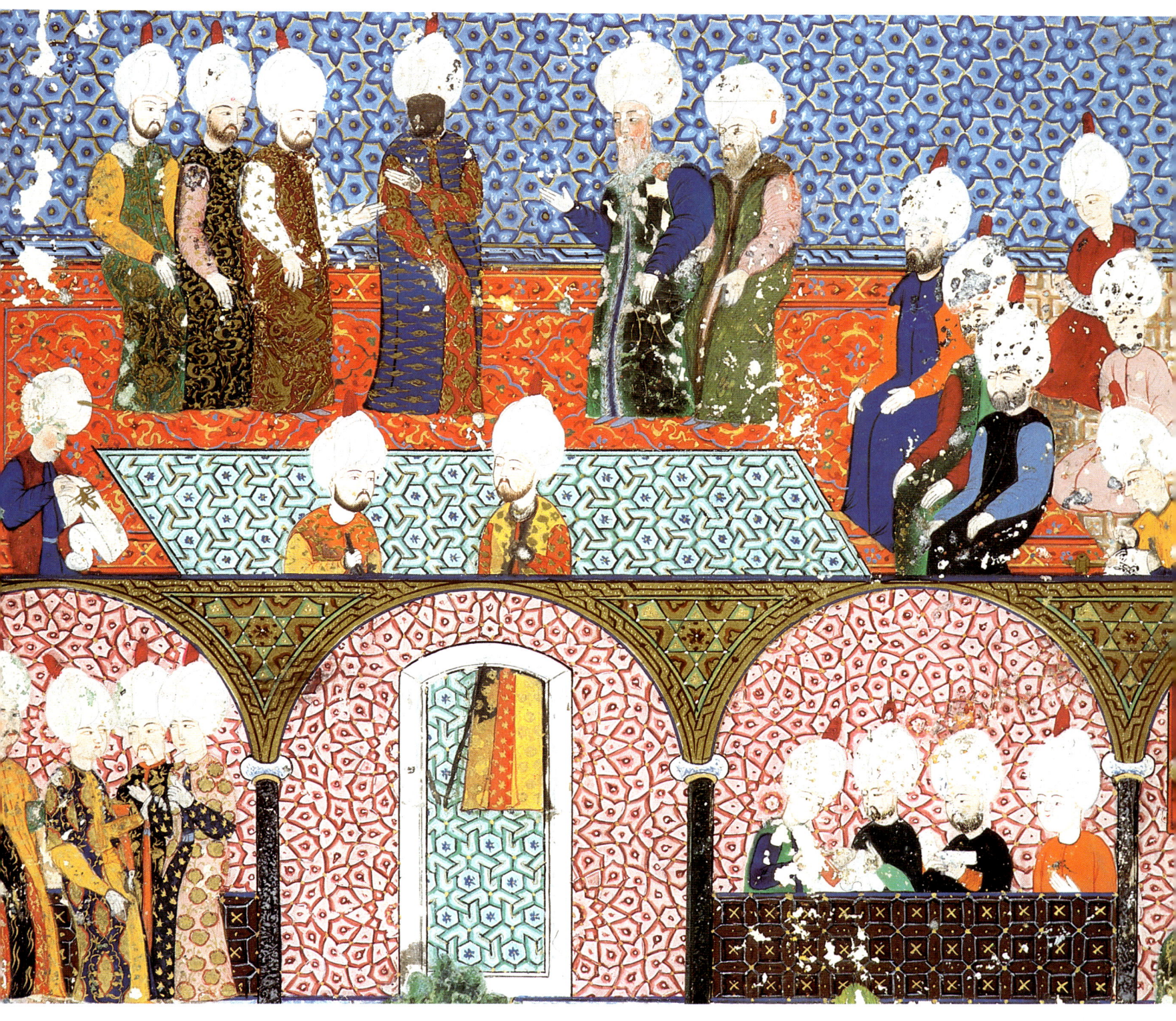

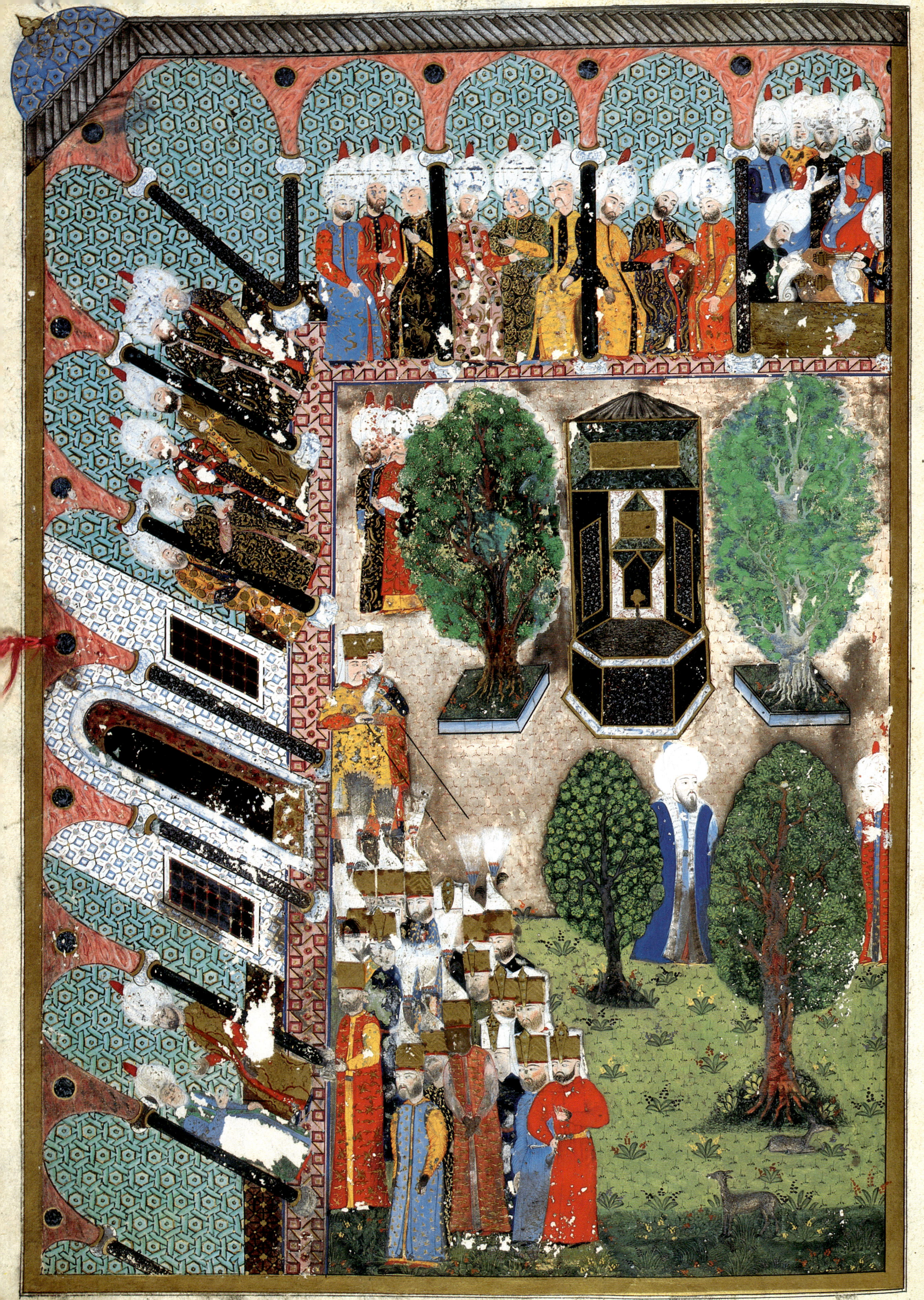

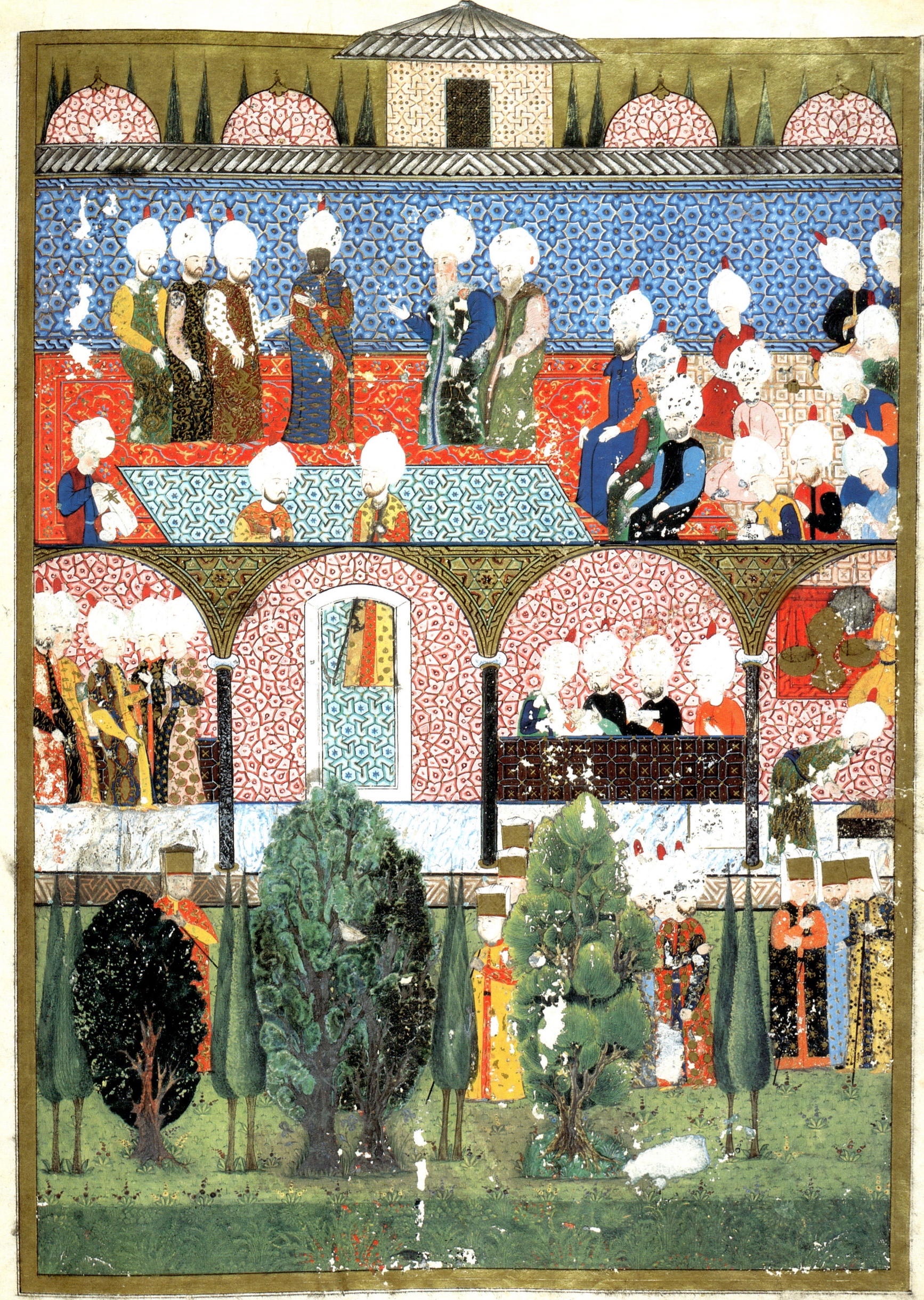

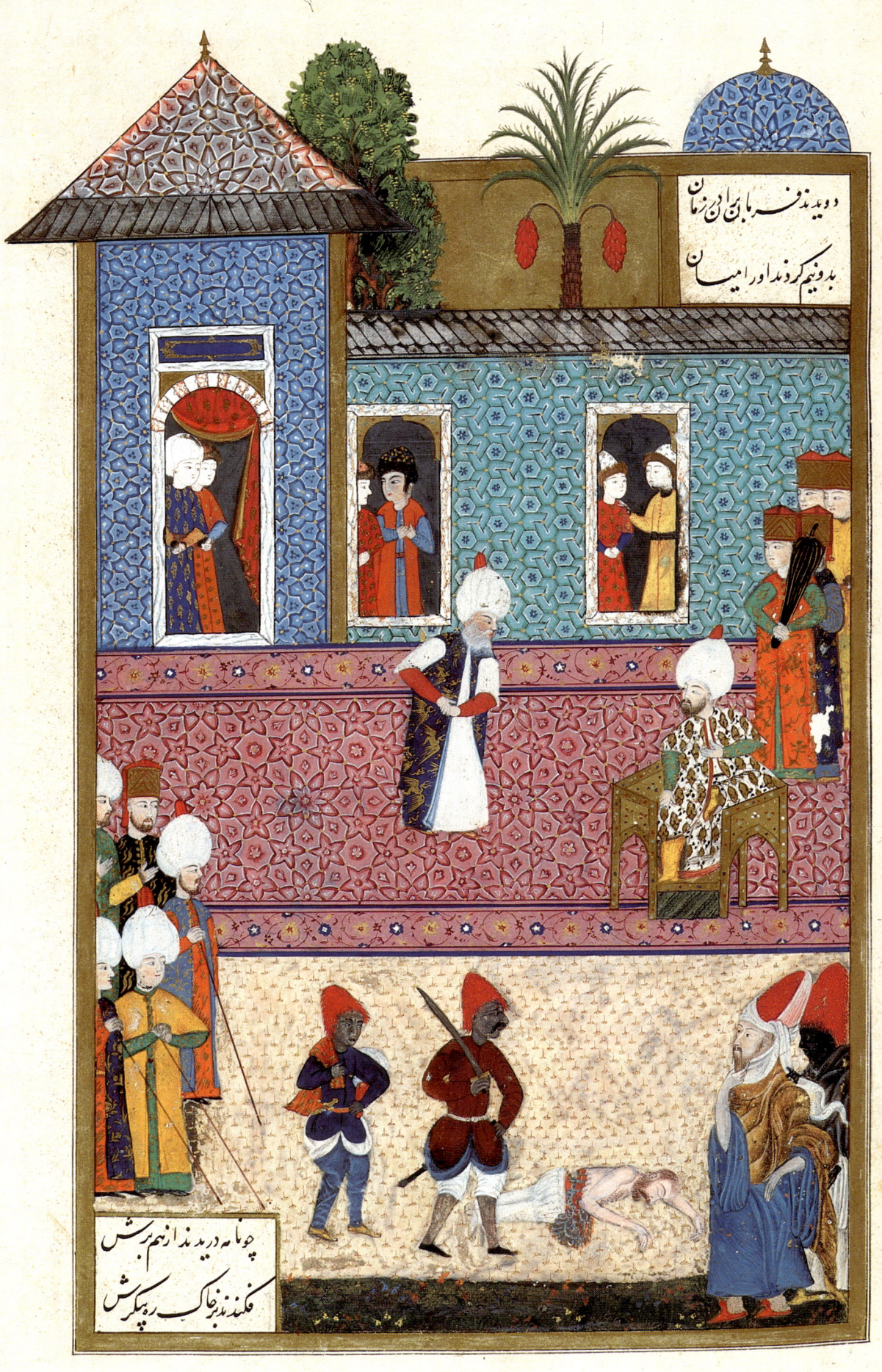

4. Execution of Canberdi Gazali's Envoy
(folio 56a)   Painter A

BEFORE Süleyman could embark on his first campaign, he had to settle an internal problem caused by the beylerbeyi of Syria, Canberdi Gazali. Underestimating the sultan, Gazali started an uprising in Damascus, which spread to other towns in Syria and Palestine in the fall of 1520. In an attempt to revive the old Mamluk empire, he wrote to Hayırbay, the beylerbeyi of Egypt, asking him to join the rebellion against the sultan. Hayırbay, loyal to the state, had Gazali's envoy killed and forwarded the treacherous letter to İstanbul to alert the sultan.

When Syria and Egypt were conquered by the Ottomans in 1517, Selim I had appointed former Mamluk officials to govern these regions. The province of Syria had its capital in Damascus and included Palestine; that of Egypt, controlled from Cairo, extended to Nubia and the Sinai Pensinsula. To retain control of these provinces was essential for both political and commercial reasons, since they extended along the eastern and southern frontiers and guarded the Mediterranean and the Red Sea.

> The painting, composed in three horizontal registers, represents Hayırbay, the beylerbeyi of Egypt, in his palace in Cairo. Seated on a gold throne with one leg bent up and placed across the other (presumably in the Mamluk fashion), Hayırbay converses with an elderly official while his attendants, one holding an encased sword, stand behind. Members of the Cairo palace, some wearing fur-brimmed caps, appear in the doorway and peer out of the windows of the structure rising in the background.
>
> In the foreground are two dark-skinned executioners, one with a bag over his shoulder, the other holding the sword with which he has just slain the unfortunate envoy sent by Canberdi Gazali, the beylerbeyi of Syria. The envoy who brought the letter inviting Hayırbay to join the rebellion against the sultan lies in a pool of blood, cut in half at the waist. He has obviously been stripped of his clothes and wears only long underpants. Two native Egyptians or Arabs—one black and one white—with loose, flowing robes and tall hats wrapped with long scarves stand on the lower right, contemplating the execution. Opposite are several courtiers with staffs and a kapıcı.
>
> As can be observed in this scene, the courts of the provincial capitals were similar to that of İstanbul, with the same set of officials attending the rulers. The location of this event is identifiable through the date palm rising above the roof and the reliance on local types to represent the executioners and the two spectators on the lower right.

5. Death of Canberdi Gazali

(folio 63b)   Painter B

UPON RECEIVING Canberdi Gazali's letter forwarded by Hayırbay, Süleyman dispatched his third vezir, Ferhad Paşa, with an army to put an end to the rebellion. Meanwhile Ali Bey, the beylerbeyi of Maraş, had moved into Syria and started pursuing the rebel forces.

When both armies met and attacked Gazali's men at Mastaba outside Damascus on 6 February 1521, Ottoman victory was inevitable. After Canberdi Gazali was killed, his followers quickly dispersed.

This internal affair was terminated just in time for the sultan to prepare his first sefer-i hümayun, which was provoked by the murder of the Ottoman ambassador, Behram Çavuş, at the court of Louis II, the king of Hungary.

> The scene, set within a landscape presumably outside Mastaba, employs a triangular composition. At the apex is an Ottoman officer holding a mace, galloping to the left while turning back. Below is another officer, who stabs Canberdi Gazali with his spear, throwing him off his horse. Gazali has lost his crownlike plumed headdress and falls with outstretched arms, his mouth open in a scream.
>
> In the foreground are a couple of his followers, dead or dying from their wounds, their hats strewn on the ground. Two groups of soldiers carrying banners and maces gather behind the hills. One group wears turbans while the other has helmets with protective hoods extending to the shoulders.
>
> The triangular formation with high hills and symmetrically placed groups of figures in the background is characteristic of the compositions of Painter B. This artist prefers to represent a few figures in his scenes and concentrates on their decorative quality, in contrast to Painter A, whose primary concern is documentation of the events.

بپوشید در بر هوا چرم دیو / ز چرم تبیره برآمد غریو
زمین بر هوا شد ز سم سوار / زمینی که گر شد هوا از غبار

بحر اجسر تیغ دشمن گداز / دلیران جبار در ترکتاز
یلان را چکاچاک تیغ از شتاب / چو بانگ چکاوک بگوش عقاب

شده دست و پا و کشش چرخ کمان / ز زاغ کمان طعمه کرکسان
ببیناند اران ز بالای زین / دلیران زغند از عدو بر زمین

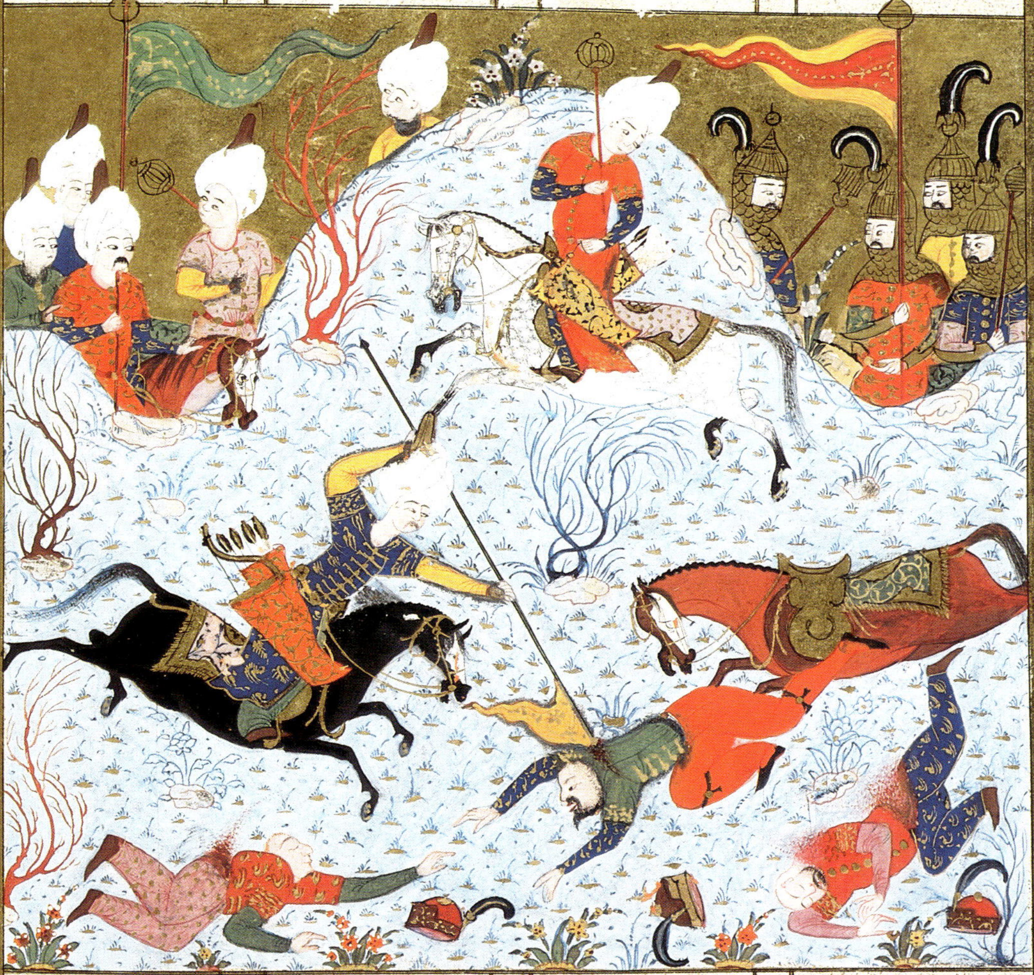

نماند ز پیکان خصم را تاب ایست / بروی زمین آسمان خون گریست
ز بس ناله زخم داران زار / دل عدو از ناله شد بیقرار

فرومایه جا بزدی شور بخت / فروماند از آن شورش کار سخت
چو زردی گرفت از افق آفتاب / شد از گرد کین لاجوردی سحاب

سمند بد اختر در آن داوری / ز سنگی مگر خورد اسکندری
نگون شد بداندیش از پشت زین / چنان خورد پشتش به پشت زمین

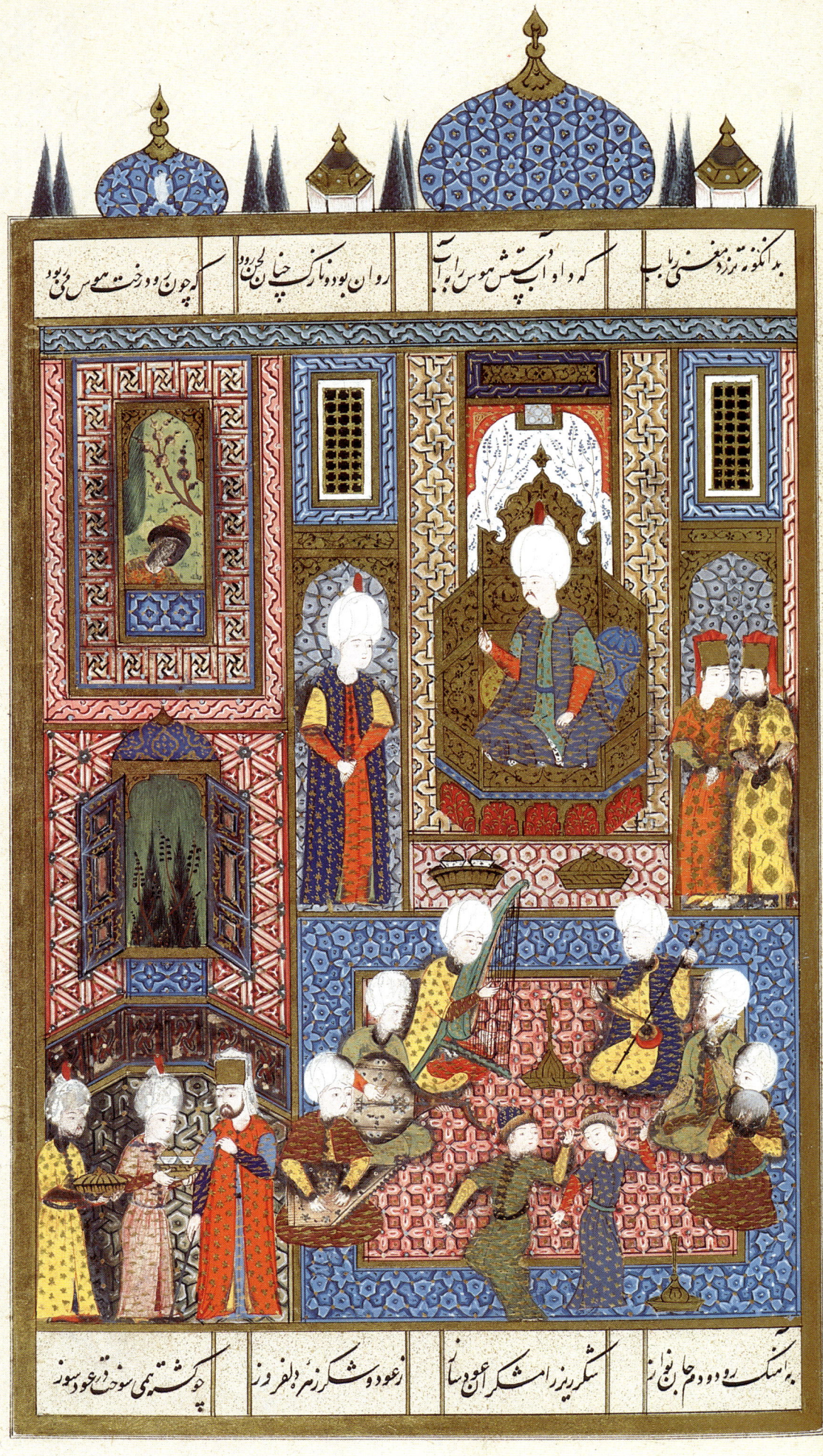

6. Süleyman Entertained

(folio 71a)   Painter A

SÜLEYMAN'S FIRST sefer-i hümayun was directed against Belgrade, an important city twenty kilometers (twelve miles) from the Ottoman border. Now the capital of Yugoslavia, this heavily fortified city had withstood three previous sieges by the Ottomans. It was ruled by Louis II, the king of Hungary, who was closely related to the Habsburgs by marriage. His murder of the sultan's envoy was just the excuse Süleyman needed to march into Belgrade.

The Ottoman army, reputed to have 30,000 camels and even some elephants carrying supplies, with provisions to purchase 10,000 wagonloads of flour and grains from the villages on the route, was supported by fifty small ships that had set sail on the Danube River under the command of the kaptan-ı derya, Danişmend Reis.

Süleyman, leading his army, left İstanbul on 18 May 1521 and arrived a week later at Edirne, where he stayed several days. He was greeted by the officials who hosted a magnificent banquet in his honor. The sultan was entertained by musicians, singers, and dancers, and was offered food and refreshments in ruby-encrusted gold and silver cups and plates.

> The painting shows the sultan being entertained by musicians and dancers in one of the pavilions of the Edirne palace. The palace at Edirne, which followed the same plan as the Topkapı Palace with three consecutive courtyards, must have contained equally sumptuous pavilions like the one in this scene.
>
> Süleyman, seated on a hexagonal gold throne, converses with an iç oğlan while two Has Oda ağas wait in attendance. Arranged in a circle in the foreground are two dancers accompanied by a six-piece orchestra. The musicians sing and play a zither, lute, lyre, small cellolike string instrument, tambourine, and cymbals or clappers. On the left is a two-storied structure in front of which a kapıcı inspects bowls of food carried by attendants; above, a figure looks out of the upper level window.
>
> The painter has constructed the scene by employing interacting circular, diagonal, and horizontal formations at the apex of which is the sultan. He has also divided the surfaces into square and rectangular compartments which fit together like a jigsaw, each section lavishly adorned with diverse geometric motifs. The attempt to create a feeling of space through arched doorways and windows opening onto a garden is overpowered by the strong two-dimensional conception of the scene.

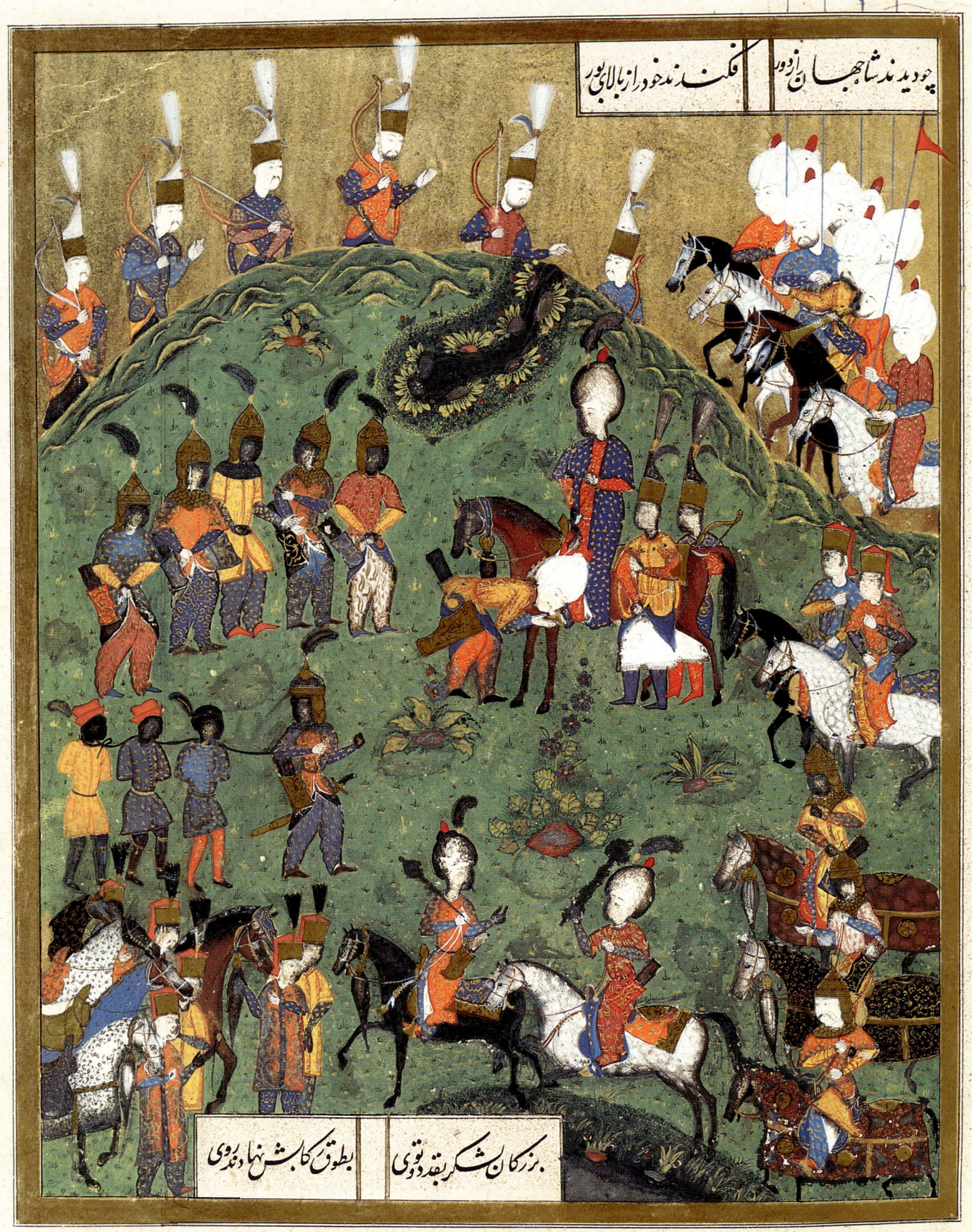

7. Arrival of Süleyman at Böğürdelen

(folio 81a)   Painter A

THE ARMY LEFT Edirne in the beginning of June and proceeded toward Filibe (Philippopolis, now Plovdiv) and Sophia, where it met with the third vezir Ferhad Paşa, who was bringing the supplies. Süleyman then moved on to Nish and arrived before the fortress of Böğürdelen (Sabacz), which had been built by the Ottomans in 1471 to support campaigns against Belgrade but was now held by the Hungarians. Joined by the units of the second vezir Ahmed Paşa, Süleyman conquered Böğürdelen on 7 June and began the reconstruction of the fortress. A few days later he built a bridge over the Sava River, crossed it with his forces, and headed toward Belgrade.

Meanwhile Hüsrev Bey had secured the road to Belgrade. He was supported by his akıncıs and sipahis as well as by a regiment of janissaries provided by the sultan. Riding ahead of the sultan was a unit headed by Hasan Bey, the beylerbeyi of Morea; following behind was the grand vezir Piri Mehmed Paşa and his forces. The navy commanded by Danişmend Reis was sailing up the Danube toward Belgrade.

> The sultan, mounted on a chestnut steed, is greeted outside Böğürdelen by one of the commanders of the armed forces waiting to join the campaign. The commander, possibly the second vezir Ahmed Paşa, bends in front of Süleyman, kissing his boot. Behind the sultan are two solaks and two mounted Has Oda ağas. Opposite are five officers in full armor waiting to greet the sultan while a sixth brings in three European prisoners, leading them by a rope tied to their necks. In the foreground are two mace-bearing cavalry commanders, flanked by several armored riders and janissaries leading horses. In the background, lined against the sky, are isolated solaks holding their bows and a massed group of cavalrymen bearing banners.
>
> Painter A utilizes a combination of rectangular, triangular, and horizontal formations, placing the sultan almost in the center of the composition. His favorite motif of a curving strip of water outlined by rocks and plants appears both on the high hills and in the foreground, providing a central axis to the scene and thus accentuating the main protagonists.

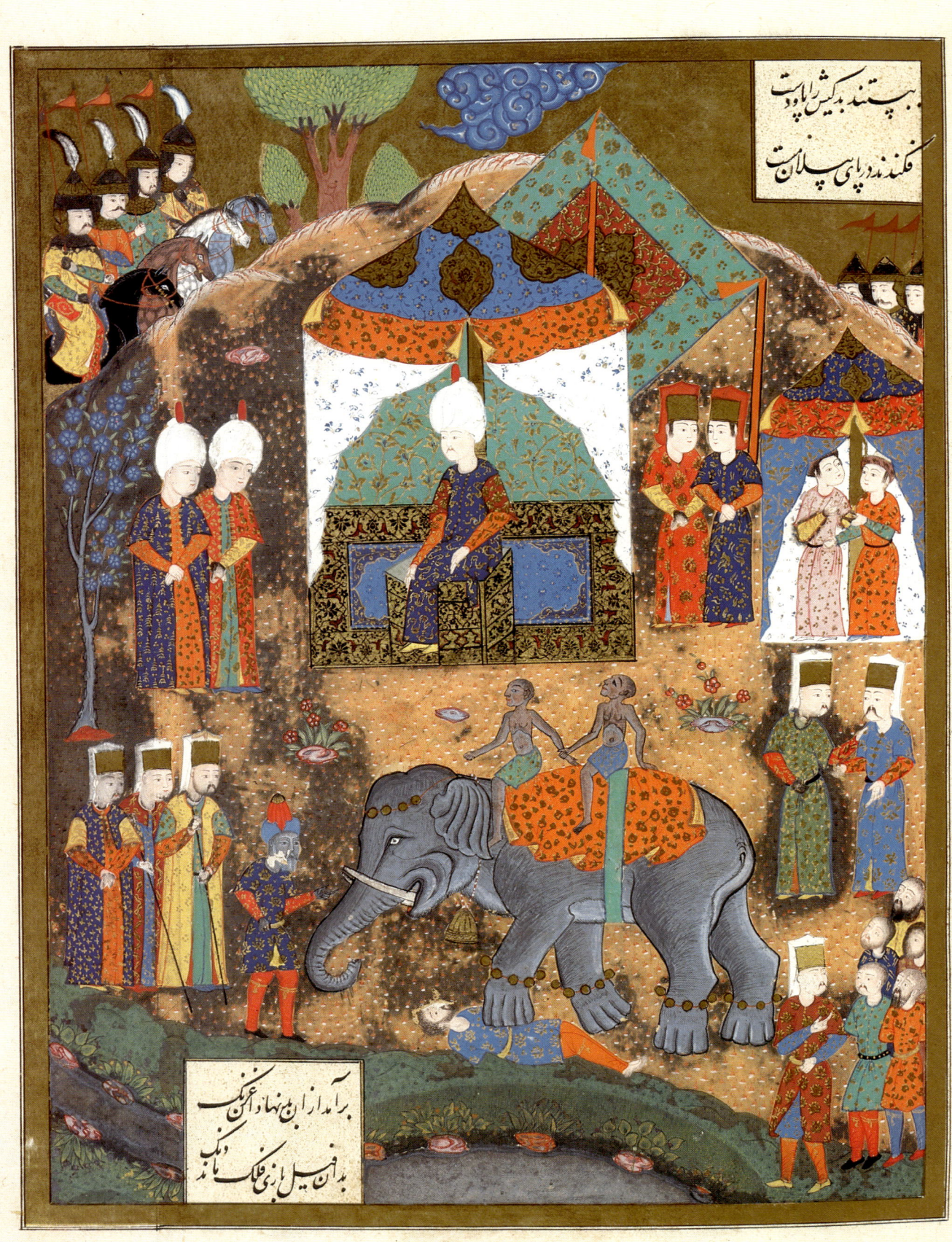

8. Execution of Prisoners
(folio 98a)   Painter A

SÜLEYMAN ARRIVED OUTSIDE Belgrade on 8 August and quickly gained control of the suburbs. The heavily defended fortress, however, held out, resisting the Ottoman siege for twenty-one days. Previous attempts by the Ottomans to take this stronghold had been unsuccessful. Its conquest was of great importance to Süleyman, both for the security of his western provinces and for his prestige as a young sultan.

Continual skirmishes took place between the Ottomans and the Hungarians outside the fortress. The Ottomans had set up camp around the city and placed their cannons at strategic locations. Piri Mehmed Paşa was in constant touch with the sultan, informing him of all developments. Bali Bey, who had joined the imperial army with his units, was succeeding in gaining ground. This officer, son of Yahya Paşa and one of Süleyman's paternal aunts, distinguished himself during the siege of Belgrade and joined the sultan's future campaigns.

> The scene, which takes place in mountainous terrain along a river, possibly the Danube outside Belgrade, depicts the sultan seated on a gold throne in the otak-ı hümayun, which has been pitched up against a high hill. He is attended by pairs of iç oğlans and Has Oda ağas; other servants appear in an adjacent smaller tent. In the foreground a prisoner is being trampled by a huge elephant led by an Asian trainer with high cheekbones and slanted eyes while two half-naked dark-skinned men ride on its back. The event is observed by groups of kapıcıs and other officials, one of whom brings in five more clearly terrified prisoners on the lower right. Other spectators include helmeted soldiers and plumed cavalry officers, who appear behind the hill in the background.
>
> The richness of the floral patterns used on the tents, furnishing, and garments of the figures harmonizes with the landscape elements, such as the blossoming fruit tree and the clusters of flowers sprinkled on the ground and along the banks of the river. The decorative quality of these features detracts from the somber theme of the scene. Even the elephant, the instrument of death, is depicted in a whimsical manner, undermining the seriousness of the event.

9. Siege of Belgrade

(folios 108b-109a)   Painter A

BELGRADE, THE KEY TO THE conquest of Hungary, fell on 29 August 1521. The explosives of the Ottoman miners had successfully breached the walls and the soldiers rushed in, capturing the outer towers. The commander of the fortress sued for peace, surrendering his entire garrison.

The following day Süleyman made a triumphal entry into the city. The cathedral of Belgrade was converted into a mosque and the *hutbe* (sermon delivered after the Friday prayer) was given in the name of the Ottoman sultan, the new ruler of the city. Süleyman stayed more than two weeks in Belgrade, supervising the reconstruction of the fortress. He installed 200 new cannons and assigned 3,000 janissaries under Bali Bey, who was given the command of Belgrade.

When the news of the fall of Belgrade reached the surrounding region, other towns and fortresses surrendered to the Ottomans. The frontier had now been extended from the Sava River to the Danube, which formed a natural border between the Ottomans and the Hungarians.

After securing Belgrade and the surrounding areas, Süleyman gathered his forces and headed back to his capital. The success of his first campaign had a tremendous impact on both his allies and adversaries. The young sultan was indeed someone to contend with and not to be taken lightly.

> The otak-ı hümayun set up outside Belgrade appears on the left half of the double folio with Süleyman and the members of his staff observing the initial assault. Opposite is the besieged city, its towers and churches filled with soldiers and priests. The Danube River that flows in the foreground unites the two halves of the scene.
>
> Süleyman, seated on a throne with his hands in his pockets, controls his excitement and anxiety about the outcome of the attack. His three vezirs, standing by the river with their hands clasped in front, share the sultan's feelings, as do the three iç oğlans on the left and the six Has Oda ağas stationed behind the throne. The same sentiment is felt by the attendants in the royal enclosure in the background, which has a fabric fence enclosing a number of tents.
>
> The city of Belgrade, protected by crenellated walls and towers, valiantly flies its flags from the rooftops. One flag represents a gold winged lion holding a book on a red ground and the other displays a series of gold fleur-de-lys on a blue ground. A fire started by the explosives of the Ottoman miners consumes the outer tower, terrifying the five Hungarian soldiers caught on the parapet. A guard protects the inner tower, around which a battalion of soldiers gather. The city, packed with basilical and domed buildings, has a large church attached to a cloister. Soldiers, monks, and residents gather in the church to pray with their bearded priest in a dark robe, imploring deliverance from the Ottomans.
>
> The scene is marvelously conceived and is charged with psychological symbolism. The majestic self-assurance and stillness that prevail in the Ottoman camp contrast with the desperate panic and commotion of the residents of the city where soldiers are caught in the burning tower, people gather in the church for prayer, and what is left of the Hungarian forces retreat to the inner tower for safety. Nevertheless, a sense of apprehension also permeates the Ottoman camp where all eyes are fixed on the city and even the sultan is nervous and has stuck his hands into his pockets. Although there is a moment of anxiety, victory is imminent for the Ottomans, as symbolized by the triumphant warrior overwhelming a lion represented on the gold and green tent behind the sultan.
>
> One of the masterpieces of Painter A, this scene illustrates how a creative artist can charge a composition with emotion and drama regardless of the restrictions of the art of manuscript illustration.

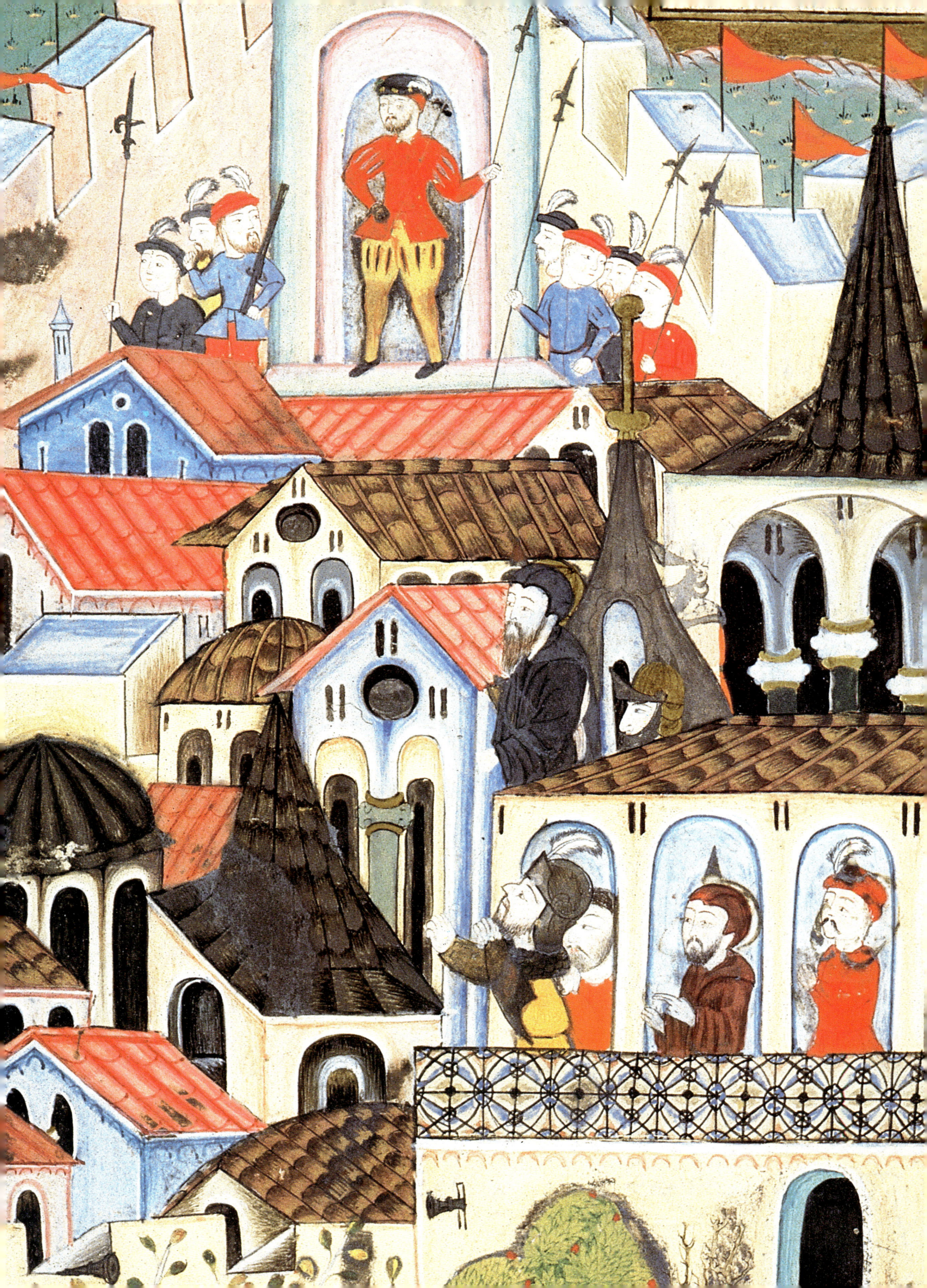

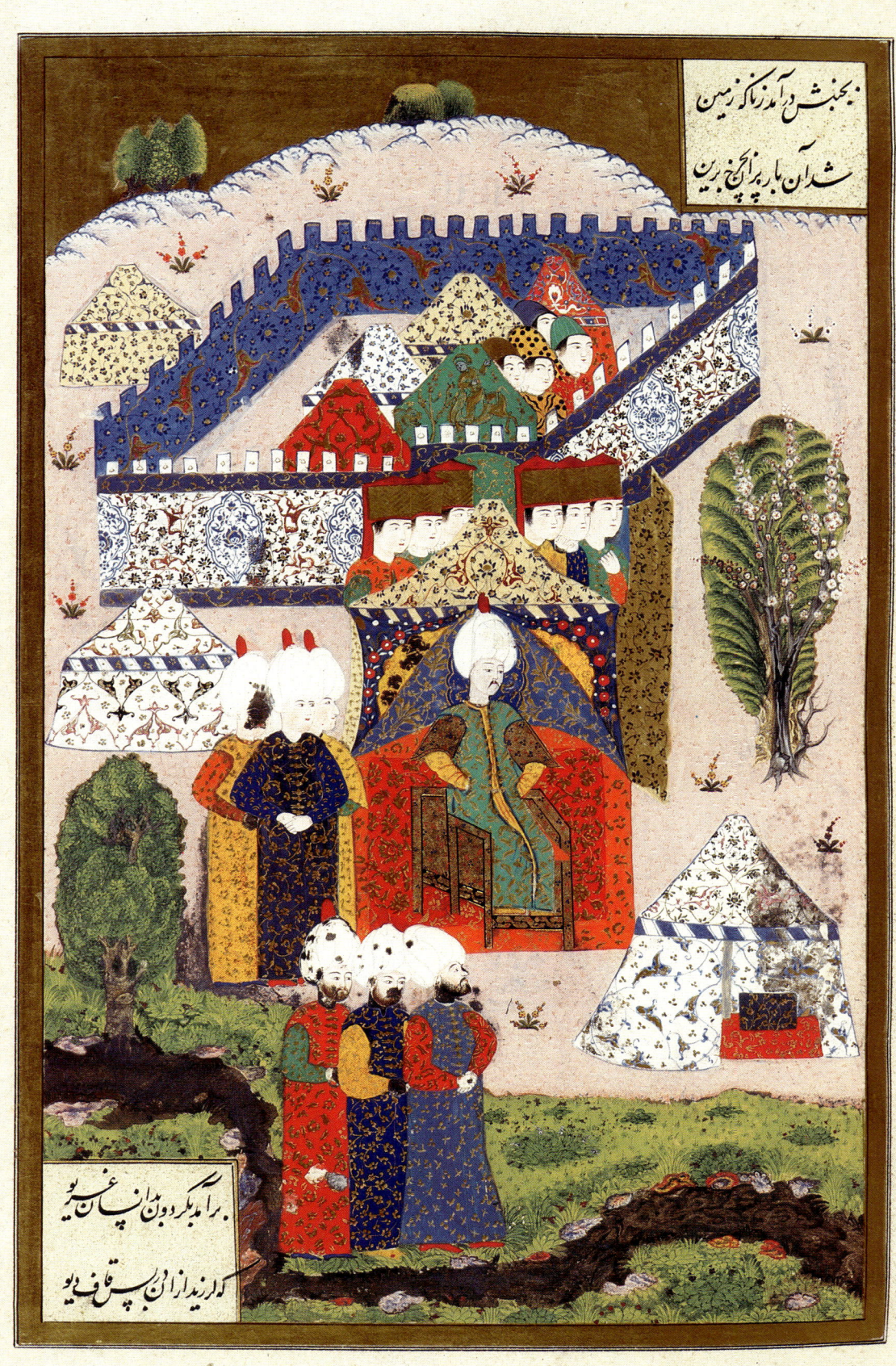

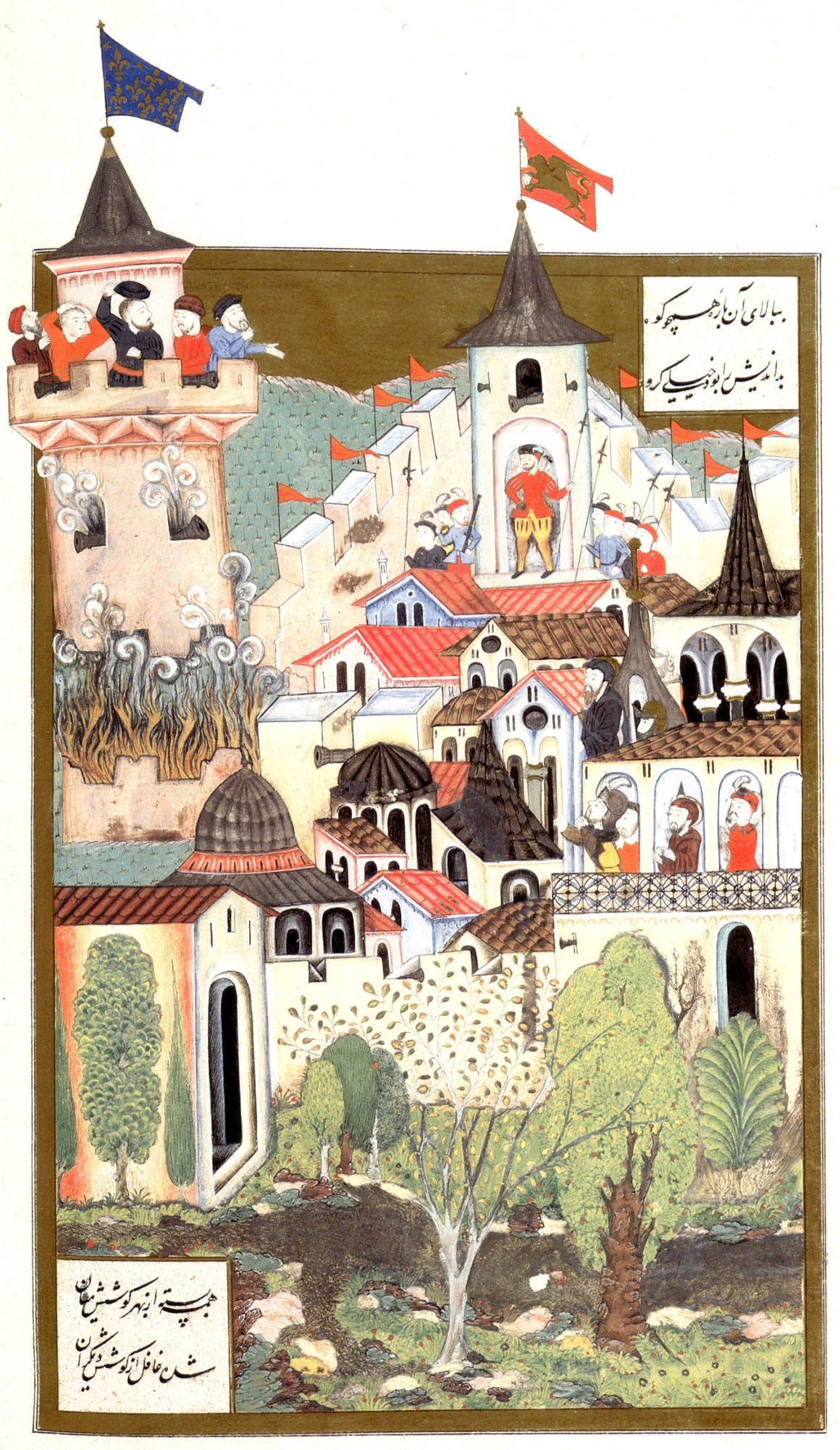

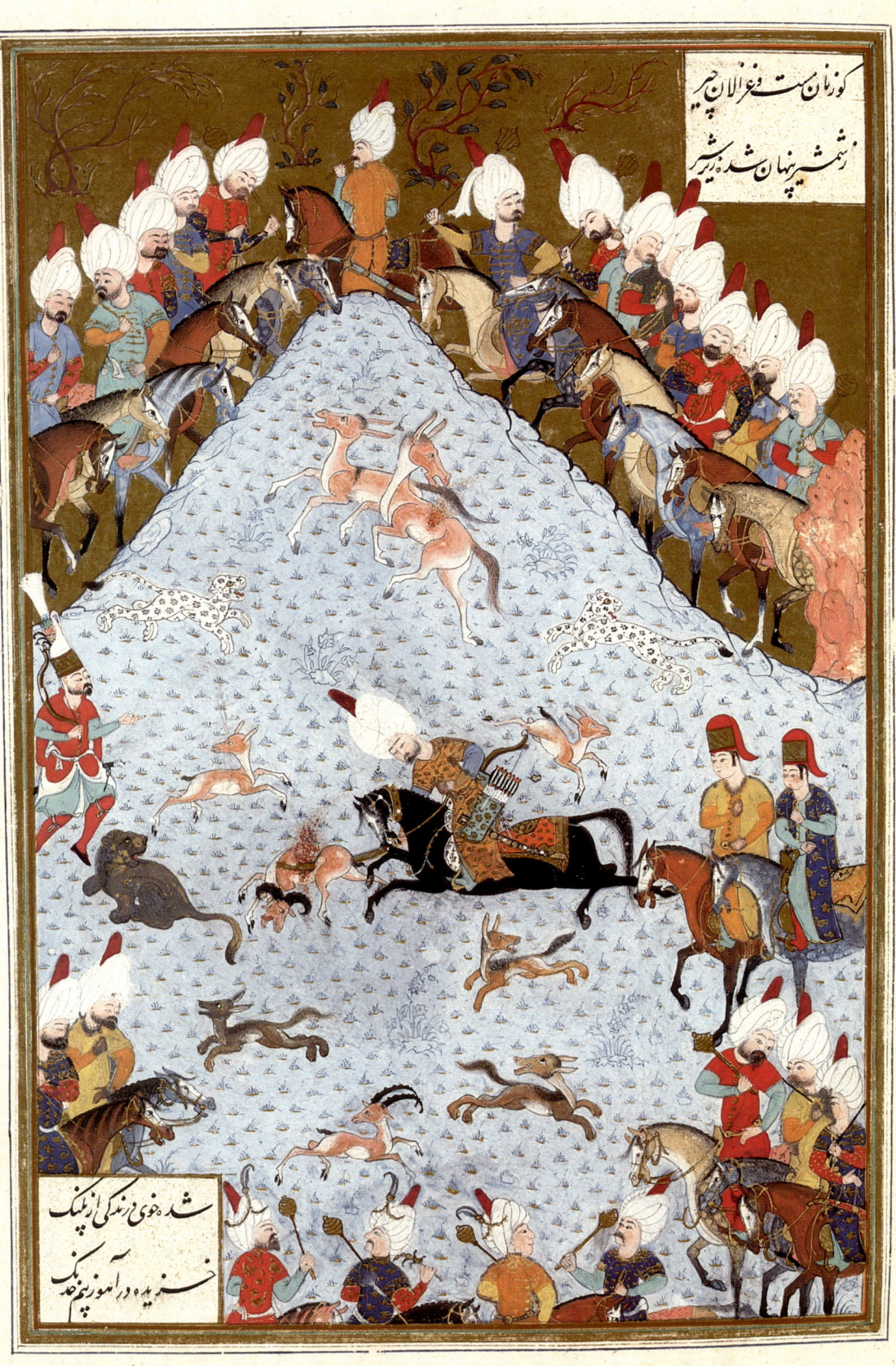

10. Süleyman Hunting

(folio 115a)   Painter B

WHEN Süleyman arrived in Nish on the way back from Belgrade, he was informed of the death of his two sons, Mahmud and Murad. Mustafa, born to Gülbahar in 1515, was now his only living son and heir. His wife Hürrem, however, was about to deliver her first child.

The sultan stopped in the Uzuncaabad Valley outside of Filibe, where he hunted wild animals, and then proceeded to İstanbul, reaching the capital on 19 October 1521. His first campaign had taken five months.

Süleyman's victorious return was celebrated throughout the empire. The residents of İstanbul came out to greet him as he approached the capital, cheering him along the road. The sultan had yet another reason to be jubilant: Hürrem had given birth to a boy he named Mehmed, after his illustrious great-grandfather Mehmed II, the conqueror of İstanbul.

A couple of months later Süleyman signed a peace treaty with the Venetians, who were anxious to secure commercial concessions. They agreed to pay a yearly tribute for the use of Cyprus and several other Aegean islands.

> Hunting scenes in the *Süleymanname* generally precede or follow victorious conquests. Süleyman, an expert hunter, obviously found the sport relaxing during his strenuous campaigns. This particular hunt takes place on the plains of Uzuncaabad, where he stopped in September 1521, after the conquest of Belgrade.
>
> The sultan, galloping in the center of the painting, slays a mountain sheep with his sword. He rides a black horse with jeweled trappings and brocaded saddlecloth, and carries a bow and a quiver full of arrows. The high triangular hill is filled with other game animals, such as onagers, leopards, gazelles, foxes, and wolves, together with a solitary lion. A pair of mounted Has Oda ağas and a solak flank the sultan while turbaned riders, some of whom bear maces, enclose the hunting field. The spectators are astounded by his prowess and openly reveal their admiration of his agility.

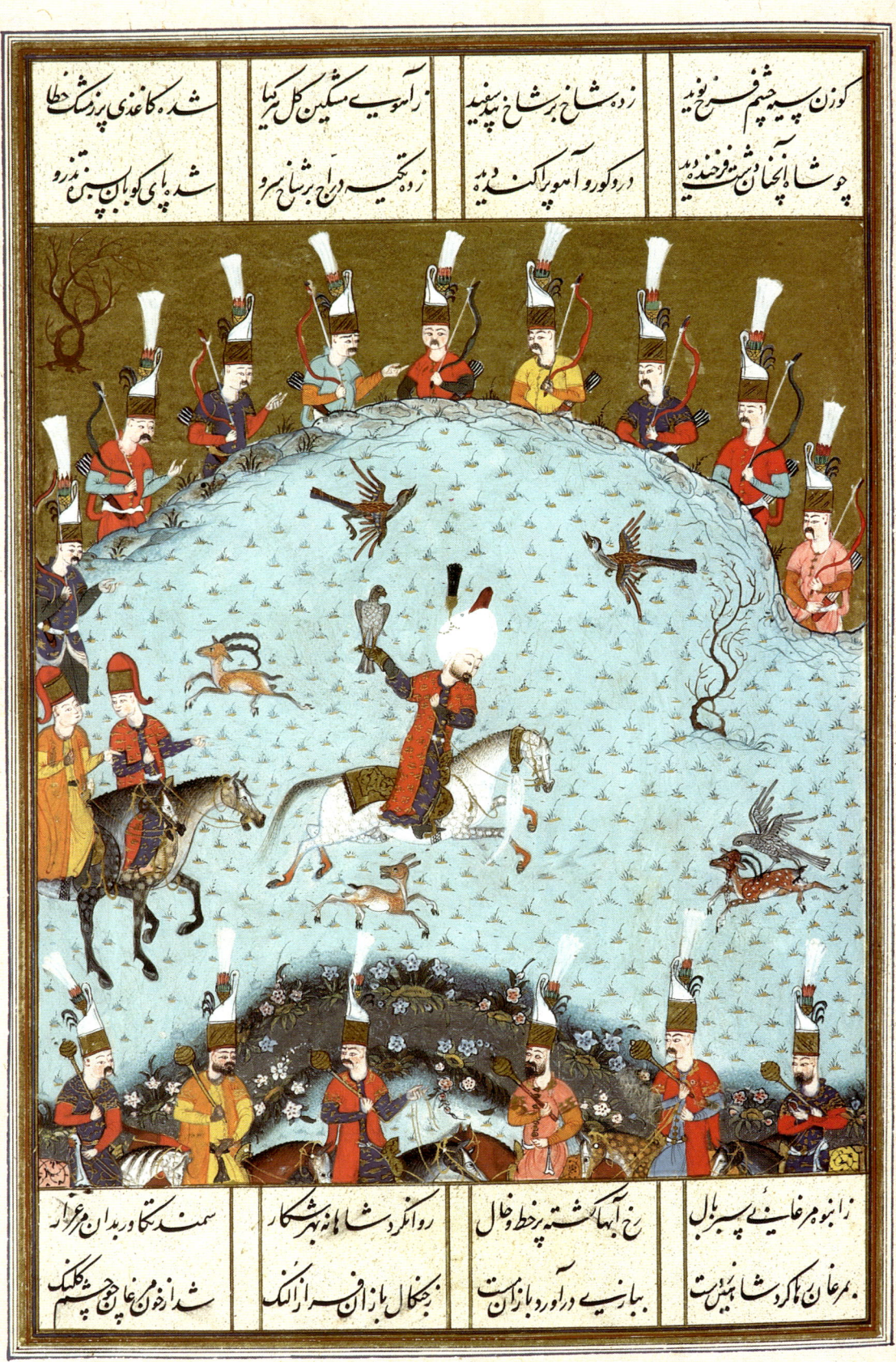

11. Süleyman Hunting

(folio 132a)   Painter B

SÜLEYMAN EMBARKED ON his second sefer-i hümayun on 16 June 1522, heading toward the island of Rhodes, the last Christian stronghold in the Islamic world and a vestige of the Crusades. Rhodes, twelve small islands, and Bodrum were controlled by the Knights of Saint John, who had settled there in 1308 after being expelled from Palestine. They were a threat to Anatolian security, pirating the Ottoman merchant fleet, attacking towns on the mainland, and supporting uprisings against the sultan, such as the one attempted by Canberdi Gazali.

The Ottoman navy, carrying a regiment commanded by the second vezir Mustafa Paşa, had left İstanbul in early June. Sailing with them was the şeyhülislam Zenbilli Ali Efendi, an unusual passenger during a campaign. Süleyman traveled with the main forces by land to Kütahya, Denizli, and Marmaris, then sailed to Rhodes. He took time off to hunt along the shores of the Menderes River before proceeding to the Aegean shore.

> The scene takes place along the shores of the Menderes River in western Anatolia, possibly near Denizli, where the sultan stopped to hunt en route to Rhodes in July 1522. During this event he is accompanied by his solaks, who line up behind the high hill in the background and ride along the banks of the river in the foreground. A pair of mounted Has Oda ağas appear on the left.
>
> The painting shows the sultan riding a white steed, with a trained falcon perched on his hand. Two birds fly above and a pair of gazelles scuttle about the hunting grounds. On the right a falcon attacks a spotted deer. In contrast to the weapons used in the previous scene, the sultan hunts here with a pair of falcons, showing his expertise in several hunting techniques.
>
> The circular formation created by the ring of attendants is repeated by the running animals and flying birds with the figure of the sultan placed at its core. The composition is almost a mirror image of the one used in the preceding illustration (10).

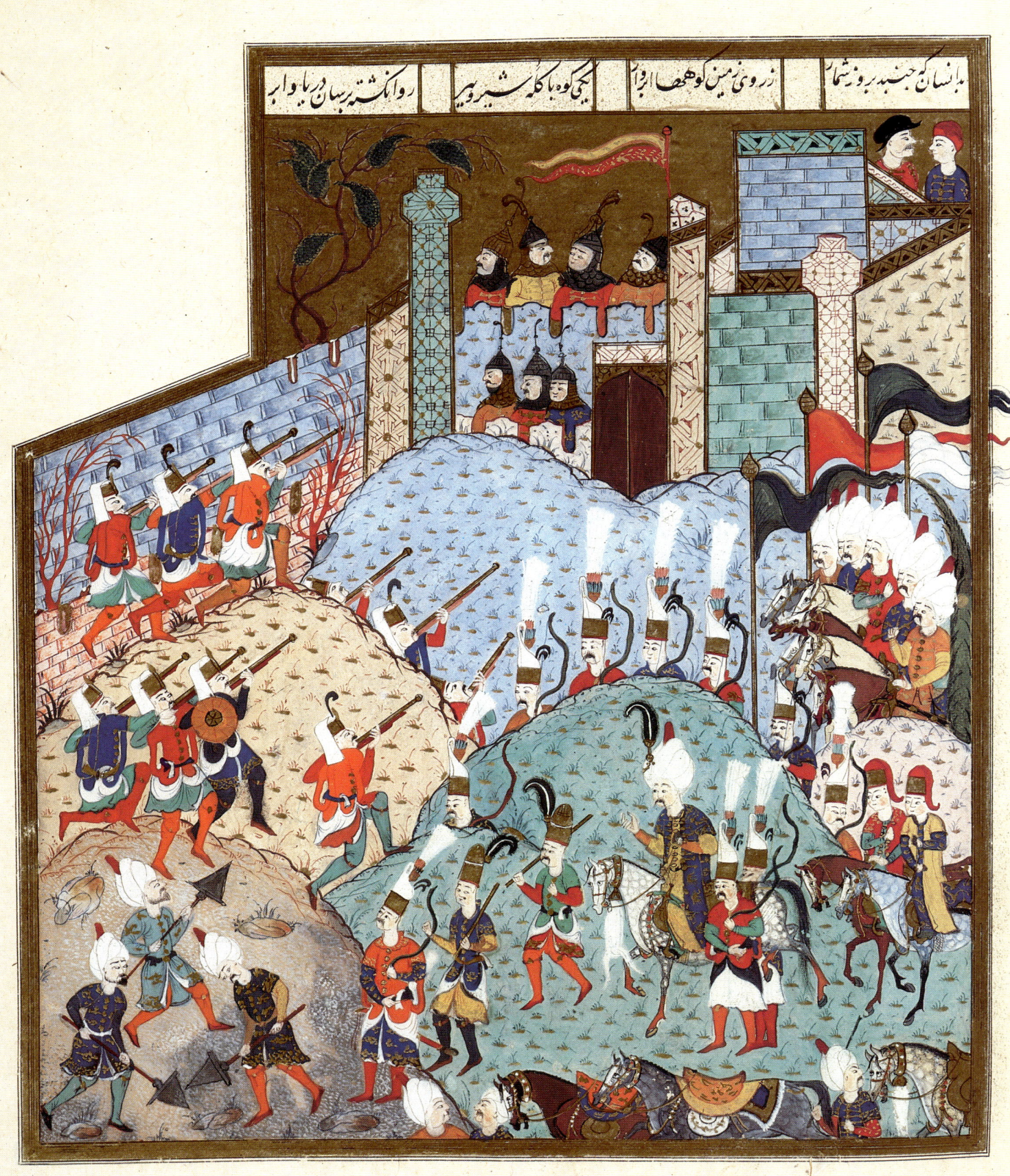

12. Süleyman Arriving at Rhodes

(folio 143a)   Painter B

SÜLEYMAN LANDED AT Rhodes on 28 July 1522 and began the siege of the fortress the following day. The ships carrying Mustafa Paşa's men had already arrived and they joined the sultan's forces. The Ottomans conquered the area around the fortress, much to the joy of the Orthodox Greek residents, who were oppressed by the Catholic knights.

The fortress of Rhodes was magnificently built; it was supplied with hundreds of cannons and had chains barricading its port. The structure had eight major bastions, each defended by the knights of a different language and country, including France, Germany, England, Italy, Spain, Aragon, Provence, and Auvergne. The grand master was an elderly Frenchman by the name of Philippe Villiers de l'Isle-Adam.

The conquest of this formidable fortress had been attempted by Mehmed II, who had besieged Rhodes without success. It was imperative that Süleyman subjugate the island; he had to surpass his predecessors, succeed where they failed in order to prove himself worthy of the Ottoman throne. He also had to eliminate the threat of the crusading knights in order to secure the Aegean and eastern Mediterranean.

> The battle of Rhodes, which lasted almost five months, was possibly the most strenuous of all Süleyman's campaigns. This critical campaign is represented by three consecutive scenes that narrate different events. The first depicts the arrival of the sultan and the preparations for the siege of the fortress.
>
> The fortress of Rhodes rises in the background, manned by soldiers wearing different types of armor and headdress. The Ottomans, gathered in the hilly terrain outside the stronghold, have begun the siege.
>
> Süleyman, accompanied by his peyks, solaks, and Has Oda ağas, approaches the fortress on horseback and instructs the miners, who have started to dig tunnels under the structure. The janissaries have taken their position behind the trenches and are ready to open fire with their rifles. The cavalry, holding maces and banners, line up behind a hill on the far right. In the foreground are attendants leading the sultan's spare horses.

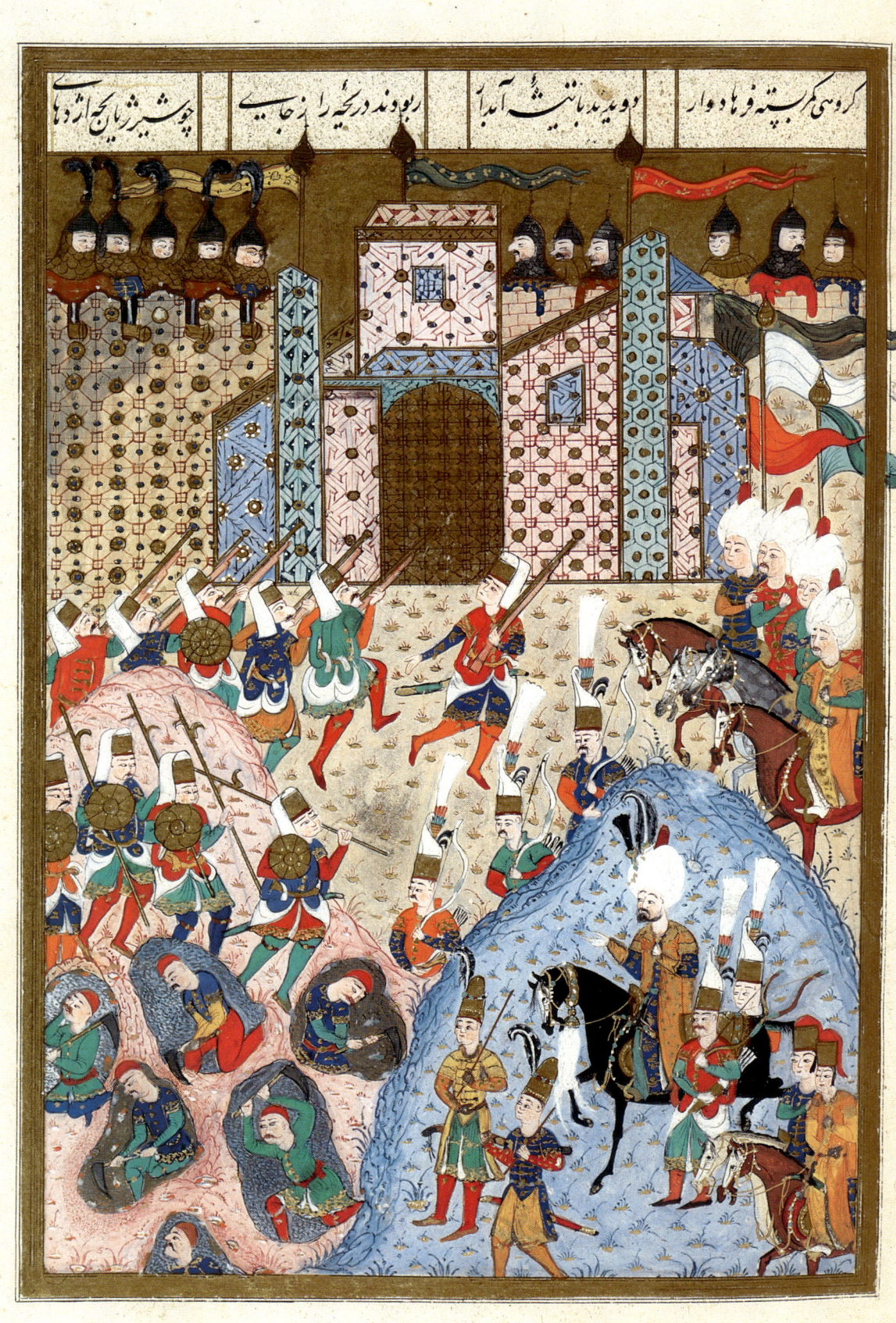

13. Siege of Rhodes

(folio 149a)   Painter B

THE BATTLE OF Rhodes was long and fierce, with many casualties on either side. About 20,000 Ottomans were reputed to have lost their lives, possibly the heaviest toll in Süleyman's reign. Hayırbay, the loyal beylerbeyi of Egypt, who had joined the sultan with his warships, was one of the casualties. Egypt was then given to Mustafa Paşa, who had been replaced by Ahmed Paşa as the commander of the naval forces.

As soon as Ottoman cannons made a dent in the walls, the breach was quickly repaired by the knights. Their powerful cannons, firing down onto the Ottoman camp, proved to be most effective. The field was littered with thousands of cannonballs. The Ottomans alone were estimated to have fired more than ten thousand at the fortress.

Both sides had their spies and knew each other's weaknesses. Each victory was counteracted by a loss. Winter was approaching and storms prevented the navy from giving effective support to the land forces.

    This painting depicts the next stage in the siege, following the same composition as the previous scene. Süleyman inspects the tunnels dug by the miners, who courageously carry out their duties despite the hazards of cave-ins and explosives. A group of janissaries continues the assault and fires at the fortress; a second group advances, holding spears and shields, ready to take over when their comrades fall. A youthful janissary gestures to his companions, discouraged by the long and fierce siege that has not yet produced any discernible results. Four of the commanders wait stoically at the side.

    The fortress of Rhodes has grown larger and more impressive, its colorful facade embellished with diverse geometric motifs. Armored soldiers look down menacingly from the parapets while flags with different designs fly from the towers and rooftops.

    Painter B, whose style is highly decorative, nevertheless manages to create the psychological atmosphere of the event. In spite of the fact that the knights have frustrated all Ottoman efforts, making the fortress of Rhodes appear impenetrable, the battle continues and the soldiers as well as the sultan valiantly persevere in their relentless attack.

14. Fall of Rhodes

(folio 154b)   Painter B

FINALLY THE GRAND master agreed to surrender the fortress, ending the battle that had begun in July. The conditions of surrender, signed on 20 December 1522, granted the knights freedom to depart in honor.

A few days later the grand master and his knights were received by the sultan, who was seated on a gold throne in the imperial otak. When the grand master prostrated himself in front of Süleyman, the sultan asked him to rise and honored him by extending his hand to be kissed. Süleyman praised the bravery of the knights and wished them well in their new life.

The Ottomans now settled in Rhodes, occupying the fortress with 4,000 janissaries under the command of the janissary ağa. The Church of Saint John was converted into a mosque and the hutbe was delivered in the name of the sultan. Leading the first prayer was the şeyhülislam Zenbilli Ali Efendi, a participant in the Rhodes campaign.

On 1 January 1523 the knights came to bid farewell to the sultan before sailing from Rhodes, terminating their two-hundred-year domination of the island. Süleyman departed from Rhodes the next day, arriving in the capital at the end of January.

> The last painting in the saga of the battle of Rhodes portrays the victory of the Ottomans and the fall of the city. The scene, by far the most complex of Painter B's work, is full of action and composed of vignettes separated by a series of hills and linked by diagonals.
>
> In the foreground is the sultan surrounded by his personal attendants, inspecting three prisoners brought in by an officer. Hanging at his side are his sword, bow, and quiver with arrows; in his right hand he holds a mace. Affected by the ferocity of the battle and the loss of so many men, Süleyman has a solemn, pensive look.
>
> The next register depicts a pair of Has Oda ağas, animatedly discussing the events, and a group of solaks. Behind them are several janissaries who have entered the fortress; one takes prisoners and another leads the captives toward four spectacularly attired commanders who have enormous feathers on their headdresses and carry large banners. Above, a skirmish continues within the fortress: janissaries fire at the enemy and a soldier slays two knights with his sword. Encircling the hill in the background are seven wailing women, who tear their hair and fling their arms, lamenting the fall of Rhodes.
>
> The zigzag composition and fluttering feathers, flags, and gesticulating figures recreate the excitement of the event. This vibrancy provides a contrast and thus accentuates the sobriety of the sultan.

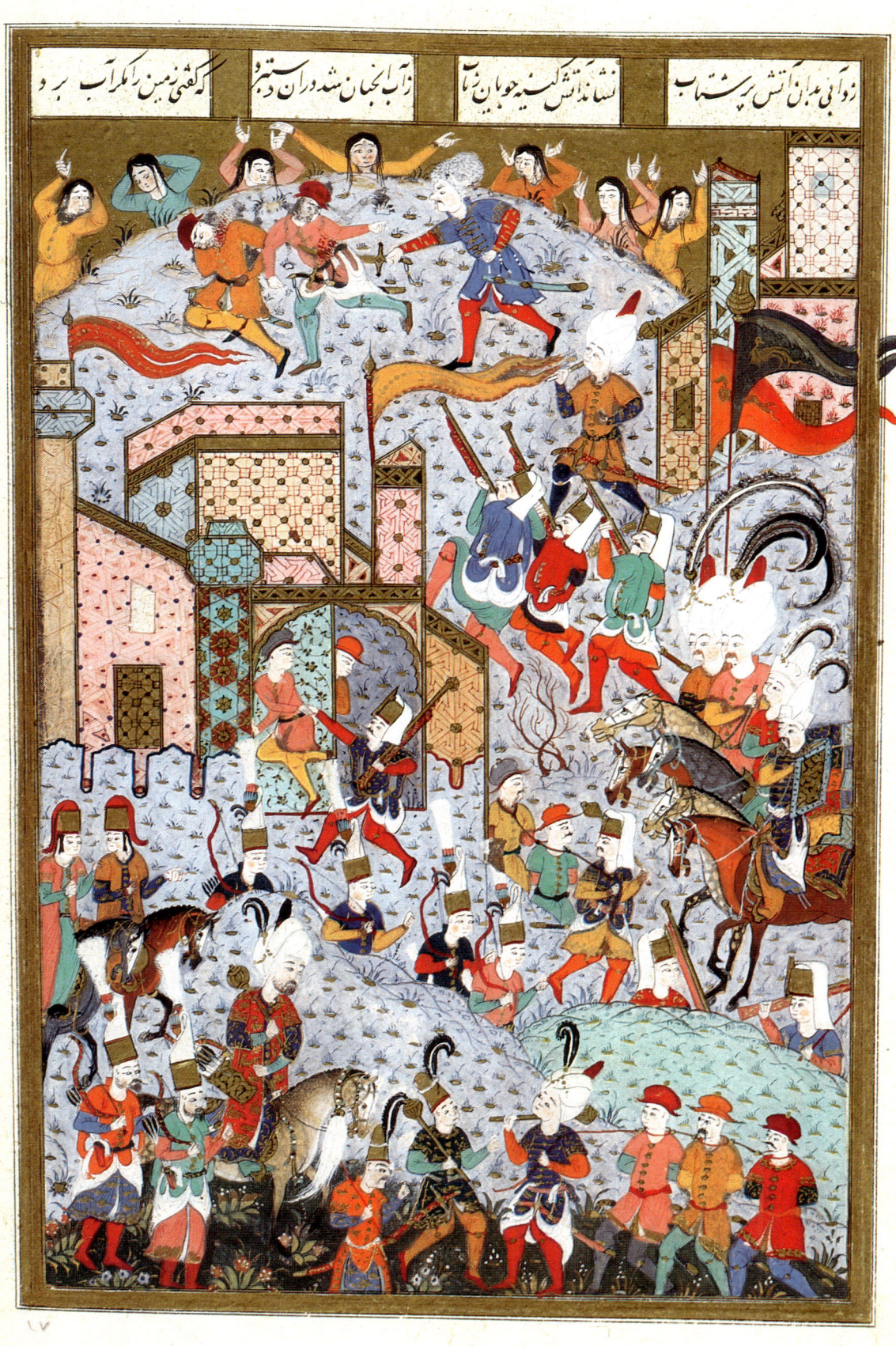

15. Death of Ahmed Paşa

(folio 170b)   Painter B

WITHIN LESS THAN a year the sultan was faced with another rebellion in Egypt, this time led by his own vezir, Ahmed Paşa. When the grand vezir Piri Mehmed Paşa retired, Süleyman appointed his childhood friend and confidant İbrahim Paşa to that post (27 June 1523). The second vezir Ahmed Paşa, next in line for the grand vezirate, was by-passed and sent as beylerbeyi to Egypt, the most important province in the empire. Angered at having been slighted, Ahmed Paşa gathered a force, captured the citadel, and proclaimed himself sultan of Egypt in January 1524. Ayas Mehmed Paşa, now the second vezir, was sent to quell the rebellion.

Kadızade Mehmed Bey, Ahmed Paşa's grand vezir in Cairo, remained loyal to the sultan and led the attack on the insurgents. He succeeded in capturing the rebel leader in August. Ayas Mehmed Paşa, seeing that the rebel had been killed and his followers dispersed, returned to İstanbul.

Süleyman dispatched İbrahim Paşa to Egypt to reestablish order. İbrahim, the same age as the sultan, had recently married Hadice, Süleyman's sister. Their wedding ceremonies took place in the İbrahim Paşa Palace overlooking the At Meydanı and was celebrated for two weeks (22 May–5 June 1524). During the festival Hürrem gave birth to Selim, adding yet another cause for celebration.

> The scene, set within an idyllic landscape with delicately curving trees filling the background, depicts in the center a beautifully attired figure mounted on a magnificent horse. He is gazing at the severed head of the rebel, Ahmed Paşa, thrown on the ground by a bearded official, who is accompanied by three other figures. In the foreground an officer leads two prisoners toward another dignitary while groups of mounted military officers stationed behind the hill observe the event. Placed around the central figure are pairs of peyks, solaks, and personal attendants resembling the Has Oda ağas.
>
> Although the main protagonists of the scene are not immediately identifiable, the presence of peyks, solaks, and personal attendants suggests that the central rider is a vezir, most likely Ayas Mehmed Paşa; the bearded figure presenting the head must be the loyal official, Kadızade Mehmed, who was responsible for the deed. Ayas Mehmed Paşa appears to have arrived on the scene shortly after the death of the rebel leader.

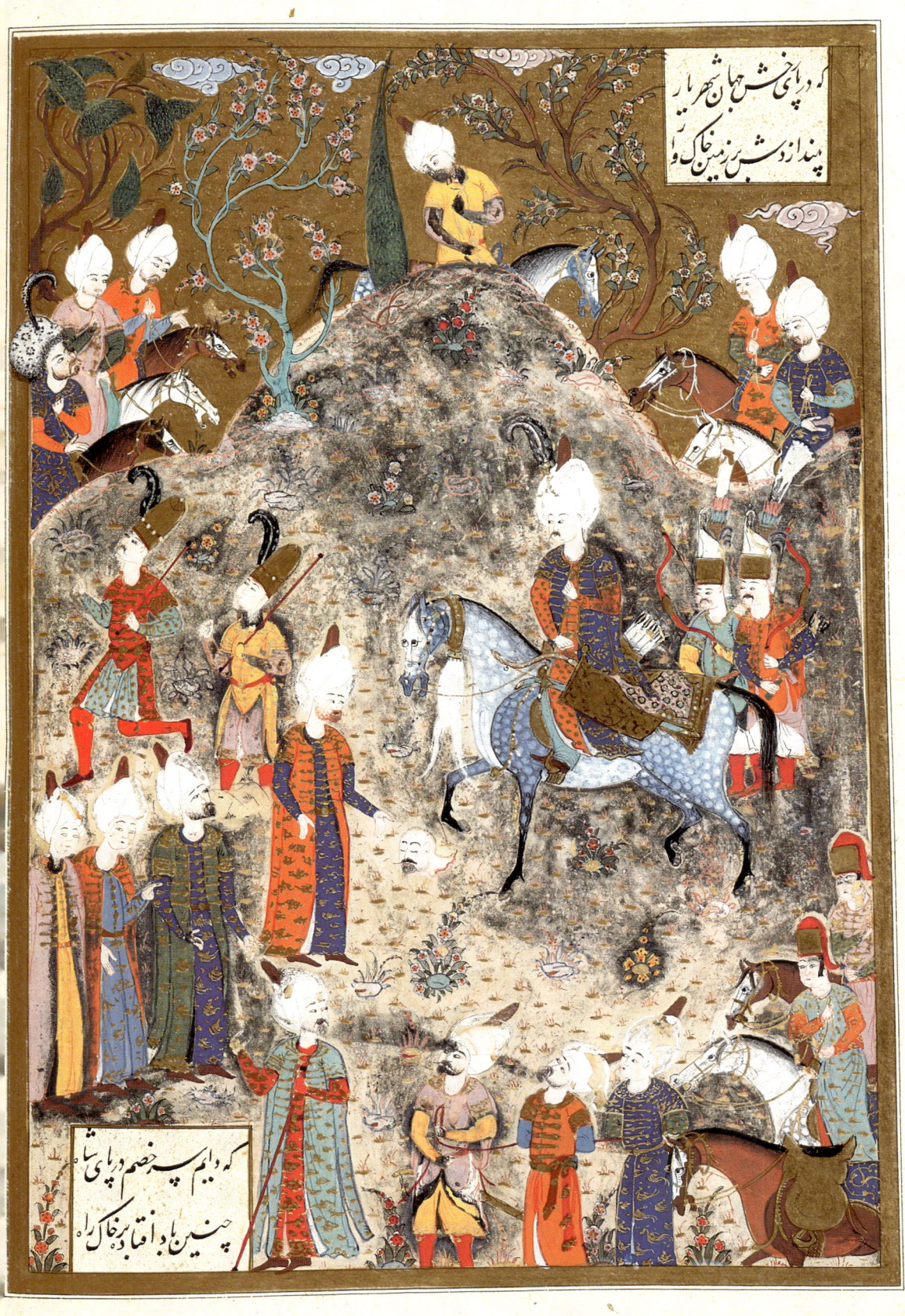

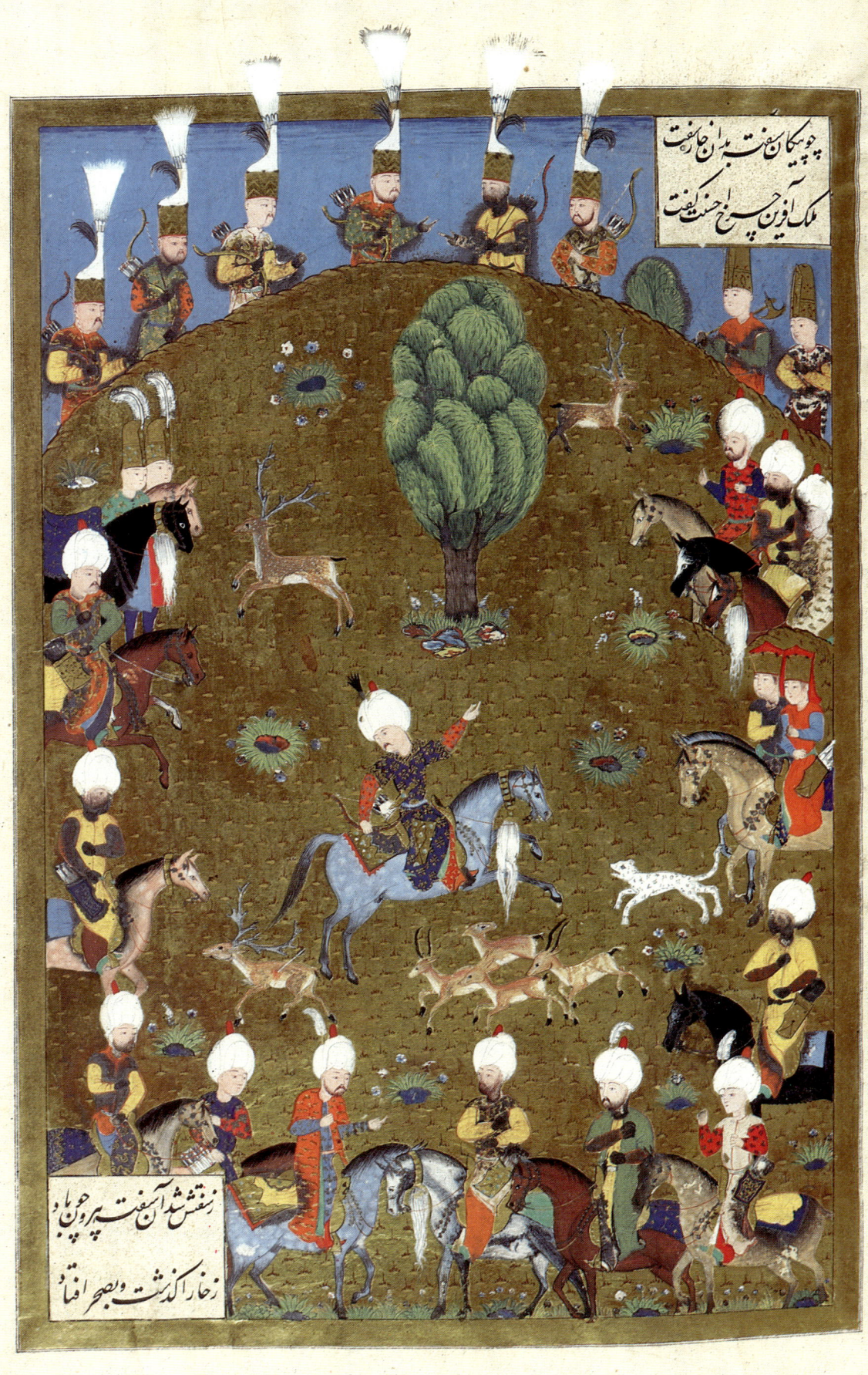

16. Süleyman Hunting

(folio 177a)   Painter A

CONFIDENT THAT HIS frontiers were well protected after the annexation of the famed fortresses of Belgrade and Rhodes and that internal security was restored in Egypt, Süleyman now turned to the administrative and legislative affairs of the state. Occasionally he took time off to relax and hunt in his favorite hunting grounds outside the provincial capital of Edirne.

These months, however, were exceptional in the life of the sultan, who soon became involved with European affairs when an envoy named Jean Frangipani arrived at the court with letters from Francis I, the king of France, and Louise of Savoy, his mother. Francis I, imprisoned by Charles V, was requesting assistance from the Ottoman sultan.

The affair had begun in 1521 when both Francis I of the Valois house and Charles V of the Habsburgs were candidates for the crown of the Holy Roman Empire, a loose but prestigious federation in Europe. Charles V won the elections, which resulted in war between the French and the Habsburgs. Europe was split between the two sides as well as between the followers of Martin Luther and the pope, the Protestants supporting Francis I and the Catholics backing Charles V. Süleyman was now being asked to join the fight and to assist Francis I.

The sultan, quick to recognize the potential benefits of a Franco-Ottoman alliance to further his own interest in Europe, sent a favorable reply to Francis I. He then prepared for his third sefer-i hümayun directed against Hungary in order to attack the Habsburgs from the rear.

> The sultan, galloping in the center of a hill encircled by his solaks, peyks, Has Oda ağas, and high court officials, has just struck a deer with an arrow and turns back to look at his prey. Running around the hunting field are other deer and gazelles together with a solitary leopard. The figure of the sultan is the pivot of the virtually centripetal composition. He is also in the center of a vertical axis created by a large luxuriant tree and strategically placed confronting pairs of figures at the top and bottom of the scene, who point to the hunter and comment on his masterful hit.
>
> The event takes place outside Edirne, before Süleyman embarked on the conquest of Hungary. One of the most spectacular paintings in the manuscript, this scene, set against a gold field with all the elements concentrated on the sultan, creates a hierarchic image. It commemorates Süleyman's two magnificent achievements, the conquests of Belgrade and Rhodes, and displays his confidence of future victories, foretelling the outcome of the Battle of Mohacs.

17. Reception of the Commanders

(folio 189b)   Painter A

SÜLEYMAN'S THIRD sefer-i hümayun, begun on 23 April 1526, was to be the first of a series of campaigns undertaken to secure Hungary. The army marched from İstanbul to Filibe and arrived on 29 May in Sophia, where the commanders of the regiments in the western provinces came to pledge their unfaltering loyalty to the sultan.

Süleyman then crossed the Sava River and moved on to Belgrade. There he met with the Ottoman navy, which had sailed up the Danube with some 800 small ships. The grand vezir İbrahim Paşa had been sent ahead to take the fortress of Varadin (Petrovaradin, Peterwardein) which lay twenty-six kilometers (about sixteen miles) northeast of Belgrade. The fortress fell at the end of July, followed by those of Ilok and Eszek. Now the region between the Danube, Sava, and Drava rivers was controlled by the Ottomans. Süleyman crossed the Drava on a newly-constructed bridge and entered the great Hungarian plain, marching toward Mohacs.

> The scene, which takes place on the plains of Sophia, depicts the reception of the commanders. Süleyman, enthroned in the imperial otak with a large canopy over its entrance, is greeted by one of the officers, who kneels in front of him, kissing the hem of his kaftan. Flanking the tent are Has Oda ağas, iç oğlans, and vezirs. Below are a pair of kapıcıs or ushers and nine other commanders waiting to be received. Beyond the hills are additional regimental officers, some holding banners. The commanders are in military attire; they wear plumes on their turbans or helmets and carry swords or bows and arrows.
>
> The triangular formation produced by the tapering hill and the imperial otak is symmetrically balanced by groups of riders and standing figures. Similar to the device used in other paintings, a vertical axis is created by a large tree at the top and confronting pairs of conversing figures at the bottom, both accentuating the sultan, who is in the core of the composition.

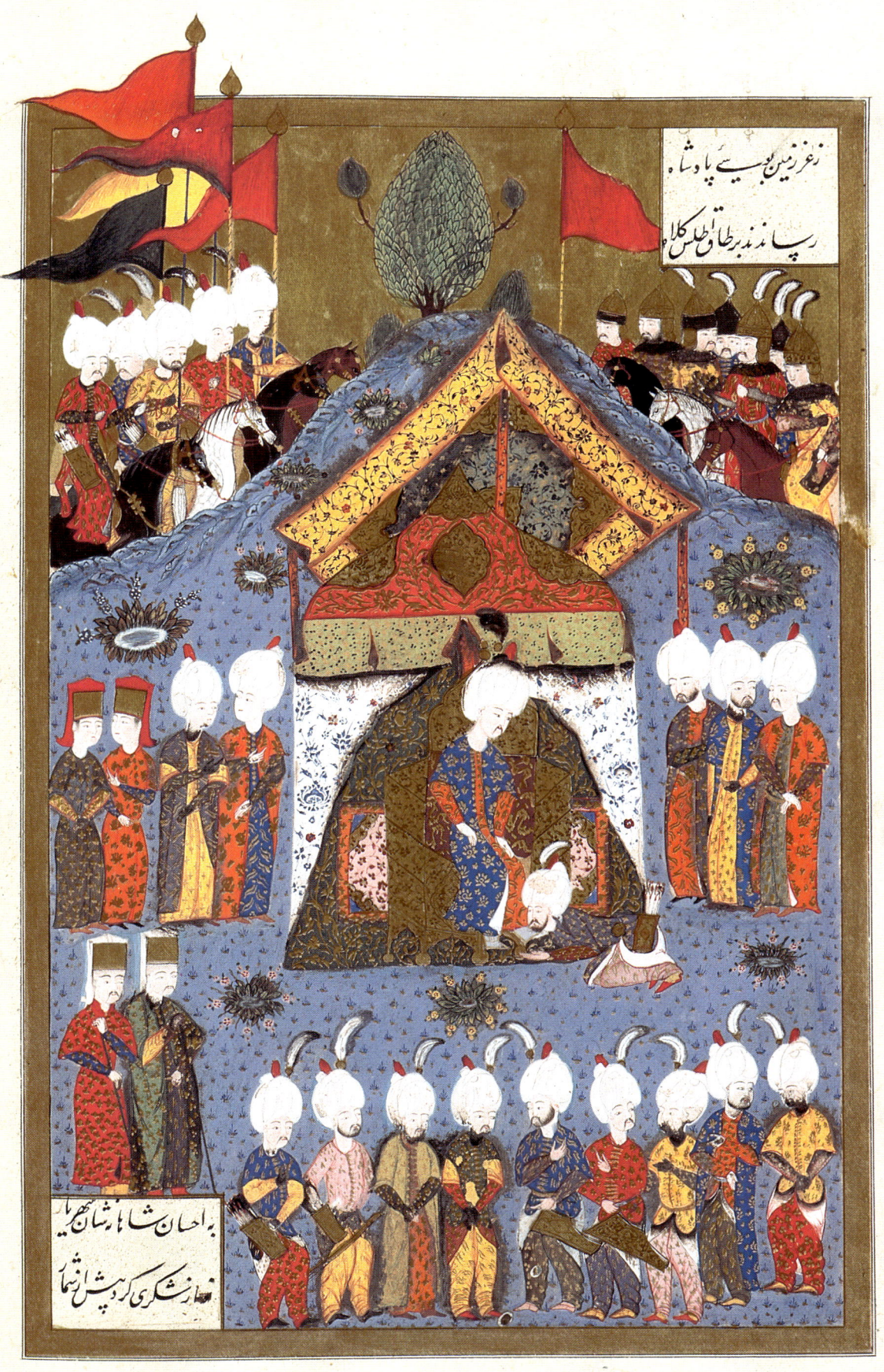

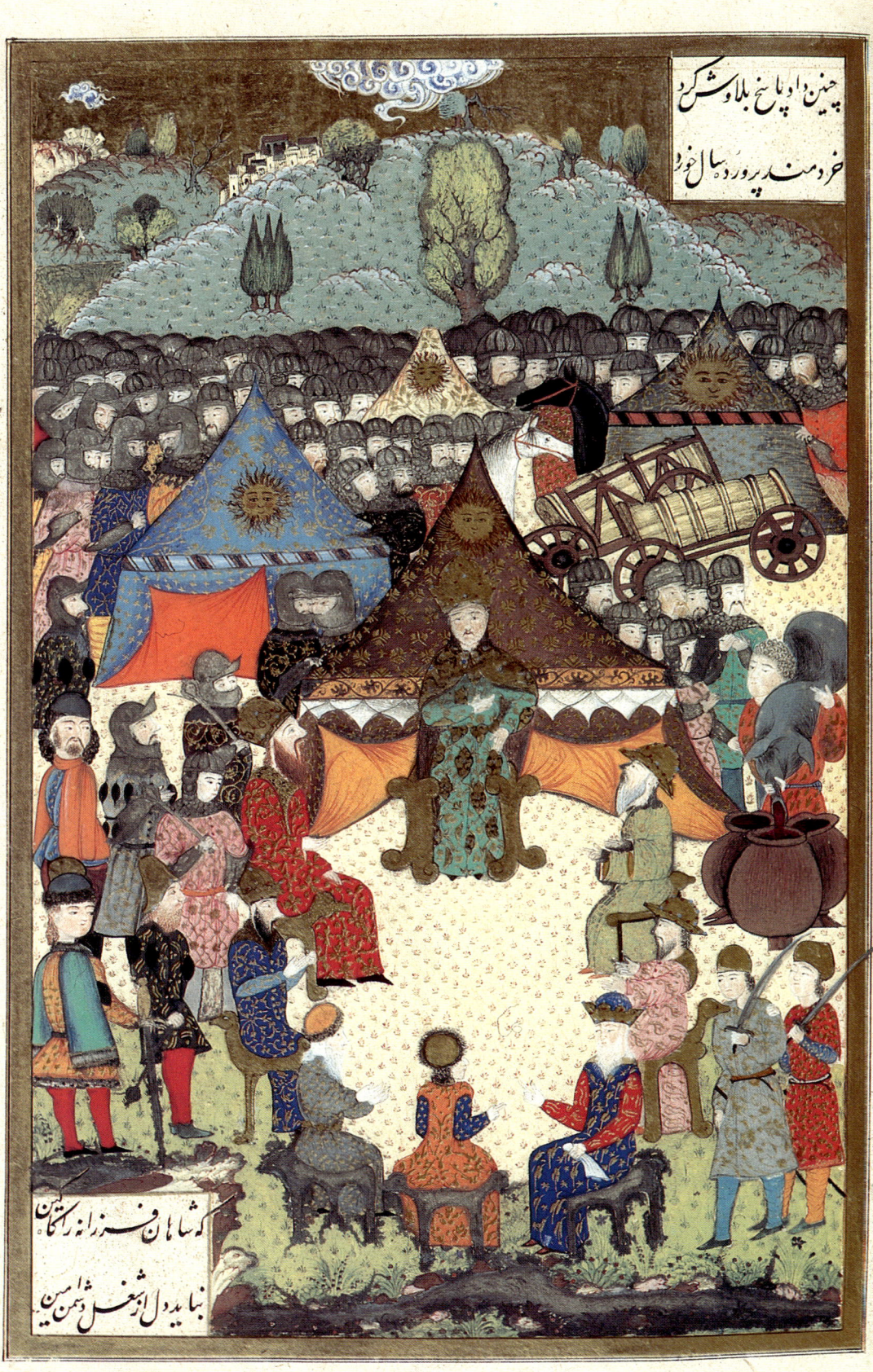

18. Camp of Louis II

(folio 200a)   Painters A and E

THE RAPID ADVANCE of the Ottoman army, with one stronghold after another falling before it, was of grave concern to the Hungarians. Louis II, a twenty-year-old king who had been enthroned at the age of ten, was a fun-loving, immature ruler inexperienced in warfare. His army had been supplemented by units sent by his brothers-in-law, Charles V and Ferdinand, and contained Hungarian, Spanish, German, and Austrian regiments. The Habsburgs, well aware of the threat of the Ottomans, had gathered a large force to confront the sultan.

Louis II moved out of his capital at Budapest and marched toward the plains at Mohacs, heading toward the advancing Ottoman army led by Süleyman.

Louis II, enthroned in front of his imperial tent, is holding a war council with the commanders of the army en route to Mohacs. He wears a large jeweled gold crown and has a cloak flung over his robe. The seven commanders seated in a ring facing the king wear various headdresses: some have crowns, others wear fur-lined caps or brimmed hats. Figures attired in various outfits surround the council; on the right is a servant emptying what appears to be red wine from a pigskin container into three large jars. Additional tents, a pair of wooden cannons, horses, and soldiers in full armor are amassed behind the king. Behind the mountains in the background are a city, possibly representing Budapest, and a windmill.

The figure types and outfits of the personages clearly identify them as Europeans. Specific elements—such as the city with a campanile and basilical building seen in the background, the symbol of the sun on the tents, and the zoomorphic chairs or thrones used by the commanders—indicate that the artist was familiar with certain European traditions. The discrepancies in the size and style of figures suggest that he relied on a number of models to represent different European types.

Louis II has a worried look while his commanders appear disorganized, arguing among themselves. The serving of wine and the two wooden cannons are an indication of the poor condition of the army, which lacks the proper discipline and the advanced technology needed to face the Ottoman forces.

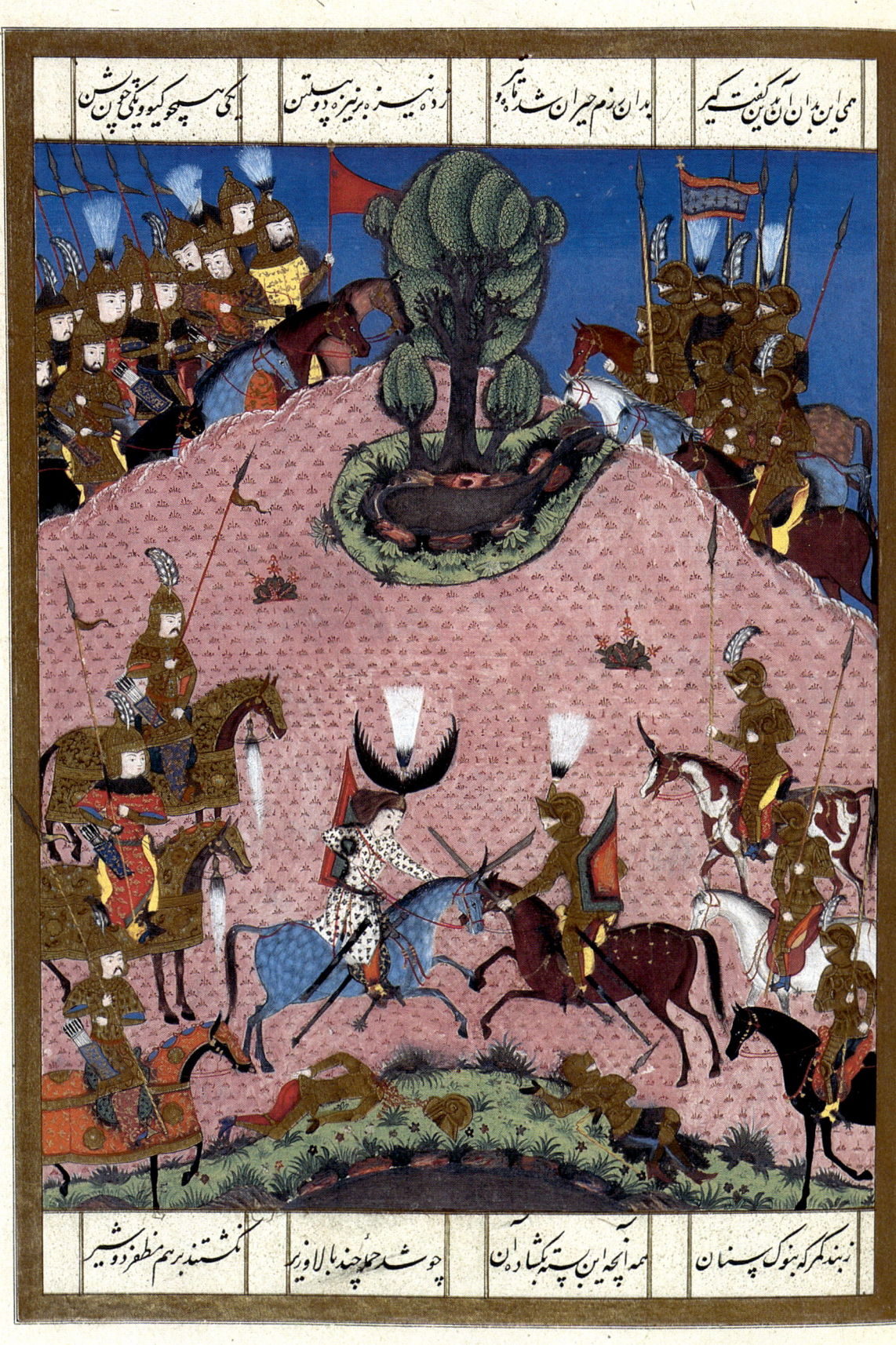

19. Battle of the Forward Attack Forces

(folio 212a)   Painter A

BALI BEY, the sancakbeyi of Semendria at the time, had joined the advance army led by İbrahim Paşa. He was in charge of the akıncıs, who raided the countryside and terrorized the enemy. One of the akıncı regiments had encountered a Hungarian corps, which it then attacked and defeated. Such encounters were called *çarha savaşı* (combat undertaken by the troops in front of the main army).

When the two armies arrived at Mohacs the Ottomans had traveled 1,500 kilometers (930 miles), crossing mountainous terrain and the Sava and Drava rivers in 128 days. The Hungarians, by contrast, had taken 38 days to march only 170 kilometers (some 105 miles) across the flat countryside from Budapest to Mohacs.

> The confrontation between the forward attack forces that takes place prior to the Battle of Mohacs is enacted by two warriors, identified as Sinan, an Ottoman delil, and Eugene, a Hungarian soldier. Sinan, wearing a leopard-skin garment and a headdress with a pair of huge wings enclosing a large plume, clashes swords with Eugene, who is in full armor with an equally impressive plume on his helmet. They both carry rectangular shields with tapering tips and are equipped with extra weapons. Flanking them are three fully armored riders on either side with additional members of the armies gathered behind the hill, separated by a group of trees growing on the banks of a river that flows down in a teardrop formation. Below are two dead Hungarians lying along the shores of a body of water, a prediction of the outcome of the battle.
>
> The Ottomans, placed on the left, wear helmets with feathers or plumes and beautifully patterned garments, their mounts protected with gold brocaded cloths. The Hungarians, shown on the right, are attired in heavy armor with helmets that cover their faces, leaving only their eyes exposed. Painter A was extremely conscientious in representing the details of military accoutrement and faithfully recreates the arms and armor used by both sides.

20. Battle of Mohacs

(folios 219b-220a)   Painter A

THE HUNGARIAN AND OTTOMAN armies arrived at the plain of Mohacs early in the morning of 29 August 1526. Incessant rain that spring and summer had swelled the rivers and flooded the countryside, turning the terrain into a vast swamp.

The Ottoman army, estimated to be 100,000 soldiers with 300 new long-range cannons, was divided into three flanks: the center was commanded by the sultan himself; the left wing with the Rumelian forces was led by the grand vezir İbrahim Paşa; and the right wing with the Anatolian forces was led by Behram Paşa, the beylerbeyi of Anatolia. The akıncıs were commanded by the sultan's two cousins, Bali and Hüsrev Beys, the sancakbeyis of Semendria and Bosnia, who created a pincer formation in the front, drawing in the enemy.

The Hungarian army, supplemented by regiments from Spain, Germany, and Austria, was recorded to number between 150,000 and 200,000 men in heavy armor, but to be equipped with only 100 obsolete cannons.

The Hungarians began the attack at noon. During the battle some thirty knights who had pledged to kill the sultan tore through the front ranks and pierced the central flank. Three of them succeeded in advancing as far as Süleyman, who had been hit by an arrow but saved from being killed by his armor. The wounded sultan fought them off valiantly with his sword and managed to slay his attackers.

The Hungarians were no match for the Ottomans with their brilliant military strategy, highly disciplined army, swift-moving light cavalry, and powerful artillery. The bulk of the Hungarian forces was devastated on the field; the remaining forces retreated toward the Karasu swamp, where their heavy armor proved to be fatal and 25,000 men drowned in the swamp. Among them was Louis II, trapped with his horse while trying to escape.

The Battle of Mohacs was concluded within a mere two hours. The Ottomans had lost some 150 men although many more soldiers were wounded. The overwhelming defeat inflicted upon the enemy enabled the sultan to extend his suzerainty over Hungary. Now Süleyman was ready to march into Budapest, the capital.

Süleyman entered Budapest on 11 September 1526. Since the city was undefended, it surrendered without a fight. The sultan spent several days there and built a bridge over the Danube uniting the two sections, Buda and Pest. Then he issued a ferman giving the crown of Hungary to John Zapolya, the voyvoda of Transylvania, who had joined the Ottomans against Louis II. Hungary became a vassal state of the sultan, similar to Wallachia and Moldavia.

> The Battle of Mohacs, commemorated by a double-folio painting, successfully recreates the fervor and excitement of this phenomenal Ottoman victory. In addition, it documents the military tactics of the army and identifies the function of the various regiments while narrating the story. The event takes place on the plains of Mohacs, in front of a beautifully executed landscape, its rolling hills abounding with different types of trees. Rivers flowing from the hills into the plain and sweeping across the foreground give the condition of the terrain, which had turned into a swamp due to the torrential rains.
>
> Süleyman, mounted on a black horse with jeweled trappings and saddle, appears in the center of the right folio, surrounded by his solaks. Riding behind him are three Has Oda ağas, a group of flagbearers, and the mehter playing horns and drums. In front of the sultan are two rows of janissaries standing behind a barricade of cannons aimed at the opposite folio. The janissaries fire their rifles or load them with gunpowder, packing it into the barrels. The youthful officer who rides next to the janissaries most likely represents either the grand vezir İbrahim Paşa who commanded the left wing of the army, or Behram Paşa, the beylerbeyi of Anatolia in charge of the right wing. Bodies of dead horses and Hungarian soldiers line the banks of the river in the foreground.

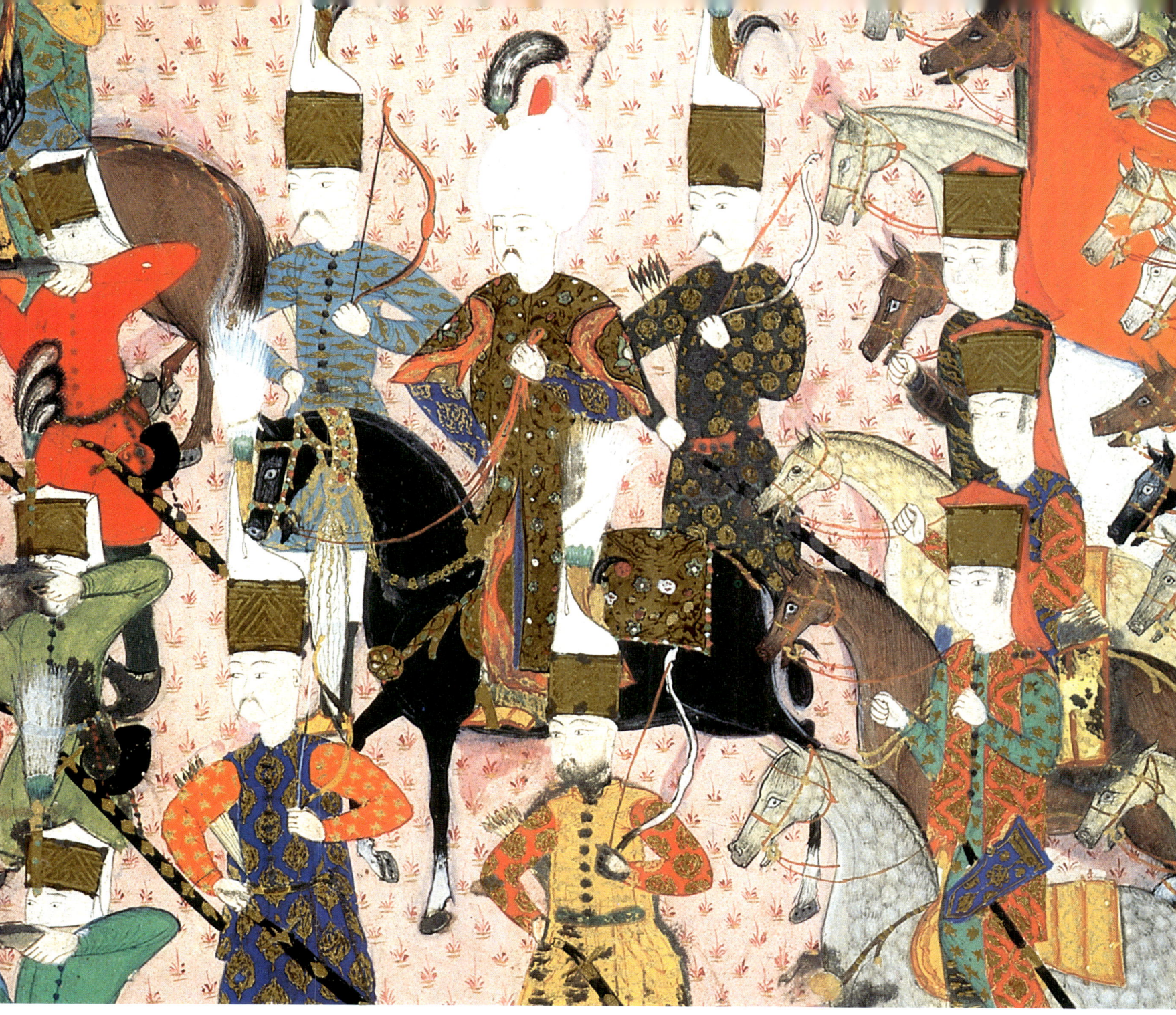

The left half of the scene is full of action and shows combatting warriors and retreating enemy groups. The general impression of disarray and fragmentation of the composition contrasts sharply with the regimentation of the sultan's forces depicted on the opposite folio. In the central field are two Ottoman commanders confronting the enemy: one wears a turban and uses a bow and arrow against his opponent, who attacks him with a spear; the other has a helmet and clobbers with his malletlike weapon the sword-bearing Hungarian, who is visibly stunned by the blow. These figures probably portray the two leaders of the akıncıs: Bali Bey, the sancakbeyi of Semendria, and Hüsrev Bey, the sancakbeyi of Bosnia. Slain and dismembered enemy soldiers thrown off their horses appear between the warriors and in the foreground. A delil, attired in the same manner as the one seen previously, courageously attacks two Hungarians on the lower left. On the left and in the background are groups of Hungarian soldiers in silver- and gold-toned armor who carry spears and banners displaying crosses and rosettes; they seem to be gathering in disoriented groups, some facing the battlefield, others turning away.

This scene is Painter A's most successful double-folio painting; the two halves are united by the field and the composition spreads horizontally across both pages, taking advantage of the extended picture frame.

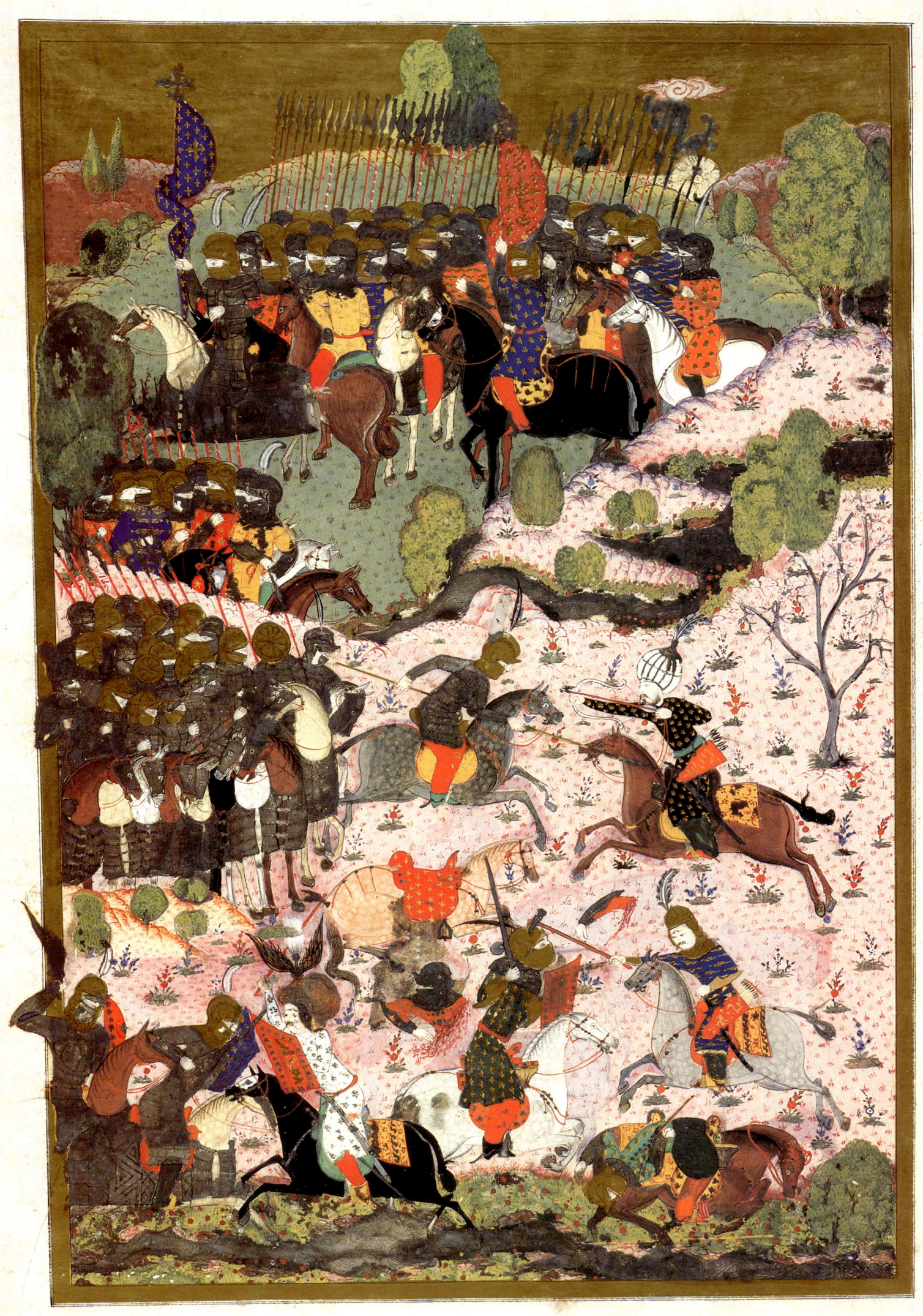

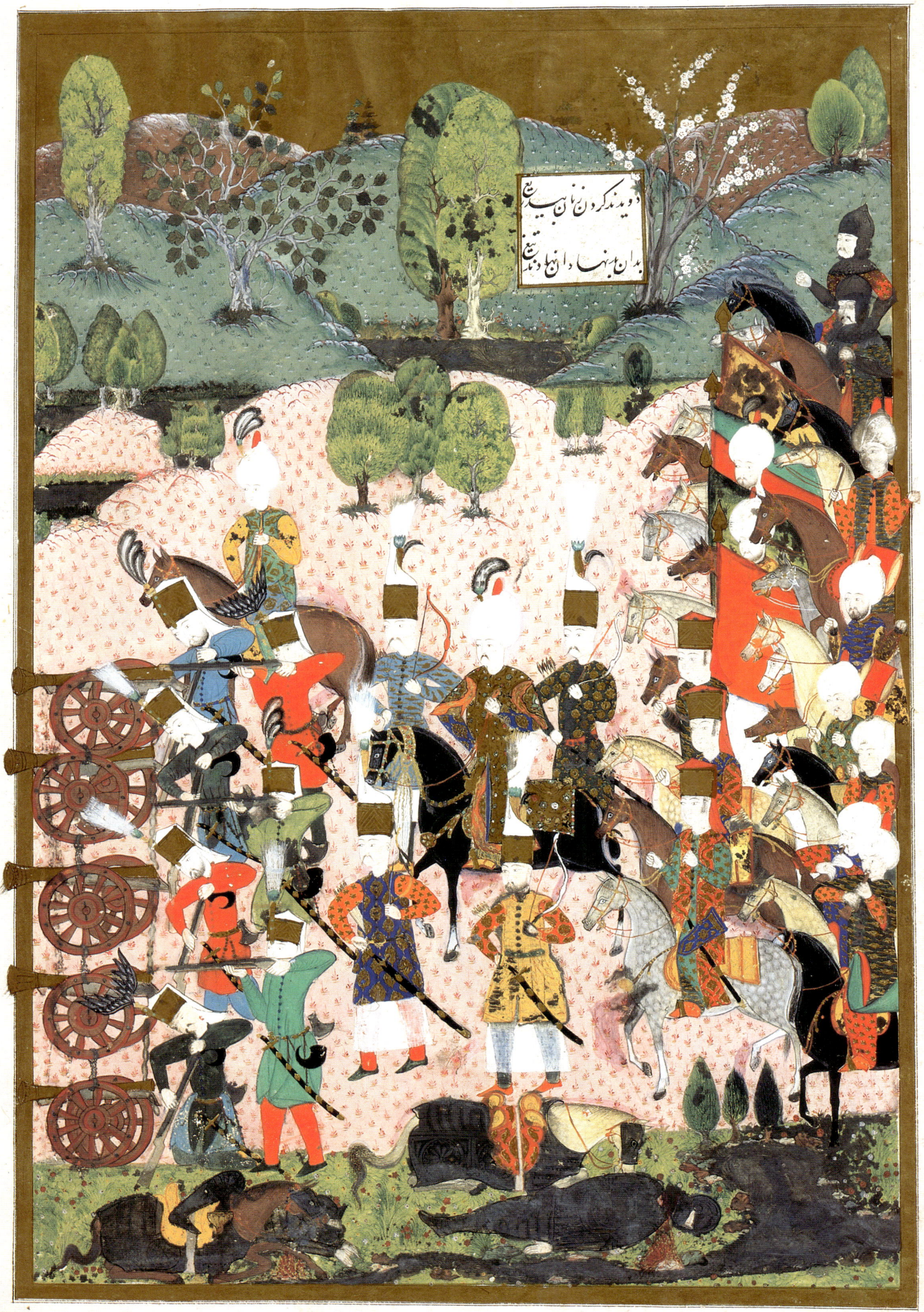

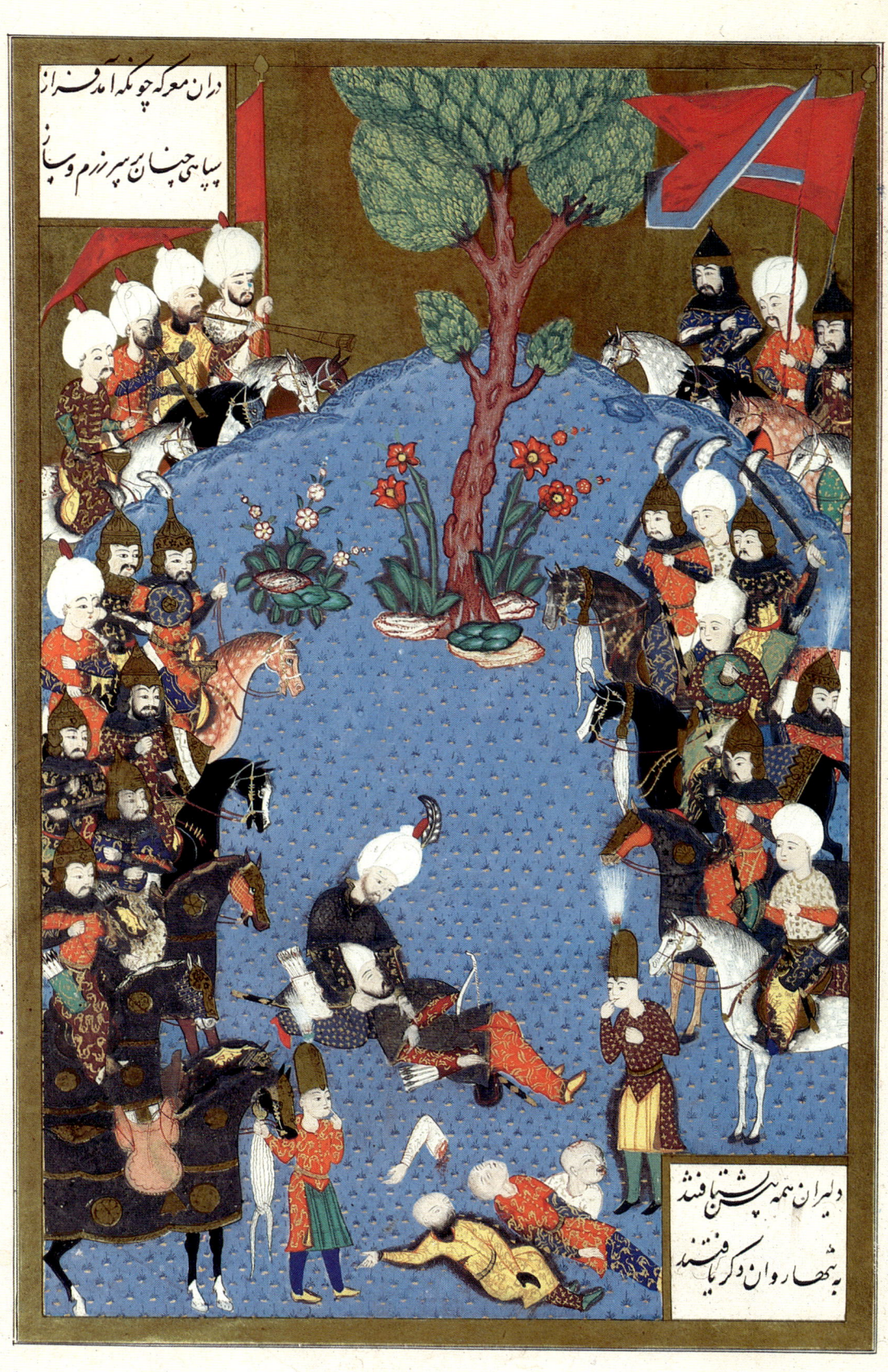

21. Death of Hüseyin Paşa

(folio 235a)   Painter A

UPON RETURNING TO İstanbul Süleyman was informed of a serious revolt in Anatolia. A group of insurgents had gathered around a leader named Baba Zunnun in Yozgat; they had attacked and killed the sancakbeyi Mustafa, who was one of the sultan's cousins. Baba Zunnun's men were spreading into southeastern Anatolia and had murdered several other officials, including Hürrem Paşa, beylerbeyi of Karaman; Ali Bey, sancakbeyi of İçel; and Behram Bey, sancakbeyi of Kayseri. Only Hüseyin Paşa, the beylerbeyi of Sivas, had been able to stop the rebels, killing their leader in the defeat he inflicted on 26 September 1526. Unfortunately, this brave officer was wounded during the battle and died near his home in Sivas, just as he was being sent relief forces led by Hüsrev Paşa.

> The painting represents the fatally wounded Hüseyin Paşa, the beylerbeyi of Sivas, dying in the arms of a fellow commander, who is most likely Hüsrev Paşa, sent by the sultan with an army to supplement his forces. Hüsrev Paşa's regiment gathers on either side of the field while several flagbearers and members of the mehter, playing horns and drums, look in from behind the hills. A large tree, with clusters of rocks and flowers growing at its roots, extends the scene vertically. In the foreground are several dismembered bodies of treacherous rebels and a pair of peyks, who express their bewilderment by biting their index fingers.
>
> The composition with the dying hero lying on the ground, his head cradled by a comrade, recalls the representation of the death of İskender, or Alexander the Great, in sixteenth-century Iranian manuscripts. Either the painter had access to these illustrations or he was trained in the same tradition before coming to the Ottoman court.
>
> The figures observing the event display sorrow, disbelief, and anger. The distress felt by Hüsrev Paşa is particularly vivid. As also seen in scenes of the death of İskender, the tree extending beyond the picture frame symbolizes the departure of the soul and its ascension into heaven.

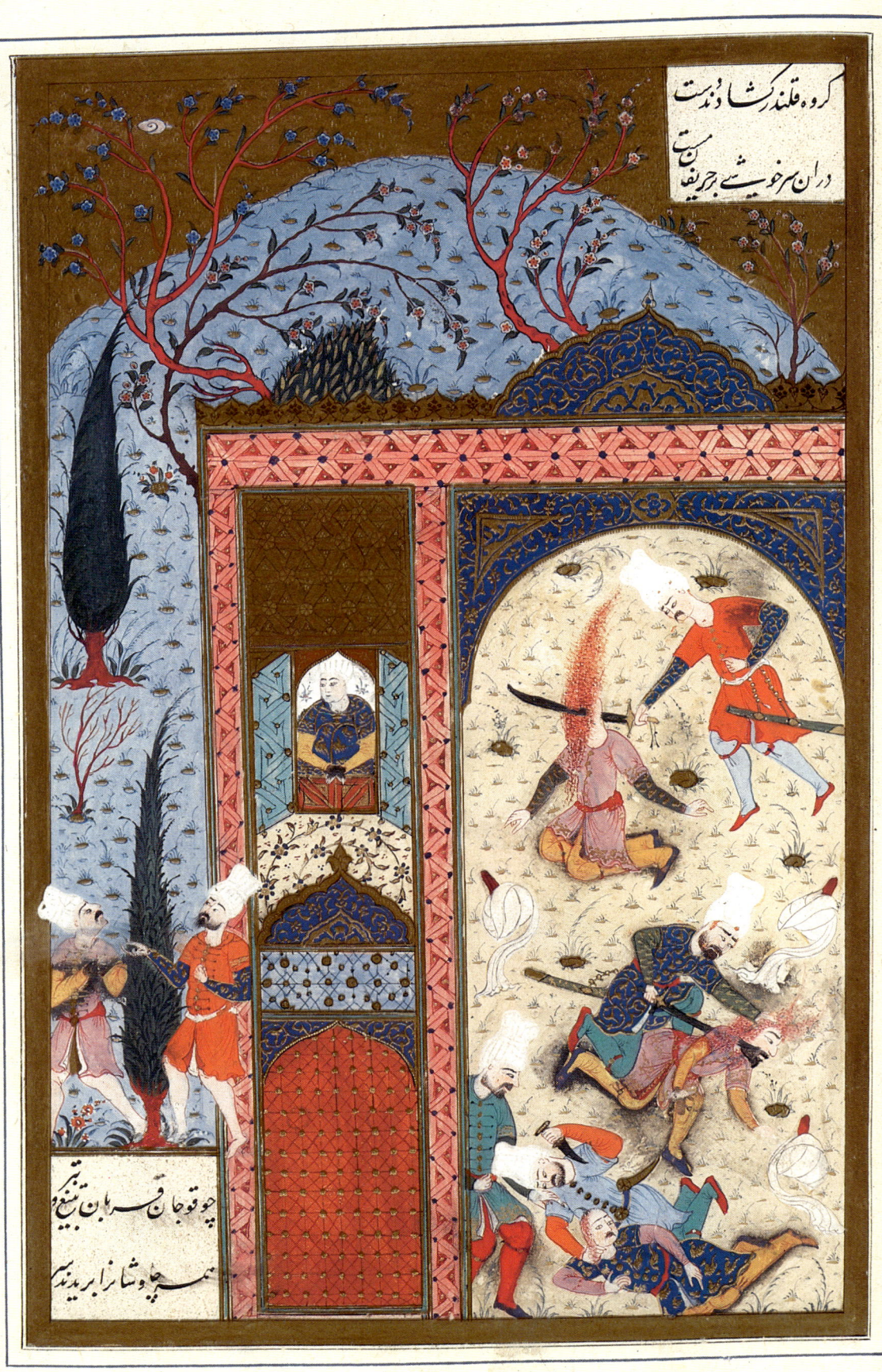

22. Kalender's Rebellion

(folio 239a)   Painter B

BY THE SUMMER OF 1527, the rebellion in Anatolia had attracted 30,000 men under the banner of a new leader named Kalender Çelebi, who was reputed to be a descendant of Hacı Bektaş Veli, the founder of the Bektaşi order of dervishes. The rebels included many shiites and were supported by Şah Tahmasp, the second ruler of the Safavid dynasty of Iran, who had been enthroned at the age of ten in 1524.

On 8 June 1527 Kalender and his followers attacked the Anatolian army at Karaçayır and killed several of the commanders. Behram Paşa, who was in charge of the Anatolian forces during the Battle of Mohacs, barely escaped with his life.

The rebels were creating a major threat to national security. Şah Tahmasp's support of them was even more disturbing; the young ruler of Iran was inciting the wrath of the sultan by interfering in internal Ottoman affairs.

> The followers of Kalender, who wear large white turbans with flat tops, are shown slaying the guards of one of the fortresses in the vicinity of Karaçayır in southern Anatolia. On the left are two rebels conversing outside the structure, which has a window above an arched entrance and a large open courtyard. Another rebel sits hugging his knees in the window while four others attack the residents in the courtyard, slashing their heads and bodies with swords and daggers. The victims are thrown down, their turbans flying around the ground.
>
> Although the scene depicts a violent and bloody episode, its gruesome effect is lessened by the decorative quality of architectural elements and landscape features.

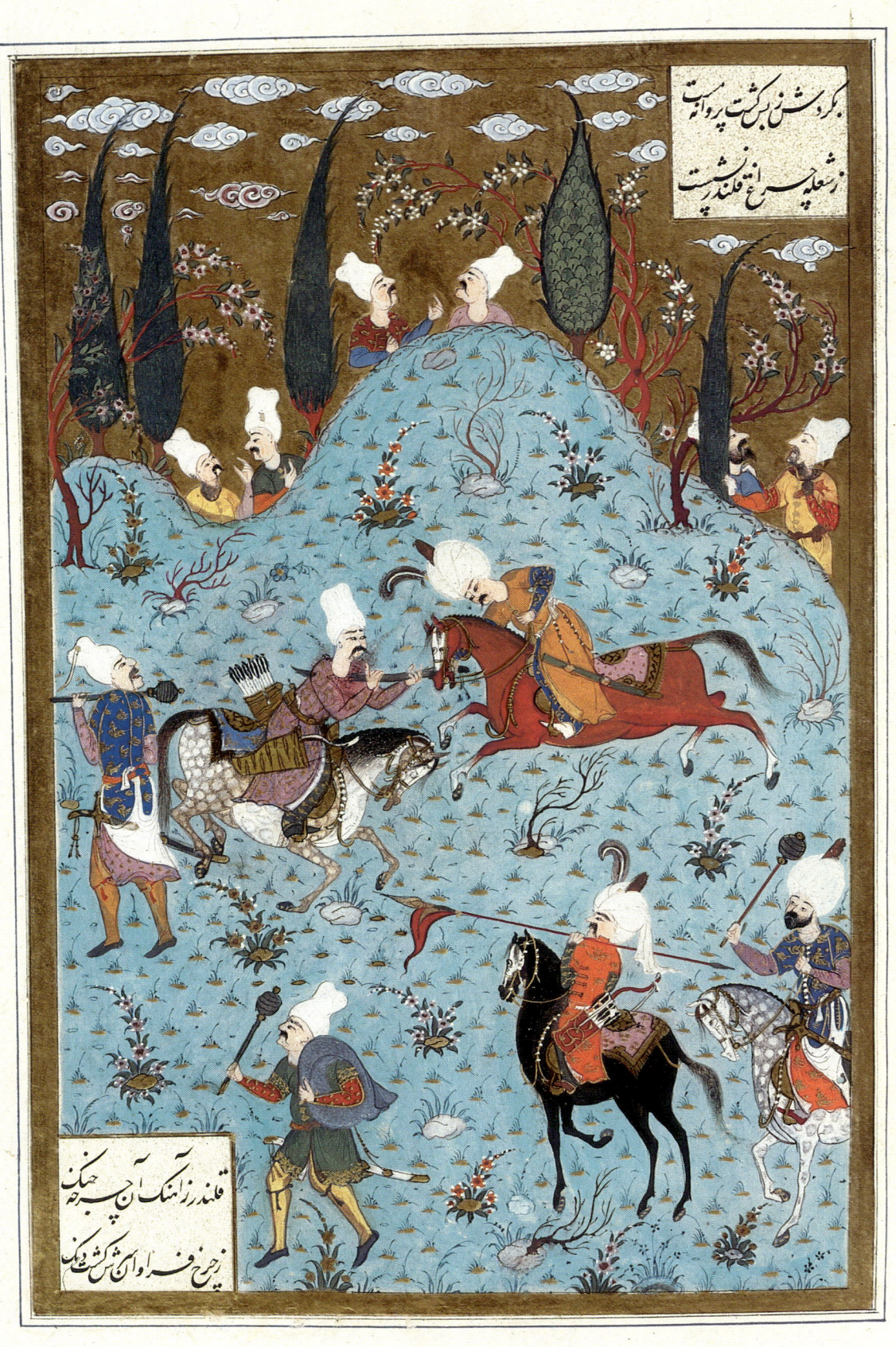

23. Death of Kalender

(folio 248a)   Painter B

SÜLEYMAN DISPATCHED HIS grand vezir İbrahim Paşa to Anatolia with 3,000 janissaries and 2,000 sipahis to put an end to Kalender's rebellion. İbrahim Paşa's forces defeated Kalender and his men at Başsaz outside Maraş on 22 June 1527. When Kalender was killed by an officer named Pervane, the rebels surrendered and were rounded up. On the sultan's orders they were not punished but given a sharp condemnation and released.

İbrahim Paşa headed back to İstanbul after restoring order in southeastern Anatolia. He was received with honors by the sultan and rewarded for his services to the state.

> This scene, which takes place outside Maraş, shows an officer named Pervane galloping towards the rebel leader Kalender and slaying him with a sword. Kalender, taken aback by the sudden attack, grabs with both hands the blade which has already pierced his chest. Two other mounted officers holding spears and maces are ready to pursue a pair of armed rebels who are fleeing on foot. One of them turns back to look at his slain leader, his mouth falling open, either in astonishment or in despair. Three pairs of other rebels appear behind the hills, animatedly discussing their fate.
>
> Painter B's efficacy in representing horses in various positions and depicting delicately intertwining trees laden with blossoms is evident in this scene. The swirling stems of the bushes and flowers covering the field create a lively movement which, together with the branches of the trees, enlivens the scene and emphasizes the action of the figures.

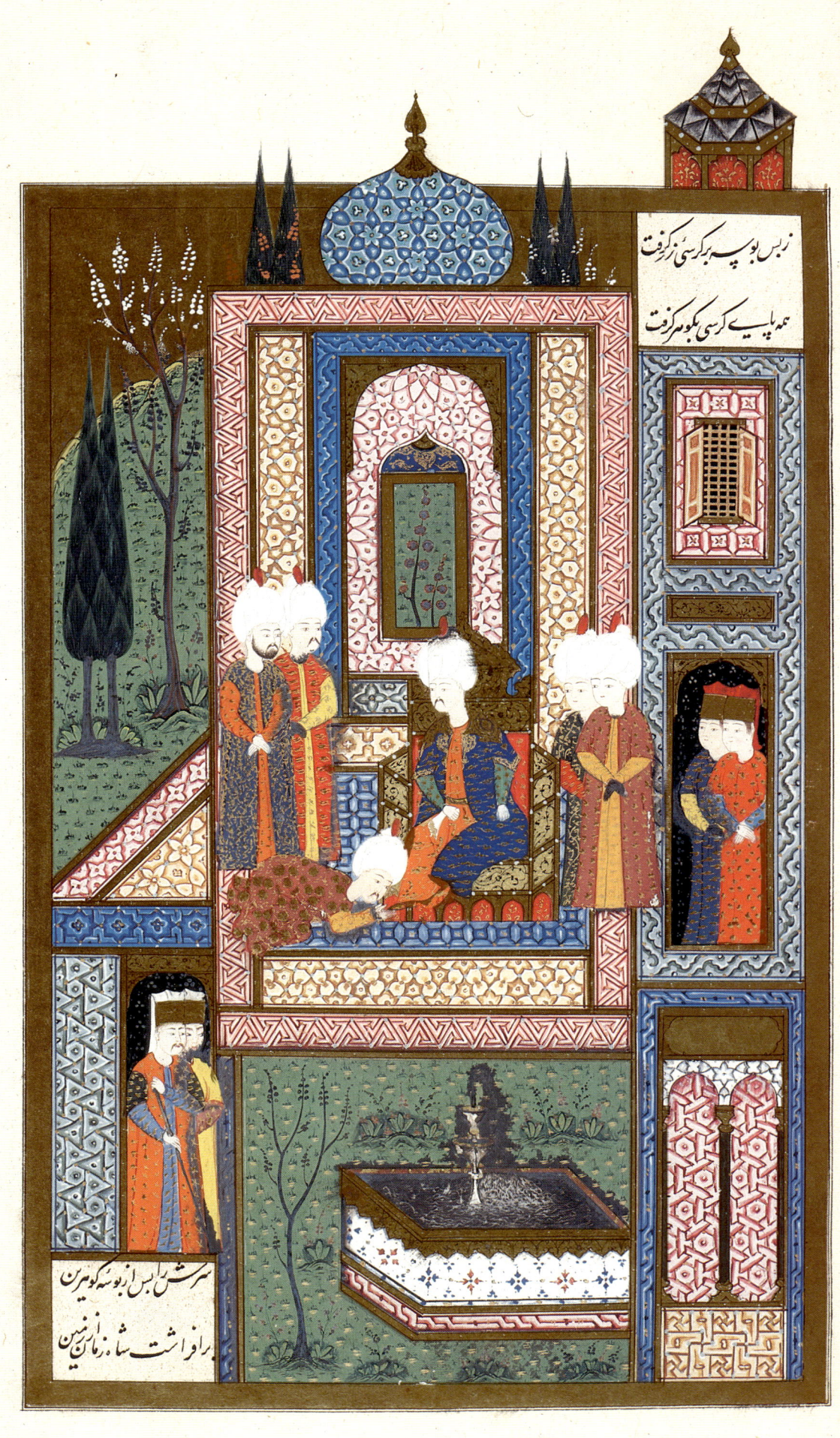

24. Reception of İbrahim Paşa

(folio 260a)   Painter A

SÜLEYMAN RECEIVED HIS grand vezir İbrahim Paşa on 11 August 1527 and praised him for quelling the rebellion in Anatolia. İbrahim Paşa was given an increase in salary and received the title of serasker.

Süleyman and İbrahim had met and become close friends when Süleyman was serving as governor in Manisa. İbrahim had been a devşirme child sold to a lady in Manisa; he had been treated as a son and given an excellent education. After Süleyman's accession, İbrahim was assigned to the Has Oda and later promoted to the post of grand vezir (1523). A highly intellectual man who was a linguist and an accomplished player of the *kemençe* (a small cellolike stringed instrument), İbrahim was also an experienced and competent military commander. He had participated in the campaigns to Belgrade and Rhodes, and successfully restored order in Egypt after Ahmed Paşa's rebellion. Respected and liked by Süleyman, he was also the sultan's brother-in-law.

The following month İbrahim was appointed the beylerbeyi of Rumelia, second in importance to that of Egypt. İbrahim was now at the pinnacle of his career and was called Makbul, meaning "the esteemed," which indeed he was. This remarkable statesman served Süleyman as the grand vezir for fourteen years. His close relationship with the sultan and his arrogance created many enemies in the court, the most formidable of which was Hürrem.

> Süleyman is shown receiving his victorious grand vezir, İbrahim Paşa, in one of the pavilions in the third courtyard of the Topkapı Palace. The jewellike domed pavilion has an arched opening that overlooks a small courtyard with a square fountain. On the left is the entrance to the courtyard, guarded by a pair of kapıcıs; opposite are the arcades of the third courtyard, behind which is a two-storied unit attached to the pavilion with two Has Oda ağas waiting in attendance in the doorway.
>
> Süleyman, flanked by two pairs of vezirs and iç oğlans, is seated on a gold throne and holds a white handkerchief. İbrahim Paşa kneels in front, kissing the hem of his kaftan. He appears grateful for the honors bestowed upon him and deeply moved to be receiving such an unusual promotion.
>
> The tone of the scene is at once intimate and formal. Only a few dignitaries are present during the reception, which makes it almost a private session; and yet the formality of the placement of the figures, the lack of human interaction, and the abstraction of the architectural setting transform the scene into a ceremonial event. The sobriety and restraint shown by the participants are quite significant, since Süleyman has just conferred upon İbrahim Paşa the title of serasker, the prerogative until now of only the sultans. This concession offended many of Süleyman's devoted officials and was later abused by İbrahim Paşa, leading to his execution.

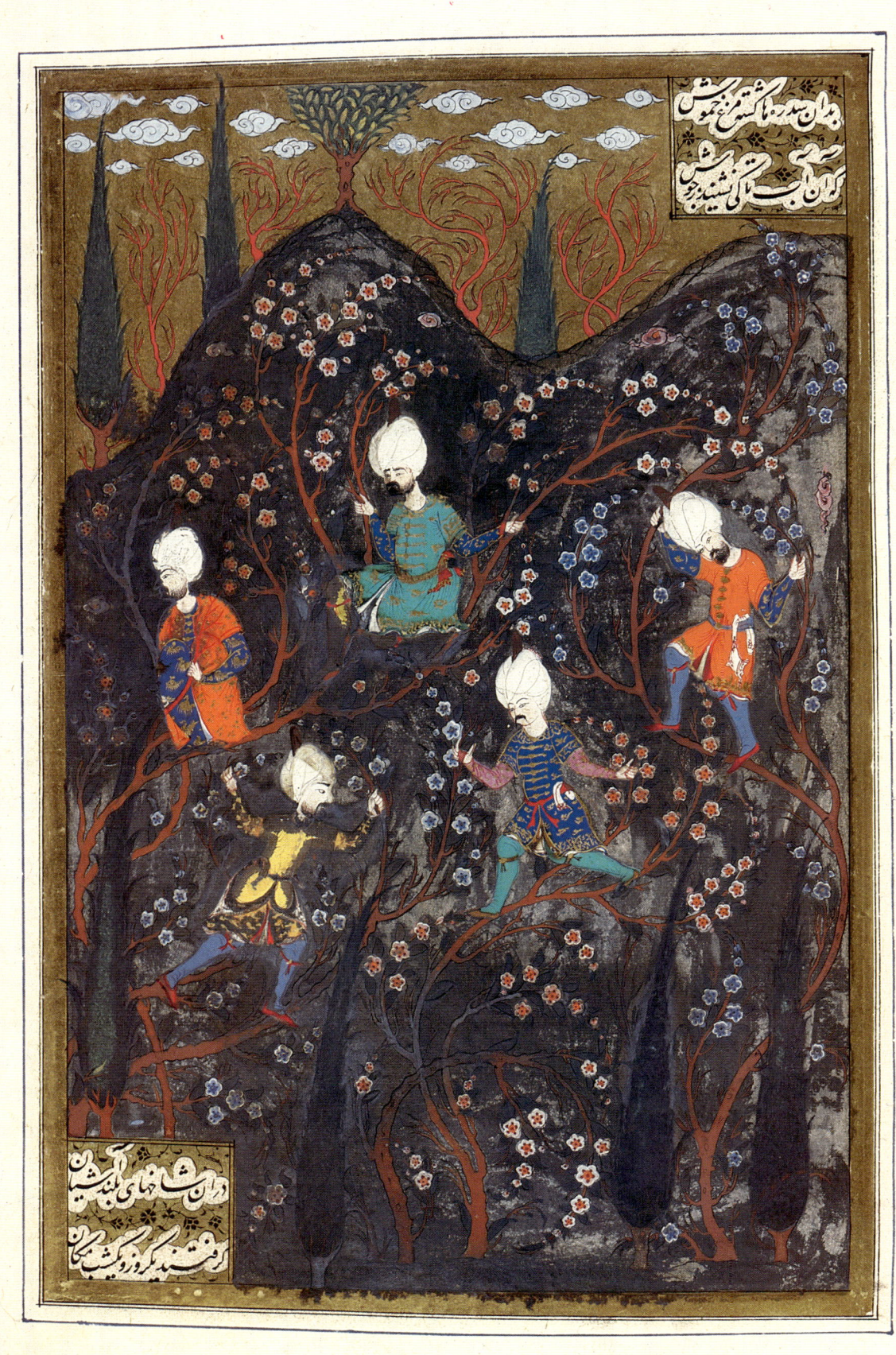

هر شاخ مرکبت زبالای من	بدو گفته طوبی قطوبی الم	گذشته زبسدر چوچرخم	زدوشاخ برشاخ کاوسپهر

بر هر شاخ ... طوفان انگیختن بود
... این عنبر آن ...
... این یاسمین ...
... این چمن و گلزار ...

در اوج آنچمن ابرمج حیات
که خوش همیخواب افتد آب
در این سلسله مرگ انخواب
چو گل یک عیش هم نبرد

...نان بادران پرست
...ریحان باران
لیکن چوهور ان
...

گرفته در آغوش شاخ درخت	نخورده می و خواب مرگ ریخته	نبسته دمی بیده هیچون جنا	کش ده نظرها بالائی

25. Soldiers Climbing Trees during a Storm

(folio 266a)   Painter B

WHILE SÜLEYMAN WAS preoccupied with the rebellions in Anatolia, Ferdinand had moved into Hungary and proclaimed himself the king of that land. Zapolya was forced to retire to Transylvania. This called for the fourth sefer-i hümayun, during which the Ottomans advanced as far as Vienna.

Süleyman gathered a massive army and departed from İstanbul on 10 May 1529. His supplies alone were transported by tens of thousands of camels and mules. Once again the army's movement was plagued by torrential spring rains, recalling the condition of the Battle of Mohacs. The army halted briefly in Edirne, Filibe, Sophia, and Belgrade before proceeding to Mohacs.

> The story of the tumultuous rains that proved to be a serious handicap to the mobility of the army en route to Vienna is the theme of this scene. According to the text, it rained incessantly that spring, causing the rivers to flood the plains. When the army stopped in Edirne, the downpour was so heavy and the ground was so wet that the soldiers had to climb trees for protection.
>
> In this unusual painting five men are shown perching on the branches of blossoming fruit trees in an attempt to take cover from the rain. The ground, once painted silver to recreate the wet terrain, has discolored with time. The original colors of the scene must have been quite striking: a silver hill set against the gold sky, accentuated by green cypresses, red branches, and varying tones of pinks and blues applied to the blossoms. It is one of the rare genre scenes of the period that represents a serious and yet amusing episode during the campaign.

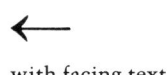

with facing text

26. Siege of Budapest

(folio 282a)   Painter B

THE ARMY SET UP camp at Mohacs, the scene of Süleyman's previous victory in Hungary. There the sultan was joined by 6,000 Hungarians led by John Zapolya. Süleyman conferred with him and İbrahim Paşa, working out a strategy. Zapolya was presented four hilats, which were placed on his shoulders one on top of another.

The army then advanced on Budapest and recaptured it after a short siege of five days, entering the city on 8 September 1529. Süleyman once again installed Zapolya on the Hungarian throne and proceeded to march into Austria, hoping for a showdown with Ferdinand.

Both Ferdinand and Charles V refused to be drawn into battle and kept evading the sultan. They knew that their forces could not hold up against the Ottomans and preferred to forestall a direct confrontation until they were more equally matched. Ferdinand withdrew to Linz, 150 kilometers (93 miles) west of Vienna, leaving the defense of his capital to the elderly Count Nicolas von Salm, assisted by Marshal Wilhelm von Reggendorf.

> The painting representing the second conquest of Budapest shows the inner fortress in the background. The fortress offers protection to several Habsburg soldiers wearing helmets as well as short-brimmed caps with white feathers. A guard stationed at the top of the observation tower scrutinizes a group of mace-bearing Ottoman cavalry officers, who advance toward the structure.
>
> In the center of the painting is the outer fortress, which has been demolished by explosives that have thrown a number of men from its walls. The soldiers fall upside down, flinging their arms and legs, and dropping their hats. Two of the men have landed in the foreground; one clutches his leg and the other, still in a swan-dive position, spreads his hands, surrendering to the officer on the lower right, who threatens him with a spear. Opposite are other cavalrymen, ready to take prisoners.
>
> Painter B portrays the enemy soldiers in a whimsical manner, representing their demise with a touch of frivolity. Even the animated rocks on the upper right appear to be amused at their clumsiness.

→

with facing text

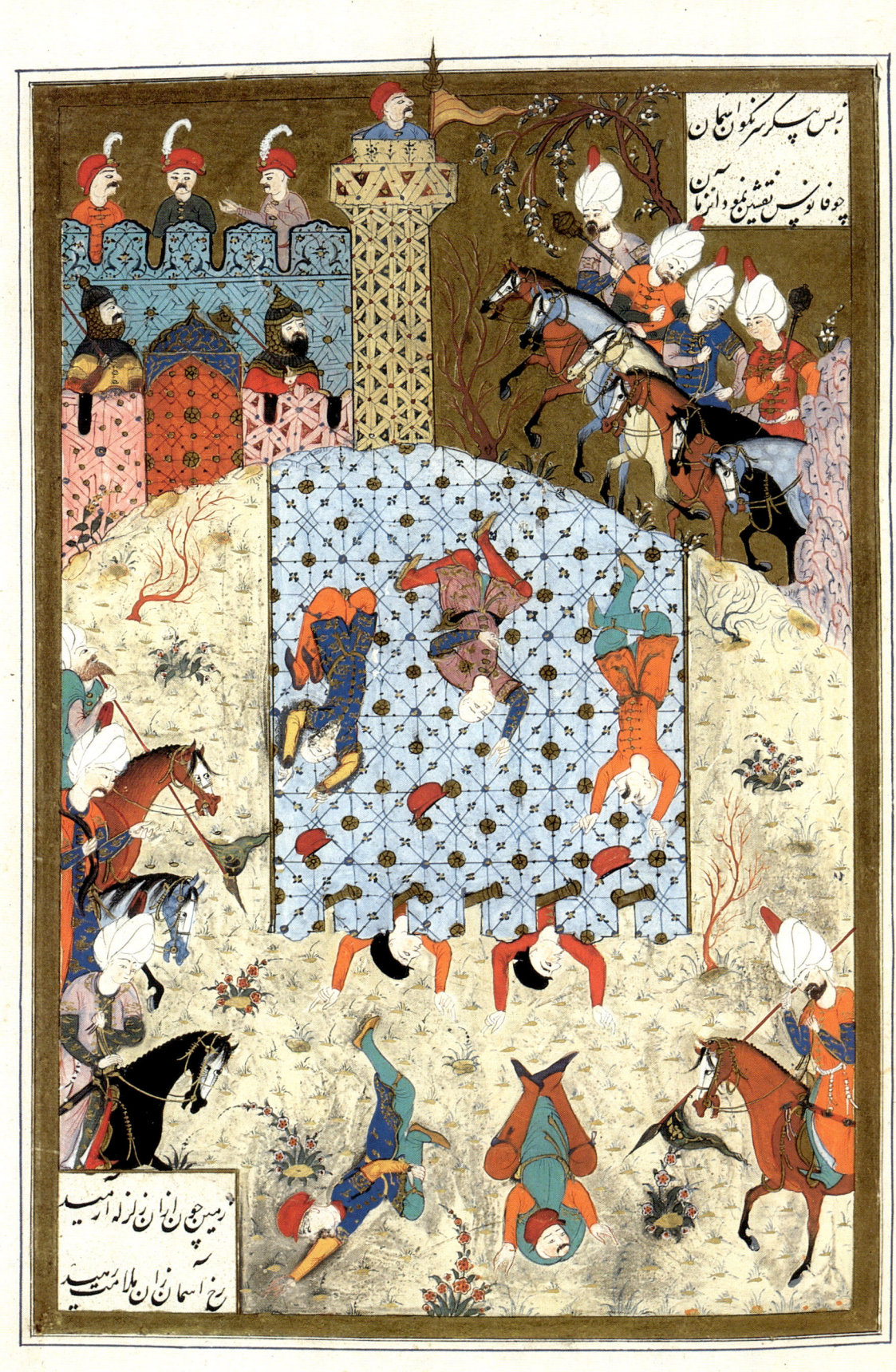

| برآمد بالای یک کوکب چو مهر | بر او اخت رایت آبنوس | هوا شد نهان اندر آن حریر درفش | نسرین شد زپولاد و پیشان بنفش |

| سپهبد بفرمود نقاب را | که از چشم دشمن برد خواب را | نهفت اندرون آتش اندر نهند | بهم آتش و باد را سرد ها |

| غریو قیامت بر افلاک شد | زهیبت دل آسمان چاک شد | کروبه دلاس باک گشتند | قیامت بپا خواست پیش |

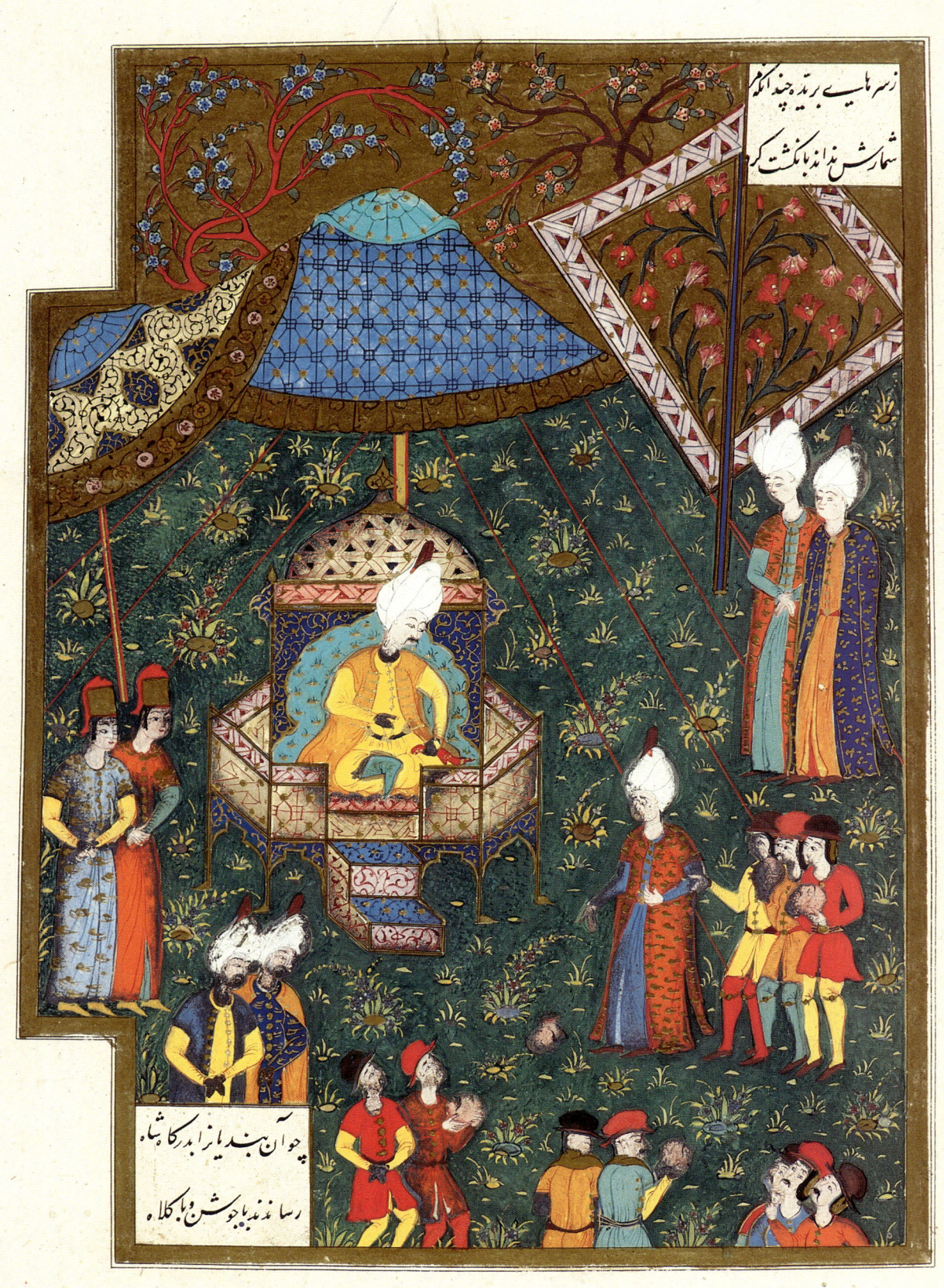

27. Süleyman Inspecting Prisoners

(folio 297a)   Painter B

THE SULTAN'S ARMY crossed the Austrian border and appeared before Vienna on 26 September 1529. The Ottomans besieged the city for over two weeks, their akıncıs raiding the countryside. The sultan's army took many prisoners and inflicted serious damage on the Austrians, causing the death of commander Nicolas von Salm. It was a matter of days before Vienna fell.

But since winter was rapidly approaching and heavy artillery had been left on the route between Vienna and Belgrade due to the swampy roads, Süleyman decided to lift the siege on 16 October. The sultan had no intention of capturing Vienna, knowing well that by the time he returned to İstanbul it would be freed by Ferdinand, who was gathering his forces in Linz. The city was too far from the Ottoman capital to be held for a long time and to be defended properly. The logistics of time and distance were against it; the city was a long and arduous journey from his headquarters and winter storms would be setting in by the time his army could undertake a lengthy siege.

Süleyman had succeeded in his mission. He had taught a lesson to Ferdinand by appearing before his capital without meeting serious opposition. He was warning the Habsburgs that he could always march into the heart of Europe if the archduke continued his belligerent attacks on Hungary.

> Süleyman, enthroned in the imperial otak set up outside Vienna, inspects three of the Austrian prisoners brought in by an official. The sultan sits crosslegged on a large hexagonal throne with a high arched back placed under a canopy. On either side are two other canopies: the rounded one protects the Has Oda ağas and the square one appears over the iç oğlans. In the foreground are a pair of officials with other groups of prisoners. The prisoners, attired in caps, short tunics, and leggings, hold in their hands several severed heads.
>
> The scene abounds with floral motifs that cover the ground and extend to the sky; various patterns embellish the shadings, the throne and its furnishings, and the garments of the figures.

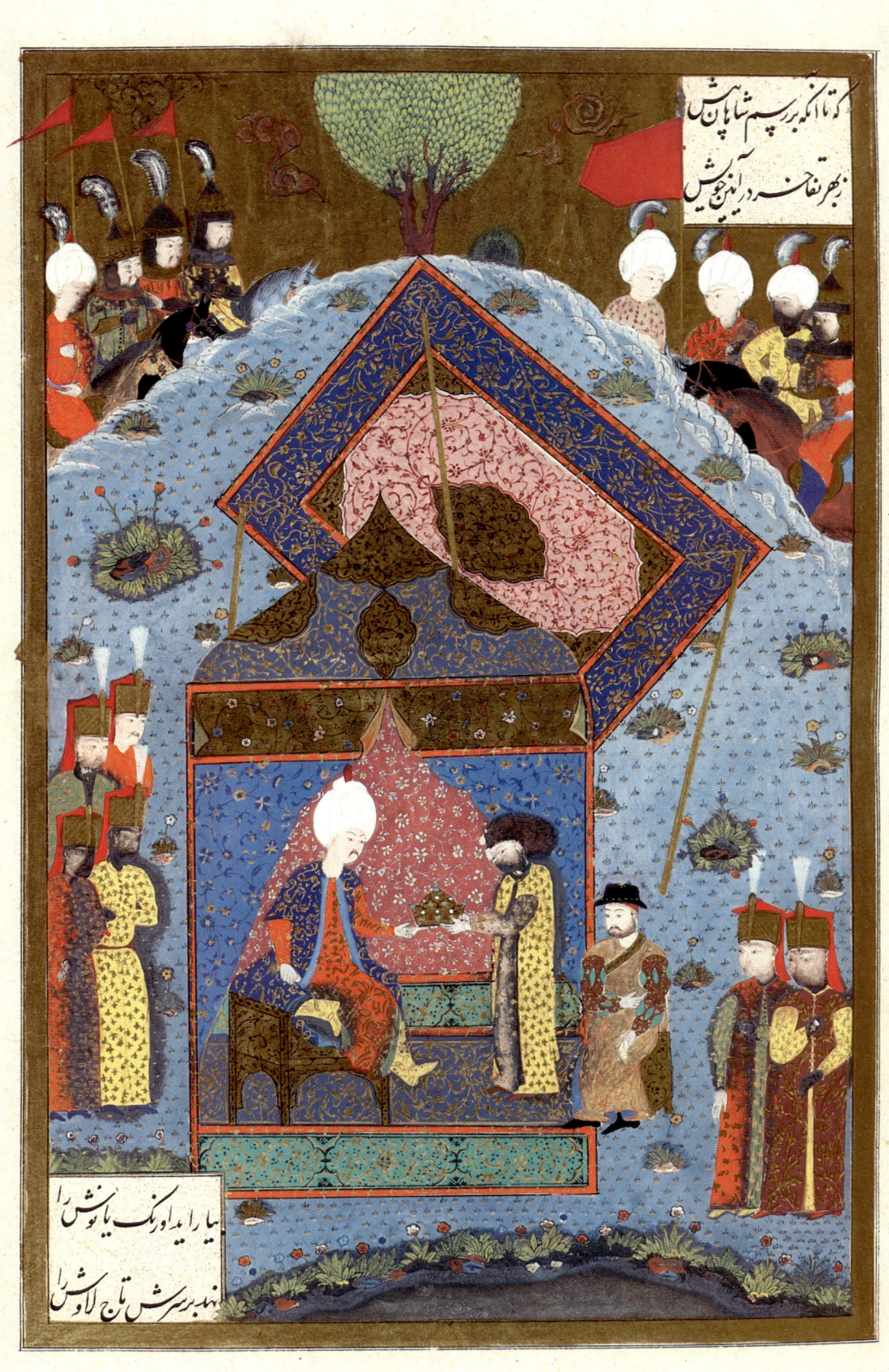

28. Süleyman Receiving the Crown of Hungary

(folio 309a)   Painter A

BEFORE SÜLEYMAN COULD head back home, he had to resolve the problem of the Holy Crown of Hungary, which had been stolen by Ferdinand's men when they withdrew from Budapest. This crown, reputed to have been made for Saint Stephen in the year 1000, was worn by all the kings of Hungary. It was imperative that it be returned and given to John Zapolya.

Süleyman had entrusted his grand vezir İbrahim Paşa with the task. An officer by the name of Küçük Bali Bey, the commander of İzvornik in Bosnia, captured the crown while it was being taken to Vienna and delivered it to the Ottoman camp on 4 September 1529. It was presented to its rightful owner, Zapolya, the following month (30 October).

Süleyman's arrival in İstanbul was a glorious event. The city celebrated his victory over the Austrians with a five-day festival, its people jubilant that their sultan's magnificence and might had struck such fear into the enemy that it was unable to face him in battle.

> Seated in the imperial otak set up outside Budapest, Süleyman is handed the famous crown of Hungary by Küçük Bali Bey, the officer who retrieved it from the Austrians. Seated at the edge of the otak is John Zapolya, waiting to receive the revered crown. Zapolya, shown as a middle-aged man with a beard, wears a short-brimmed hat and a gold-banded translucent coat over a robe with split seams on its sleeves and holds a handkerchief.
>
> Witnessing this ceremonial event are several military officers who stand on either side of the tent while others, riding horses, appear behind the hill rising in the background. A large tree at the apex of the composition and a river flowing in the foreground accentuate the three protagonists.
>
> The jeweled gold crown presented to Süleyman has a domical top and a crenellated diadem. The original crown of Saint Stephen is slightly different, with semicircular and triangular units placed above a plain diadem and its dome surmounted by a cross. Here, the artist represents a type of crown resembling those worn by Louis II and his commanders during the war council prior to the Battle of Mohacs (18).

29. Süleyman Entertained

(folio 321b)   Painter C

IN JUNE 1530 the court celebrated the circumcision of the three oldest princes: Mustafa, Mehmed, and Selim. Circumcisions of Ottoman princes were always commemorated with great festivities in which both the court and the public participated. There would be processions of the court officials and parades of the guildsmen, who marched with their floats and displayed their arts and crafts; mock battles, races, and various athletic competitions; and all sorts of circus acts, concerts, musical plays, firework displays, and banquets.

The fete organized for Şehzades Mustafa, Mehmed, and Selim took place in the At Meydanı, which was to become the traditional site for future circumcision festivals. The sultan and his court viewed the activities from the balcony of the palace of İbrahim Paşa, which had been completed in 1521. The three-week program included banquets, games, firework displays, presentations of gifts, and a procession of the sultan and the princes from the Topkapı Palace to the At Meydanı. During this festival Nasuh, one of the Enderun ağas and a renowned mathematician, historian, painter, and swordsman, created the game of matrak, an invention which earned him the honorific Matrakcı.

> The symmetrically composed scene represents a domed pavilion with an arched opening, in front of which is a hexagonal throne with a high lobed back placed on a large rug. Süleyman sits crosslegged on the throne, holding a red rosebud. He is listening to the music of the quartet gathered around the pool in the foreground. Three of the entertainers play musical instruments—a tambourine, a small cellolike stringed instrument, and a lute—while the fourth, holding a book of poems, is singing. Placed in front of the throne are three gold trays containing a pair of porcelain bowls with lids, a tall-necked jeweled bottle, and small glass or gemstone cups. Flanking the sultan are a pair of Has Oda ağas and a solitary iç oğlan.
>
> The composition and style of painting are based on the generalized enthronement scenes found in mid-sixteenth-century Iranian manuscripts executed in Tabriz and Kazvin. Painter C, who produced this illustration, must have been trained in those centers prior to coming to İstanbul. His other contribution in the *Süleymanname* also reflects the same tradition (see 39).

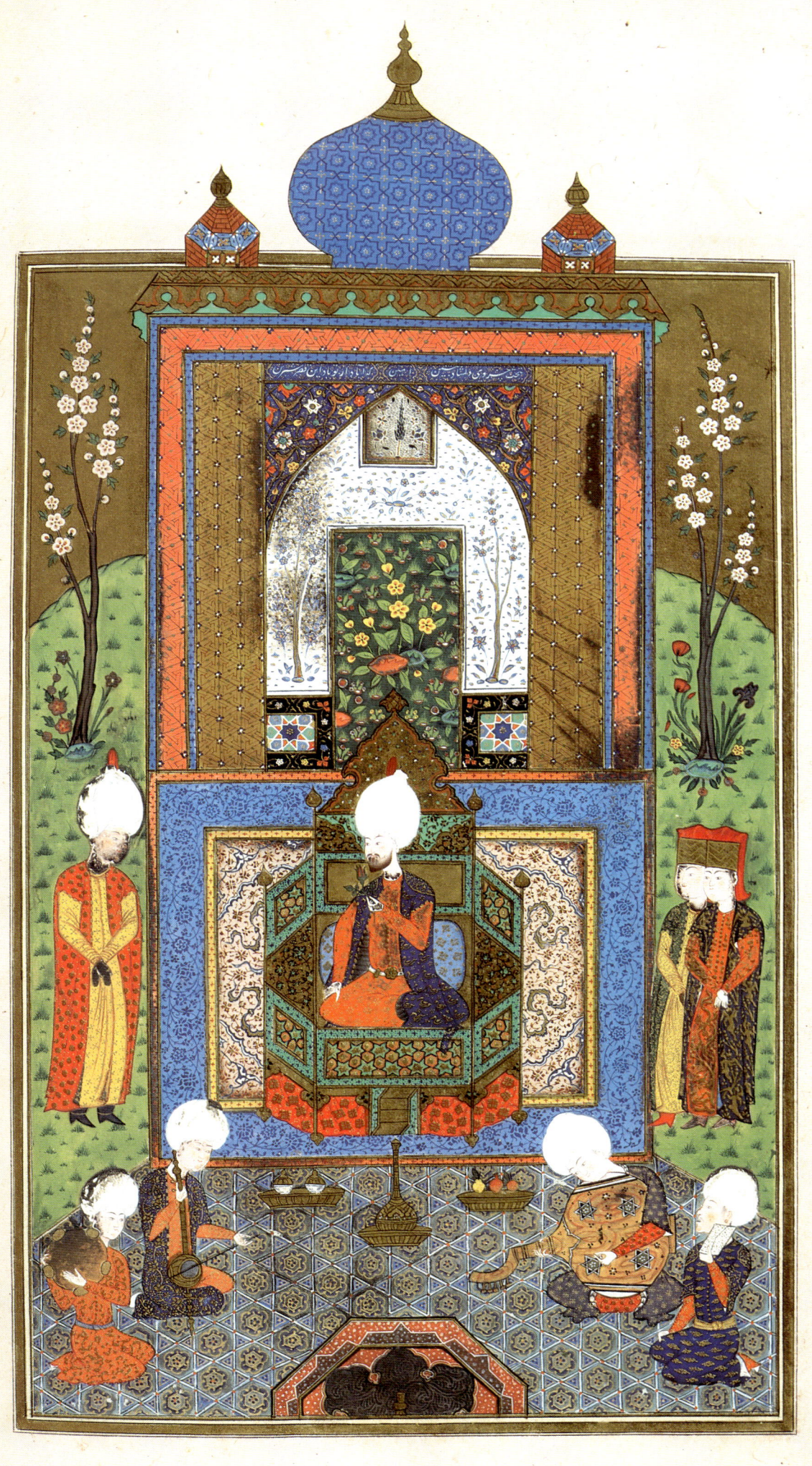

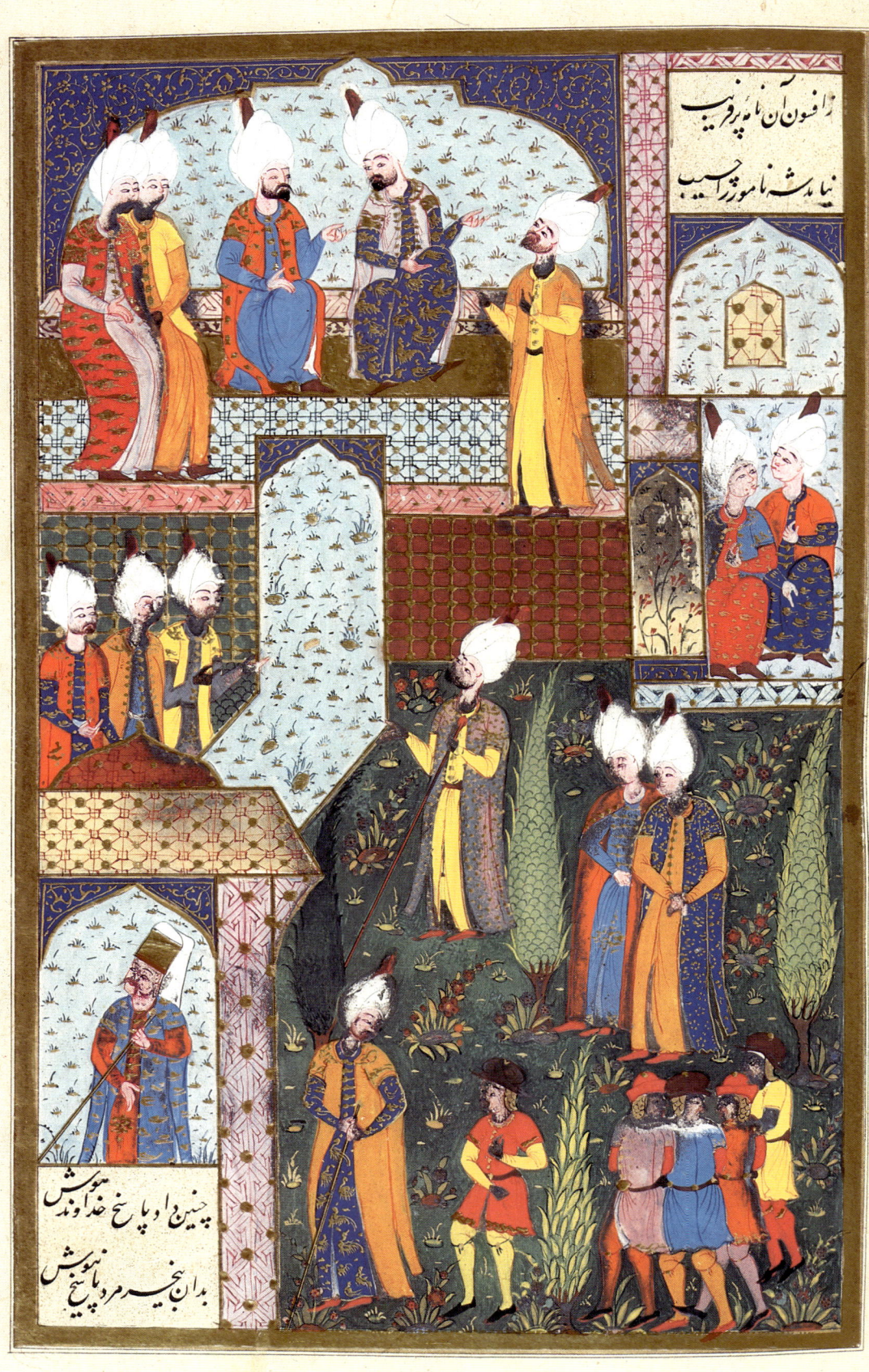

30. Arrival of the Austrian Ambassadors
(folio 328a)   Painter B

MEANWHILE, Ferdinand had started campaigning in Hungary; he refused to acknowledge Zapolya and claimed himself as its king. He sent to İstanbul a delegation of twenty-four envoys, headed by the commander of Güns, General Nicolas Jurischitz, and the Count of Lamberg, Joseph von Schneeberg.

The Austrian mission arrived in the capital on 17 October 1530 and was received by the grand vezir İbrahim Paşa at the end of the month. The envoys presented Ferdinand's letter requesting that the sultan expel Zapolya and recognize his right to the Hungarian crown.

The members of the Divan deliberated for weeks. They could not accept Ferdinand's claims and considered him the ruler only of Austria. Hungary had been conquered twice (in 1526 and 1529) by the sultan and would remain a tributary state of the Ottomans.

The scene takes place in the second courtyard of the Topkapı Palace with a kapıcı guarding the Babüsselam on the lower left. In the courtyard are five of the Austrian envoys, their leader conversing with an official, who is either an usher, a protocol officer, or a translator. Behind them are other court officials, waiting to be summoned by the Divan.

The Kubbealtı appears in the background with five ministers attending the Divan. The dignitaries are discussing the letter from Ferdinand brought by his envoys. The personage seated in the center, wearing a richly brocaded blue kaftan, most likely is the grand vezir İbrahim Paşa, who is refusing to grant any of the archduke's requests. The pair of courtiers in the chamber on the far left seem to be speculating on the outcome of the proceedings.

The painter builds up the composition by relying on diagonal lines that are repeated in the gestures and gazes of the figures and that culminate at the top with the ministers. These formal devices also create a tension, reflecting the anxiety of the participants about the decision of the council. In spite of this, the artist has produced a two-dimensional and highly abstract image devoid of any spatial progression by employing the motif of tufts of grass outside the structures as well as within the chambers.

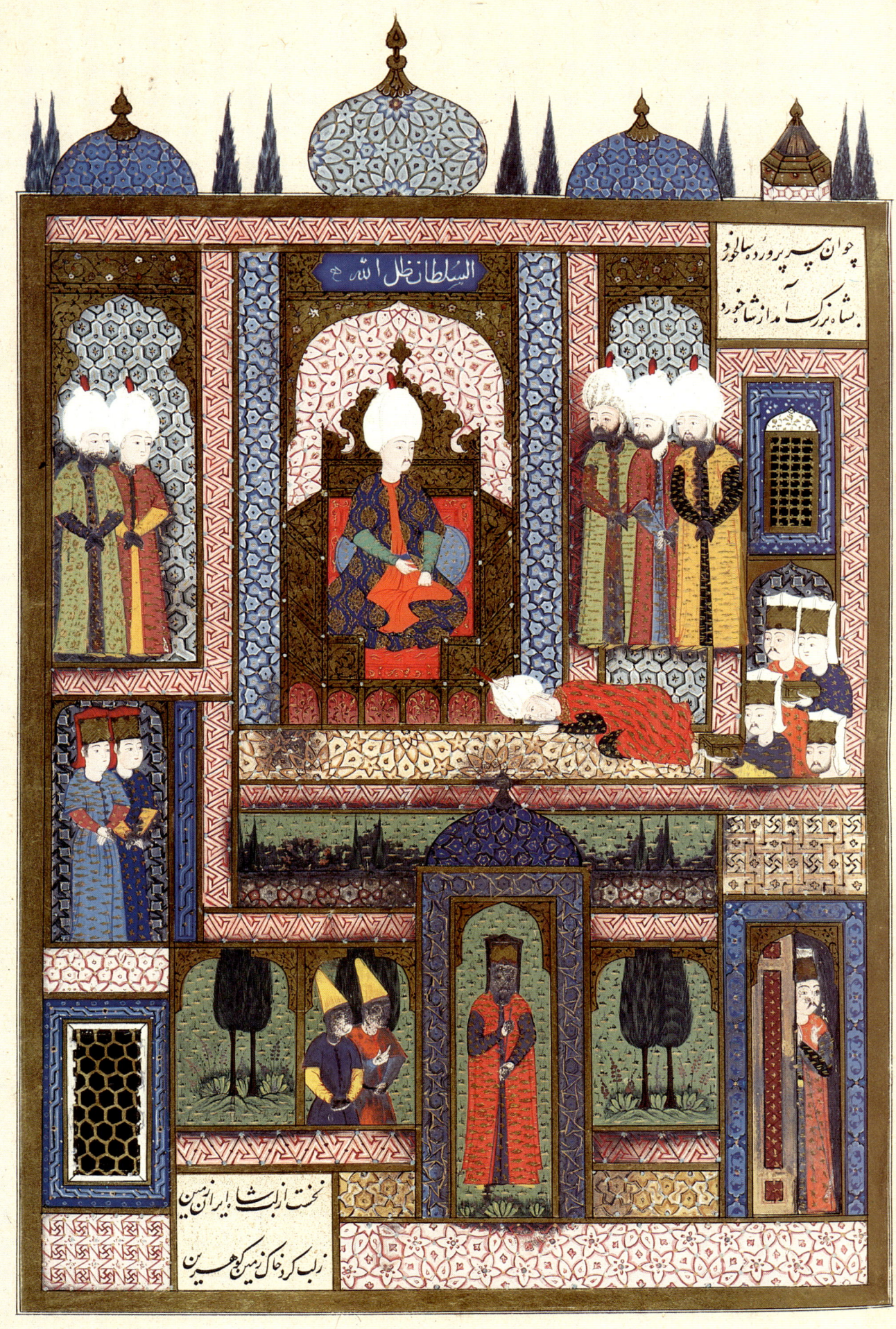

31. Reception of the Iranian Ambassador

(folio 332a)   Painter A

FERDINAND TRIED TO form an alliance with the Safavid ruler, Şah Tahmasp, attempting to put pressure on the Ottomans from both sides. He wrote to the şah, asking him to join forces against the sultan. When Tahmasp sent him a favorable reply, Ferdinand exposed the confidential answer. The şah, afraid that his outright support of Ferdinand might be detrimental to his own security, sent an envoy to İstanbul to apologize to the sultan. Süleyman reprimanded the şah but accepted his regrets.

The sultan soon embarked on his fifth sefer-i hümayun (his third to secure Hungary), leaving İstanbul on 25 April 1532. The army took the same route as before, traveling through Edirne, Filibe, Sophia, and Nish, heading this time towards Güns, the Austrian stronghold.

Süleyman, attended by his ministers and servants, is receiving Şah Tahmasp's envoy in the Arz Odası immediately behind the Babüssaade, the gate leading into the third courtyard of the palace. The sultan, seated on a throne placed slightly off-center, gestures towards the elderly Safavid ambassador, who prostrates himself on the ground. A pair of iç oğlans and three vezirs participate in the ceremony. Behind the envoy are several officers who carry two jeweled boxes as a part of the gifts presented on behalf of the şah. Standing below the iç oğlans are the sultan's Has Oda ağas. In the foreground a kapıcı guards the domed entrance to the third courtyard while two servants walk in the garden. An officer looks out from a doorway on the lower right, his gaze directed beyond the picture frame.

The solemn expressions of Süleyman and his ministers suggest that they have some reservations in accepting the şah's apology. Displeased with Tahmasp's attempt to join their arch-enemy Ferdinand, they accept his expression of regret without much enthusiasm. The indisputable superiority of the Ottoman sultan over his opponents, particularly over the Safavids, is stressed by the inscription placed over the throne: *el-sultan zillullah*, "the sultan, the shadow of God," a title emphasizing his preeminence among the Muslim rulers.

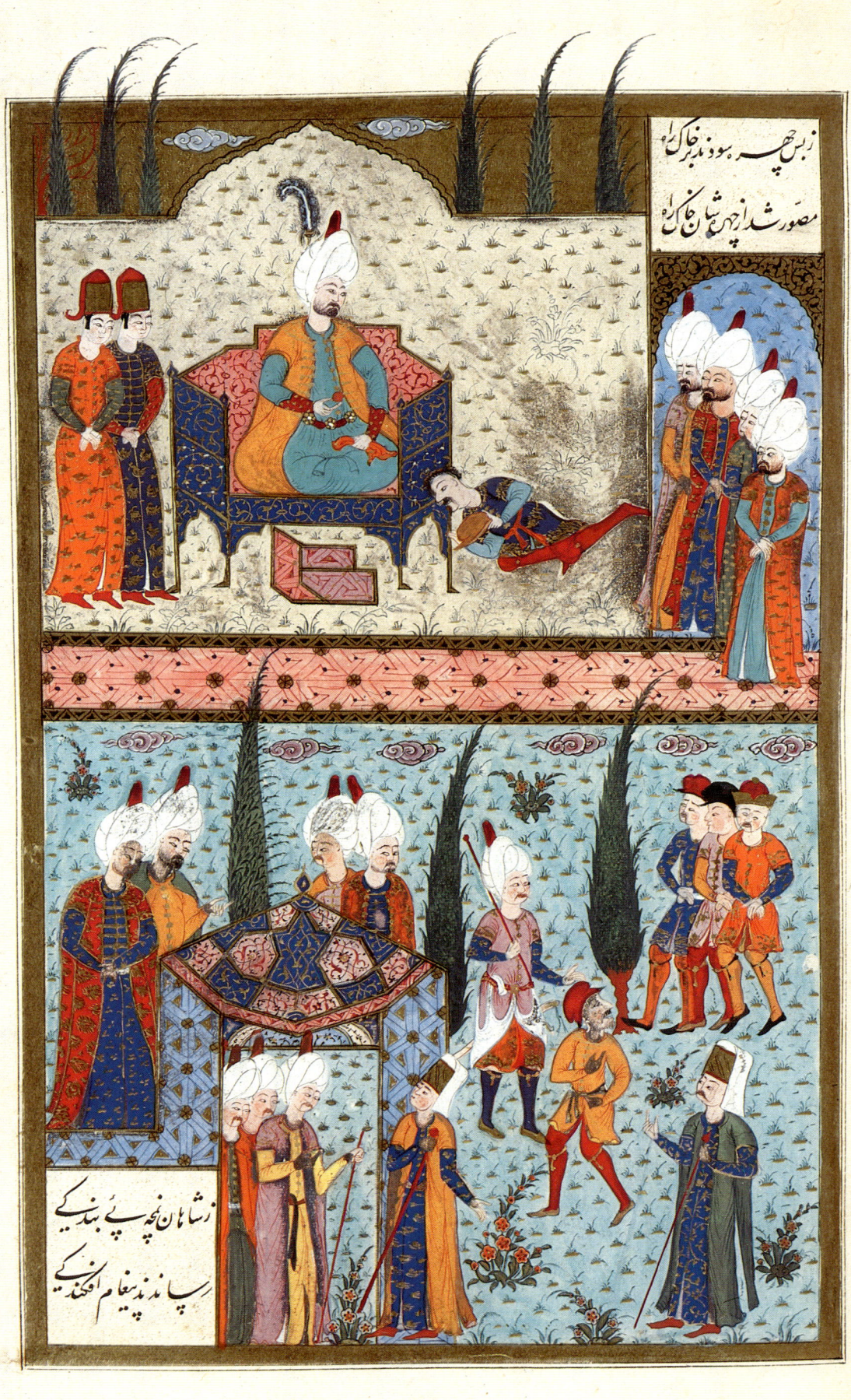

32. Reception of the Austrian Ambassador
(folio 337a)   Painter B

WHEN SÜLEYMAN stopped at Nish on 12 June 1532, an Austrian delegation came to his camp to discuss a peace treaty. It included the Count of Lamberg, who had been sent to İstanbul two years before. Süleyman received the delegation, listened to their offers, and refused to accept the conditions, which were more or less similar to those presented on the earlier mission. Also, it would have been difficult to accept any peace proposals from the Austrians in view of the belligerency they had shown in besieging Budapest during the winter of 1530-1531. The Ottoman garrison, supplemented by the divisions under the Semendria sancakbeyi, Mehmed Bey, had successfully defended the city.

Süleyman dismissed the Austrian delegates and moved on to Belgrade, where the army halted for about two weeks between 25 June and 8 July.

> The scene takes place in an abstracted setting with landscape elements and architectural components illogically juxtaposed. The background shows the sultan enthroned under a lobed arch with the Austrian ambassador kneeling on the ground while clutching his hat. A pair of Has Oda ağas and four vezirs attend the reception. The field of the chamber is covered with tufts of grass. Separated by a horizontal band of geometric decoration, identical tufts of grass reappear in the courtyard in the front, creating an ambiguity of interior and exterior spaces.
>
> In the foreground is a domed gateway leading into the courtyard where the kapıcıs, ushers, officers, and Austrian envoys converse casually in groups. The Austrians wear low-brimmed hats or caps, belted short tunics, and leggings. The three young delegates are visibly uncomfortable while their leaders appear more at home, animatedly joining the conversation.
>
> Painter B has chosen to show the 1532 reception of the Austrians in a setting recalling that of the Arz Odası in the Topkapı Palace, the traditional location for such ceremonies, even though the event takes place in the vicinity of Nish after Süleyman left the capital.

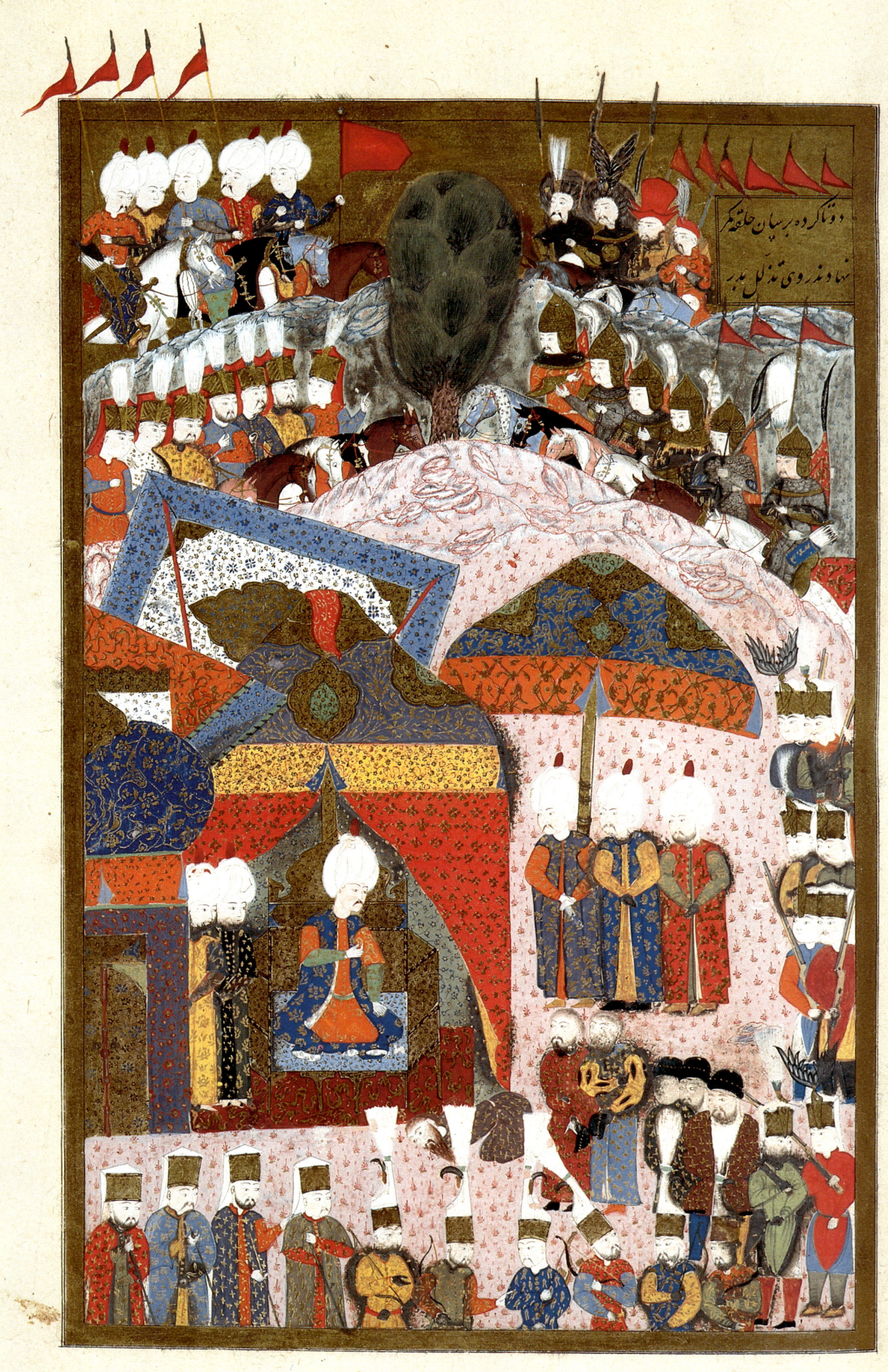

33. Reception of the French Ambassador

(folio 346a)   Painter A

WHEN THE ARMY halted in Belgrade, Süleyman received the French delegates sent by Francis I, now free in Paris. The French were greeted ceremoniously and a parade of the armed forces was arranged in their honor. The delegates, headed by Antonio Ricon, toured the Akıncı and Janissary Corps, visited the Anatolian and Rumelian regiments, and met with the commanders and vezirs. After being received by the sultan and allowed to kiss his hand, they presented Francis' letter reaffirming the Franco-Ottoman alliance.

The contrast between the receptions of the French and Austrian envoys was intentional: Süleyman was demonstrating to both Francis I and Ferdinand that his allies were always treated with honor and respect whereas his adversaries were demeaned and slighted.

> The magnificent reception of the ambassadors of Francis I, Süleyman's ally, takes place outside Belgrade, where the Ottoman army halted en route to Güns. The sultan, seated on a jeweled throne set up in a stunning otak and surrounded by other equally elaborate tents and canopies, is attended by his iç oğlans and vezirs. The chief of the delegates kneels before the sultan while five other Frenchmen wait their turn. Enclosing the reception area are various officers such as kapıcıs, solaks, and janissaries.
>
> Lined up behind the high hill with animated rocks are various regiments of the armed forces, including the akıncıs, flagbearers, armored cavalry, and janissary officers, all attired in their ceremonial garments.
>
> The French delegation wear small black hats and long robes. It is possible that the robes were meant to be hilats presented by the sultan. It was customary to place an expensive kaftan—sometimes two or more—on the shoulders of deserving dignitaries.

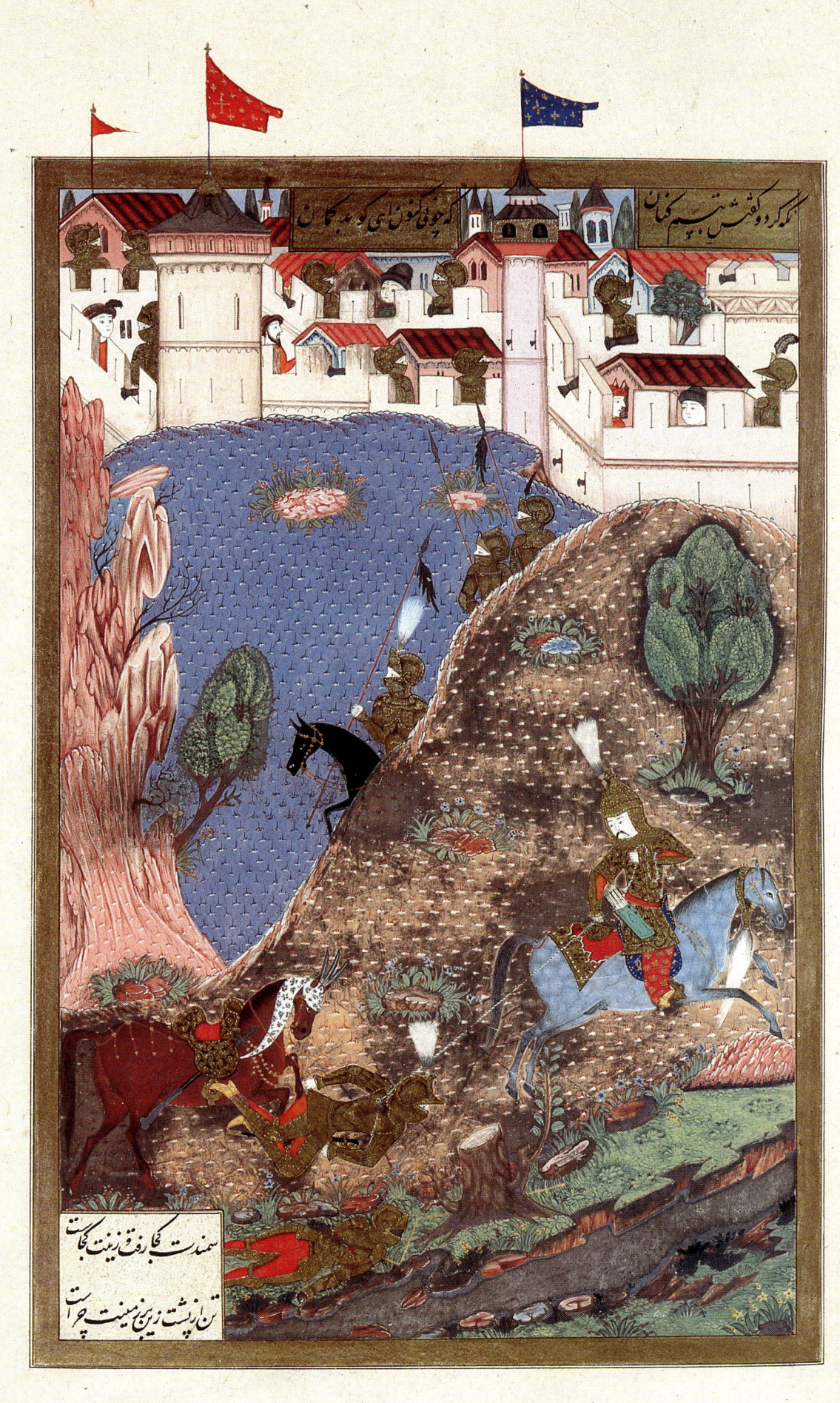

34. Battle of Güns

(folio 353a)   Painter A

GÜNS, ONLY NINETY kilometers (about fifty-six miles) south of Vienna, was defended by Nicolas Jurischitz, who had headed the 1530 delegation sent to İstanbul. The Ottomans arrived before the fortress on 10 August 1532 and laid siege.

The battle that followed resulted in casualties on both sides. Güns was able to withhold until 28 August. After its fall, the Ottoman army proceeded to capture Graz together with several other fortresses on the Güns-Graz road.

When Süleyman returned to İstanbul on 21 November, the city celebrated his victorious campaign with a five-day festival. The success of the campaign, however, was overshadowed by the news that Andrea Doria, a Genoese admiral once serving Francis I and now commanding the naval forces of Charles V, had attacked ports in Algeria and sailed through the straits of Messina, capturing Coron on the southwest coast of Morea. Ottoman supremacy in the Mediterranean was seriously threatened by this unexpected Habsburg victory.

In the beginning of 1533 another Austrian delegation arrived in İstanbul to discuss a peace treaty. The negotiations lasted until 22 June 1533, when a treaty was signed in which Ferdinand agreed to give up all claims to Hungary and to recognize the rule of John Zapolya, the sultan's vassal.

> The illustration represents one of the battles that took place during the siege of Güns. The scene, divided diagonally by a hill, depicts in the background the fortress with flags displaying crosses hoisted on its towers. Helmeted soldiers and civilians roam around the buildings, which are basilical in shape, have arched openings, or are attached to campaniles. Three fully armored soldiers, half hidden behind the hill, patrol the meadow in front of the city.
>
> In the foreground an Ottoman warrior gallops toward the right and lassoes an Austrian, pulling him off his horse. The body of another Austrian lies along the river that flows on the lower edge of the folio. The Ottoman, identified in the text as the akıncı Turhan Bey, wears a large plume on his helmet and a chain mail tunic. His captive, mentioned as being named Anton, the commander of the fortress, has a full body armor, similar to that worn by the other Austrian soldiers.
>
> The strong diagonal division of the scene is an unusual device in the illustrations of Painter A, who generally uses triangular or horizontal formations. A feeling of depth is created by the sharp drop from the high hill and crags down to a meadow leading to the fortified city in the background.

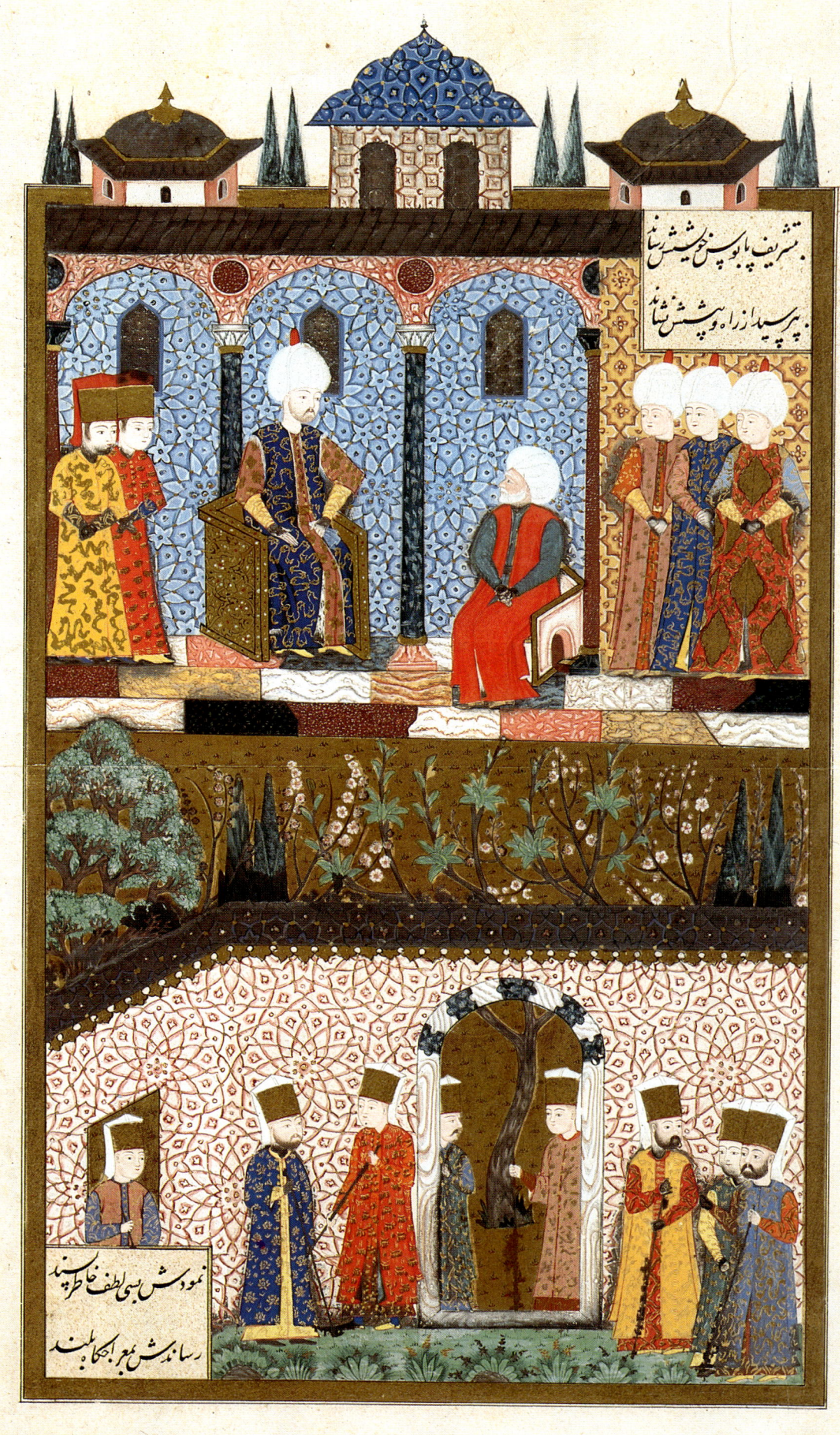

35. Reception of Barbaros Hayreddin Paşa
(folio 360a)   Painter A

SÜLEYMAN, CONCERNED ABOUT Andrea Doria's naval victories, invited to his court Barbaros Hayreddin, the famed seaman who ruled in Algiers. Barbaros Hayreddin landed in İstanbul with eighteen of his admirals on 27 December 1533. He put on a magnificent display, parading hundreds of prisoners carrying bags of money and objects made of silver and gold, beautiful female slaves dressed in valuable silks and bedecked with jewels, camels loaded with gifts, and rare and exotic African animals led by their keepers. Walking behind them were Barbaros Hayreddin and his admirals, dressed in modest attire. Thousands of residents lined the streets to watch the spectacle put on by this formidable sixty-three-year-old seaman.

The next day Barbaros Hayreddin and his retinue were received by the sultan and were presented hilats. The sultan discussed with him the problem caused by Andrea Doria and assigned him the task of finding a solution. Barbaros Hayreddin did not disappoint the sultan, for he immediately set about rebuilding the navy, adding over sixty new warships, and captured Coron and Tunis the following summer. In recognition of these achievements, he was then given the title of beylerbeyi and put in command of the imperial navy, becoming the kaptan-ı derya. The next decade proved to be the greatest period for Ottoman victories at sea under the able and energetic command of this remarkable admiral.

One of the most intimate scenes in the manuscript, this painting shows the sultan conversing with Barbaros Hayreddin in front of the arcades of the third courtyard. Süleyman, reserving a jeweled gold chair for himself, has allowed his esteemed guest to be seated in his presence, giving him a similar but simpler piece of furniture. The event takes place after the formal reception in which Barbaros Hayreddin and his admirals were greeted by the members of the Divan. Now Süleyman confers with the renowned seaman, discussing in detail Mediterranean policies and the problem created by Andrea Doria. There is a sense of privacy and intimacy to the scene despite the presence of the Has Oda ağas and iç oğlans.

The foreground is a high wall with an entrance guarded by a number of kapıcıs, who quietly converse among themselves, echoing the relaxed atmosphere of the meeting above. Beyond the wall is a delightful garden abounding with flowering trees.

Barbaros Hayreddin sits obediently with his hands clasped on his lap looking up at the sultan. His face with a white beard and wrinkled skin appears to have been painted from life.

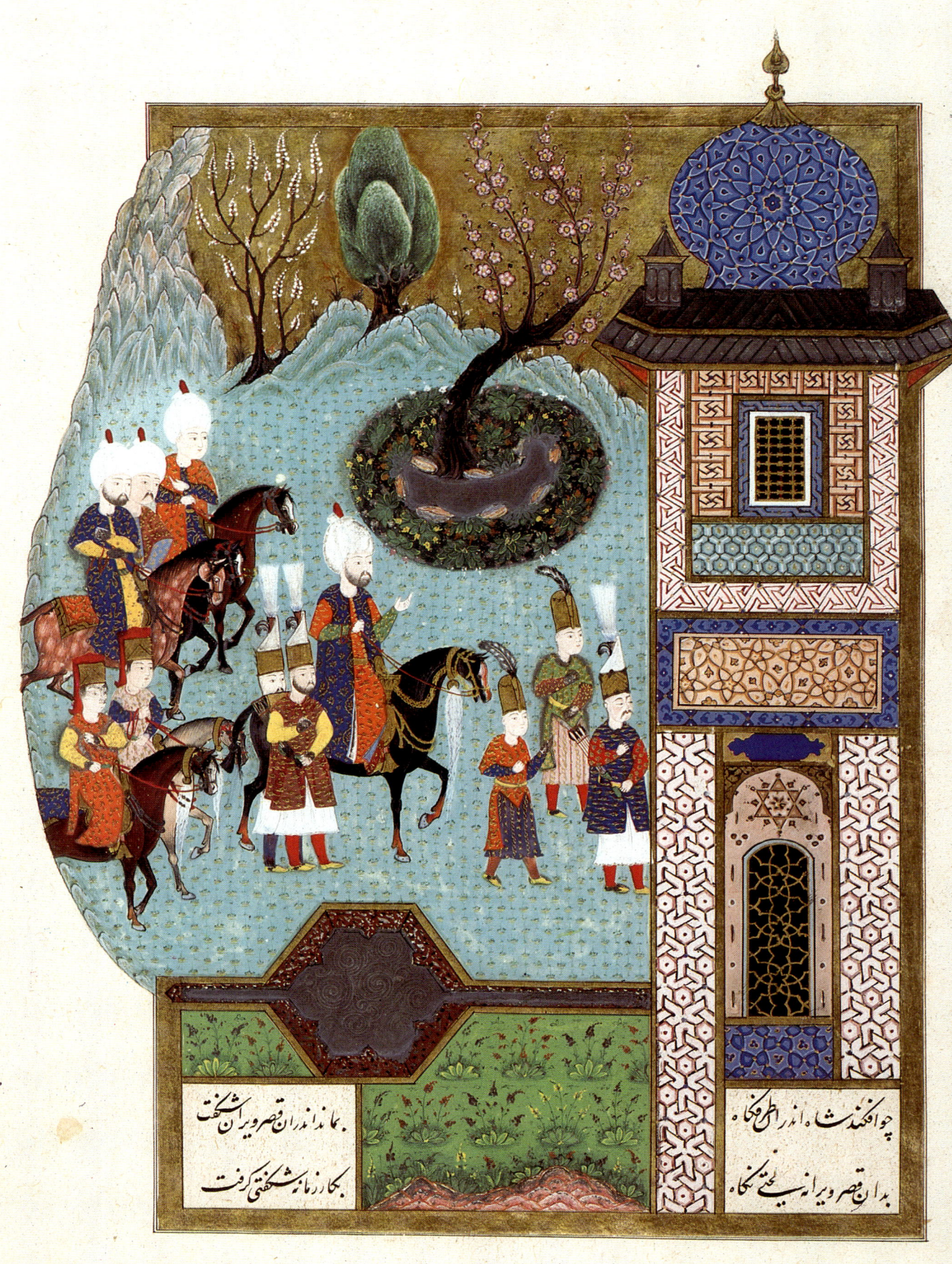

36. Arrival of Süleyman at Kasr-ı Şirin

(folio 367a) Painter A

CONFIDENT THAT HIS naval forces were in good hands, Süleyman now turned his attention to the troublesome affairs on his eastern frontier. His sixth sefer-i hümayun, directed against the Safavids, was long overdue and delayed because of the involvements with the Habsburgs in the west. Recently, the ruler of Bitlis had joined the şah, adding to the great number of disturbances.

Süleyman left Şehzade Mustafa in charge of the capital and departed on 11 June 1534, traveling through Konya, Sivas, and Erzurum. The grand vezir İbrahim Paşa had left İstanbul on 21 October 1533, proceeding toward Aleppo. When he arrived outside Tabriz in mid-July 1534 the city opened its doors to the Ottomans. Soon after, the emirs of Şirvan and Gilan also proclaimed allegiance to the sultan.

Süleyman arrived at Tabriz at the end of September and joined forces with İbrahim Paşa. The Ottoman army marched to Sultaniye, Kasr-ı Şirin, and then on to Baghdad. The sultan made a triumphal entry into Baghdad on 30 November 1534. He stayed there until April 1535, rebuilding a number of monuments, including the tomb of Ebu Hanife, the founder of the Hanefi sect of Islam to which the Ottomans belonged. Among the residents of this esteemed cultural capital was Fuzuli, the famous poet, who composed an ode commemorating Süleyman's arrival in Baghdad and later joined the sultan's court in İstanbul.

> During his campaign in Iran and Iraq, the sultan stopped at Kasr-ı Şirin to spend a night on the way to Baghdad. This site was named after the ruins of a Sasanian palace thought to have been built by the legendary king, Hüsrev (Khosrau), for his beloved, Şirin.
>
> Mounted on a black horse and attended by his peyks, solaks, and Has Oda ağas, Süleyman leads a group of three officials toward a magnificent building rising on the right. The two-story domed structure has a garden with a hexagonal pool fed by water channels in the front. The dome of the structure appears to be covered with blue tiles whereas the facade is decorated with panels composed of diverse geometric motifs.
>
> The landscape in the background is composed of delicately painted mountains, hills, and trees, and contains a pond from which a blossoming fruit tree rises. The meadow curves out into the left margin, wrapping around the riders.
>
> Süleyman is obviously remarking on the beauty of the building, which is indeed one of the more striking structures in the manuscript. The composition of the scene recalls the arrival of Hüsrev at Şirin's castle frequently depicted in sixteenth-century copies of Nizami's *Hamse* both in Safavid and Ottoman manuscripts.

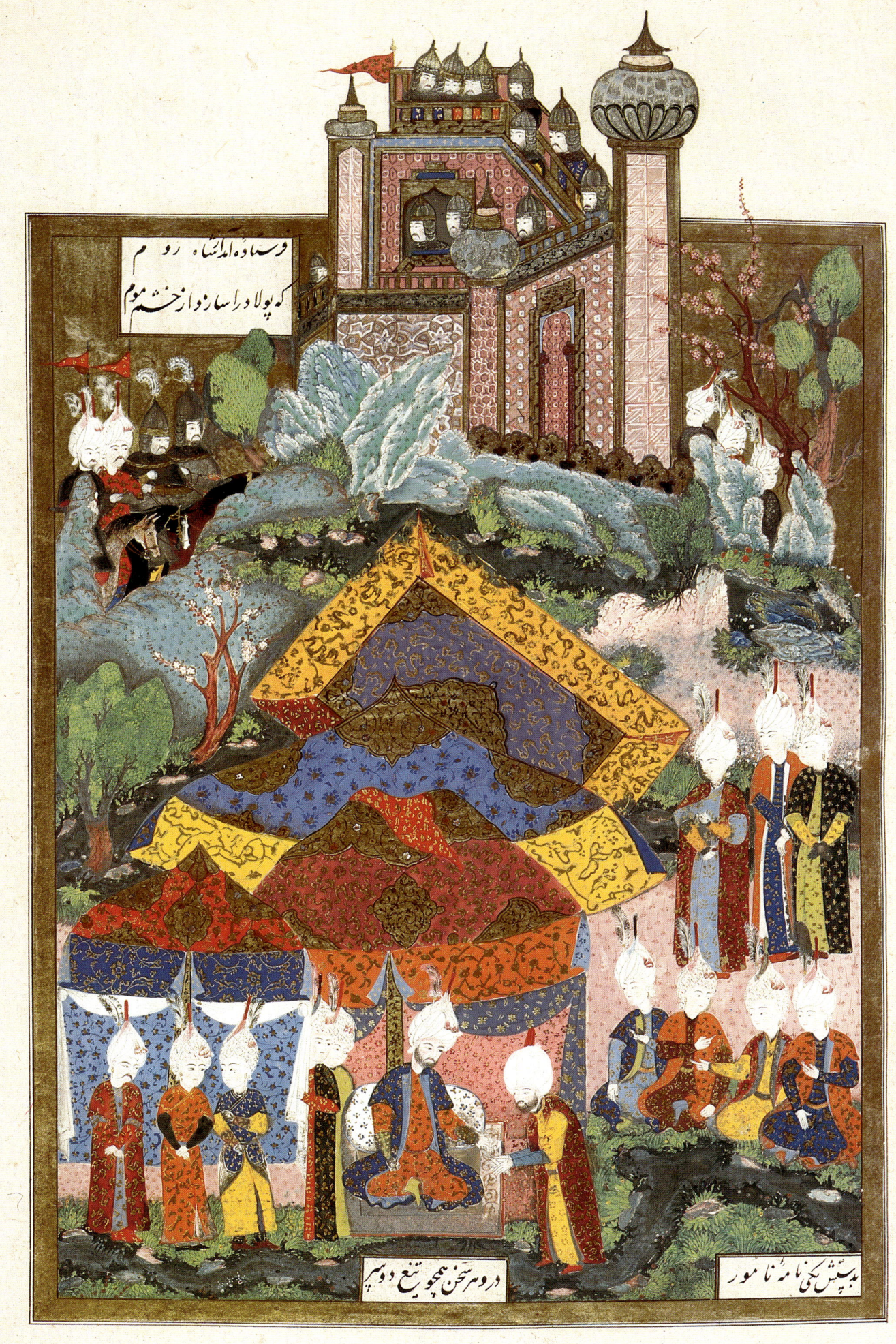

37. Tahmasp Receiving the Ottoman Ambassador

(folio 374a)   Painters A and D

WHILE SÜLEYMAN WAS occupied with the restoration of Baghdad, Tahmasp's forces captured Tabriz. On June 1535 the Ottomans reentered the capital of Azerbaijan, proclaiming supremacy over Tabriz for the third time (the first conquest was by Selim I in 1514, the second by İbrahim Paşa a year earlier). Tahmasp moved his court to Kazvin, then to Isfahan, withdrawing into the center of the country. During this campaign Sam Mirza, one of the şah's younger brothers, joined the Ottomans together with several commanders of such key fortresses as Bekir, Suhrab, and Gülgün.

Süleyman and Tahmasp exchanged emissaries but could not agree upon specific terms for a peace treaty. After Süleyman departed from Tabriz on 27 August, Tahmasp was back in the city. The conquest of the Irakeyn, or the two Iraqs as it was called in contemporary histories—one Irak-ı Arab (Arabian Iraq) with its capital at Baghdad and the other Irak-ı Acem (Iranian Iraq) with its traditional center at Hamadan—added Azerbaijan, the emirates of Şirvan and Gilan together with all of Iraq and its capital Baghdad to the Ottoman Empire. The Ottomans could not hold on to Tabriz. This status quo was unofficially accepted by both sides.

Süleyman was back in İstanbul on 8 January 1536, his first campaign against the Safavids concluding victoriously and resulting in substantial territorial gains.

Although this illustration appears in the portion of the text that describes the voluntary submission of several Safavid fortresses and the presentation of the keys of these strongholds to the sultan, the camp depicted here cannot represent that of the Ottomans due to certain iconographic features. The elaborate tents set up along the banks of a river flowing in the foreground enclose a personage sitting on the ground, in contrast to the sultan who is always shown enthroned. This personage, as well as his attendants, courtiers, and commanders, wears an elongated turban that tapers toward the thin tall baton which was fashionable in the Safavid court. The same headdress appears on the figures flanking the spectacular fortress soaring above the rocky mountains in the background.

In addition, not a single figure is attired in an outfit worn by Ottoman officers and attendants such as Has Oda ağas, peyks, solaks, and janissaries, with the exception of the dignitary bending in front of the seated personage and presenting a letter. This figure is shown wearing the rounded turban associated with the Ottoman court. The painting obviously represents the camp of the Safavids with Şah Tahmasp receiving an envoy from Süleyman. It refers to a previous episode in which the sultan sent a message to the şah.

The fortress in the background projects over the frame. It has a large entrance portal flanked by two minarets and the facade is covered with tiles and brickwork, both of which are characteristic of sixteenth-century Safavid architecture. The fortress probably represents Tabriz, which changed hands a number of times during the campaign. It is guarded by helmeted soldiers, presumably belonging to the Safavid army. Tahmasp appears to have retained Tabriz while forced to give up Iraq and parts of Georgia and Azerbaijan.

Painter A's hand is visible in the overall composition as well as in architectural and landscape features, decorative furnishings, and select figures, including the şah and the Ottoman ambassador. His assistant, Painter D, was responsible for the attendants and courtiers and for the grouping of the figures. His reliance on Iranian models and training in Tabriz is also visible in the other scenes on which he collaborated with Painter A (see 51 and 56).

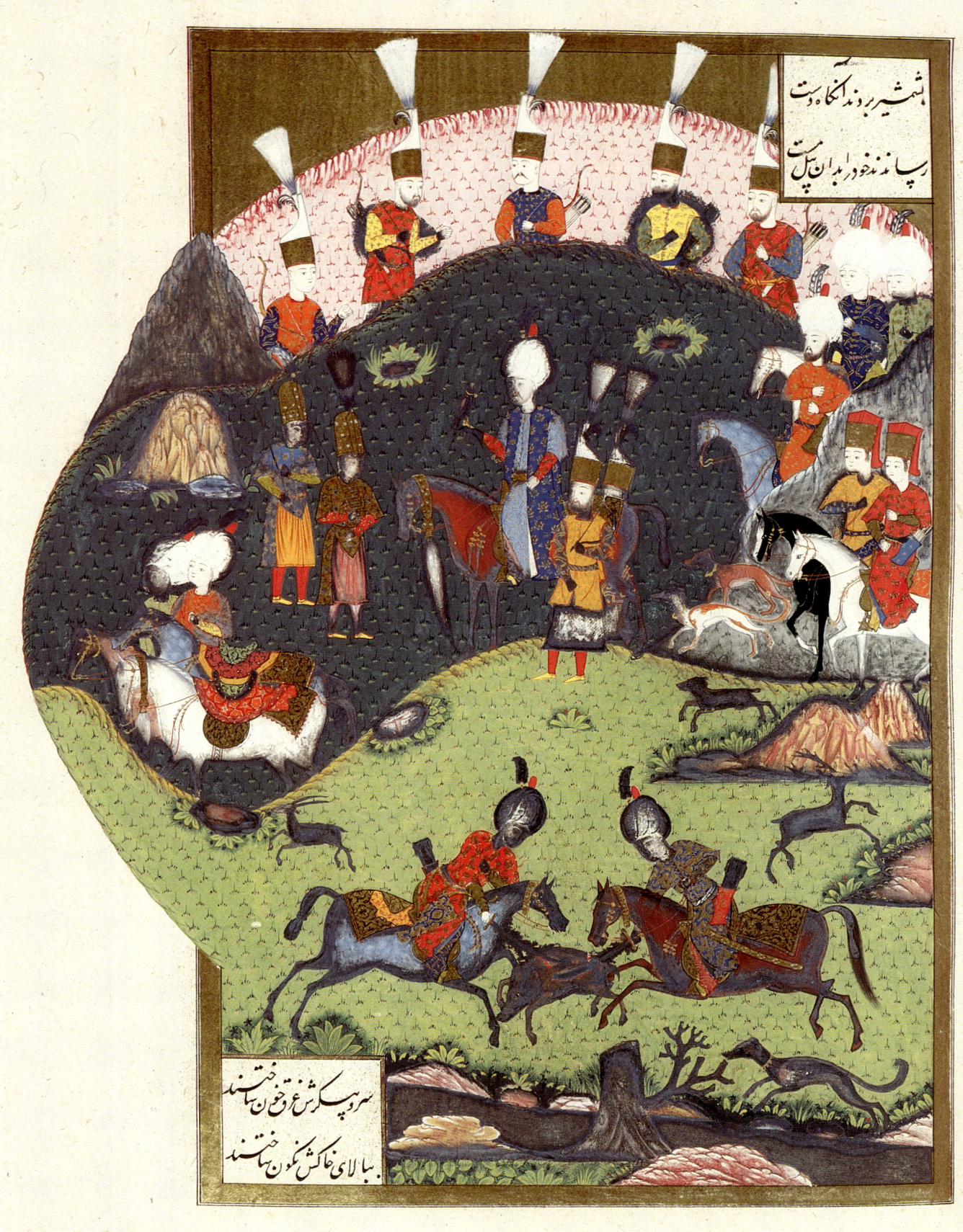

38. Süleyman Hunting with Mehmed and Selim

(folio 393a)   Painter A

ALTHOUGH THE CAMPAIGNS to Iraq and Iran extended the Ottoman frontier to the Arabian Gulf, İbrahim Paşa was blamed for failing to secure Tabriz. He had also made a number of hasty and overreaching decisions and proclamations that were considered treacherous; and he had aroused the enmity of the other vezirs and, more significantly, of Hürrem by his arrogance and delusion of grandeur. Accused of treason, he was executed on 15 March 1536 and replaced by Ayas Mehmed Paşa.

The following year Süleyman embarked on his seventh sefer-i hümayun. The capture of Tunis by Charles V and Venetian activities at sea provoked his only naval campaign, which was directed against the island of Corfu on the Adriatic Sea. On 17 May 1537 Süleyman, joined by Şehzades Mehmed and Selim, led the army to Filibe and Avlonya (Valona). Barbaros Hayreddin Paşa, commanding the navy, had already set sail for Italy.

This campaign, called the Pulya (Pulia) campaign since it was designated as a prelude for the conquest of Italy, was inconclusive and Süleyman had to abandon the siege on 6 September. He returned home by way of Manastır (now Bitola) and Salonica, stopping at Yenice (twenty-seven kilometers or some seventeen miles northwest of Salonica) on the Vardar River to hunt with his sons.

> The painting of Süleyman hunting with his sons along the Vardar River is divided into three horizontal registers by the rolling hills and depicts the princes galloping towards each other in the foreground. Şehzade Mehmed and Şehzade Selim have caught a wild boar, which they slay with swords. Other game animals, including a deer and gazelle, scramble about the field while a hunting dog, assisting the princes, runs along the shores of the river placed at the bottom of the folio.
>
> Süleyman, with a hawk perched on his hand, rides behind the hill, accompanied by his peyks and solaks. Extending into the margin on the far left are attendants leading spare horses. Opposite are more hunting dogs, a pair of mounted Has Oda ağas and other officers. Additional solaks placed between the hills in the background stand in a semicircular formation, enclosing the scene.

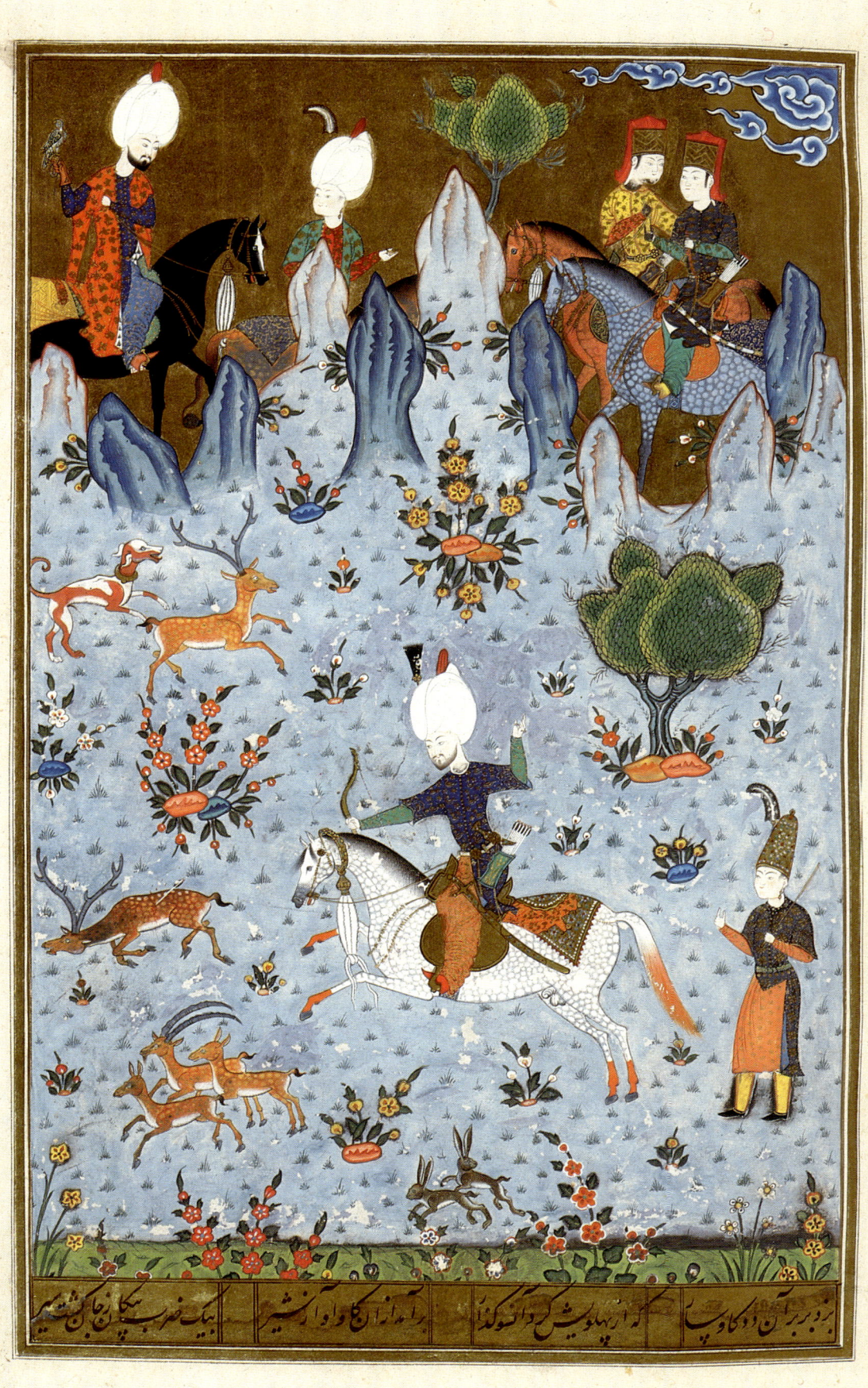

39. Süleyman Hunting Deer

(folio 403a)   Painter C

SÜLEYMAN'S EIGHTH sefer-i hümayun took place between 8 July and 27 November 1538, and resulted in the annexation of Bucak (southern Moldavia). On the way back Süleyman was given the news of the Ottoman naval victory at Preveza. On 28 September Barbaros Hayreddin Paşa had defeated the armada commanded by Andrea Doria, which was composed of the combined naval forces of the Holy Roman Empire, the papacy, Venice, Genoa, Florence, Portugal, and the Knights of Saint John at Malta. Barbaros Hayreddin Paşa had devastated the enemy in merely five hours, inflicting such a blow that it could not recover for nearly four decades.

During the campaign the emir of Basra had accepted Ottoman suzerainty and presented the key to his domain when Süleyman stopped in Edirne in late July. Now that the Ottomans were masters in the Mediterranean and the Arabian Gulf, they were able to extend their power to the other seas as well, including the Indian Ocean. Hadım Süleyman Paşa, who set sail on the Indian Ocean against the Portuguese, conquered Aden on the way and landed at Gujerat that summer. He established an Ottoman outpost in Yemen on his way back the following year.

> The second illustration executed by Painter C (see also 29) represents the sultan hunting at Babadağ in Dobruja en route to Moldavia. Süleyman rides in the center of the scene, hitting a spotted deer with his arrow. A peyk joins him on the field, which is covered with clusters of flowers and has a rounded tree growing from a group of rocks; scattered around are running hares, a buck with two does, and a dog chasing a deer. Behind the craggy rocks in the background are several riders, including a pair of Has Oda ağas and an officer holding a hawk.
>
> The sparse and uncomplicated composition with a few large and slim figures reflects the hand of an artist trained in the style of Kazvin. The formulaic hunt could have illustrated any number of Iranian epic or literary texts had it not been for the Ottoman types—the peyk and the Has Oda ağas—included in the scene.

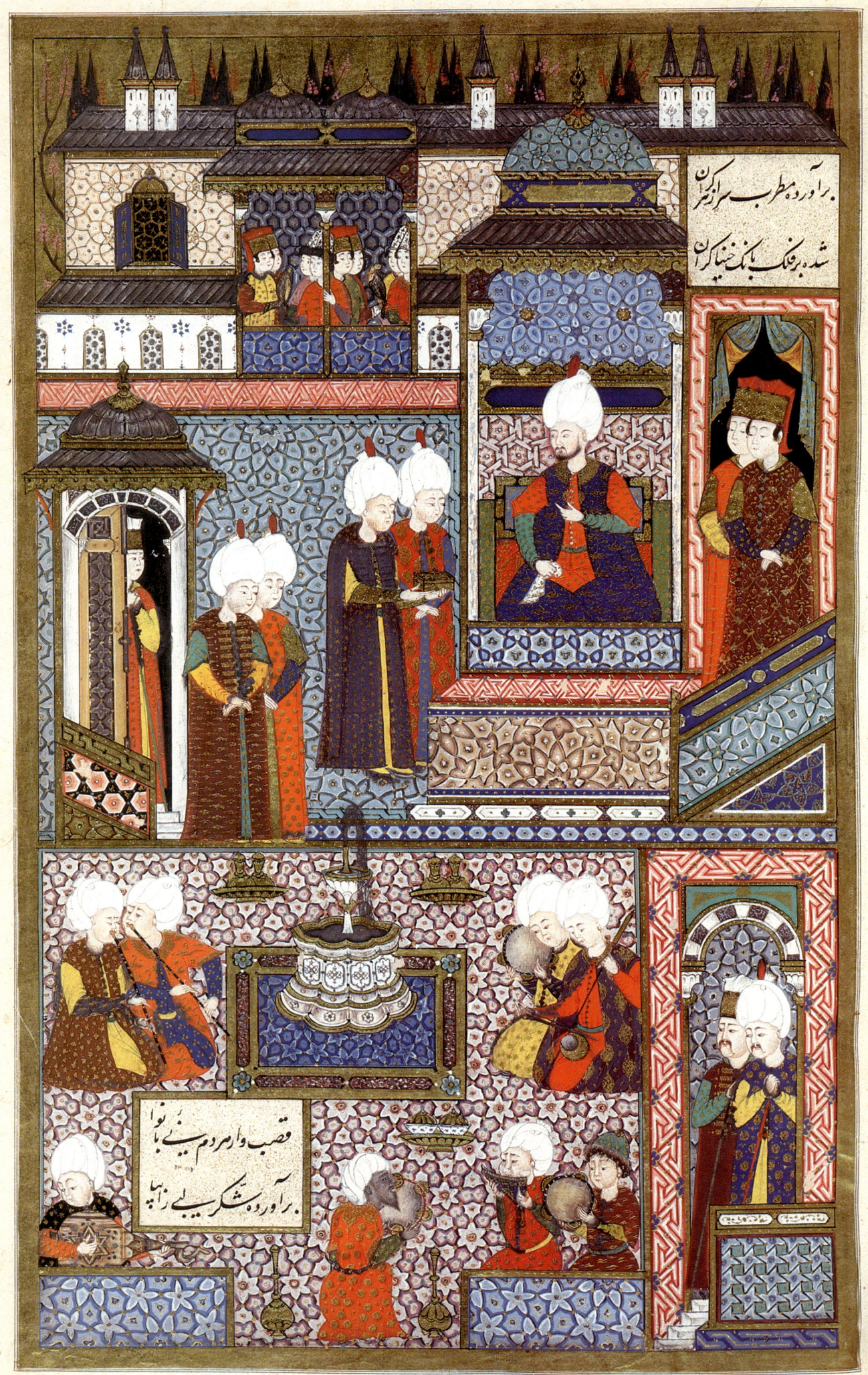

40. Circumcision Festival of Bayezid and Cihangir

(folio 412a)   Painter A

ON 11 NOVEMBER 1539 the two younger princes, Bayezid and Cihangir, were circumcised. The festival arranged in their honor was doubly joyous since it also celebrated the marriage of Süleyman's daughter Mihrimah to Rüstem Paşa, who was later to become the grand vezir.

Similar to the festival of 1530 given in honor of the elder princes, Mustafa, Mehmed, and Selim, this two-week event took place at At Meydanı and included a variety of performances, competitions, and games.

Süleyman, whose first two decades of rule had justly earned him the title Magnificent, was now a seasoned monarch, loved and respected by his subjects, and feared by his enemies. His navy had just conquered Castelnuovo, forcing the Venetians to sign a peace treaty in which they paid substantial sums of money and gave up a fortress on the Dalmatian coast together with a number of islands in the Aegean.

One of the masterpieces of Painter A, the scene is built up of various highly ornate units that represent different architectural components and create a kaleidoscopic effect. A vibrating spatial relationship is produced by receding and advancing planes; depth is suggested by arches and doorways with half-hidden figures in the background. But as in some of the other interior scenes by this painter, strong decorative elements counteract the depth and lend the work a two-dimensional quality.

The event most likely takes place in the Has Oda in the third courtyard of the palace. This pavilion has a marble fountain in the antechamber and a domed built-in throne in the corner of the elevated inner chamber. The composition, divided into three horizontal registers with some overlapping elements, shows the entrance to the Has Oda on the lower right, guarded by two officials. Gathered around the fountain nearby are eight musicians. On the lower left a lute player plucks the strings of his instrument while directing his gaze outward. In the center a dark-skinned man holds a tambourine; he faces a pair playing panpipes and a second tambourine. The dark-skinned figure, shown in profile with his mouth open, appears to be an Egyptian or Arabian singer. Other pairs of musicians play flutes, a tambourine, and a small stringed instrument. Bottles and trays with small bowls and jars are placed between the figures.

Süleyman is seated on the large elevated throne surmounted by a dome. In one hand he holds a handkerchief and with the other gestures toward the two iç oğlans presenting him with a jeweled box. A pair of Has Oda ağas stand in a doorway next to the throne, its opening covered by curtains. To the left are two more court attendants and a kapıcı looking out from behind a half-open door in a domed entrance that leads into the two-storied structure in the background. This structure contains a series of stained-glass windows and chimneys, together with a double-domed chamber that has an arcaded balcony overlooking the Has Oda. Seen behind its columns are four pairs of falconers and attendants.

The artist individualizes the figures and employs modeling in their faces. The depiction of the sultan is particularly remarkable: its specificity reveals a life study. Süleyman has an oval face with prominent cheekbones, aquiline nose, arched eyebrows, and almond-shaped eyes; he wears a mustache and trimmed beard.

The painting commemorating the circumcision of Bayezid and Cihangir is a tribute to the magnificence of the sultan and his court. Süleyman, forty-five-years old at the time, is portrayed as a mature and self-assured ruler of great stature who has successfully doubled the boundaries of his empire and multiplied the holdings of his treasury.

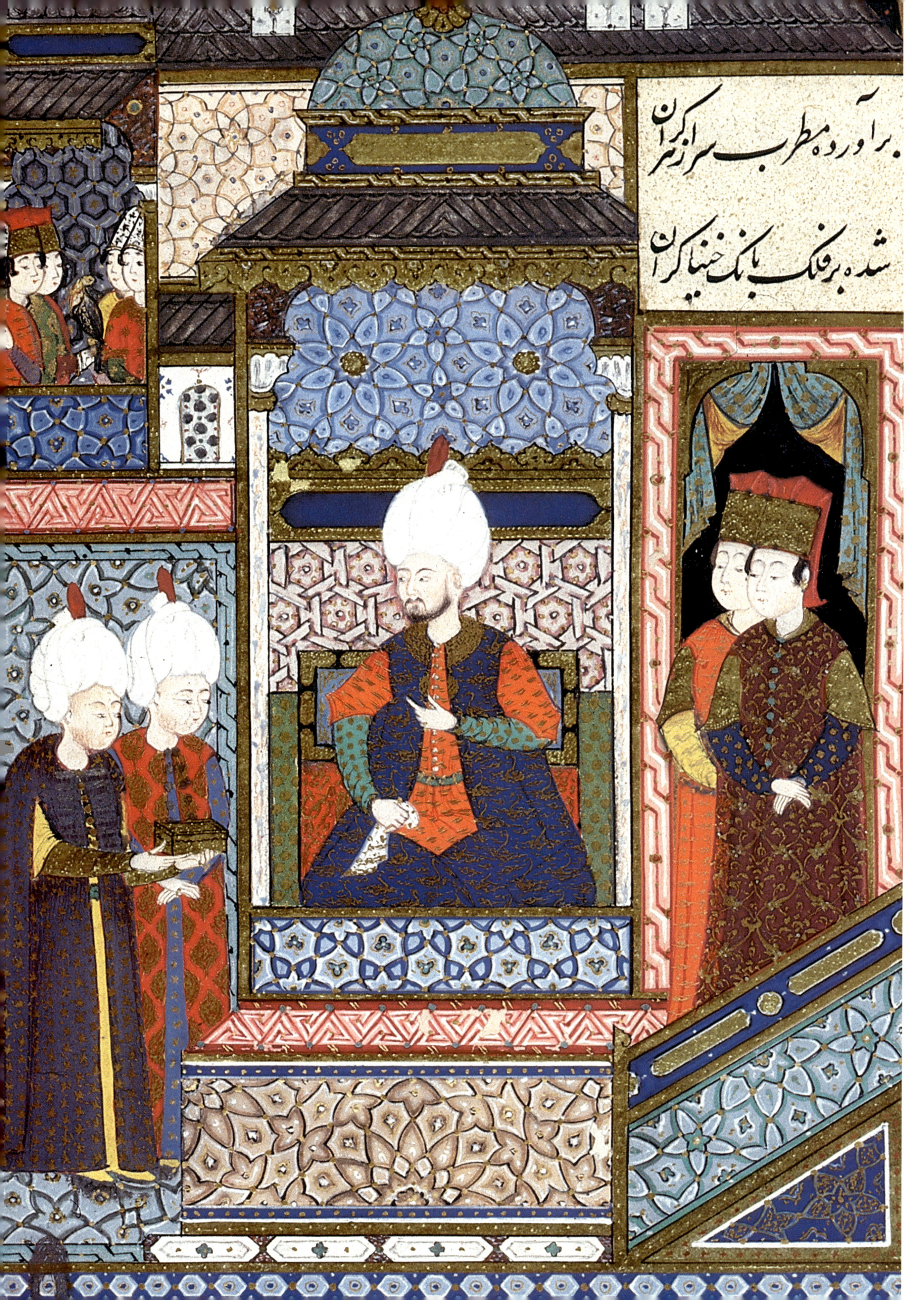

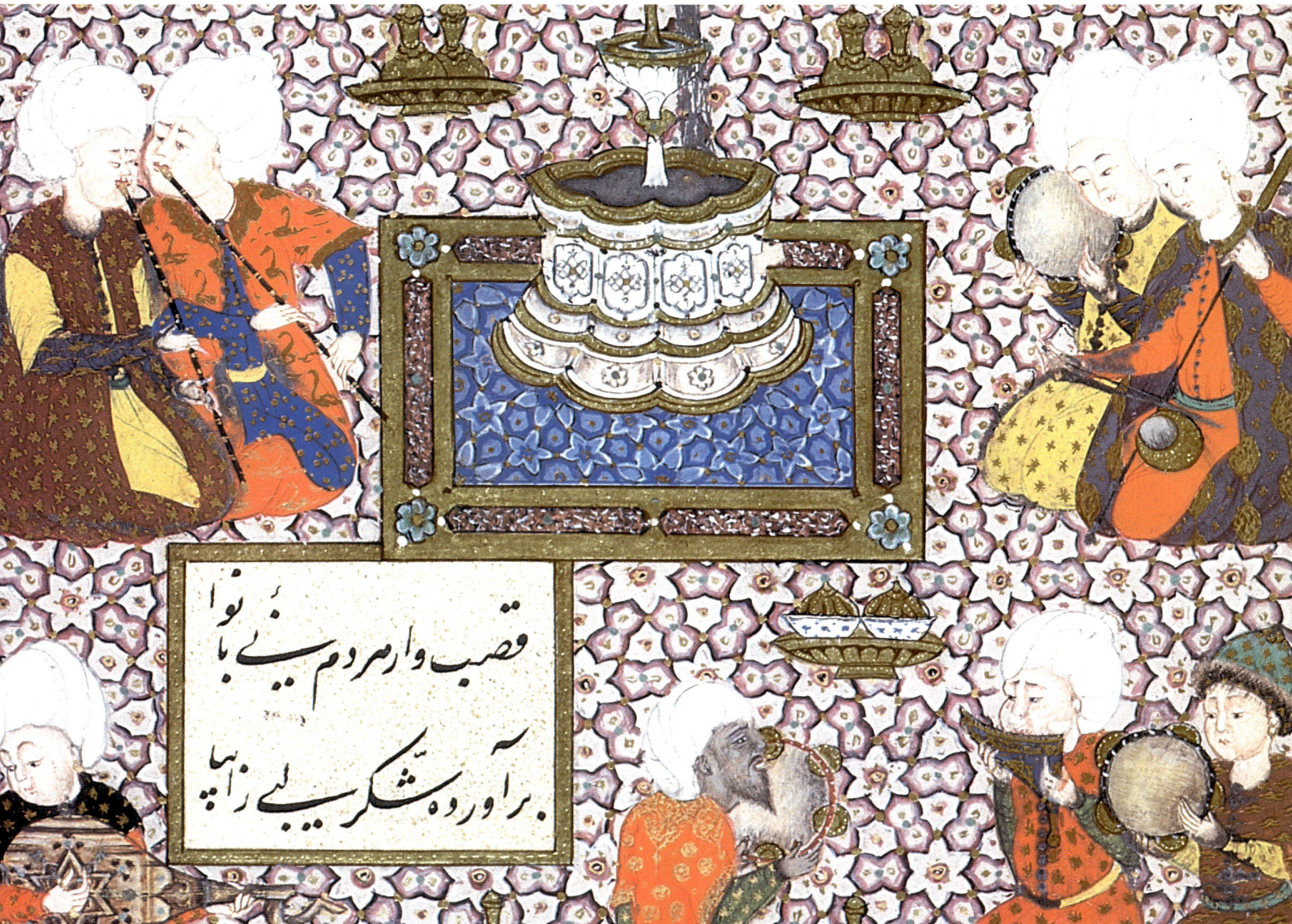

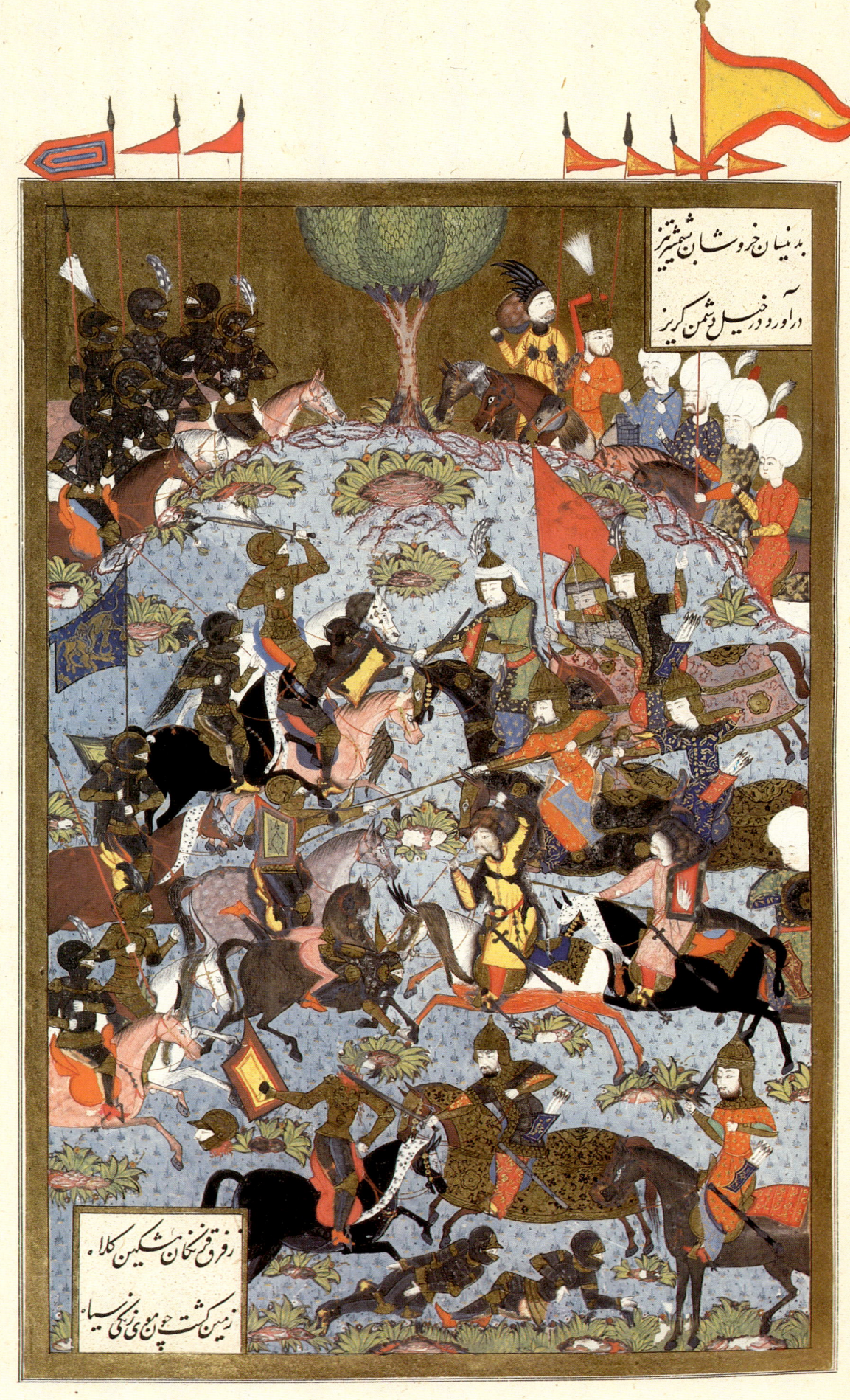

41. Battle of the Ottomans and Austrians

(folio 422a)   Painter A

THE DEATH OF John Zapolya in 1540 provided yet another opportunity for Ferdinand to lay claim to Hungary. Zapolya's wife, Isabella, the daughter of the king of Poland, Sigismund I, had given birth to a son weeks before his death. The infant Stephen Zapolya was now the king of Hungary and the voyvoda of Transylvania.

Ferdinand, refusing to accept the legitimacy of the child, took advantage of the situation and sent an army commanded by General von Reggendorf into Hungary. Mehmed Bey, the commander of the akıncı forces, was dispatched to aid the city.

Süleyman left İstanbul with his army on 20 June 1541. Joining him on his ninth campaign were his sons Selim and Bayezid, as well as the kazasker of Rumelia, Ebussuud, who was to become the empire's most celebrated şeyhülislam. The sultan had sent in advance an army commanded by the vezir Mehmed Paşa and the beylerbeyi of Rumelia Hüsrev Paşa together with a naval force led by Kasım Paşa.

The battle in which Mehmed Bey led his forces against Ferdinand's army under General von Reggendorf takes place on the hills outside Budapest. The two armies rush in from either side, clashing in the center in four irregular registers, their lively action recreating the sound and fury of the encounter. The Ottomans, leaping in from the right, attack the enemy with swords, spears, and arrows. Some of the soldiers wear light armor and helmets, others wear turbans or the soft flowing caps of the akıncıs. Mehmed Bey, distinguished by a white kerchief wrapped around his plumed helmet, holds a shield while slashing his opponent with a sword. Behind him is a flagbearer carrying a red banner.

The Austrians, wearing full armor and helmets, also use swords and spears. Their banner depicts a pair of gold lions attacking a horned animal on a blue ground. Two slain soldiers lie in the foreground; another is decapitated above, his head rolling off; and a third is speared and thrown from his horse. The Austrians are obviously losing the battle, their forces overwhelmed by the valor of the sultan's army.

Riding behind the hill in the background are additional groups of soldiers separated by a central tree. The Ottomans, on the right, consist of the mehter playing cymbals and drums, flagbearers, a delil with a feathered cap, and a janissary officer. Confronting them on the other side are the Austrians, all of whom wear heavy armor, some with feathers on their helmets. The delil and janissary seem oblivious of the approaching enemy, their attention drawn by an event that takes place beyond the picture frame.

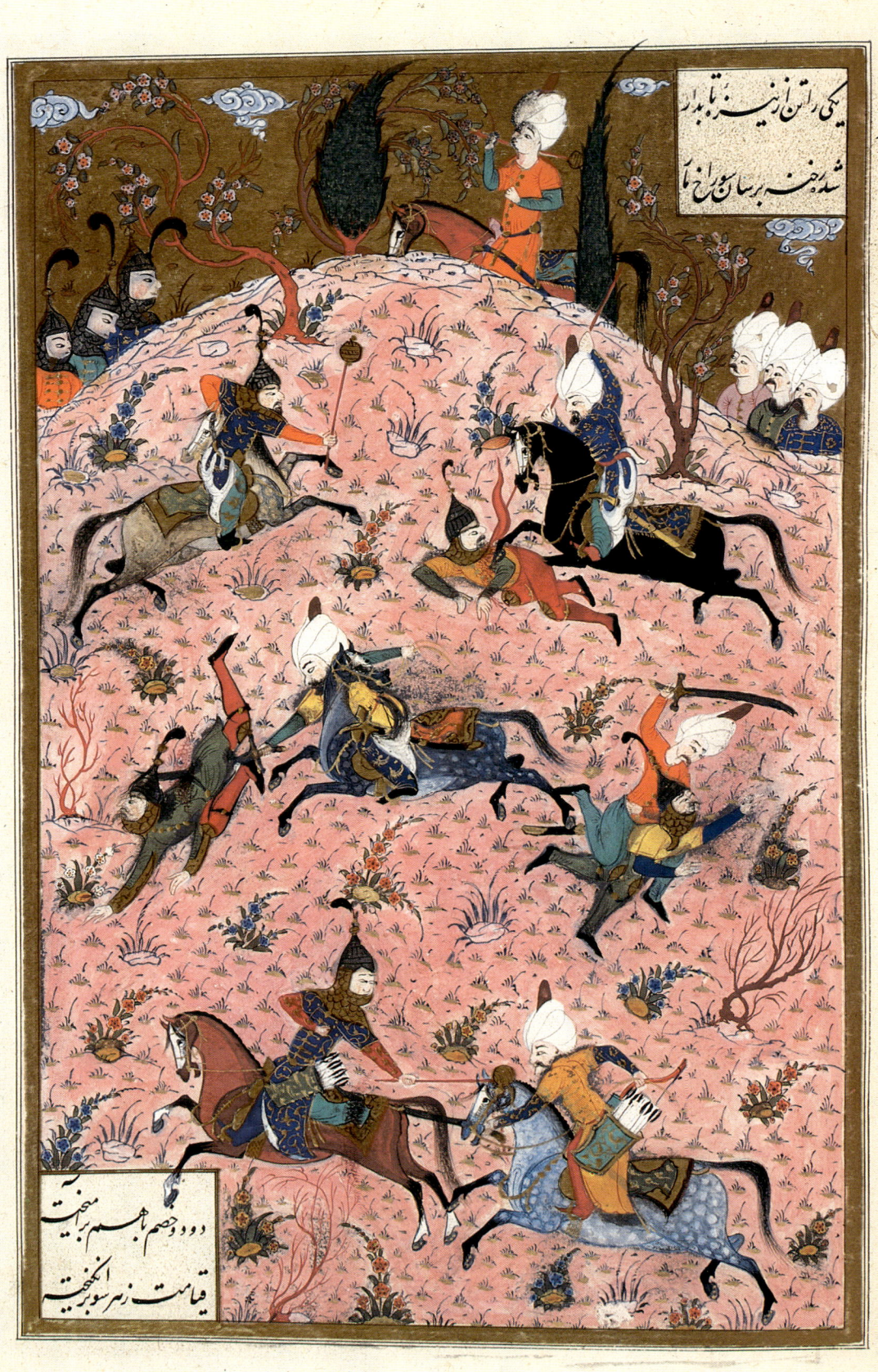

42. Battle of İstabur

(folio 433a)   Painter B

DURING THE BATTLE between the Ottomans and the Austrians outside Budapest, General von Reggendorf gathered his men on a hill, consolidating his forces. The Ottomans, led by Mehmed Bey, positioned themselves to create a square around the enemy and dug their trenches. This strategy, called *istabur* or *tabur*, gave its name to the celebrated battle.

The battle was won on 22 August 1541. General von Reggendorf was wounded and the Austrians started running away; they were pursued by the Ottomans, who captured many enemy soldiers. By the time Süleyman arrived in Budapest on 26 August, the city was under firm control.

> A battle that takes place during the sultan's ninth campaign to Hungary is represented as a sequence of individual confrontations, placed in three registers against a high hill. In the foreground an Ottoman holding a sword is pursuing an Austrian, who turns back to strike at him with his spear. Above, a pair of Austrians is being attacked by two Ottoman soldiers, one riding on a horse and the other jumping on the back of the enemy. On the top of the hill another Ottoman spears a fallen Austrian, whose comrade rushes to help him, swinging his mace. Additional members of the opposing armies stand behind the hill, in the center of which is a mace-bearing Ottoman officer.
>
> In contrast to the group attack represented in the previous scene, Painter B here shows several vignettes of fighting men, revealing a different approach to the depiction of battles. His scene is equally vivacious, but lacks the massive impact of his colleague's illustration.

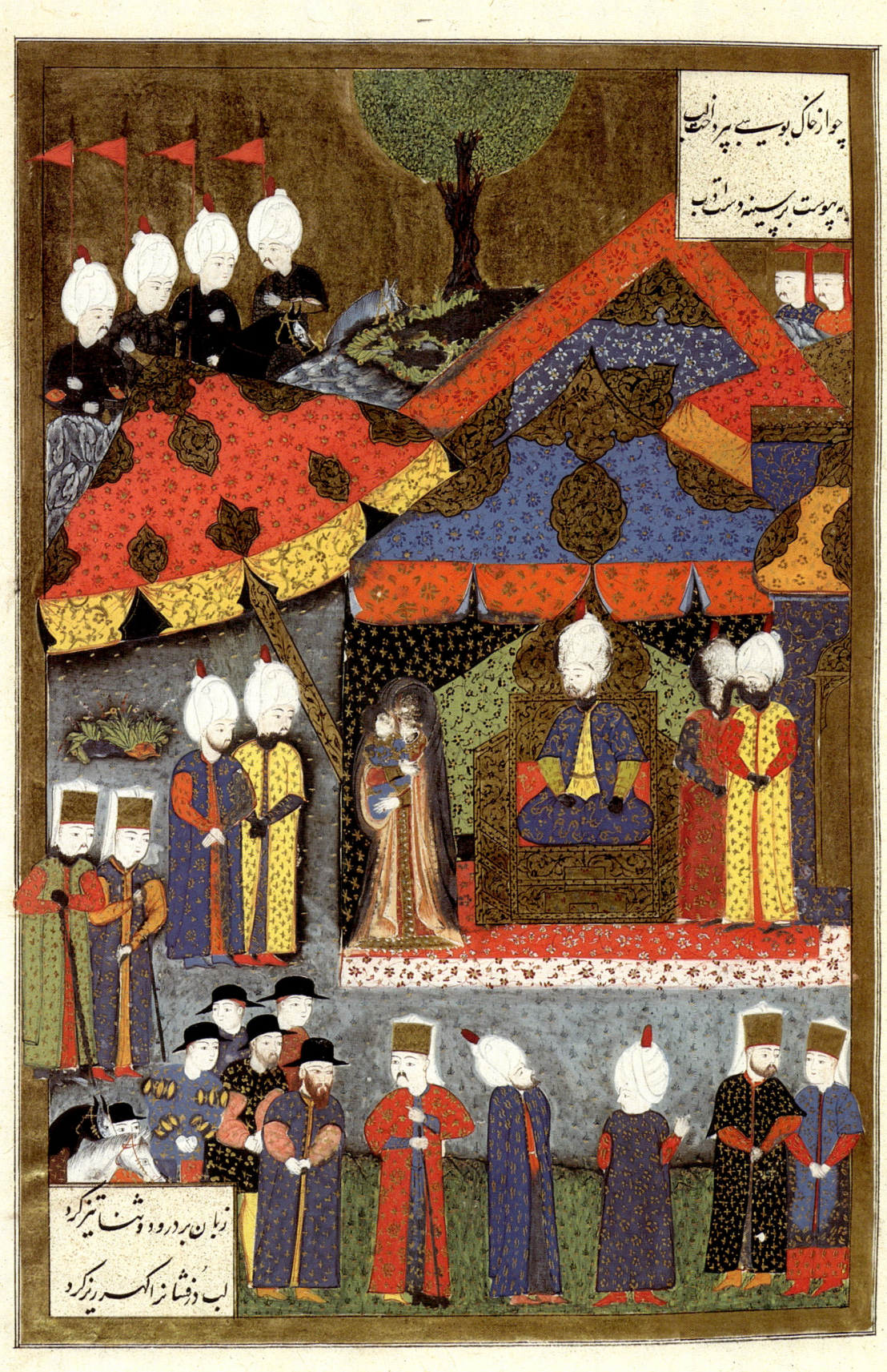

43. Reception of Queen Isabella and Infant Stephen

(folio 441a)   Painter A

SÜLEYMAN ORDERED THE imperial otak to be set up outside Budapest and received the infant king Stephen on 29 August 1541. The child was accompanied by dignitaries and the head bishop of Varadin, Martinuzzi, who had been appointed regent.

Süleyman held the thirteen-month-old Stephen (called Szigmund Janos) and patted his head. Şehzades Selim and Bayezid also held the child and played with him. Then the sultan's declaration that Hungary was to be formally annexed and become an Ottoman province was read to the citizens of the city. Stephen was allowed to retain the title of king and Ramazanoğlu Uzun Süleyman Paşa was appointed beylerbeyi of Budapest.

The sultan entered the city on 2 September and participated in the Friday prayer led by Ebussuud Efendi in the newly converted mosque. A few days later Queen Isabella and her son, together with Martinuzzi and the Hungarian court, moved to Lipva in Transylvania. Süleyman, feeling that he had secured Hungary for good, left Budapest and returned to İstanbul, arriving there on 27 November 1541.

> Süleyman, seated on his throne in the imperial tent set up outside Budapest, is conversing with Queen Isabella who carries in her arms the infant Stephen, heir to the Hungarian throne. Attending the sultan are two iç oğlans. Standing next to the queen are two princes; Bayezid, the older of the two, is bearded and Selim has a long mustache. Below them are two kapıcıs.
>
> Other kapıcıs, vezirs, and officers appear in the foreground, some turning in toward the sultan. One of them instructs a group of attentive Hungarian dignitaries wearing brimmed hats and short tunics or long robes. The foremost figure with a full beard most likely represents Martinuzzi. In the background is a hill with a tree and four cavalrymen, who are partially hidden by the canopy of the sultan's otak.
>
> The figure holding the infant recalls the Madonna-and-Child theme found in Christian painting. Isabella is attired in long flowing robes with a hooded cloak and carries her son in the crook of her arm.
>
> The scene is unique in that it represents a female monarch conversing with an Ottoman sultan. One wonders whether this tribute given to the queen, who was a Polish princess, was not in part intended to honor Süleyman's wife, Hürrem, also of Polish descent. It should be noted that whereas Arifi's text states that Isabella brought her son to the sultan, the other historians of the period state that the child was carried to the imperial otak by his nurse.

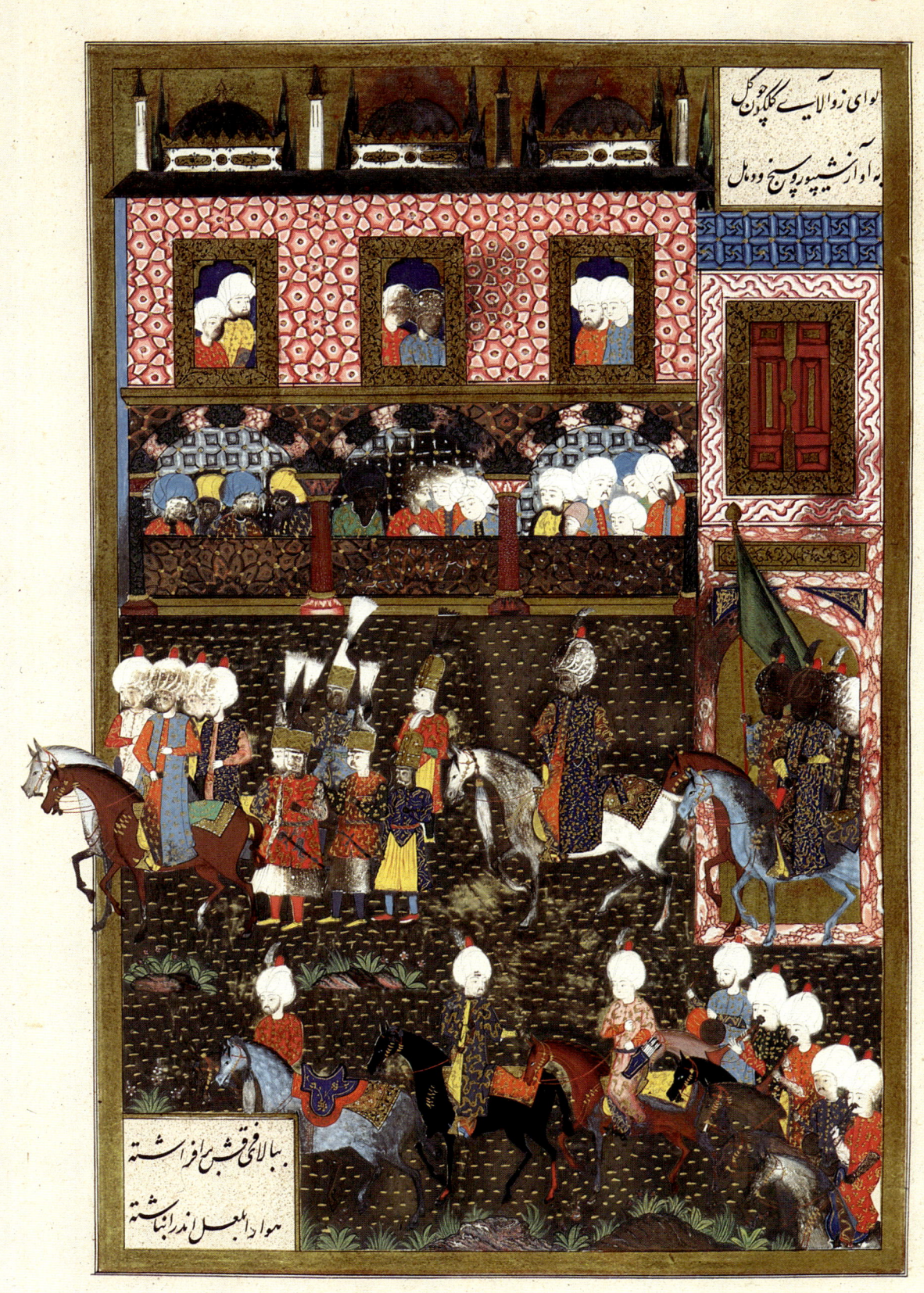

44. Princes Leaving for Their Provinces
(folio 445a)   Painter A

IT WAS TRADITIONAL FOR Ottoman princes to be assigned sancaks in the provinces and start their training in administrative, legislative, and military affairs at an early age. Süleyman himself had served as a sancakbeyi in several cities and his sons were given similar assignments.

In 1541 Şehzade Mustafa, the son of Gülbahar and the heir presumptive, was transferred from Manisa to Amasya. Şehzade Mehmed, the eldest son of Hürrem, was assigned to Manisa, a prestigious sancak traditionally given to the crown princes because of its proximity to the capital. This change of posts in favor of Şehzade Mehmed was thought to have been engineered by Hürrem, her first victory in her endeavor to assure the throne for one of her own sons.

The princes had a retinue similar to that of the sultan and were attended by solaks, peyks, and a small mehter. Their departure to a new post was always the occasion for a celebration. The princes, accompanied by their attendants, officers, and regiments, paraded through the city in a magnificent array of colorful banners and outfits before heading out to their provincial capitals.

> The scene represents a group of riders emerging from one of the gateways of the Topkapı Palace and proceeding in front of a structure with figures looking out from its windows and arched openings. In the center is a beautifully attired prince riding a white horse, preceded by solaks and peyks, who walk behind the four mounted officers heading the procession, their horses extending beyond the picture frame. Other officers pass through the gateway, one carrying a green banner. In the foreground are the mehter playing drums and horns, and additional riders, who either converse or lead one of the spare horses.
>
> The text merely states that "the elder princes departed for their sancaks," without identifying the individuals. The central figure portrayed here is either Mustafa, the crown prince humiliated by being transferred to Amasya, or Mehmed, who replaced him in Manisa.
>
> The excitement created by this shift in posts, which indicates a change in the designation of the heir to the Ottoman throne, is reflected by the figures gathered in the background. The population of İstanbul, aware of the significance of the sultan's decision, observe the departure of the prince to his new assignment with great interest.

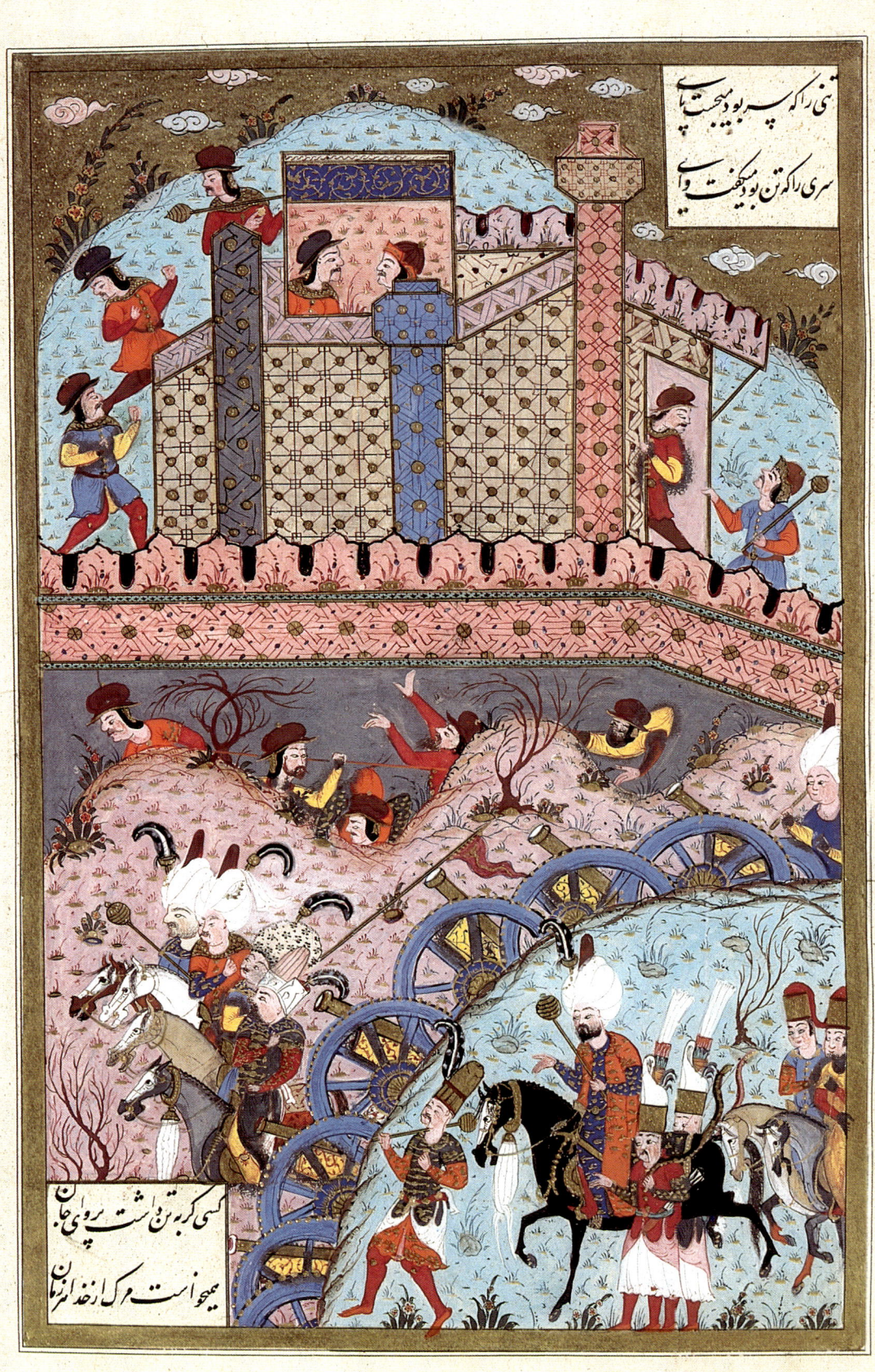

45. Siege of Estonibelgrad

(folio 459a)   Painter B

FERDINAND'S REPEATED aggressions in Hungary followed by yet another attempt to take Budapest provoked Süleyman's tenth sefer-i hümayun, once again directed against the Austrians.

The sultan departed on 23 April 1543 from Edirne, where he had spent the winter with Şehzade Bayezid. The navy with some 370 ships set sail on the Danube River and joined the sultan in Budapest. After securing Budapest, Süleyman went on to conquer Pecs, Siklos, and Estergon. The latter fell after a siege of twelve days and cost the life of Bali Paşa, recently appointed beylerbeyi of Budapest. The celebrated battle gave its name to this campaign, the Estergon Seferi.

Then the army marched on to Estonibelgrad, a sacred city where the Hungarian kings were crowned and buried in its cathedral. The city was besieged for two weeks and fell on 4 September. Süleyman received the commander, allowed his hand to be kissed, and granted him his freedom. The main church was converted into a mosque and the first hutba was delivered in Süleyman's name. The cathedral and its treasury, however, were left untouched.

Estonibelgrad became a sancak under Budapest. Its new governor was Ahmed Bey, the youngest brother of Bali Paşa; another brother, Mehmed Paşa, was now the beylerbeyi of Budapest. Süleyman left a garrison of 4,000 men at Estonibelgrad and started back home, arriving in İstanbul on 16 November.

> The siege of Estonibelgrad recalls that of Rhodes (see 12 and 13), with a stylized fortress in the background and the Ottoman army gathered behind the hills in the foreground. Süleyman, accompanied by his guards and Has Oda ağas, approaches the battlefield on the lower right, holding a mace in one hand and gesturing towards the artillery with the other. Ottoman cannons are lined up behind the hill with four commanders riding off to supervise the attack.
>
> Beyond a second hill is a moat with several enemy soldiers swimming in the water, climbing on the shore, and waving their arms. They appear to be running away from the besieged fortress and abandoning their comrades.
>
> In the background the fortress of Estonibelgrad rises above a crenellated wall with a number of soldiers holding maces walking around a structure that has an entrance and several towers. Inside are two figures conversing in what appears to be an open courtyard. The enemy soldiers are attired in brimmed hats or helmets and wear short belted tunics. The commotion created by swimming, gesticulating, and roaming figures provides a contrast to the rigidity of the Ottoman forces with their artillery and officers lined up in an orderly fashion.

46. Süleyman Hunting with Selim

(folio 462b) Painter B

UPON RETURNING HOME, Süleyman was grief-stricken on hearing that Şehzade Mehmed, his first son born to Hürrem, had died in Manisa on 6 November 1543. The twenty-two-year-old prince, recently assigned to that city, was very dear to the sultan, who was deeply affected by his loss. Süleyman had his son's body brought to İstanbul and buried in the district that was to be called Şehzade after the prince. He then commissioned the royal architect Sinan to construct a mosque and a mausoleum there in his son's memory.

Süleyman later met with his second eldest son, Şehzade Selim, and had long discussions with the prince. Selim was now assigned to the privileged sancak of Manisa.

During the following three years the sultan negotiated with the Habsburgs, finally signing a peace treaty in 1547. All the cities conquered by the Ottomans would be kept by the sultan; Austrians would not attack Ottoman lands; Ferdinand was recognized as the ruler of Austria while Charles V was considered the king of Spain.

Meanwhile Rüstem Paşa, greatly favored by his mother-in-law, Hürrem, was appointed grand vezir, replacing Hadım Süleyman Paşa. He was to be the most influential person in the court for the next two decades, serving as grand vezir from 1544 to 1553 and again from 1555 to 1561.

> This hunt illustrates the portion of the text narrating the meeting of Süleyman with his son Selim that took place after the death of Şehzade Mehmed in the fall of 1543. Among the most successful compositions of Painter B, the scene is conceived as three horizontal planes defined by hills. These planes are joined by strong diagonals created by figures who ride into the field and confront the hunters.
>
> In the foreground are two riders, who project out over the frame on the lower right, while a third rider gallops in from the left, oblivious of the pair of leopards crouching in the center. Behind the hills are three hunters with the bearded sultan riding a black horse, turning around to shoot a pair of gazelles with an arrow. His companions are youthful figures, who either use a bow and arrow to aim at gazelles or slay a spotted deer with large antlers, while other animals (including two hares and a wolf) scurry about. An officer rides in from the upper left, rounding up the prey and gesturing towards one of the hunters. Groups of figures, including peyks, Has Oda ağas, and officers with spare horses, observe the scene from behind the hills.
>
> Although Süleyman is immediately recognizable, Şehzade Selim, who also participated in the hunt, is not as easily identified. He must be the youth on the chestnut horse who turns back to shoot and is pointed out by the officer riding in from the upper left.

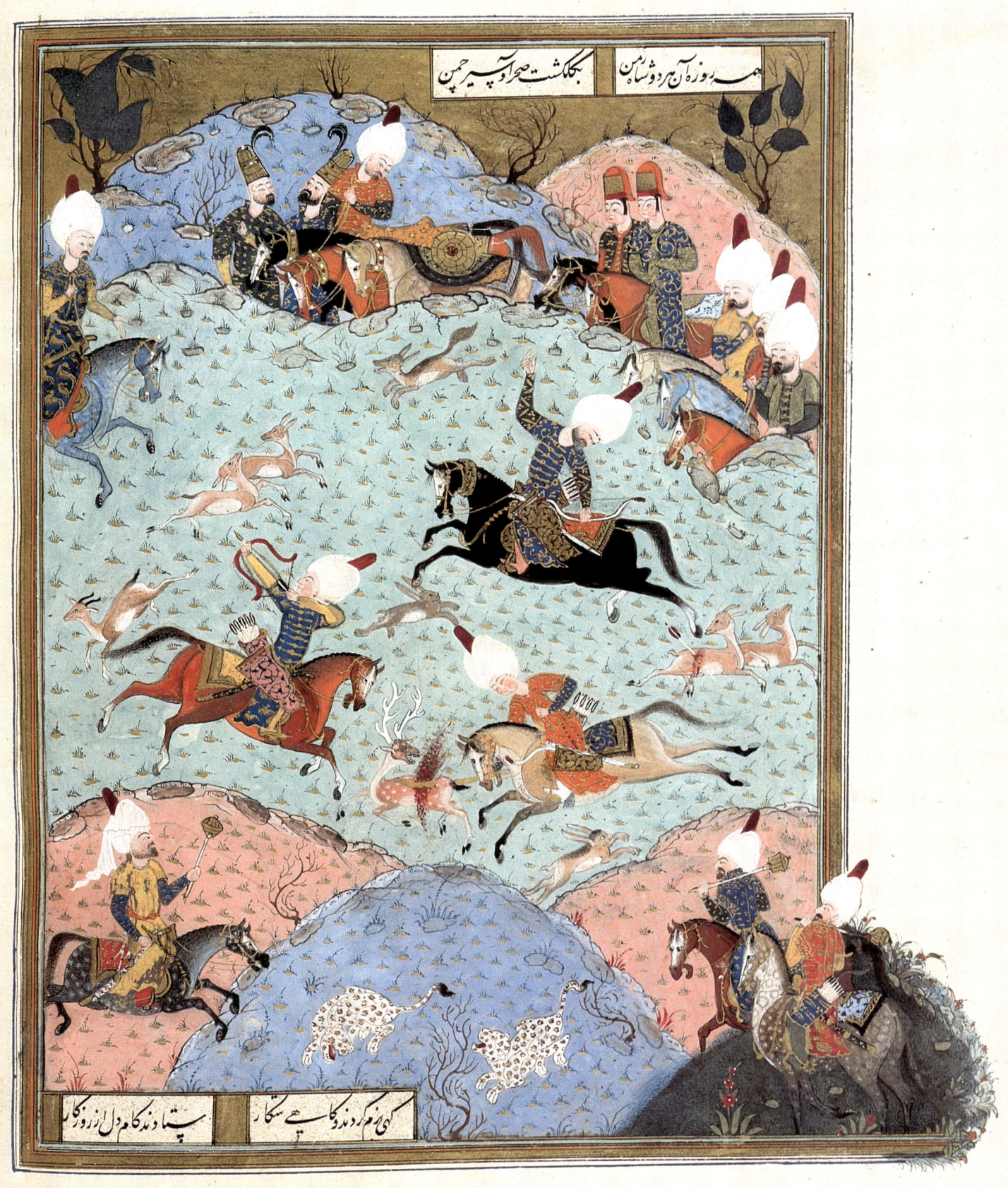

47. Reception of Elkas Mirza

(folio 471b)   Painter B

THE FIVE-YEAR TREATY signed between the Ottomans and the Habsburgs in 1547 resulted in a long break in hostilities. Although there would be battles on the western front, Süleyman did not embark on a major campaign against the Habsburgs for another two decades. The Franco-Ottoman alliance was renewed by Henry II, who had been crowned king of France after the death of Francis I. Süleyman was now free to devote his attention to the problems on the eastern front—in particular the Safavids, who were ravaging the southeastern regions and Georgia.

The same year Süleyman was visited by Elkas Mirza, the twenty-seven-year-old adventurous brother of Tahmasp. Elkas, the governor of Şirvan, had rebelled against the şah and escaped via the Caucasus and the Crimea to İstanbul after being defeated. He had brought his court with him and was offering Süleyman his services. Included in his retinue were the poets Arifi and Eflatun, both of whom became the official court biographers of the sultans.

Süleyman, who was in Edirne when Elkas arrived in İstanbul, entered the capital with a spectacular parade, displaying all the wealth and power of his empire. Elkas, duly awed by the sultan's magnificence, was received by Süleyman and the Divan. The sultan was pleased to have Elkas' support against Tahmasp, thinking that he would serve as a loyal ally on the Safavid throne.

> The reception of Elkas Mirza takes place in the Arz Odası. Süleyman, sitting on a throne and attended by his Has Oda ağas and vezirs, has permitted the Safavid prince to be seated in his presence. Both the sultan and his guest wear ceremonial outer kaftans with long panels hanging at the back and inner kaftans with attached sleeves. In the foreground are the arcades of the second courtyard and the domed Babüssaade which opens into the third courtyard. Several officers including a kapıcı, four iç oğlans, and three *zülüflü baltacıs* (special corps of guards) with conical caps and long locks of hair wait outside the gate.
>
> The architecture is extremely elaborate and consists of various interlocking components adorned with diverse geometric and floral motifs. The logical progression from the gateway to the throne room is intentionally counteracted by rich and varied decorative units, creating an ambiguity between open and closed spaces and between advancing and receding planes.
>
> In contrast to the stylized and abstract setting, the face of the sultan reveals an unusually realistic depiction with its aquiline nose and slightly graying beard. Süleyman is portrayed as a middle-aged monarch, beginning to show his advancing years.

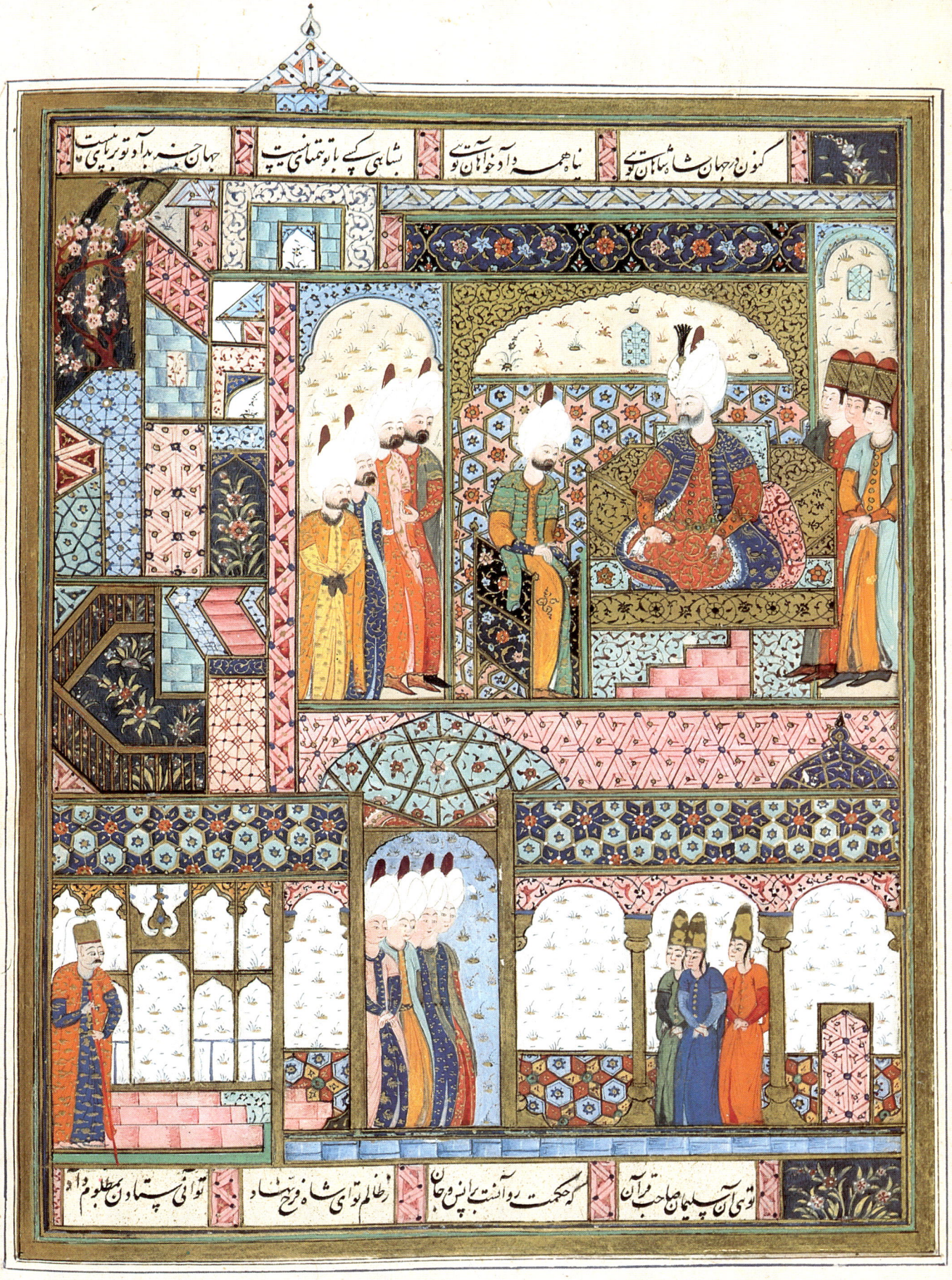

48. Süleyman Conversing with Mustafa

(folio 477b)   Painter B

SÜLEYMAN EMBARKED ON his eleventh sefer-i hümayun on 29 March 1548, this time marching east to Tabriz. Elkas had been sent ahead with an army, advancing as far as Hamadan, Isfahan (now the Safavid capital), and Kaşan. Another Safavid prince, Burhan-ı Ali, whose mother was Tahmasp's sister, had also joined the Ottoman forces against the şah.

Süleyman's youngest son Cihangir was accompanying his father on this campaign. When the sultan stopped at Seyyidgazi near Eskişehir, he arranged to meet Şehzade Selim, who was being sent as a regent to Edirne while the sultan was involved in the east. A few days later Süleyman met Şehzade Bayezid at Akşehir; the prince rode with his father's army as far as Kayseri before returning to his own sancak in Kütahya. Then Şehzade Mustafa, the eldest prince, arrived from Amasya and traveled with the sultan for several days. Süleyman took time out to enjoy the company of his sons and discussed the affairs of the state with each prince.

The sultan continued toward Tabriz, taking the city on 27 July for the fourth time. Then he marched to Van, which had fallen to the Safavids. He reaffirmed his control over the city on 25 August and appointed İskender Paşa as its beylerbeyi. Süleyman then moved to Aleppo, where he spent the winter of 1548-1549.

> The meeting of Süleyman with one of his sons takes place in a three-storied pavilion overlooking a garden. The sultan sits in a cantilevered balcony supported by columns; holding a bow and arrow, he gazes at the pair of ducks swimming in the square fountain in front of the pavilion. Seated behind him is the prince with a pair of Has Oda ağas in attendance. Placed on the floor are bowls of fruit and a single-handled jug. Below, two bearded officials converse in the arched entrance of the structure. In the foreground, flanking the fountain, are musicians who play a lute and tambourine. A bottle and two bowls of fruit are placed on the ground in front of them.
>
> The text states that Süleyman traveled with Şehzade Bayezid to Kayseri, where he found his eldest son, Mustafa, waiting for him. The sultan stayed in Kayseri three or four days, where he was entertained in the rose gardens. The bearded prince represented here is most likely Şehzade Mustafa, the heir presumptive.
>
> The contemplative appearance of the sultan, who holds weapons of destruction in his hand while enjoying the beauty of the garden and the songs of the musicians, creates a pensive mood rarely found in manuscript illustrations. It is as if the sultan has a premonition of the death of Şehzade Mustafa, who sits behind him, trusting and obedient.

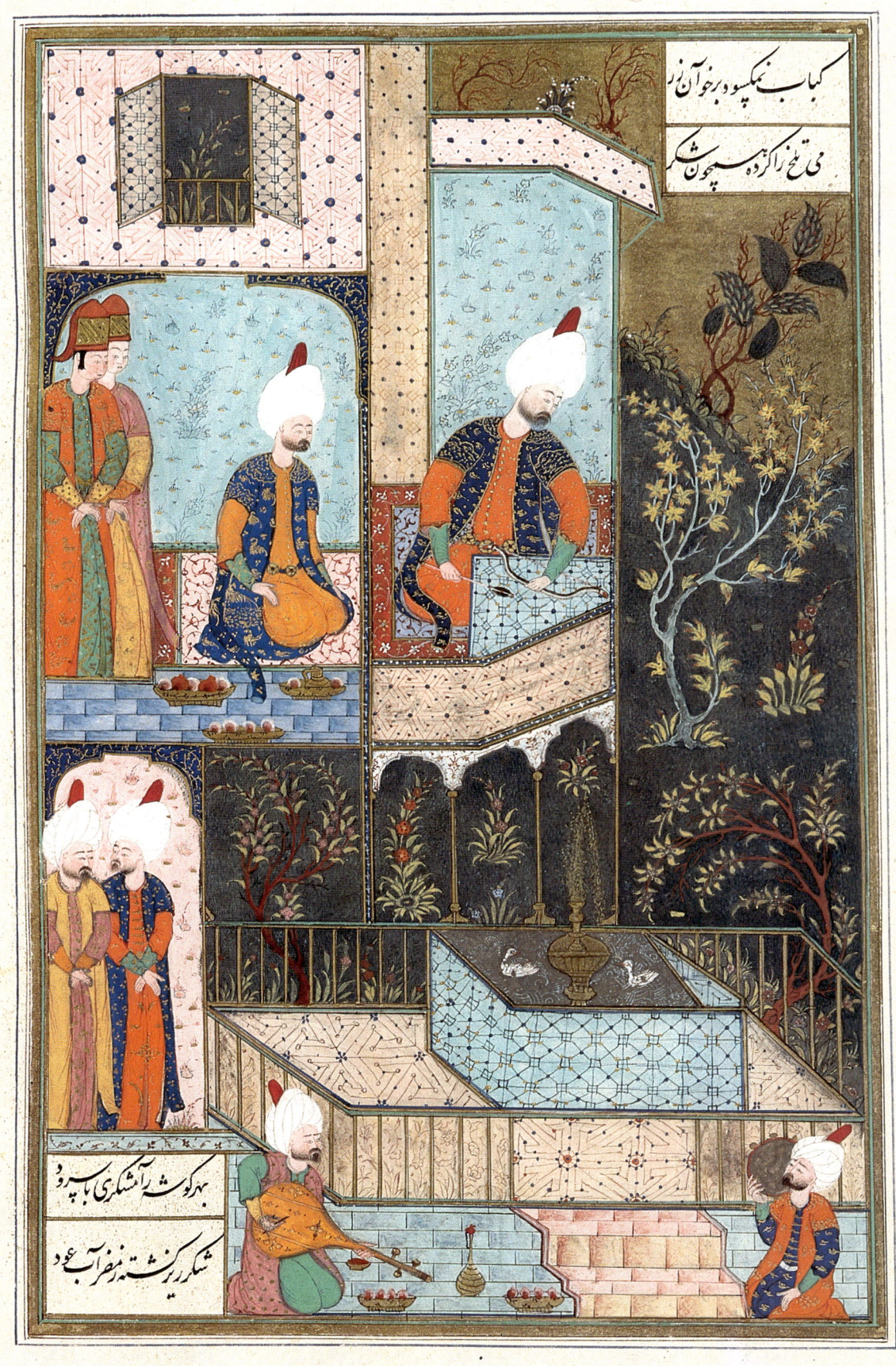

49. Arrival of Gifts from Elkas Mirza

(folio 498b)   Painter B

WHILE SÜLEYMAN WAS wintering in Aleppo, Elkas Mirza sent him the booty he had taken during his raids into Iran. The list, according to Arifi, included such valuable items as Korans transcribed by Yakut and Abdullah Sayrafi, renowned thirteenth- and fourteenth-century calligraphers; rare manuscripts with jeweled bindings, some made in Herat and Şiraz containing the calligraphy of Sultan Ali and the paintings of Behzad; large quantities of pearls, diamonds, rubies, and musk; gold belts, swords, horse trappings, saddles, cups, ewers, bows, and maces; Chinese fabrics and Iranian silks, including a unique satin tent canopy; beautiful maidens; and many other treasures. These were received by the court and properly recorded.

Süleyman always enjoyed staying in Aleppo. This time he spent six months there and asked Şehzade Bayezid to join him. Father and son participated in a number of hunting parties, the favorite sport of the sultan. He also took time out to visit Hama, Homs, and Antioch.

> The presentation of gifts sent by Elkas Mirza takes place in a setting resembling the second courtyard of the Topkapı Palace and recalls the reception of Austrian ambassadors (see 30), utilizing a pronounced zigzag composition. Servants bearing gifts wrapped in *bohças* (cloths) walk in the foreground, then proceed along the diagonal path leading to the council chamber, which is attended by ushers and protocol officers. The Divan is informed of their arrival by an official standing on the upper right. The figure in the center, presumably the grand vezir Rüstem Paşa, pokes the arm of a dignitary holding an open book, possibly the defterdar who has a list of the gifts.
>
> The interactions of the figures, particularly that of the grand vezir and the defterdar, are skillfully described. Rüstem Paşa, renowned for his avarice and passion for riches, is clearly impressed by the gifts while the defterdar, who is wise to the wealth of the empire, scorns the value of Elkas Mirza's presents.
>
> Although the text states that Elkas sent the gifts to the sultan in Aleppo, Painter B uses as his setting what appears to be the Divan chambers in the Topkapı Palace. He is either relying on a previously employed setting to depict the Aleppo palace or interprets the text, showing the arrival of the gifts in the capital after they were received by the sultan.

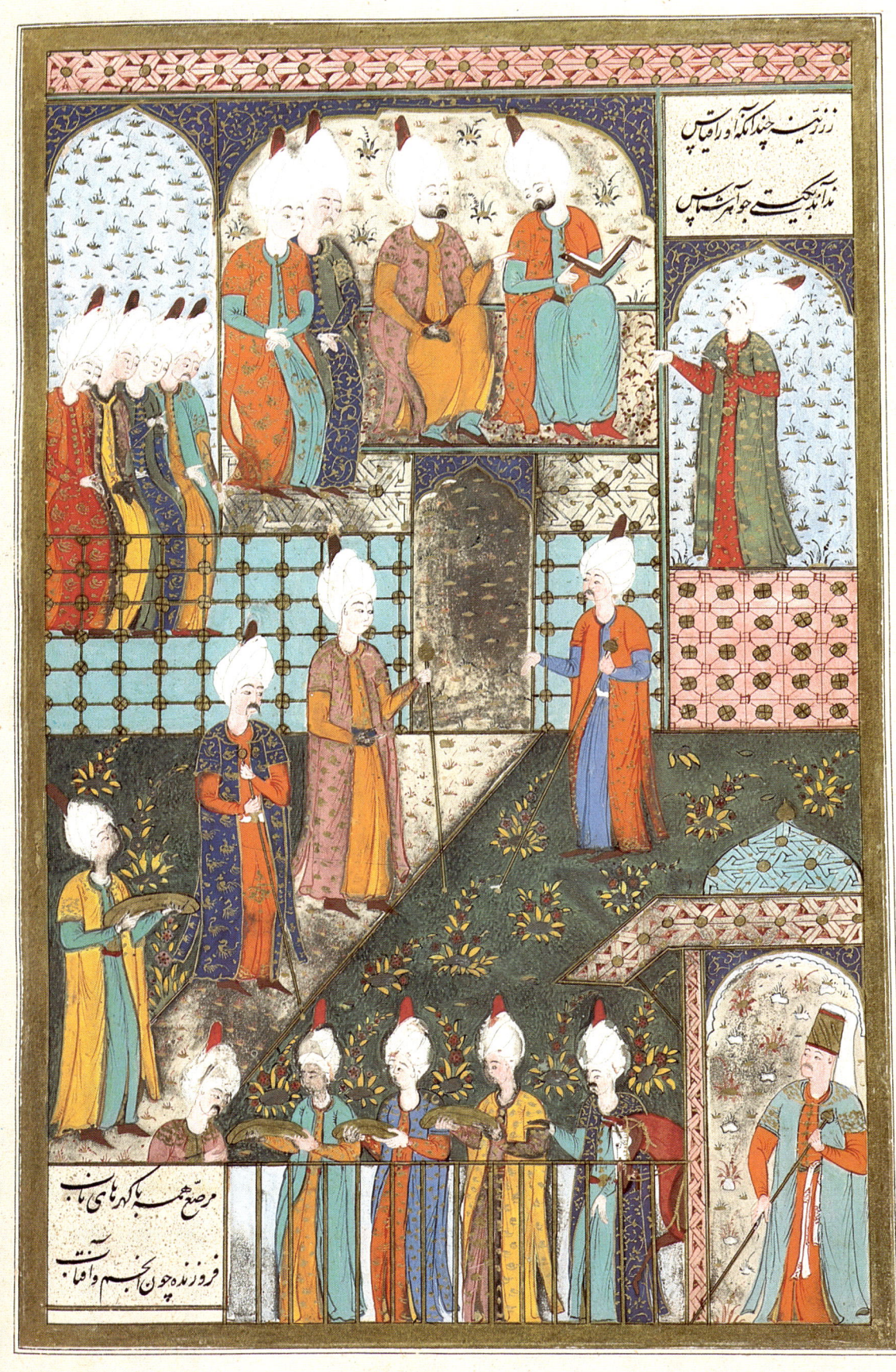

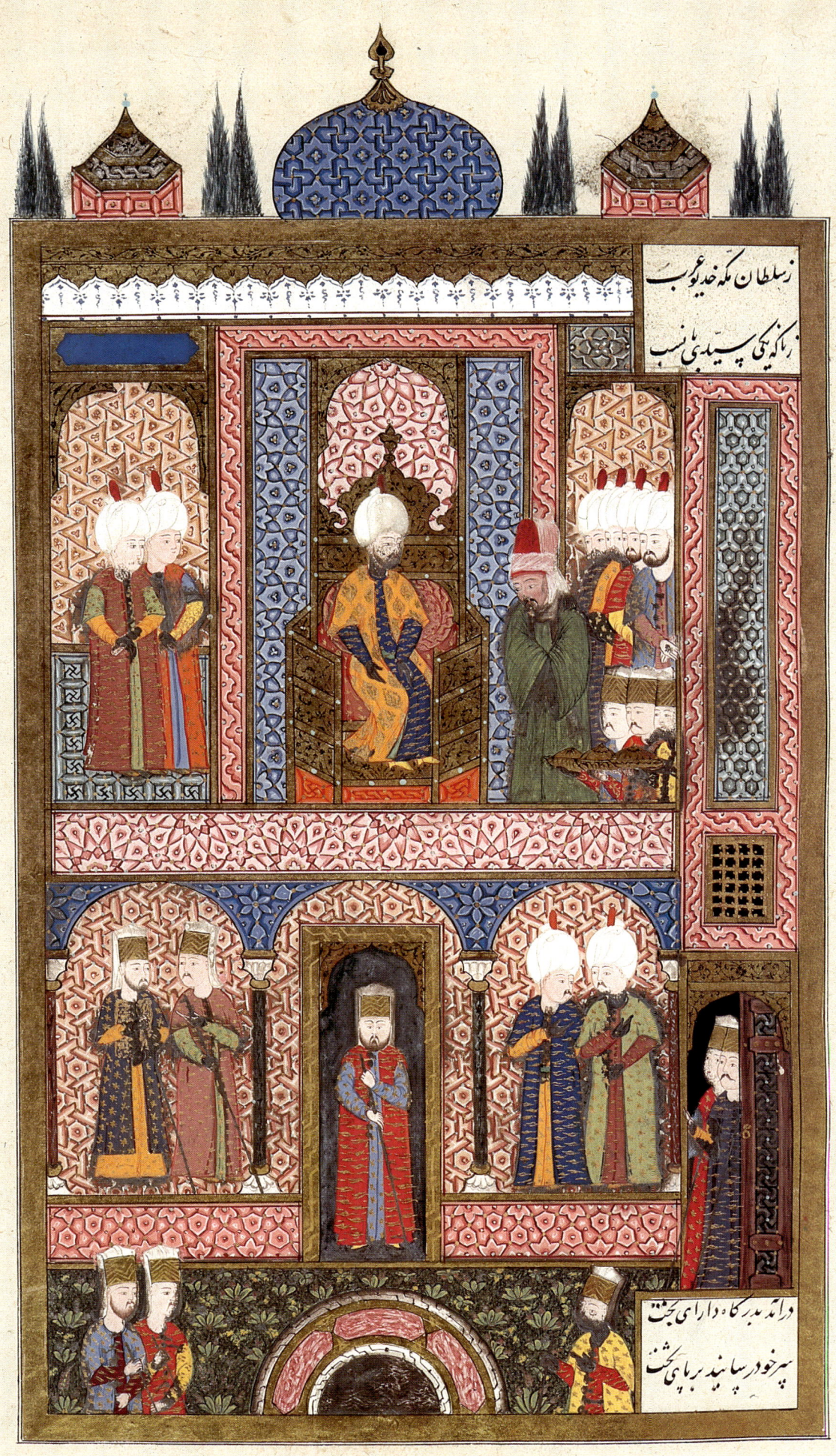

50. Reception of the Ambassador of the Hijaz

(folio 503a)   Painter A

WHEN IN Aleppo Süleyman was paid a visit by the ambassador of the şerif of Mecca, who was in charge of the Hijaz. The Hijaz with its Holy Cities of Mecca and Medina had voluntarily accepted Ottoman rule after the conquest of Egypt by Selim I in 1517. The envoy was reaffirming his master's loyalty to the Ottoman sultan.

After the ambassador presented gifts on behalf of the ruler of the Hijaz and departed, Süleyman received the envoys sent by the emir of Taşkent, who was a descendant of the Mongol ruler Cengiz (Genghiz) Han.

The oath of allegiance on the part of these Muslim rulers was significant during this campaign. Süleyman, the sultan of the Ottomans and the protector of Islam, was waging war on another Muslim ruler, the şah of Iran.

> Süleyman, enthroned in a domed chamber and flanked by his iç oğlans and ministers, receives the ambassador from the Hijaz and accepts the gifts carried in by court attendants. The envoy is attired in a long loose robe and a tall hat wrapped by a kerchief, the characteristic garments worn by the Arabs (see also 4). He stands in front of Süleyman with his head bent and his hands hidden under the sleeves of his robe in humble submission. Below are kapıcıs guarding the entrances to the reception chamber and an adjacent structure while a couple of palace officials converse beneath the arcades beyond the circular pool.
>
> Receptions of ambassadors followed a rigid ceremony and took place in similar settings, which accounts for the repetitiveness in the composition of the scenes representing these events (see 31, 32, 47, and 53). The painters vary the compositions by changing the position of the vezirs and attendants, as well as the juxtaposition of architectural components, trying to create distinctive compositions.
>
> According to the sequence of events described in the text, this episode takes place in Aleppo during the winter of 1548-1549. It appears that the palace in Aleppo had a domed reception chamber with an arcaded facade opening into a courtyard, identical to the Arz Odası in the Topkapı Palace. Here, however, there is a circular fountain in front of the chamber.

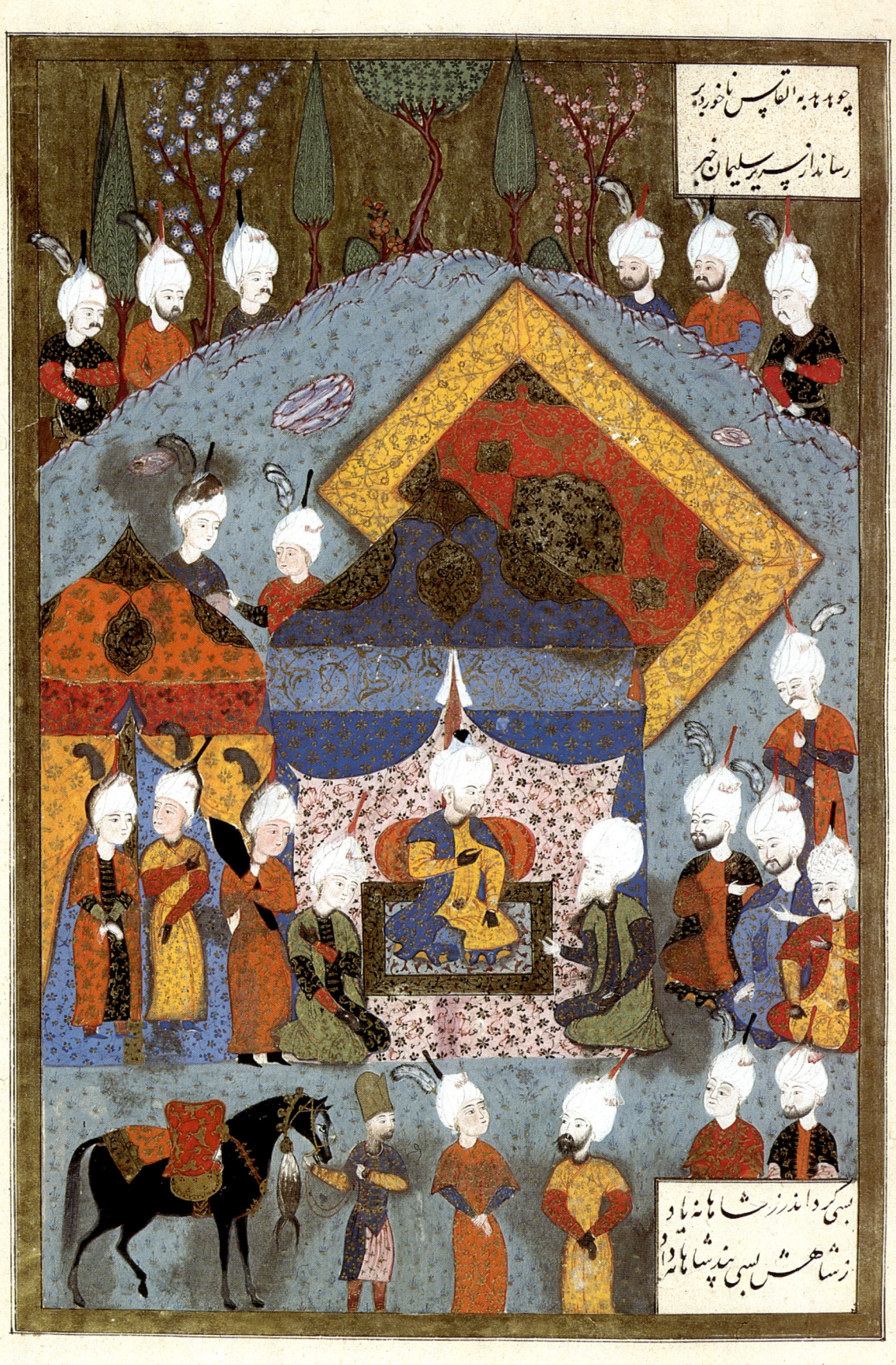

51. Elkas Mirza Receiving the Sultan's Envoy

(folio 506a)   Painters A and D

ELKAS MIRZA, moving with the Ottoman army into the heart of Iran, was in continual touch with the sultan. Before Süleyman left Aleppo for Diyarbakır on June 1549, he dispatched an envoy to Elkas. The envoy's name was Derviş Mehmed, whose son Arifi was the şahnameci of the sultan.

Derviş Mehmed arrived at Elkas Mirza's camp on 3 July 1549 and presented the sultan's message to his former master. Süleyman was recalling Elkas, who had been acting too independently and had not been following orders. Elkas, afraid of the sultan's reprimand, sought refuge among the neighboring tribes. In the following month, he was captured and turned over to the şah. Tahmasp imprisoned him in the fearsome fortress at Alamut where he died thirty years later.

Although the contribution of Elkas Mirza to the sultan's political activities was negligible, his arrival in İstanbul with his retinue left an impact on Ottoman art. Arifi, one of the poets of his court, not only wrote the official biography of Süleyman but also chose a specific group of painters, establishing a precedent for the production of future illustrated histories of the sultans.

> The central personage in this outdoor reception scene is Elkas Mirza, who sits in his tent, conversing with the elderly envoy, Derviş Mehmed, sent by the sultan. Although the composition and grouping of figures are similar to those in the imperial otak scenes, a number of iconographical features identify this scene as the camp of a personage other than the sultan. In contrast to the sultan who is always enthroned in his tent, Elkas sits on the ground; the figures holding encased swords next to him wear Safavid turbans, not the characteristic headdress of the imperial Has Oda ağas; other servants as well as the courtiers also wear elongated turbans with thin, tall batons fashionable in the Safavid court. Elkas and the envoy, however, wear the more rounded turbans of the Ottomans, possibly due to their official status. The peyk leading a spare horse in the foreground also stresses their association with the sultan's forces.
>
> The composition of the scene as well as the landscape elements, furnishings of tents, and select figures—such as the peyk and most of the officers standing behind the hill—reveals the hand of Painter A. He was assisted by Painter D, who represented Elkas together with the figures around the tents and in the foreground in the style characteristic of mid-sixteenth-century Iranian painting.

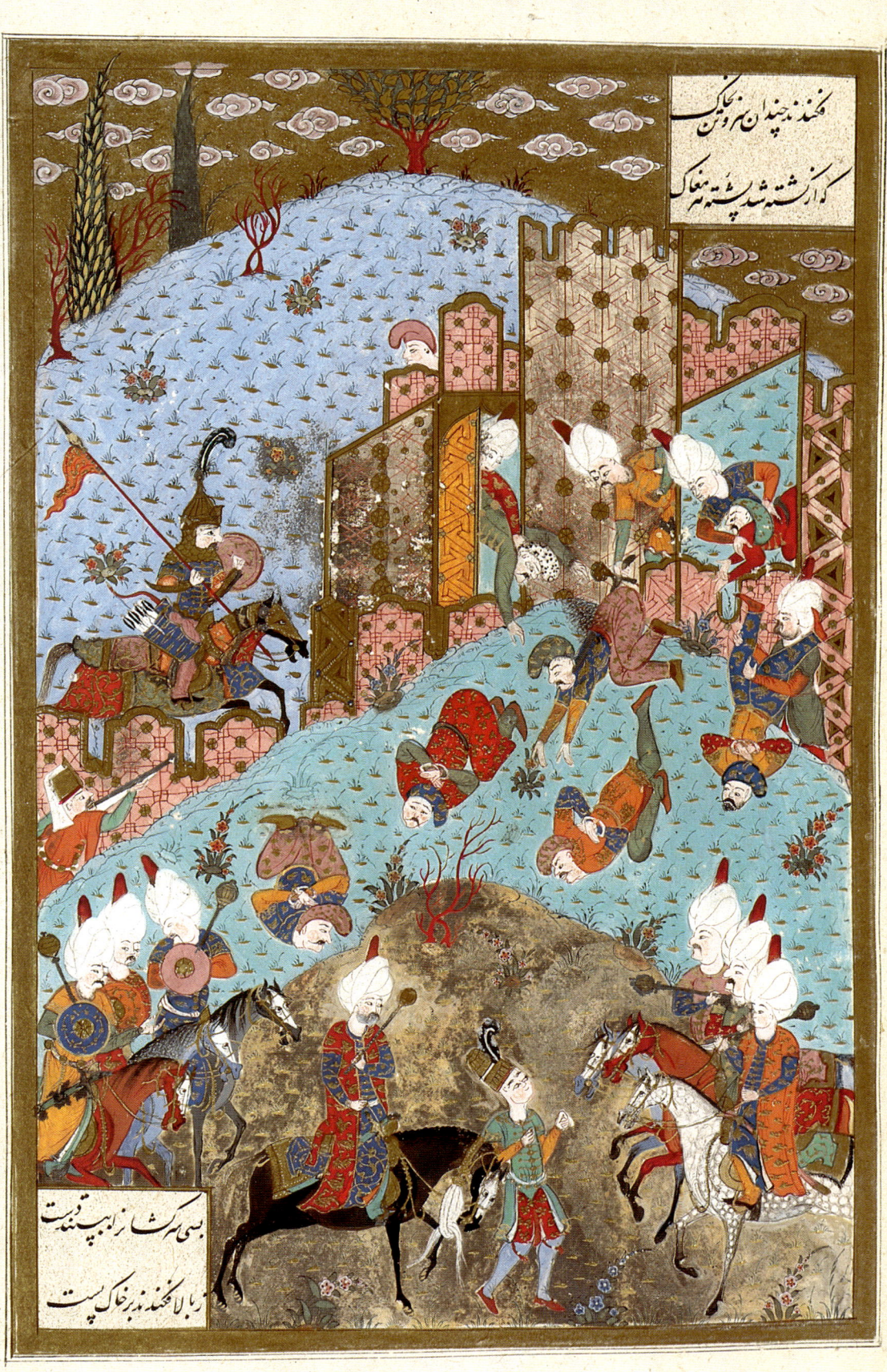

52. Battle of the Ottomans and Georgians
(folio 514a)   Painter B

DURING THE IRANIAN campaign the Ottomans launched a major offensive with an army headed by the third vezir Kara Ahmed Paşa and supplemented by the regiments from Karaman, Sivas, Maraş, and Erzurum. The Ottoman forces moved into Georgia in August 1549, successfully capturing over forty other fortresses in the next months, including those of Tortum, Akçakale, and Livana, each of which became a separate sancak. Kara Ahmed Paşa and his army caught up with the sultan in Diyarbakır in October as Süleyman was heading back. The campaign of 1548-1549 was inconclusive since Tahmasp had refused to be drawn into battle. The only benefit to the state was the establishment of the beylerbeyi of Van and the conquest of several fortresses.

Süleyman arrived in İstanbul on 21 December 1549, after being on the road for twenty-one months. On the way home, he stopped to receive the ambassador sent by the han of Bukhara and to meet with his sons, Bayezid and Selim.

> During the Iranian campaign, Kara Ahmed Paşa, the third vezir of the court, successfully captured a number of Georgian fortresses, including the one at Akçakale represented here. The commander, who holds a mace, rides in the foreground, attended by a peyk. On either side are groups of cavalry officers with maces and shields. The Akçakale fortress, seen in the background, has fallen and a few Ottoman soldiers wearing turbans have entered the city. They are putting an end to the last resistance by slaying the Georgians with their swords and unceremoniously dumping them over the walls with their hands tied behind their backs. On the far left are an armored rider and a janissary, continuing the attack.
>
> Painter B depicts the enemy thrown off the ramparts in a whimsical manner (see also 26). Wearing soft floppy hats and tunics, the Georgians are flung head first and land on the ground in an assortment of contorted and exaggerated postures. These caricature figures provide a lighthearted touch to the battle, indicating that the Georgians were not a serious threat to the Ottomans.

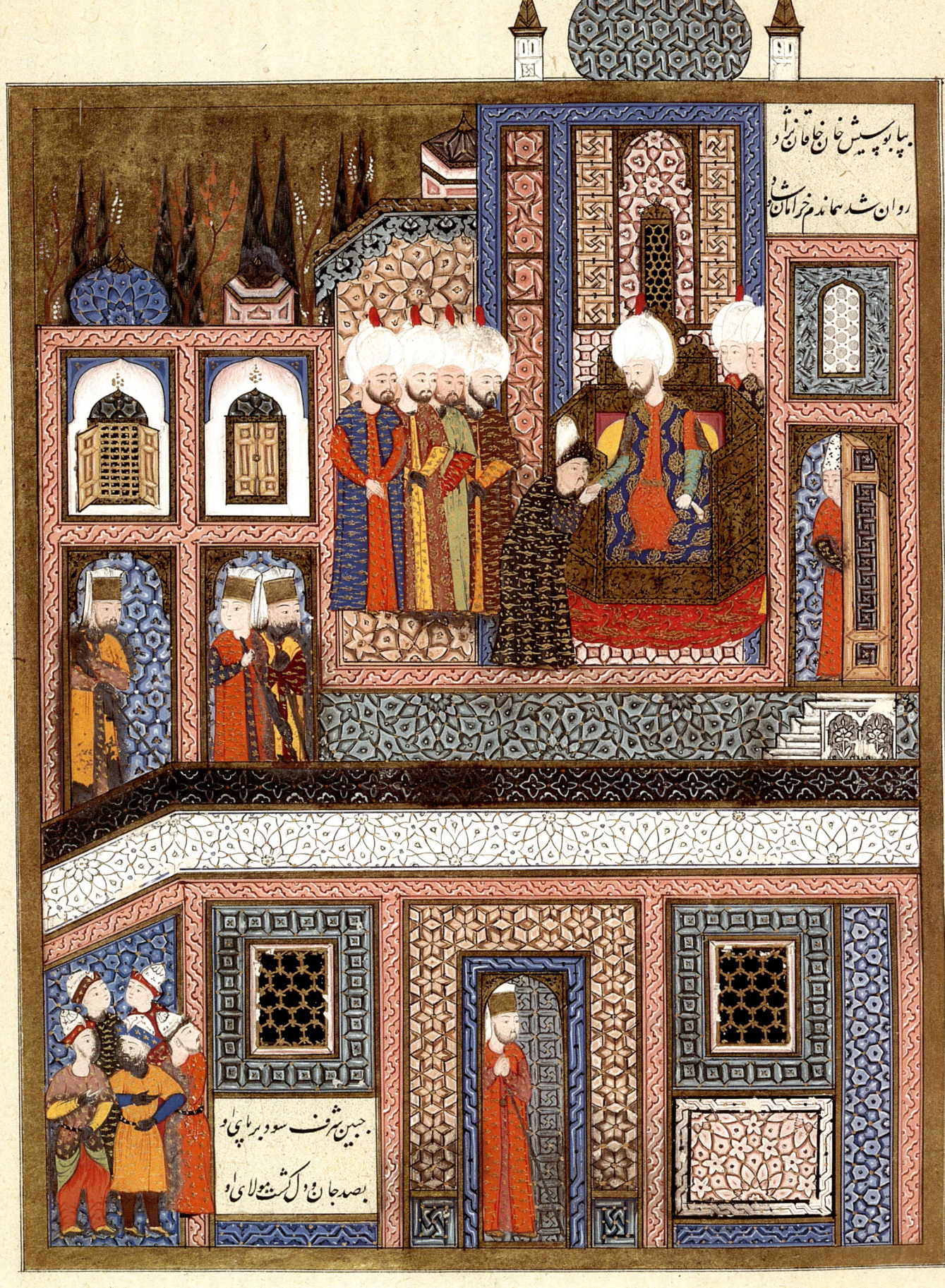

53. Reception of Devlet Giray Han

(folio 519a)   Painter A

AFTER RETURNING TO İstanbul, Süleyman commissioned Sinan to build the Süleymaniye Complex, which included a monumental mosque, mausoleums for himself and his wife, and a number of units housing educational, charitable, and social institutions together with residences for students, staff, and caretakers. The foundation for this truly imperial complex was laid in 1550 with the şeyhülislam Ebussuud Efendi blessing the event.

The following year the sultan was paid a courtesy visit by Devlet Giray Han, who had recently ascended to the throne of the Crimean hanate. Devlet Giray, a strong and reliable ally, was related to the sultan through Süleyman's mother, Hafsa, who was the daughter of Mengili Giray, Devlet's grandfather.

In the same year war broke out in Transylvania when Bishop Martinuzzi, the regent of Stephen Zapolya, decided to assert his independence by playing the Ottomans and the Habsburgs against each other, much to the annoyance of both Süleyman and Ferdinand. Martinuzzi, supported by the pope and promoted to the rank of cardinal, first allied himself with the Habsburgs, to whom he ceded Lipva, the capital of Transylvania. Sokollu Mehmed Paşa, then the beylerbeyi of Rumelia, moved into Transylvania and succeeded in recapturing Lipva.

The Arz Odası beyond the Babüssaade is the setting for this reception in which Süleyman, seated on a gold hexagonal throne, extends his hand to be kissed by Devlet Giray Han, the ruler of the Crimean Tatars and his maternal cousin. Devlet Giray wears a tall cap with a fur brim, the traditional headdress of the Crimeans, and a kaftan decorated with a çintemani pattern consisting of a series of double wavy lines and triple balls. This design, popular in the Ottoman court in the sixteenth century, was based on ancient talismans and symbolized the might and power of tigers and leopards. It is highly probable that Devlet Giray is wearing a hilat presented by the sultan.

Attending the reception of the esteemed ally are four vezirs and a pair of iç oğlans. The entrances to the Arz Odası and adjacent chambers are guarded by kapıcıs and servants.

The foreground depicts the walls of the second courtyard and the Babüssaade with its guard. On the lower register is a group of five Crimeans wearing split-brimmed hats. They huddle together, converse, and gesture toward the gateway, obviously awed by the splendor of the sultan's palace and its ceremonial procedures.

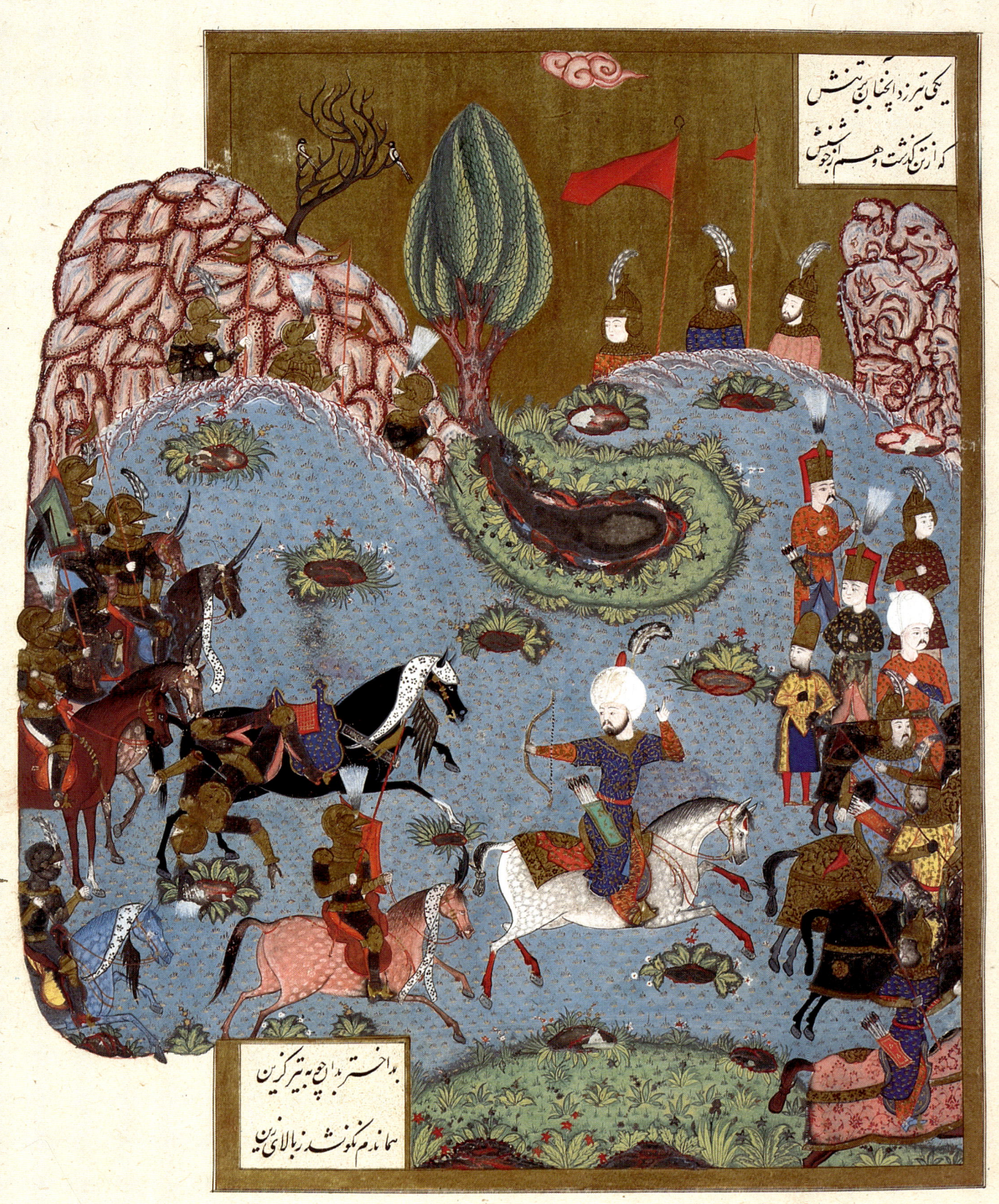

54. Ottomans Leaving Lipva

(folio 527a)   Painter A

SOKOLLU MEHMED PAŞA had left Ulama Paşa in charge of Lipva with a garrison of 5,000 men before moving on to Temesvar, which he besieged on 16 November 1551 without success.

Meanwhile the Habsburgs sent a force of 10,000 soldiers to recapture Lipva. Ulama Paşa fought valiantly against the attackers, but when his forces were reduced to only 1,500 men, he asked for a cease-fire. The Habsburg commander agreed to allow the Ottomans to leave the fortress in peace. As Ulama Paşa was evacuating the city with his men on 5 December, the enemy ambushed the retreating Ottomans. Ulama Paşa was wounded and barely escaped with his life to Belgrade, but not before inflicting serious casualties on the Habsburgs.

Martinuzzi, whose avarice had provoked the resumption of hostilities between the Habsburgs and the Ottomans, now decided to change sides and to join the Ottomans. This ambitious man was finally assassinated on Ferdinand's orders.

> The painting represents the Habsburg army breaking the armistice and ambushing the Ottoman forces after they evacuated the fortress of Lipva. Ulama Paşa, the beylerbeyi of Bosnia who was left in charge of Lipva, rides in the foreground, twisting back in his saddle to shoot at the treacherous enemy. His arrow has found its mark, fatally wounding the commander of the attackers, who falls off his horse. The Ottoman army—consisting of riders wearing helmets and turbans, in addition to janissaries, peyks, and soldiers walking on foot—retreats on the far right with several members turning back to look at Ulama Paşa's chivalrous act. The attacking enemy, in full armor, moves in from the left.
>
> Several other Habsburg and Ottoman soldiers appear behind the hills in the background, separated by a teardrop-shaped body of water with a large tree growing along its shore. The enemy forces are hidden by the craggy mountains while the Ottomans are exposed, indicating that they were unexpectedly ambushed. The animated rocks on the upper right, full of sinister human faces, provide additional commentary on the perils hidden among the mountains.
>
> A lively movement is created by the galloping horses and the orientation of the figures with all the elements progressing to the right. This is accentuated by the spread of the painting into the left margin, its massed weight appearing to push the figures forwards into the scene. The swoop of the pond in the background not only assists in accelerating the movement but also draws attention to the main protagonist, whose contrapuntal posture links the two units.

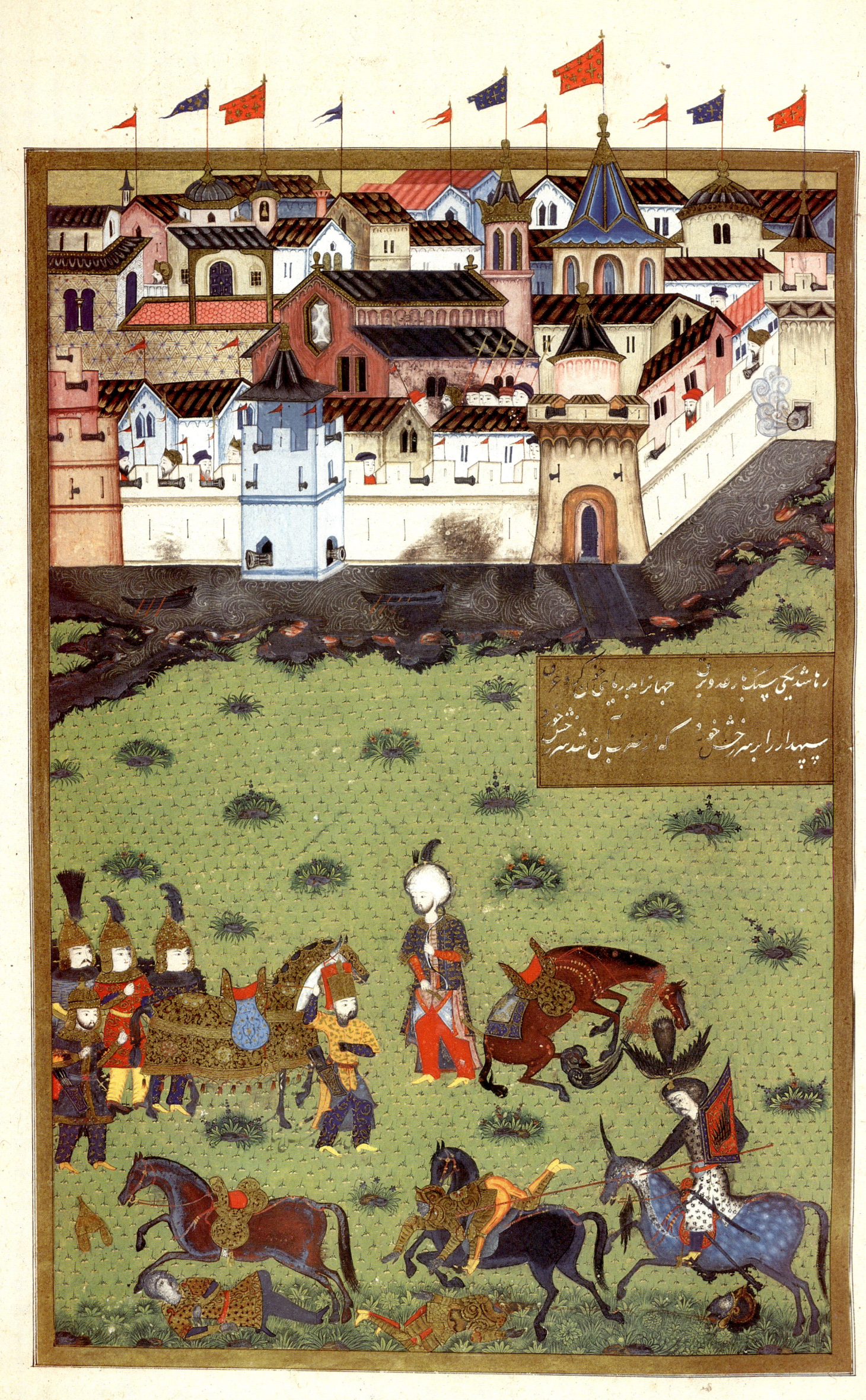

55. Siege of Temesvar
(folio 533a)   Painter A

ON APRIL 1552 Sokollu Mehmed Paşa was replaced by Kara Ahmed Paşa as the commander of the Transylvanian campaign. Kara Ahmed Paşa immediately resumed the siege of Temesvar on 28 June and entered the city the following month. Temesvar was declared a beylerbeyi, losing its formal status as a semiindependent vassal city. Kara Ahmed Paşa then proceeded to conquer Lipva and a number of other fortresses in Transylvania and Hungary.

Kara Ahmed Paşa's victories on the western front were overshadowed by his failure to take Erlau, a strategic city in northern Hungary. Erlau was to be captured in 1596 by Süleyman's great-grandson, Mehmed III.

The siege of Temesvar is represented by two separate episodes that take place in horizontal registers on the lower portion of the folio while the impressive fortress soars in the background. The lowest register depicts a delil with huge wings on his head spearing an enemy soldier, flinging him off his horse. Lying on the ground is a warrior with a severed head and another enemy soldier, who lost his helmet when he fell off his fleeing mount.

Immediately above is Kara Ahmed Paşa, standing next to his horse, which appears to have been beheaded by a direct hit from a cannon. A janissary and several helmeted soldiers bring him a new mount, beautifully decorated with a jeweled saddle and brocaded coverings. This episode takes place in a meadow, beyond which is a large moat surrounding the fortified city rising in the background. Temesvar, heavily guarded with cannons and soldiers peering from its towers and crenellated walls, has a drawbridge over the moat, leading to a gateway in a fortified tower. The city is packed with domed and pitch-roofed structures, in the center of which is a large basilica with a campanile. Flags displaying large crosses surrounded by smaller ones fly from the rooftops. The cannon in the tower on the upper right has smoke coming out of its barrel, indicating that it was recently fired and caused the death of Kara Ahmed Paşa's horse, which is directly in front of its firing line.

Painter A has illustrated three different features of the battle in a most ingenious manner: on the top is a general view of Temesvar, providing the setting; in the center is an episode that took place during the siege, individualizing the scene; and in the foreground is a symbolic victory, foretelling the eventual defeat of the enemy. This is the last painting in the manuscript devoted to the Ottoman-Habsburg hostilities, which came to a halt between 1552 and 1556. The sultan's attention was now concentrated on eastern campaigns and the Iranian wars, which are described in the subsequent scenes.

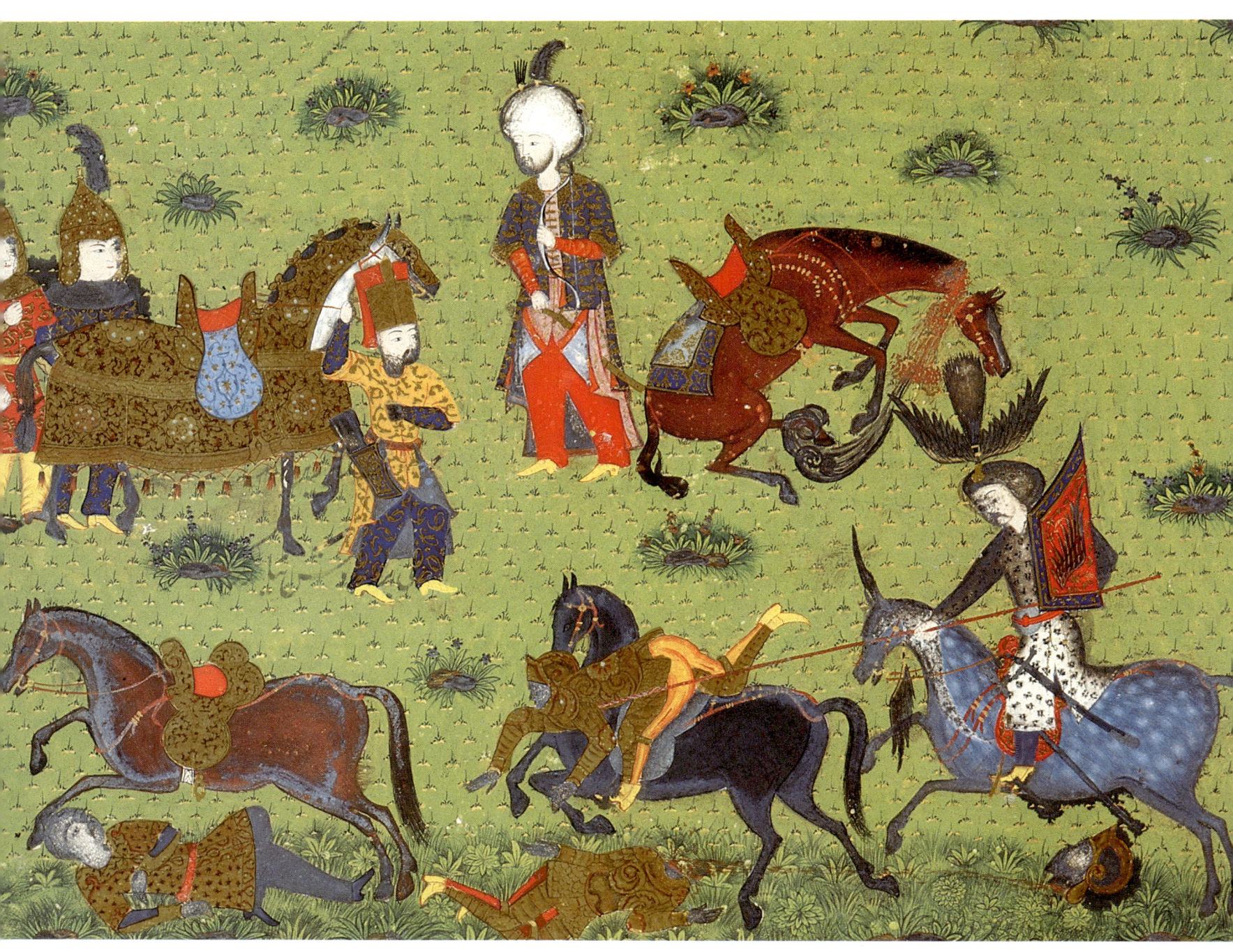

212

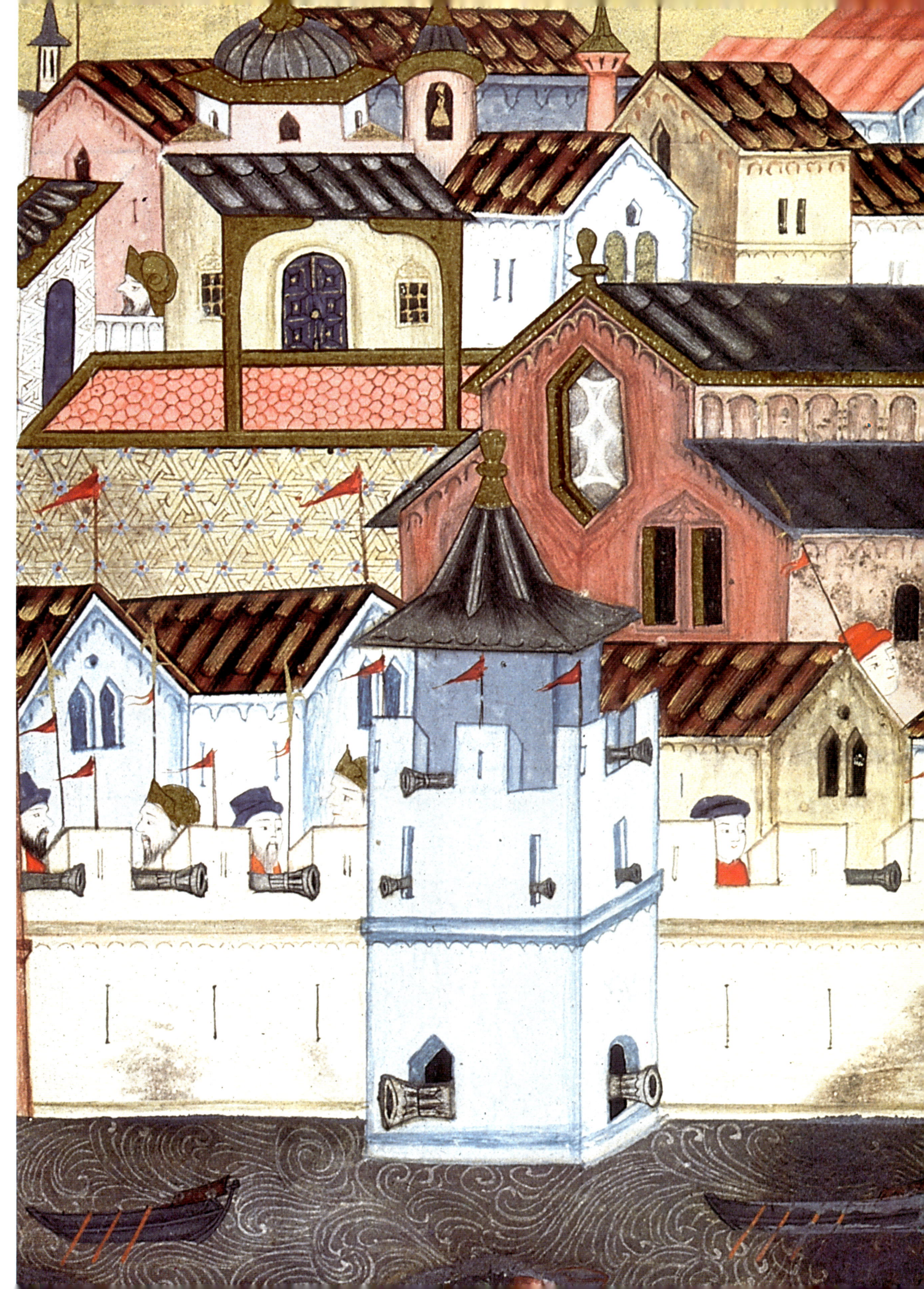

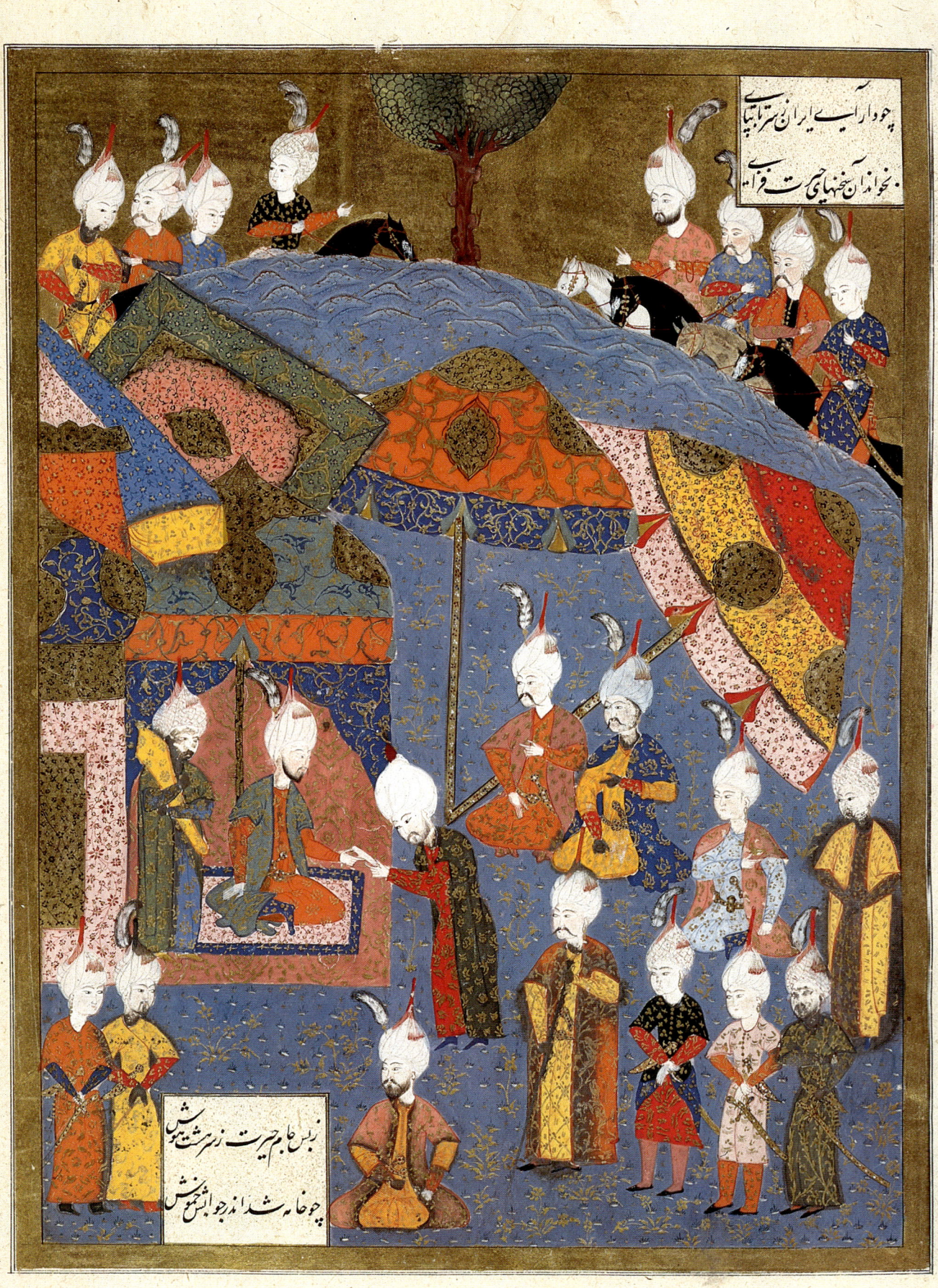

56. Tahmasp Receiving the Ottoman Ambassador

(folio 550a)   Painters A and D

MEANWHILE Tahmasp, taking advantage of the involvement of the Ottoman army in Hungary, advanced to Van, devastating the countryside. Under the command of his son Ismail Mirza, the Safavids captured the fortress of Ahlat and besieged Erzurum. İskender Paşa, recently appointed the beylerbeyi of Erzurum, valiantly defended the city and repelled the şah's army although his men were outnumbered by the Safavids.

In the ensuing battle İskender Paşa surrounded the fortress of Ardanuç (Ardanuchi) in Georgia, where a treasured ruby cup called *cam-ı Cemşid* was hidden. This cup (called *cam-ı cihannüma* in this text) was thought to have belonged to the legendary founder of the Iranian empire, Cemşid, and was associated with Alexander the Great. Cherished throughout the centuries, it had passed from one king of Iran to another as a symbol of power and legitimacy of rule.

İskender Paşa insisted that Tahmasp relinquish all claims to this treasure and sent an envoy to the şah's court with a letter containing his request. He then captured the fortress of Ardanuç, located the famous cup, and sent it to İstanbul.

> The saga of the cam-ı Cemşid is the subject of this and the following painting. The episode illustrated here shows Tahmasp handing to the envoy sent by İskender Paşa a letter in which he forfeits his claim to the precious cup and surrenders it to the Ottomans.
>
> As in the other camp scenes, the imperial tents are set up in front of a hill with groups of figures gathered around the central personage while riders appear in the background. Tahmasp sits on rugs or textiles spread on the ground, attended by his swordbearer. The şah is surrounded by courtiers who either sit crosslegged on the ground or stand around the tent. Tahmasp and his courtiers wear the elongated Safavid turbans and have jeweled daggers tucked into their belts, a tradition alien to the Ottomans. İskender Paşa's envoy bends his head while receiving the letter, knowing well its contents.
>
> The forfeiture of the cam-ı Cemşid symbolizes the superiority of the Ottomans, who not only inflicted serious military defeats upon the Safavids but were also powerful enough to confiscate their revered national treasure, striking an even more painful blow.
>
> It was Painter D who collaborated once again with Painter A and represented the Iranian types in this painting (see also 37 and 51).

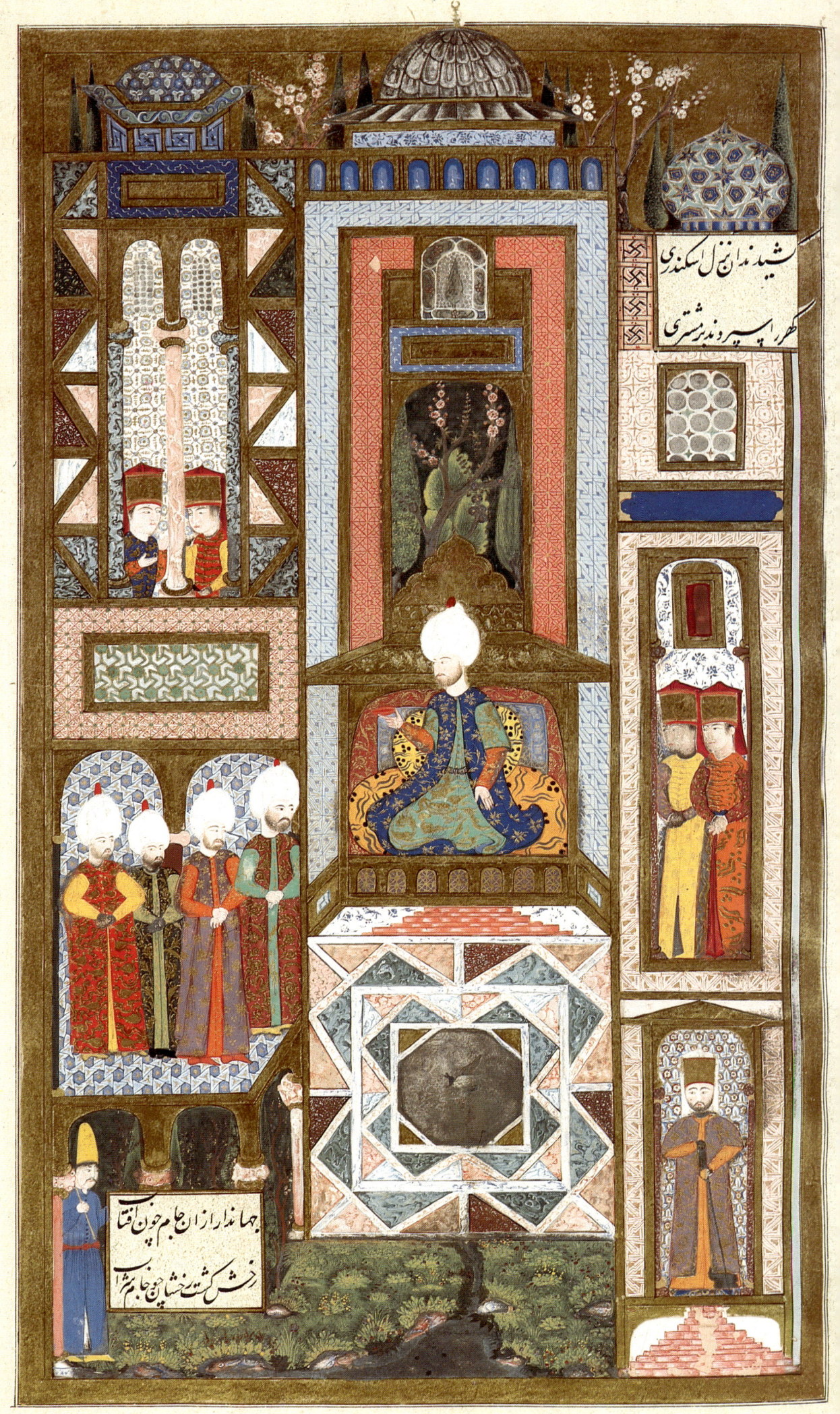

57. Süleyman Presented with the Ruby Cup

(folio 557a)   Painter A

SÜLEYMAN MUST HAVE BEEN pleased to have gained the famed cup of Cemşid on the eve of his preparations for his twelfth sefer-i hümayun, called the Nahçivan campaign, which was directed once more against the Safavids. When the cup arrived in İstanbul, it was presented to the sultan in a formal ceremony.

Süleyman embarked on his Iranian offensive on 28 September 1553. During this campaign, which lasted until 31 July 1555, the sultan traveled via Kütahya and Ereğli; wintered in Aleppo; returned to Kars, Karabağ, and Nahçivan; and marched back to Erzurum, Sivas, and Amasya, where he spent the second winter and negotiated peace treaties with both the Safavids and the Habsburgs.

This was a strenuous and exhausting war for Süleyman, who was suffering from ill health. The Nahçivan campaign was also to be emotionally draining, coinciding with the deaths of two of his sons.

> The painting is composed of three vertical sections subdivided horizontally by a number of architectural units showing various gates, entrances, windows, gardens, courtyards, arcades, terraces, balconies, and domes. Each component is elaborately decorated; some designs are highly abstract while others clearly constitute stained-glass windows, tiled walls, marble columns, and pavements. Süleyman sits in the center of this fantastic setting on an elaborate gold throne rising above a marble-inlaid courtyard with a central fountain; behind the throne is an archway opening onto the gardens in the background, above which is a stained-glass window with a central cypress tree. The sultan, resting on çintemani-patterned cushions, holds the renowned ruby cup in his hand, displaying it to the four vezirs, who stand in reverence on the left. Kapıcıs, Has Oda ağas, and other attendants guard the gardens and entrances; the pair standing in the triple-columned balcony on the upper left discuss the arrival of the fabled item, pointing at the cup.
>
> The possession of the mythical cup of Cemşid, the symbol of Ottoman power and victory over the Safavids, is fully exploited by the painter, who uses this opportunity to display the majesty of the sultan and the splendor of his court. Süleyman here is indeed the magnificent sultan of three continents and the inheritor of the realm of Cemşid. This famous ruby cup disappeared in later years and the fate of the cam-ı Cemşid remains a mystery.

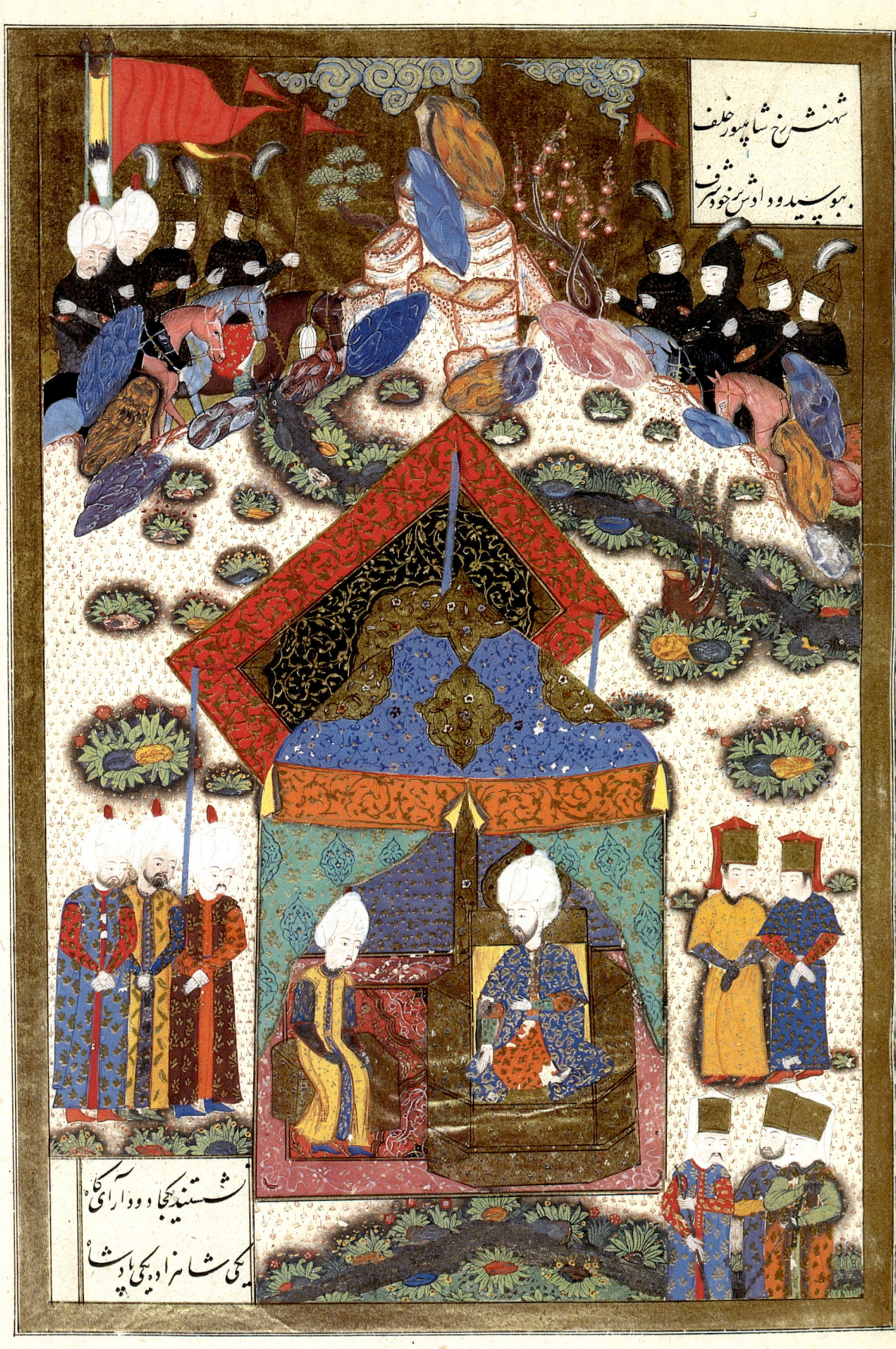

58. Süleyman Conversing with Bayezid

(folio 570a)   Painter A

SHORTLY AFTER DEPARTING from İstanbul in September 1553, Süleyman stopped at Yenişehir outside Bursa where he met with Şehzade Bayezid and entrusted the European provinces of the empire to the young prince by sending him to serve as regent in Edirne. After spending a few days with his father, Bayezid departed with his army, heading toward the capital of Rumelia.

The sultan next moved on to Ereğli, where one of the greatest personal tragedies of his life took place. Şehzade Mustafa, now serving as governor in Amasya, had been accused of plotting to overthrow his father and proclaiming that the sultan was old and sick and therefore unfit to rule. This accusation was further aggravated by the immense popularity of the prince with the army. Hürrem, backed by her son-in-law Rüstem Paşa and the other vezirs, had convinced the sultan that Şehzade Mustafa was a serious threat and should be dealt with before civil war broke out. She was obviously looking after the welfare of her sons as well as that of her husband.

When Şehzade Mustafa arrived to meet his father at Aktepe near Konya, he was cheered by the soldiers. The next day, 6 October, he was ushered into the imperial tent, where executioners were waiting for him. His death created a tremendous uproar among the janissaries, who held Rüstem Paşa responsible and demanded a reprisal. Süleyman was forced to expel his grand vezir and replace him with Kara Ahmed Paşa, the hero of recent military engagements in the west.

> The painting represents Süleyman receiving his son Bayezid at Yenişehir, where the army halted on the sultan's twelfth campaign, the third directed against the Iranians.
>
> The imperial otak has been pitched beside a river and inside Süleyman converses with his son, who is seated on a gold chair next to him. On both sides of the tent vezirs and Has Oda ağas discuss the meeting of father and son. Flanked by cavalrymen carrying flags, a mountain with rocks lying precariously at its summit rises in the background. A river flows down the mountain, its curve counteracting the sharp lines of the rectangular canopy over the tent.
>
> Süleyman is instructing the prince in state affairs and discussing tactics for handling the continuous threats from the Habsburgs. Şehzade Bayezid, by now an experienced commander and administrator, listens obediently to his father's advice before departing for Edirne.

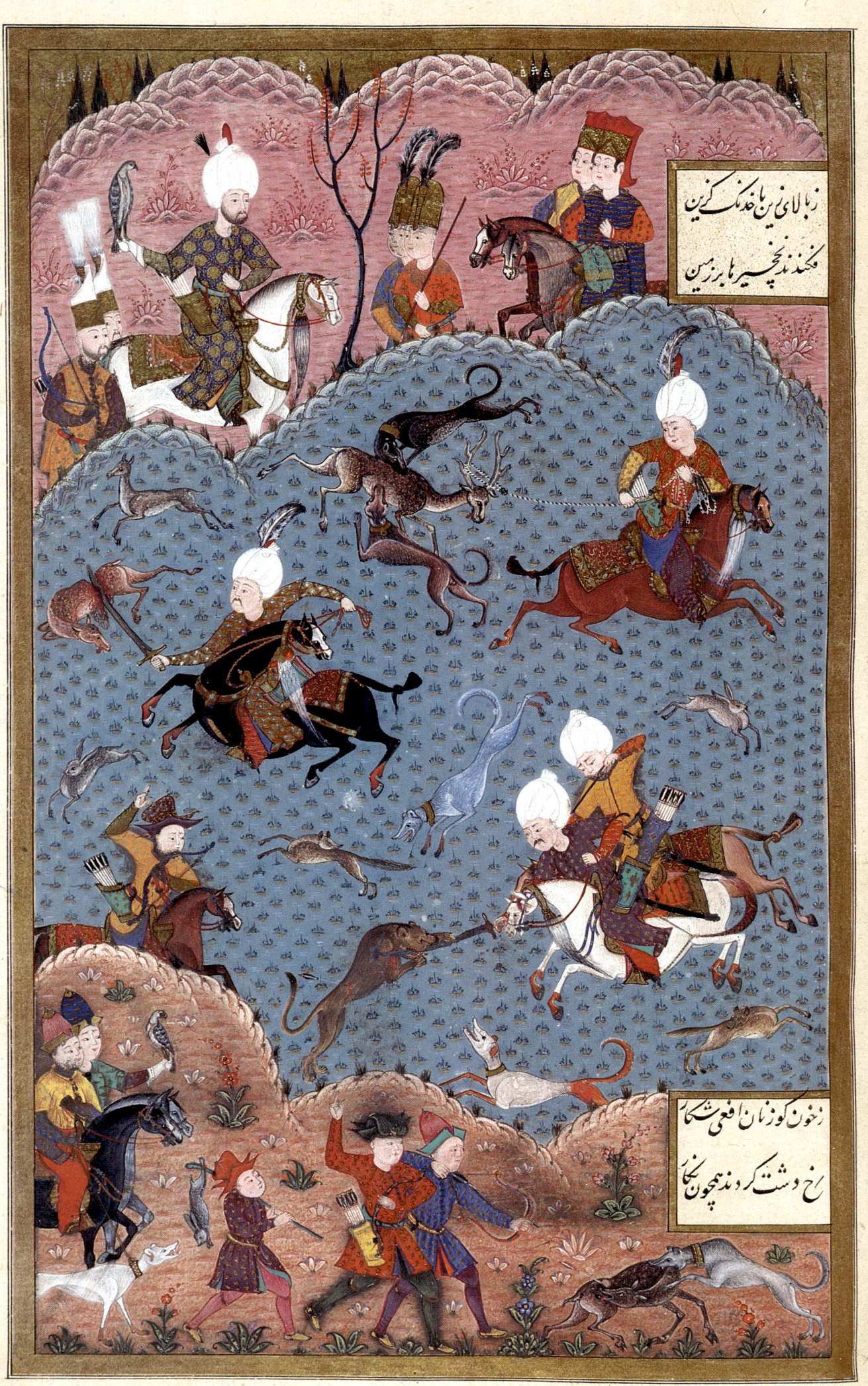

59. Süleyman Hunting with Selim
(folio 576a)   Painter A

SÜLEYMAN DECIDED TO spend the winter of 1553-1554 in Aleppo, where his youngest son, Cihangir, was serving as governor. Here a second personal tragedy struck the sultan when Şehzade Cihangir died on 27 November. This frail prince was devoted to his step-brother Mustafa and could not recover from the shock and grief caused by his execution. Cihangir's body was sent to the Şehzade Mosque complex in İstanbul to rest beside that of his brother Mehmed, who had died ten years earlier. Süleyman later commissioned Sinan to build the Cihangir Mosque in his son's memory.

Süleyman now had only two living sons, Bayezid and Selim. He asked Selim, who was wintering in Maraş with his forces, to join him in Aleppo. Şehzade Selim left his soldiers there and came to spend the winter months with his father. Süleyman tried to find some distraction by hunting with his son.

> This hunting party takes place outside Aleppo, where Süleyman spent the winter with his son Selim, who was the new crown prince since Mustafa's execution for treason a month earlier.
>
> Organized in three horizontal registers, the painting depicts hunters, game wardens, and falconers in the foreground; a lively hunt with the crown prince accompanied by other riders appears in the central field; and the sultan, attended by his solaks, peyks, and Has Oda ağas, is placed in the background. Thus the painter builds up the composition in progressive planes as well as in social hierarchy.
>
> One of the most successful scenes of Painter A, it reveals a masterful interplay of horizontals and diagonals, harmonious integration of separate vignettes, and energetic movement. The exceptionally skillful depiction of the figures and animals in the foreground suggests that the artist was inspired by European hunting scenes.
>
> Şehzade Selim, who rides a black horse, slashes a gazelle with his sword while his companions lasso a buck or slay a lion. They are assisted by several hunting dogs which chase hares, gazelles, and foxes. Süleyman silently observes the hunt with a hawk perched on his hand, his majestic stillness contrasting with the almost frenzied activity taking place in the field. His mood seems solemn, detached, and even depressed. He is probably reflecting upon the recent loss of his two sons and the events that caused their deaths.

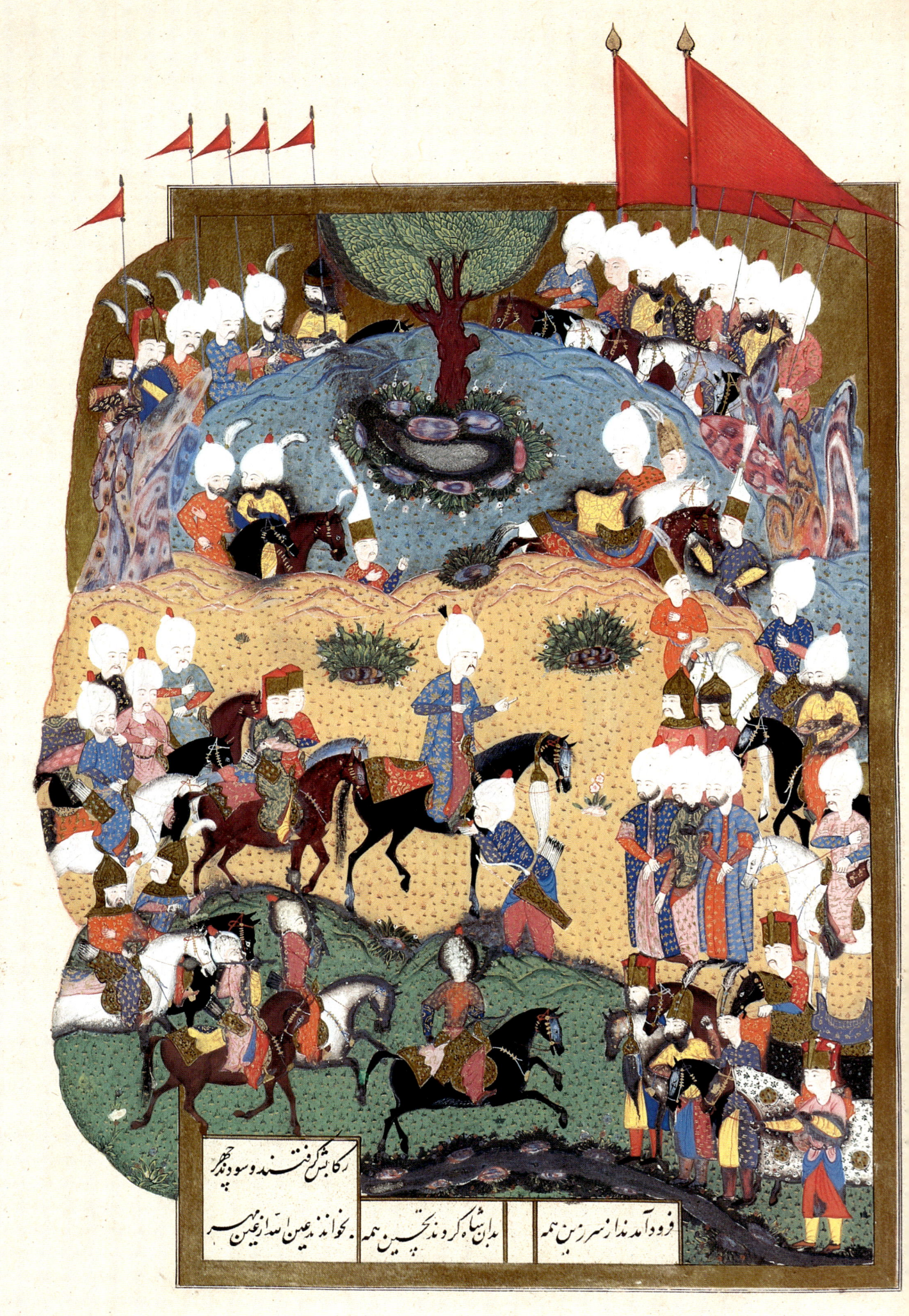

60. Selim Greeted by the Commanders

(folio 583a)   Painter A

SÜLEYMAN MOVED OUT of Aleppo in April 1554 and proceeded to Diyarbakır, where other regiments joined the main army. Şehzade Selim was to lead the right flank with the Anatolian cavalry, a prestigious command given to the new heir presumptive to the Ottoman throne.

After Şehzade Selim arrived with his provincial regiments and met with the commanders of the Anatolian division, he joined the sultan's camp. Süleyman addressed the massive army gathered outside Diyarbakır; he explained the significance of the campaign and praised the valor of his units in such an eloquent and emotional speech that he brought tears to everyone's eyes. The soldiers shouted that they would follow the sultan to the end of the world and were prepared to die in his service. Süleyman, riding at the head of his forces, marched out of Diyarbakır on 20 May.

> After various units of the Ottoman army gathered for the Iranian campaign, Süleyman held a war council outside Diyarbakır. The painting shows the arrival of Şehzade Selim's regiment and the reception of the new crown prince by the commanders of the Anatolian army, one of whom pays homage by kissing his boot.
>
> Şehzade Selim, mounted on a black horse, rides in front of his personal attendants and officers. Some of the commanders have dismounted and wait to greet him; others are still arriving on horseback. The field is surrounded by soldiers from various regiments who ride or walk in the foreground and gather behind the hills in the background. They include turbaned and helmeted cavalrymen, janissaries, peyks, solaks, and their leaders. The bright red banners projecting above together with the figures and landscape elements extending into the left margin help to accentuate the massiveness of the Ottoman forces. By showing the units partially hidden behind rows of rolling hills, the artist suggests that greater numbers exist beyond the picture frame.

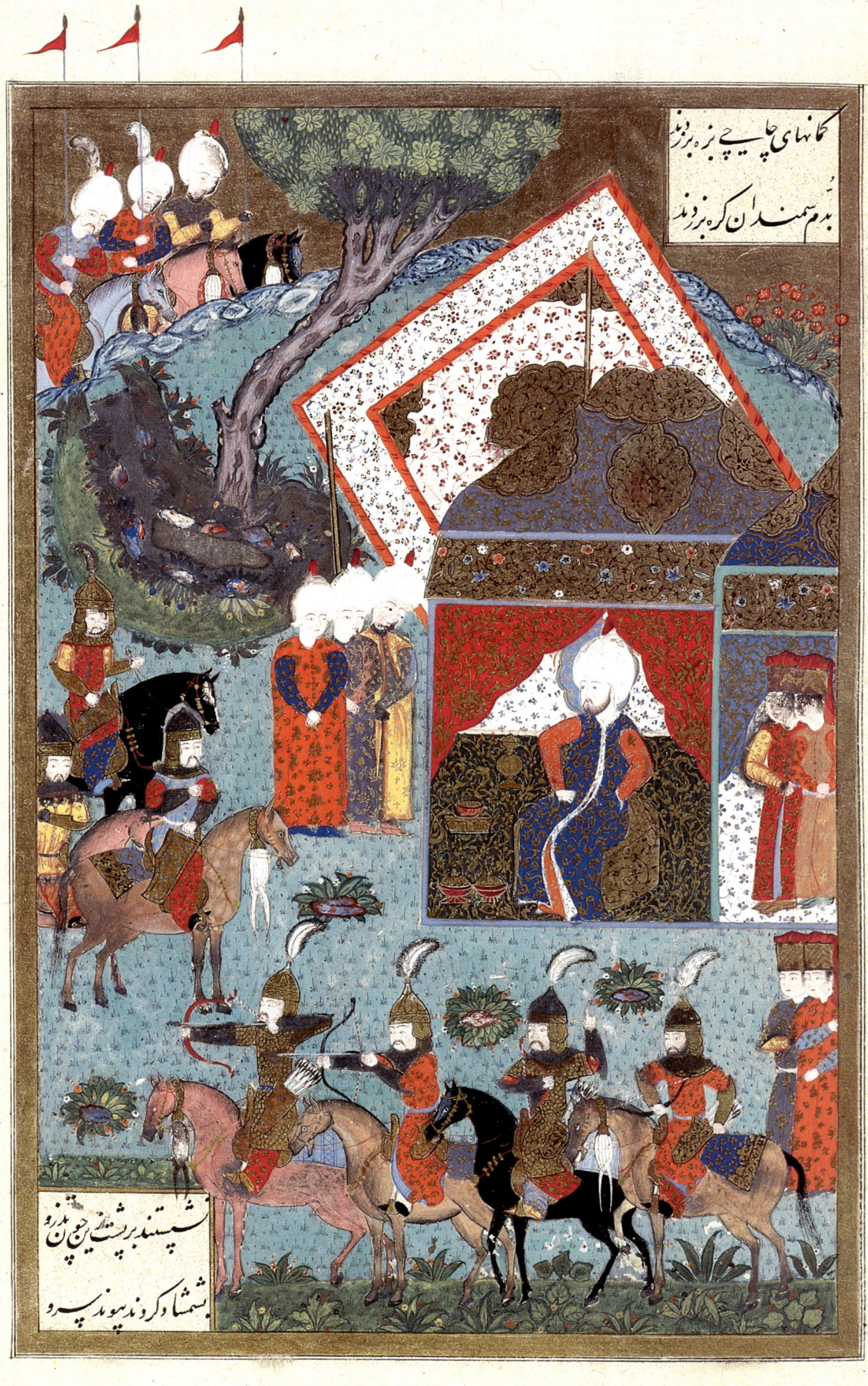

61. Performance of the Archers
(folio 588a)   Painter A

THE OTTOMAN FORCES halted briefly in Erzurum, where the regiments of the vezirs, beylerbeyis, and Şehzade Selim paraded before the sultan. The sultan had amassed a formidable army, superbly disciplined and trained. Süleyman had sent word to Tahmasp, demanding a confrontation, but the şah refused to be drawn into battle and kept withdrawing. Süleyman followed his official declaration of war by marching into the Caucasus, heading toward Revan and Nahçivan.

> On the way to Nahçivan, the army halted in a valley called Pasinabad outside Erzurum. Here the *bahadırs* (archers) put on a display. Süleyman, enthroned in his otak and attended by his Has Oda ağas and iç oğlans, watches the bahadırs, who are lined up in the foreground. The archers wear helmets with plumes and protective coverings over their arms; some also wear chain mail tunics. Additional members appear on the left, waiting for their turn.
>
> Cavalrymen carrying banners look in from behind the high hill, which has a large tree, its trunk echoing the curve of the lining of the sultan's kaftan. Süleyman, taking a brief period of rest, is shown in a beautifully decorated tent with jugs, bowls of fruit, and refreshments placed on the black and gold floor covering.

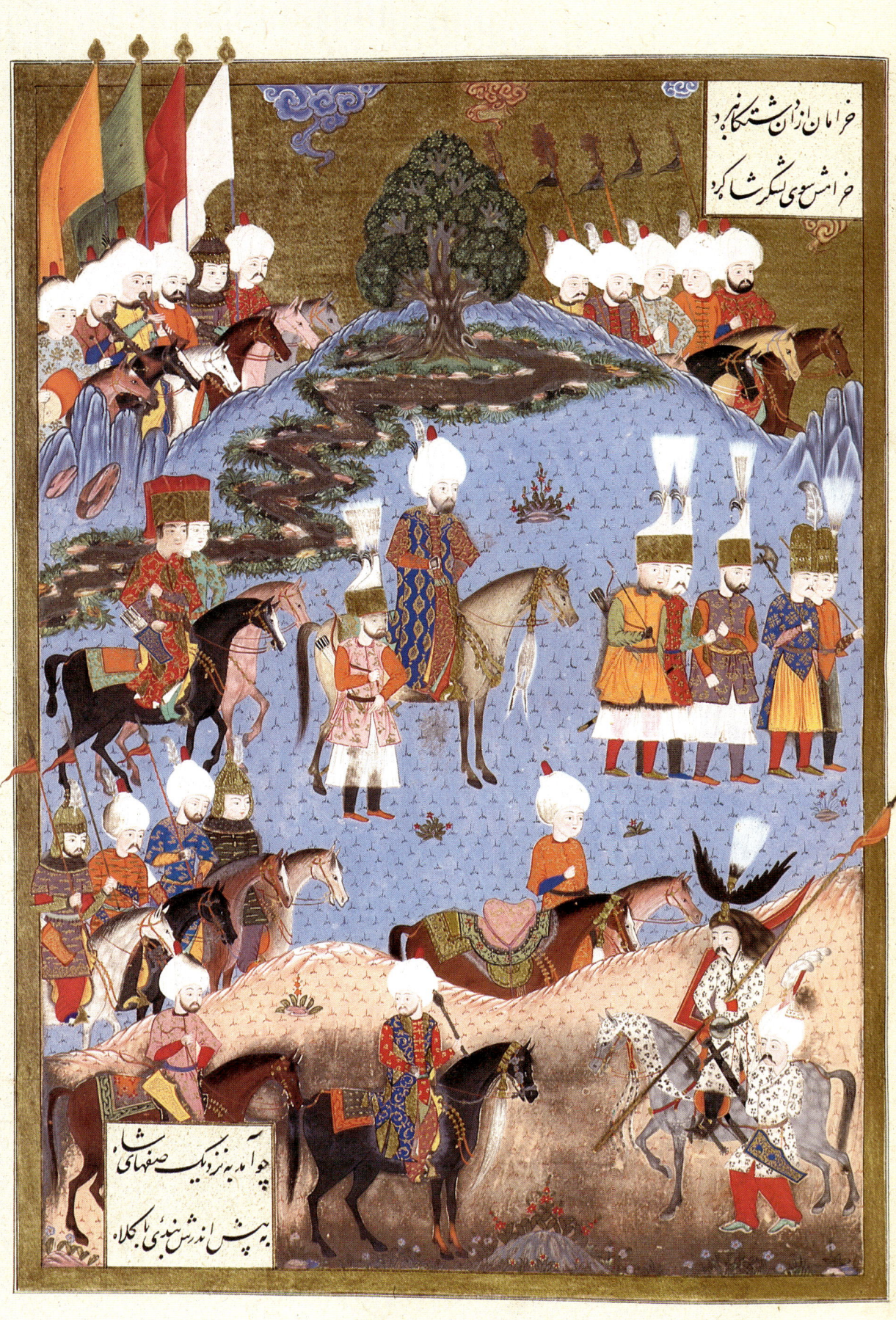

62. Süleyman Marching with the Army

(folio 592a)   Painter A

SÜLEYMAN ARRIVED AT Nahçivan at the end of July 1554. His commanders were inflicting serious defeats on the Safavids and capturing many cities and towns in the region. The Ottomans won a major battle against the Safavids at Taht-ı Süleyman, after which Tahmasp sued for peace.

During his twelfth sefer-i hümayun the sultan annexed a major portion of the Caucasus, extending the eastern frontier of his empire. Satisfied with the results of the campaign, Süleyman began to withdraw his forces and headed back via Erzurum and Sivas, arriving at Amasya at the end of October. There he dismissed his forces after rewarding them for courageously carrying out their duties.

Although the text accompanying this painting describes the battle between a delil named Divane-i Rumeli and a Safavid commander, the artist presents this as a minor episode, concentrating instead on the representation of the sultan marching with his forces. On the lower right is the delil with huge wings on his headdress; he has overcome the Safavid commander and taken him prisoner. Riding toward him are two officers, one of whom carries a mace.

The Ottoman army appears in the field behind the hill in the foreground. Süleyman rides in the center, flanked by two solaks. A pair of peyks holding halberds and three other solaks with bows and arrows precede him on foot while two Has Oda ağas ride behind. Below is a youthful attendant leading the sultan's spare horse and a group of turbaned and helmeted officers.

The mehter playing drums and horns appears on the upper left together with the flagbearers. Opposite are the cavalry officers with banners attached to their spears. Separating the two groups is a tree growing at the pinnacle of the hill with a river at its roots that flows down in a zigzag formation. Planes separated by hills and the flow of the river help to create a sense of depth and spaciousness.

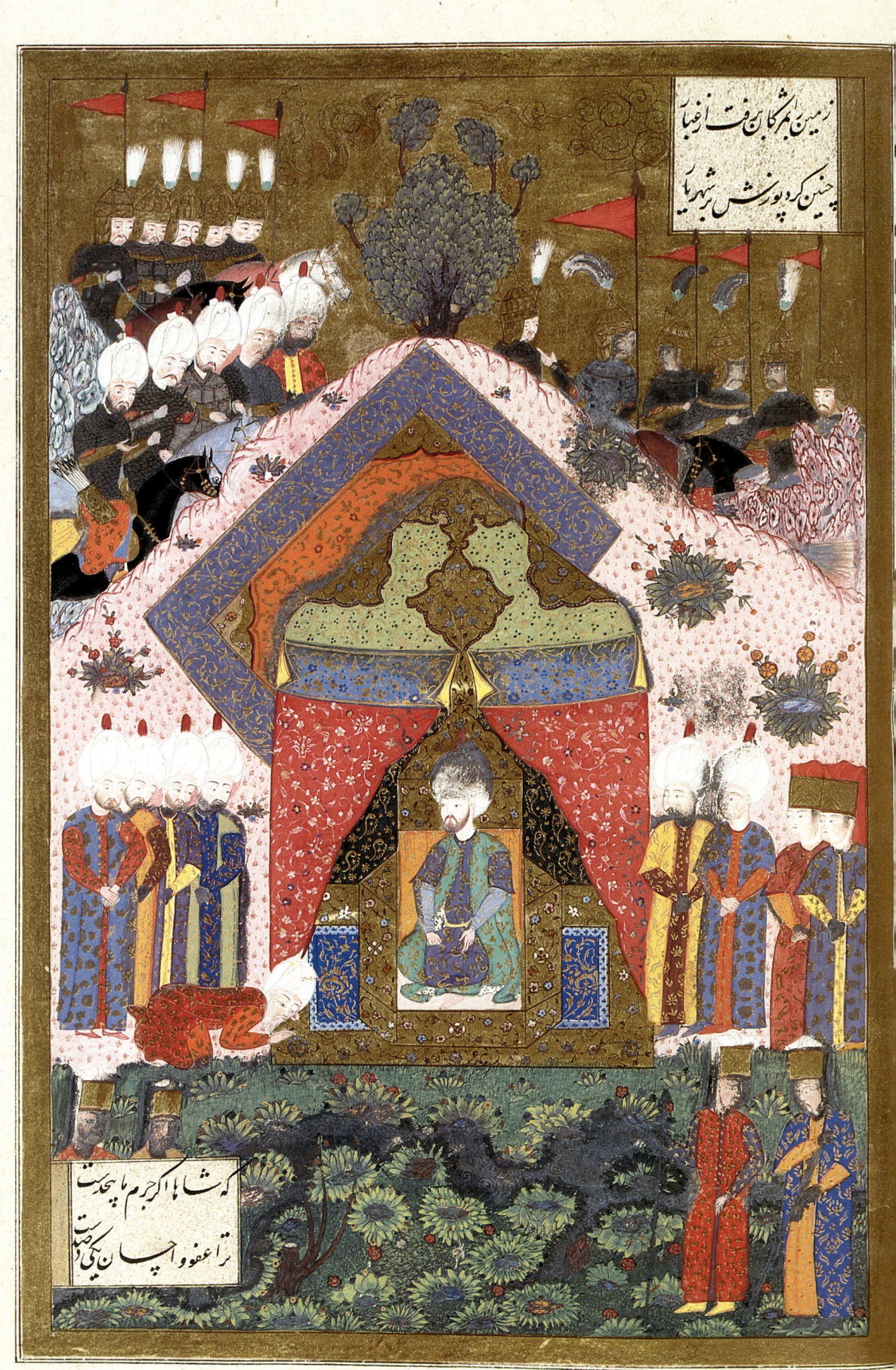

63. Reception of the Iranian Ambassador
(folio 600a)   Painter A

SÜLEYMAN SPENT THE winter of 1554-1555 in Amasya. He attended to the political and administrative affairs of the state, taking time off to hunt for relaxation. He was getting on in years and feeling the strain of continual campaigning on two frontiers. His primary concern was to end the long and inconclusive wars with the Safavids.

Süleyman and Tahmasp exchanged a number of ambassadors, trying to find a solution that was acceptable to both sides. Safavid envoys came with a series of proposals from the şah and returned with the sultan's counteroffers.

> The reception of Şah Tahmasp's elderly envoy takes place in the imperial camp set up on the banks of a river outside Amasya. Standing in the foreground along the river are two pairs of kapıcıs. Süleyman, enthroned in the tent placed in the center of the painting, is flanked by his iç oğlans, Has Oda ağas, and vezirs. The ambassador, identified in the text as Sinan, kneels in front of the sultan, relaying Tahmasp's request for an armistice. Rising behind the tent is a hill, at the summit of which is a large tree with officers carrying banners gathered on each side.
>
> The symmetrical composition contains a triangular formation, in the center of which is the sultan seated on a gold throne, surrounded by rich furnishings. He dominates the composition just as he triumphs over the Safavids from whom he accepts submission.

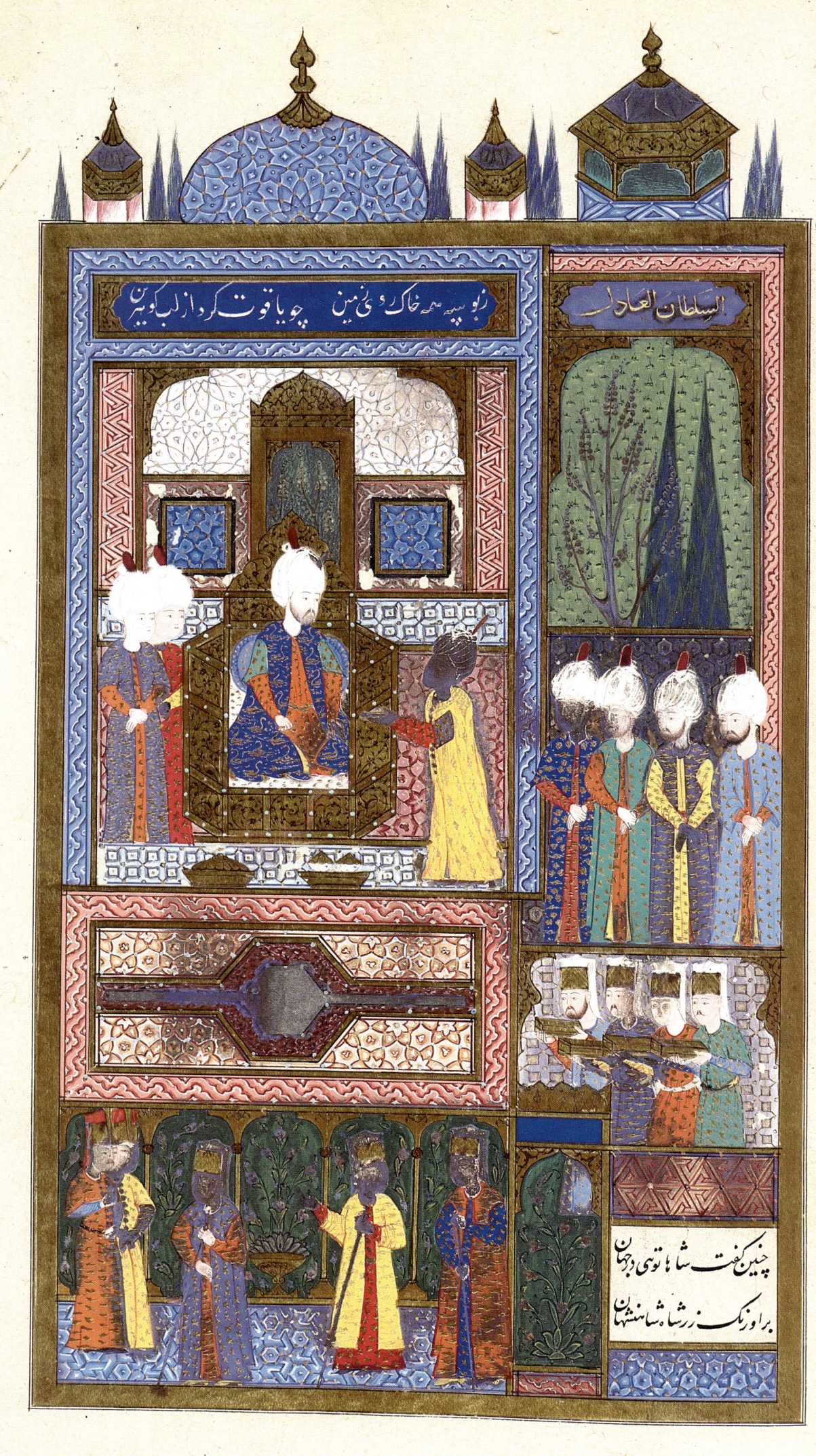

64. Reception of the Iranian Ambassador

(folio 603a)   Painter A

FINALLY Süleyman and Tahmasp agreed on the terms of the armistice. The şah sent as his ambassador Ferruhzade Kemaleddin Bey, who arrived in Amasya on 10 May 1555 with Tahmasp's offer of friendship. According to Arifi the şah also sent valuable gifts, including a gold-embroidered canopy for a tent resembling a rose garden, caskets filled with gold coins, silks with figural representations, jewelry, bows, and countless other unusual and rare items. After meeting with the vezirs of the Divan, the Safavid envoy was received by Süleyman. The peace treaty signed on 29 May determined the frontier between the Ottomans and the Safavids.

Meanwhile the French delegation representing Henry II had arrived in Amasya together with a group sent by Ferdinand. The Austrians, headed by the renowned statesman Baron Ogier de Busbecq, were able to obtain only a six-month cease-fire before returning to Vienna.

After concluding his diplomatic meetings, Süleyman left Amasya and arrived in İstanbul on 31 July. The sultan did not embark on a military expedition for the next eleven years. His thirteenth and last sefer-i hümayun was to be undertaken in 1566, from which he did not return.

> Süleyman, enthroned in the reception chamber of the Amasya palace, converses with the Safavid ambassador, who is pleading the şah's terms. The setting resembles the Arz Odası with a pavilion rising behind an arcade, its entrance placed to the side. Here, however, is a marble courtyard with a fountain in front of the pavilion, recalling the layout of the Has Oda. Participating in the ceremony are four vezirs and a pair of iç oğlans. Walking in front of the arcade are several officers and kapıcıs holding staffs. Four attendants have entered the complex, carrying jeweled gold boxes and containers sent by Tahmasp.
>
> Similar to Painter A's other representations, the pavilion is composed of various elaborately decorated units, some of which open into the gardens in the background. Inscribed above the arch on the upper right are the words *el-sultan el-adil*, "just sultan," referring to Süleyman's renowned legislative acts. The presence of refreshments in the pavilion—a large covered bowl and two small porcelain cups on a tray—indicates that the negotiations are almost over and the celebrations about to begin.

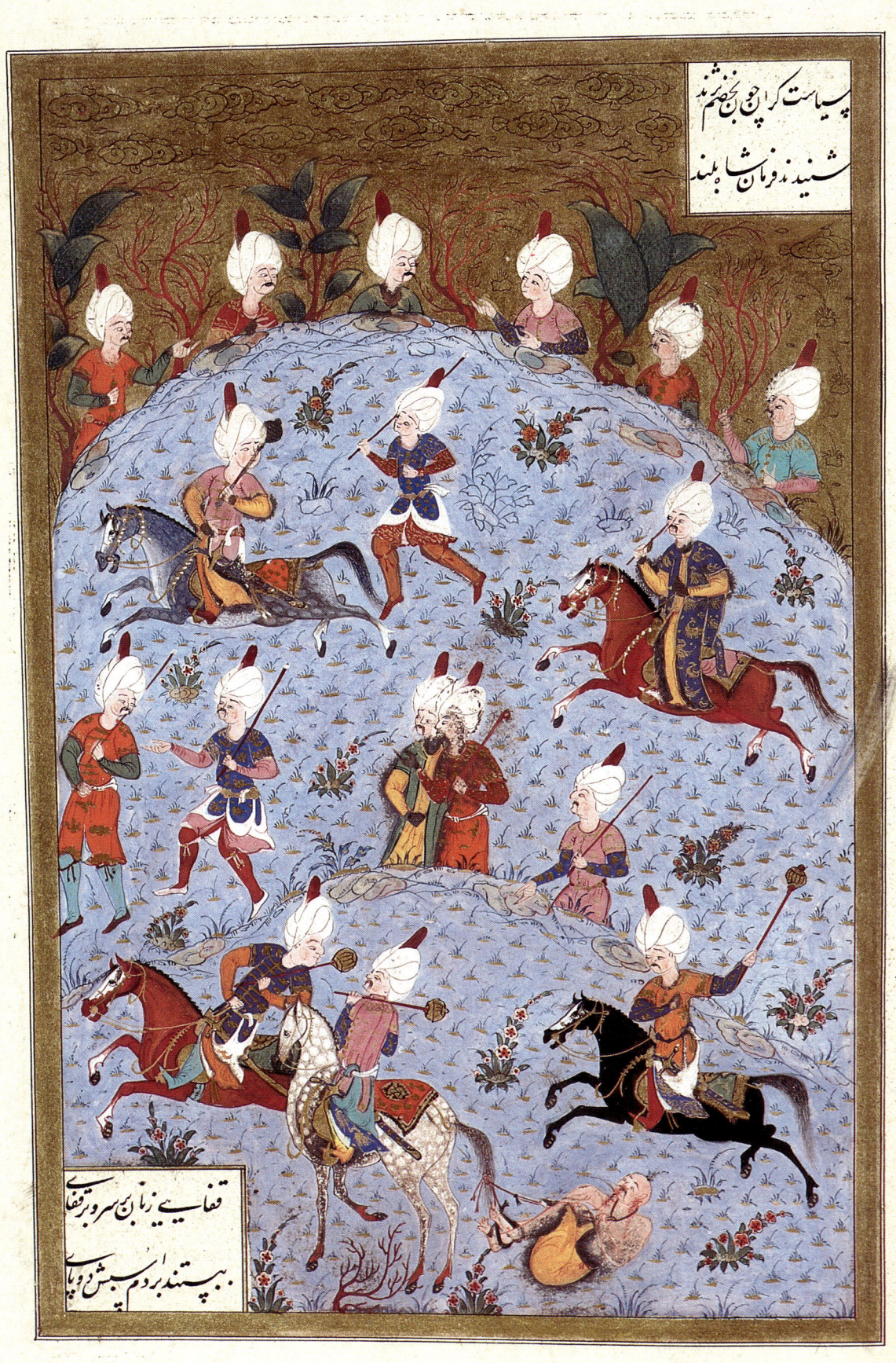

65. Death of Contender Mustafa

(folio 611a)   Painter B

WHILE SÜLEYMAN WAS preoccupied with diplomatic negotiations in Amasya, a man who resembled the executed Şehzade Mustafa impersonated the prince, inciting an uprising in Salonica. Şehzade Bayezid, stationed in Edirne, sent a force against him.

Upon returning to İstanbul, Süleyman entrusted the third vezir Sokollu Mehmed Paşa with the contender Mustafa affair. The impersonator was caught and brought to İstanbul to be tried at the end of July 1555.

Shortly after this affair the grand vezir Kara Ahmed Paşa was executed, accused of supporting the unjust activities of the beylerbeyi of Cairo and undermining the authority of the sultan. Rüstem Paşa was reinstated on September 1555, beginning his second term as the grand vezir, a post he held until his death in 1561.

The last scene of the manuscript shows the death of the man who impersonated Şehzade Mustafa and led an uprising against the sultan. He was caught outside Salonica and brought to İstanbul. In the foreground the half-naked prisoner, tied to the tail of a horse, is dragged on the ground with his hands and feet bound. The officer on the horse converses nonchalantly with his colleague, while a third rider moves toward them. Other riders and foot soldiers holding maces or sticks appear on the next plane. Several figures lined up behind the hill in the background discuss the fate of the contender.

The illustration is typical of Painter B's scenes: the setting and the figure types are generalized, and the composition is built up of parallel horizontal registers. A lively action is created by the beautifully rendered galloping horses and conversing figures.

Appendices

CHRONOLOGY

1494	Süleyman born in Trabzon (6 November).
1509	Süleyman governor in Bolu; accession of Henry VIII.
1510	Süleyman governor in Kefe.
1512	Abdication of Bayezid II and accession of Selim I (24 April); Süleyman called to İstanbul; death of Bayezid II (26 May); Selim I fights brothers Korkud and Ahmed.
1513	Süleyman governor in Manisa.
1514	Selim I embarks on campaign to Iran; Süleyman asked to serve as regent in Edirne; conquest of Tabriz.
1515	Birth of Mustafa to Gülbahar; Francis I becomes king of France.
1516	Selim I embarks on campaign to Syria and Egypt; Süleyman asked to serve as regent in Edirne.
1517	Conquest of Syria and Egypt; end of Mamluk rule; caliphate passes to Ottoman sultans.
1520	Death of Selim I (22 September); Süleyman arrives in İstanbul (30 September); accession ceremonies (1 October); marries Hürrem; Canberdi Gazali rebellion in Damascus.
1521	Gazali rebellion quelled (6 February); Ottoman ambassador, Behram Çavuş, killed in Hungary by Louis II; first campaign (18 May-19 October) to Belgrade; conquest of Böğürdelen; conquest of Belgrade (29 August); death of Süleyman's two sons, Murad and Mahmud, and unnamed daughter; birth of Mehmed to Hürrem; Charles V becomes emperor of Holy Roman Empire.
1522	Second campaign (16 June 1522-30 January 1523) to Rhodes; conquest of Rhodes (21 December), Bodrum, and Aegean Islands; birth of Abdullah and Mihrimah to Hürrem.
1523	Süleyman returns to İstanbul; İbrahim Paşa becomes grand vezir; Ahmed Paşa rebellion in Egypt.
1524	Death of Ahmed Paşa; İbrahim Paşa marries Hadice, Süleyman's sister; birth of Selim to Hürrem (28 May); Tahmasp on Safavid throne.
1525	Francis I taken captive and imprisoned by Charles V; birth of Bayezid to Hürrem (14 September).
1526	French ambassadors in court with letters from Francis I and Louise of Savoy; third campaign (23 April-13 November) to Mohacs; victory at Battle of Mohacs (29 August); death of Louis II; Süleyman receives John Zapolya in Budapest, appoints him king of Hungary (10 November); rebellion in Anatolia; death of Şehzade Abdullah.
1527	Kalender rebellion quelled; Ferdinand occupies Budapest.
1529	Fourth campaign (10 May-16 December) to Vienna; Budapest taken (8 September) and John Zapolya enthroned (14 September); Süleyman besieges Vienna (26 September-16 October); crown of Saint Stephen returned to Hungary.
1530	Festival for the circumcision of Şehzades Mustafa, Mehmed, and Selim (18 June); Süleyman receives Austrian ambassadors.
1531	Ferdinand besieges Budapest; birth of Cihangir to Hürrem.
1532	Fifth campaign (25 April-21 November) to Güns; Andrea Doria captures Coron (8 August); conquest of Güns (28 August); alliance with Poland.
1533	Peace treaty with Ferdinand (22 June); governor of Bitlis joins Tahmasp; İbrahim Paşa leaves for Iran.
1534	Death of the queen mother Hafsa Sultan (19 March); Barbaros Hayreddin Paşa becomes grand admiral, conquers Coron and Tunis; sixth campaign (11 June 1534-8 January 1536) to Iran and Iraq; conquest of Van, Tabriz (July), and Baghdad (November); annexation of

	Azerbaijan and Iraq; governors of Gilan and Şirvan join Süleyman; Süleyman spends four months in Baghdad, reconstructing the city; Tahmasp takes Van and Tabriz.
1535	Süleyman reenters Tabriz; Charles V takes Tunis (21 July); Sam Mirza joins Ottomans.
1536	Süleyman returns to İstanbul; Ottoman-French treaty (February); execution of İbrahim Paşa (15 March); Barbaros Hayreddin Paşa campaigns on coast of Italy; war with Venice.
1537	Seventh campaign (17 May-22 November) to Corfu; siege of Corfu (25 August); Barbaros Hayreddin Paşa conquers Mediterranean ports.
1538	Eighth campaign (9 July-27 November) to Moldavia; Barbaros Hayreddin Paşa's victory at Battle of Preveza (29 September); annexation of southern Moldavia (4 October); governor of Basra joins Süleyman; Hadım Süleyman Paşa campaigns in India; annexation of Aden.
1539	Hadım Süleyman Paşa establishes an Ottoman province in Yemen; conquest of Castelnuovo (10 August); circumcision festival for Şehzades Bayezid and Cihangir, and wedding of Mihrimah and Rüstem Paşa (11 November).
1540	Peace treaty with Venice; death of John Zapolya; birth of Stephen Zapolya; Ferdinand invades Hungary.
1541	Ninth campaign (20 June-27 November) to Hungary; Süleyman in Budapest (2 September); Hungary annexed; Barbaros Hayreddin Paşa defeats Charles V in Algiers.
1542	Ferdinand's army besieges Budapest; Austrians repelled by Ottomans and city saved.
1543	Tenth campaign (23 April-16 November) to Hungary; conquest of Pecs, Siklos, Estergon, and Estonibelgrad; Barbaros Hayreddin Paşa lands in Marseilles and Toulon, captures Nice; death of Şehzade Mehmed in Manisa (6 November).
1544	Sinan begins construction of the Şehzade Mehmed Mosque; Mehmed Paşa conquers fortresses in Hungary; Rüstem Paşa becomes grand vezir.
1545	Armistice with Ferdinand; Ebussuud Efendi becomes şeyhülislam (until 1574).
1546	Conquest of Taiz in Yemen; death of Barbaros Hayreddin Paşa; Sokullu Mehmed Paşa appointed grand admiral; death of Martin Luther.
1547	Five-year treaty signed with Habsburgs, papacy, Venice, and France (1 August); Sanaa conquered by Özdemir Paşa; Elkas Mirza arrives in court with Arifi and Eflatun; death of Francis I; accession of Henry II; accession of Ivan IV; death of Henry VIII.
1548	Eleventh campaign (29 March 1548-21 December 1549) to Iran; Elkas Mirza advances in Iran; conquest of Tabriz (28 July) and Van (25 August); completion of the Şehzade Mehmed Mosque.
1549	Elkas Mirza captured and imprisoned by Tahmasp; conquests in Georgia; Süleyman returns to İstanbul.
1550	Foundation laid for the Süleymaniye Mosque; Koca Sinan Paşa becomes grand admiral.
1551	Campaigns in Transylvania against Ferdinand; conquest of Lipva; Turgud Reis captures Tripoli (14 August); fall of Lipva.
1552	Ahmed Paşa captures Temesvar and Lipva, besieges Erlau; Tahmasp attacks Van and Erzurum; Piri Reis attacks Hormuz and Muscat.
1553	Franco-Ottoman naval allegiance; Turgud Reis attacks Corsica; twelfth campaign (28 August 1553-31 July 1555) to Iran and Georgia; execution of Şehzade Mustafa at Aktepe (6 October); death of Şehzade Cihangir (27 November); expulsion of Rüstem Paşa; Kara Ahmed Paşa becomes grand vezir.
1554	Conquest of Nahçivan and Revan; rise of the contender Mustafa; death of Piri Reis; death of Koca Sinan Paşa; Piyale Paşa becomes grand admiral (until 1568).
1555	Süleyman spends winter in Amasya; Busbecq arrives in Amasya; treaties signed with the Safavids (29 May) and Habsburgs (2 June); sultan returns to İstanbul (July); death of contender Mustafa; execution of grand vezir Kara Ahmed Paşa (28 September); Rüstem Paşa reinstated; Ottoman navy active in the Mediterranean; first coffee shops open in İstanbul.
1556	Continuation of warfare with Ferdinand; Ottoman navy conquers Oran in Algeria.
1557	Dedication of the Süleymaniye Mosque (15 August).
1558	Naval campaigns in Balearic islands; death of Hürrem (15 April); completion of the *Süleymanname* (late June-early July); death of Charles V; Ferdinand becomes Holy Roman Emperor; accession of Elizabeth I.
1559	Civil war between Şehzades Bayezid and Selim; Bayezid, defeated at Konya (June), flees to Iran; received in Kazvin by Tahmasp.
1560	Tahmasp imprisons Şehzade Bayezid; Ottoman navy besieges Malta; conquers Jerba on north African coast.

1561 Death of Rüstem Paşa (12 July); execution of Şehzade Bayezid (25 September).

1562 Peace treaty with Austria.

1564 Death of Ferdinand.

1565 Siege of Malta (20 May-11 September); death of Turgud Reis; Sokollu Mehmed Paşa appointed grand vezir (until 1579).

1566 Thirteenth campaign (1 May-7 September) to Szigetvar; death of Süleyman (7 September); conquest of Szigetvar; accession of Selim II (30 September); burial of Süleyman (28 November).

GENEALOGY

FATHER: Selim I (born 1470 in Amasya; accession ceremonies 24 April 1512; died 22 September 1520)

MOTHER: Hafsa (born ?; valide sultan 1520-1534; died 19 March 1534)

BROTHERS: Abdullah, Mahmud, Murad (mothers unknown; all three died 1514?); Üveys (unrecognized since born after mother given as wife to another official; died 1546)

AUNTS (PATERNAL):
Hadice (married İbrahim Paşa 1524)
Selçuk (married Ferhad Paşa)
? (married Yahya Paşa)

COUSINS:
Bali (son of unknown aunt and Yahya Paşa; died 1543)
Mehmed (son of unknown aunt and Yahya Paşa; died 1551)
Ahmed (son of unknown aunt and Yahya Paşa)
Hüsrev (1480-1541; son of Selçuk and Ferhad Paşa)

WIVES AND CHILDREN:
Gülfem
  1. Mahmud (1512-1521)
  2. Murad (1519-1521)
  3. daughter (died 1521)
  4. daughter (?)

Gülbahar (married 1515 ?; died 3 February 1581)
  1. Mustafa (1515-1553; married ?; three children; son Mehmed or Murad died 1553)

Hürrem (born 1500?; married 1520?; died 15 April 1558)
  1. Mehmed (1521-1543; married Aya)
  2. Abdullah (1522-1526)
  3. Mihrimah (1522-1578; married Rüstem Paşa 1539; daughter married first Semiz Ahmed Paşa, then Ahmed Feridun Paşa)
  4. Selim (born 28 May 1524; accession ceremonies 30 September 1566; died 15 December 1574; married Nurbanu; son Murad reigned 1574-1595; daughter Esmahan married Sokollu Mehmed Paşa)
  5. Bayezid (1525-1561; married ?; sons Abdullah, Mahmud, Mehmed, and Orhan died 1561)
  6. Cihangir (1531-1553)

CONTENTS OF THE SÜLEYMANNAME

Arifi's *Süleymanname* contains 30,000 verses based on the meter of Firdausi's *Şahname* and opens with the traditional münacat, prayers found at the beginning of literary or epic works. Here the author has selected certain verses from the Koran that pertain to Solomon, thus implying a parallel between the patriarch and the sultan, both of whom have the same name and fame. This section also includes prayers devoted to the fortune, majesty, justice, and leadership of the ancient prophets, associating these deeds with the life and activities of the sultan.

The münacat is followed by a prologue that ends with the accession ceremonies of Süleyman. The remaining portion of the text is divided into 171 major sections, which contain a summary at the beginning under the heading of *matla-ı dasıtan* (beginning of the epic), and 608 subsections identified by descriptive subheadings. Each major section comprises one to thirty subsections of varying length.

Arifi follows the chronology of Süleyman's reign closely, giving occasional dates in the subheadings. Although in a few places he breaks the sequence with a flashback to an episode that took place earlier, he generally adheres to a strictly sequential account of the events. Occasionally he indulges in poetic excursions and hyperboles, extolling the qualities of such subjects as the seasons and the climate. When compared with other historical sources, Arifi's accounts have a high degree of accuracy, with the exception of a few instances. For example, the author describes Queen Isabella as being present during the 1541 meeting of Süleyman and Stephen Zapolya (see 43), whereas all the other historians state that the infant king was brought by his nurse, not by his mother.

Arifi begins the epic history with the events of September 1520, when Süleyman is informed of the death of his father, and terminates it in September 1555, when the grand vezir Kara Ahmed Paşa is executed and Rüstem Paşa reinstalled. The end of the text is followed by a eulogy to the sultan and the colophon.

The following is a listing of the major sections of the text with a summary of the subsections; the illustrated subjects are marked with an asterisk; figures on the right refer to the folios where these sections begin.

	Zahriye (Dedication)	1b
	Münacat (Prayers)	2b
*	Prologue: praises of the sultan; death of Selim I; arrival of the sultan in İstanbul; accession ceremonies.	4a
1.	Body of Selim I arrives in İstanbul; the new sultan addresses the army.	19a
2.	The sultan restores confiscated goods to merchants; execution of kaptan-ı derya for injustice.	24a
3.	Ottoman laws.	26a
4.	"Mansur" soldiers and those paid by the state.	27a
5.	Laws and ranks of the military classes; their ranks in the palace.	28a
*6.	Laws and ranks of the non-Muslims.	31a
7.	Laws and ranks of the judicial and learned classes.	33b
8.	Traditions and regulations of the students of the learned class.	34b
*9.	Laws of the Divan.	36a
10.	Description of ranks and duties of various military and administrative personnel.	40a
11.	Description of defense forces, gunners, and riflemen.	46a
12.	Description of the types of ships.	48b

13.	Introduction to the book; story of Rüstem appearing in Firdausi's dream; description of famous grand vezirs.	50a
*14.	Rebellion of Canberdi Gazali.	54a
15.	Canberdi Gazali advances to Aleppo.	57a
16.	Canberdi Gazali's battle with Karaca Paşa.	58b
17.	Qualities of fire and description of winter; continuation of Gazali's rebellion.	59a
*18.	Continuation of Gazali's rebellion; death of Gazali; year 927.	61b
19.	Beginning of the campaign to Belgrade.	64a
*20.	The sultan declares war; departs from İstanbul; is entertained in Edirne; arrives in Filibe.	66b
21.	The sultan calls for a Divan; discussions among the vezirs.	74a
22.	The sultan arrives in Sophia.	76b
23.	Ahmed Paşa sends soldiers to Böğürdelen; janissaries burn enemy vessels on the Danube; Piri Mehmed Paşa advances to Belgrade.	78a
*24.	Conquest of Böğürdelen.	79b
25.	The sultan orders bridge to be built; Piri Mehmed Paşa relates conditions of Belgrade; heavy artillery placed under outer fort; conquest of outer fort.	83a
26.	The sultan sends word asking to see Piri Mehmed Paşa.	89a
27.	Mustafa Paşa conferring with Piri Mehmed Paşa.	90a
28.	Other events involving Piri Mehmed Paşa.	91a
29.	Battle between Piri Mehmed Paşa and soldiers of Belgrade.	92b
*30.	Completion of bridge in ten days; collapse of bridge during rains; prisoners executed by an elephant.	96a
31.	The sultan advances toward Belgrade; description of attack; the sultan orders bridge on the Sava; outer fort falls.	98b
*32.	The sultan orders mines to be dug; bridge on the Sava completed; prisoners sent by Bali Bey from Hungary arrive; miners successful in blowing up towers; Ottomans enter fortress.	105a
33.	Conquest of Belgrade, year 927; booty taken by the sultan.	111b
*34.	Death of Şehzade Murad; the sultan hunts at Uzuncaabad.	113a
35.	Death of Şehzade Mahmud; murder of the governor of Yemen, İskender, by Kemal Bey; death of Bıyıklı Mehmed Paşa.	115b
36.	Reasons for campaign to Rhodes.	117a
37.	Qualities of spring; strength of fortification of Rhodes; the sultan sends Ferhad Paşa to Sivas after Şehsuvarzade Ali Bey.	118a
38.	Soldiers sent to Rhodes.	122a
39.	The sultan visits Eyüp Sultan; embarks for Rhodes. Hüsrev Paşa, governor of Diyarbakır, sends word that Menuçihr, the king of Georgia, accepts the sultan's sovereignty; the sultan arrives in Kütahya.	123b
40.	Mustafa Paşa arrives at Rhodes; begins fighting.	127b
*41.	Description of summer heat; the sultan travels at night; hunts at the Menderes River.	130b
42.	Conquests of Herke and Iskaradan fortresses; Ferhad Paşa sends word of death of Şehsuvarzade Ali Bey.	132b
43.	The sultan arrives at Marmaris.	134b
44.	The sultan requests surrender of knights; orders siege of fortress.	135b
45.	Ships arrive from Egypt.	137a
46.	Description of the fortress of Rhodes.	138a
47.	Description of the trenches and fortifications.	138b
48.	Work of the Ottoman miners; disposal of excavated earth; enemy's counteroffensives.	139b
*49.	Continuation of mining; piles of earth outside fortress; the sultan orders massive attack; death of the governor of Avlonya.	142a
50.	Ahmed Paşa praises janissary ağa; opposed by beylerbeyi of Rumelia.	145b
51.	Birth of Şehzade Mehmed.	147a
*52.	Ottoman cannonball ignites enemy ammunition dump and blows up tower.	147b
53.	Death of Hayırbay, beylerbeyi of Egypt; Mustafa Paşa sent to Cairo; fortress defenses divide into four units; the sultan sends navy to Marmaris due to winter storms; bombardment of fortress; repairs by enemy.	149b
*54.	Breach in the walls; Ottomans attack, then retreat due to rains; Bali Ağa, the janissary commander, encourages his men to attack.	152b

55.	Knights sue for cease-fire; the sultan accepts their offer; arrival of enemy ships; the sultan's anger at kaptan-ı derya; the arrival of Ferhad Paşa and his forces; fall of Rhodes, year 929.	156b
56.	The sultan rewards army; Ahmed Paşa professes friendship to İbrahim Paşa.	161a
57.	Reasons for the expulsion of Ferhad Paşa; retirement of janissary commander Bali Ağa.	162b
58.	Battle between Ahmed and İbrahim Paşa over the grand vezirate; Mustafa Paşa quells rebellion in Egypt; Ahmed Paşa sent to Cairo; Ahmed Paşa rebels in Egypt.	165b
*59.	Army in Egypt refuses to support Ahmed Paşa; death of Ahmed Paşa at the hand of his soldiers, year 930.	169a
60.	Decapitated head of Ahmed Paşa sent to İstanbul; Kasım Paşa assigned to Egypt; İbrahim Paşa sent to Egypt.	171a
*61.	The sultan hunts at Yanbolu; displays great feats; hunts at Edirne; execution of Ferhad Paşa; janissaries loot İstanbul at night; birth of Şehzade Selim, year 932.	172b
62.	Reasons for Hungarian campaign; İbrahim Paşa encourages war with Hungary.	180a
63.	Arrival of French ambassadors and presentation of French king's letter.	182b
64.	The sultan prepares for Hungarian campaign; description of the Crimean han; the sultan leaves İstanbul for Hungary.	184b
*65.	The sultan arrives in Sophia; commanders arrive with their mehters to greet the sultan; tribute arrives from Moldavia and Chios.	188a
66.	İbrahim Paşa sent with Rumelian army in advance; Bali Bey, son of Yahya Paşa, joins İbrahim Paşa.	190a
67.	Rumelian army crosses the Sava and arrives at Sirem Island; distribution of arms to soldiers; nightfall and capture of enemy; the sultan frees prisoners.	191b
68.	Battle of Varadin; enemy burns city and escapes to inner fort; conquest of Varadin; the sultan receives and rewards commanders.	193b
69.	Conquest of Ilok fortress; enemy sues for peace and surrenders; conquest of Sirem fortress.	196b
*70.	Louis II hears that the sultan is approaching.	198b
71.	The sultan orders a bridge over the Drava; prisoners taken from Louis' army.	202a
72.	İbrahim Paşa crosses Drava with army; the sultan crosses Drava and orders bridge destroyed.	204a
73.	Louis II sends Tomor Pavli to destroy bridge over Drava; Pavli finds bridge already destroyed.	205b
74.	İbrahim Paşa requests Bali Bey to find out Hungarian strategy; Bali Bey's answer; İbrahim's idea of unloading equipment on battlefield.	207b
*75.	Descriptions of the Anatolian and Hungarian camps; Louis II advances with armored army.	209b
*76.	Hungarians begin attack; battle of the Hungarian and Rumelian armies; Louis II advances and retreats; the sultan orders advance to Louis II's camp.	216a
77.	Ottoman victory; the sultan distributes rewards; moves on to Budapest.	222b
78.	The sultan arrives at Budapest, year 932; part of city burns.	224b
79.	The sultan hunting; assembles Divan in the former king's palace.	226a
80.	The sultan allows soldiers to attack; conquest of Szegedin and Tetel fortresses.	228b
81.	Conquest of Pecs fortress; death of the janissary ağa.	230b
**82.	Rebellion in Bozok; Behram Paşa sent against the rebels; Hüseyin Paşa fights the rebels; rebellion quelled; death of Şehzade Abdullah; Kalender's offensive.	232a
83.	Battle between Kalender and Fil Yakub.	239b
84.	The sultan sends İbrahim Paşa against Kalender; Behram Paşa prepares for battle; arrival of forces from Karaman and Aleppo.	241b
85.	Death of the governors of Karaman, Alaiye, and Bireci.	243b
86.	Good news arrives from Anatolia.	245a
*87.	Death of Kalender by Pervane, year 933.	246b
88.	The sultan rewards soldiers.	248b
89.	Kasım Paşa appointed the beylerbeyi of Rumelia; Bali Bey sends word to John Zapolya; Ferdinand defeats Zapolya.	249b
90.	Zapolya requests the sultan's aid; Ferdinand sends letter demanding Budapest.	252a
91.	The sultan embarks for Hungary for the second time.	255b
*92.	İbrahim Paşa becomes serasker; comes to kiss the sultan's foot.	256b
93.	İbrahim Paşa gives banquet to military commanders; death of Mustafa Paşa.	260b
94.	The sultan leaves İstanbul; increases the number of sancaks.	262b

*95.	Torrential rains; rivers overflow; the sultan crosses the Meriç River.	263b
96.	Ruler of Croatia joins Ottomans; news of victory from Mehmed Bey; İslam Han defeated by Saadet Giray Han.	267a
97.	Ferdinand sends letter to court; the sultan's answer.	269a
98.	Zapolya arrives at Mohacs; parade of the army; Zapolya astonished at army's might.	271a
99.	Commander of Estergon joins Ottomans; İbrahim Paşa besieges Budapest.	274a
100.	Battle between forces of İbrahim Paşa and commander of Budapest.	275b
101.	Prisoners give information on fortress to İbrahim Paşa.	276b
102.	İbrahim Paşa creates conflict between Austrians and Hungarians.	279a
*103.	Mines dug beneath towers of Budapest fortress; mines exploded; Austrians flee to inner fortress; Austrians sue for peace; send message to İbrahim Paşa.	280b
104.	Story of Halid b. Velid in Mecca used as an example.	286a
105.	The sultan arrives at Budapest; İbrahim Paşa goes to Beşkırad fortress for crown of Hungary.	286b
106.	İbrahim Paşa sends envoy to Beşkırad fortress; commander of Beşkırad comes with the stolen crown.	289a
107.	The sultan bestows Hungary on Zapolya; enthronement of Zapolya, year 934.	291a
108.	Conquest of fortresses; İbrahim Paşa sends soldiers to Vienna.	293b
*109.	Battle between the Rumelian army and the Austrians.	295b
110.	The sultan is informed that Ferdinand has escaped; Austrians attack at night.	297b
111.	The sultan's dream; inspects Vienna on horseback; reasons for lifting siege.	301a
112.	Qualities of cold; the sultan asks İbrahim Paşa to find the crown of Hungary.	304b
113.	Zapolya greets the sultan at Budapest.	306a
114.	Zapolya presents gifts and kisses the sultan's foot; is presented the crown of Hungary.	307a
*115.	Birth of Şehzade Bayezid, year 934.	308b
116.	Circumcision festival for princes, year 936; festivities at At Meydanı (banquets, games, firework displays, and gifts); arrival at At Meydanı of the sultan and princes from Topkapı.	310b
117.	Death of Behram Paşa, beylerbeyi of Rumelia; Mustafa Paşa appointed to that post; birth of Şehzade Cihangir.	317a
*118.	Entertainment of the sultan; description of hunt.	320a
119.	The sultan informed of Ferdinand's offensive against Zapolya; Ferdinand apologizes.	323a
*120.	Ferdinand sends letter to court; the sultan's response.	325b
121.	Ferdinand communicates with the şah of Iran; announces content of the şah's letter.	329a
*122.	Iranians apologize; the sultan departs for Austria.	331b
*123.	French envoys en route; reception of Austrian ambassadors.	335a
*124.	Increase of sancaks; army parades for French ambassadors who visit various divisions and vezirs, and meet with the sultan.	337b
125.	Battle of Güns; mines placed; fortress conquered.	348a
*126.	Church burns; battle of Turhan and Anton.	350b
127.	Conquest of Bicani fortress; reasons for the sultan's return from Austria.	354a
128.	The sultan returns from Austria; alliance of the Spanish king and the pope; dispatching of Andrea Doria with the armada; conquest of Coron and Patros.	355b
*129.	Reason for campaign to Iran; arrival of Barbaros Hayreddin Paşa at court; he is sent to Aleppo and meets with İbrahim Paşa; the sultan leaves for Iran.	358a
*130.	The sultan arrives at Ucan Valley; reception of the ruler of Gilan; Mehmed Han of Dulkadir joins Ottomans; defeat of Iranians; the sultan arrives at Kasr-ı Şirin; arrives at Baghdad; Ulama Paşa fights Iranians at Van.	361b
*131.	Execution of İskender Çelebi; Iranians send forces to Van; the sultan sends letter to the şah; the rulers of Bekir, Suhrab, and Gülgün fortresses join the Ottomans; the şah sends envoy to İbrahim Paşa, suing for peace.	370b
132.	The sultan ravages Iran and returns home.	376a
133.	Execution of İbrahim Paşa; Ayas Mehmed Paşa becomes grand vezir; Barbaros Hayreddin Paşa captures Coron; the sultan departs for Avlonya; Mustafa and Hüsrev Paşas fight against Albanians; defeat of Albanians.	379a
134.	Lütfi Paşa's battle with Venetians at sea.	388a
135.	Lütfi Paşa conquers Castro fortress; the sultan departs for Corfu; winter begins and the sultan lifts siege.	389a
*136.	The sultan hunts at Vardar Yenicesi; entertained at Ilıca and hunts at Serez Çayır, Gümülcine, Karaçayır, Çatalca, and Yanbolu.	392a

*	137.	Campaign to Moldavia; the sultan hunts at Babadağ; reception of the ambassadors from India; battle of Barbaros Hayreddin Paşa and Andrea Doria; Doria takes Castelnuovo.	401a
	138.	Fire in İstanbul; Venetians sue for peace; the sultan hunts at Yalova and Bursa.	408a
*	139.	Circumcision of Şehzades Bayezid and Cihangir, year 946; the sultan hunts at Ipsala.	411a
	140.	İstabur campaign; Ferdinand requests Budapest be given to him.	413a
	141.	Ferdinand asks that Budapest be taken away from widow of Zapolya.	415b
	142.	Battle between forces of Ferdinand and the queen; treaty between the two; the sultan is informed of the queen's dilemma; departs for Edirne.	417a
	143.	Mehmed Bey sent to Budapest to aid the queen.	419b
*	144.	Battle between forces of Mehmed Bey and Ferdinand; description of spring; the sultan hunts at Yanbolu; calls for meeting of the Divan.	420b
	145.	The sultan orders Hüsrev Paşa to build a bridge over the Danube.	425b
	146.	Süleyman Paşa goes to Artukabad; the sultan departs from İstanbul; qualities of rain and flood.	426a
*	147.	Mehmed Paşa arrives in Budapest; attacks enemy; soldiers dig into trenches; battle of the forward attack forces.	428a
	148.	Mehmed Paşa's offensive.	433b
	149.	Continuation of the offensive.	435b
*	150.	The sultan arrives at Budapest; rewards Mehmed Paşa and army; converses with the queen.	437b
	151.	Ferdinand apologizes to the sultan; battle between forces of Hasan, beylerbeyi of Algiers, and the king of Spain.	441b
*	152.	Princes depart for their provinces.	444a
	153.	Herzogovinians join the battle of Budapest and are annihilated.	446a
*	154.	Barbaros Hayreddin Paşa fights the enemy at Nice; the sultan departs for campaign; conquest of Lipva, Siklos, Estergon, and Estonibelgrad.	447a
*	155.	Death of Şehzade Mehmed; the sultan converses with Selim; conquest of Georgia; expulsion of Süleyman and Hüsrev Paşas; death of Barbaros Hayreddin Paşa; conquest of Basra.	460a
*	156.	Elkas sends message to the court; the sultan arrives from Edirne; receives Elkas; departs for Iran; the Austrian ambassador comes with peace treaty; construction of Şehzade Mehmed Mosque begun.	466b
*	157.	The sultan converses with Bayezid; entertained with sons at Kayseri; converses with Mustafa.	475a
	158.	Commanders greet the sultan; the sultan converses with Elkas and vezirs; Erciş joins the Ottomans; Tahmasp sends letter to Elkas; Elkas answers.	480a
	159.	Battle of Elkas at Kırkale; the sultan arrives at Azerbaijan; returns to Van and Diyarbakır; Elkas moves into Iran.	489a
***	160.	Elkas raids Iran; the ambassador from India arrives in İstanbul with gifts; İskender Paşa, beylerbeyi of Van, sends head of Hacı Dünbülli to İstanbul; Elkas sends gifts to İstanbul; Elkas requested to return; reception of the ambassador from Hijaz; Derviş Mehmed sent to Elkas as envoy; the sultan departs for Diyarbakır; correspondence between Ismail Mirza and İskender Paşa; defeat of Elkas.	495a
	161.	Death of Elkas.	512a
**	162.	Battle of Ahmed Paşa and the Georgians; reception of the ambassador from Bukhara; the sultan departs from İstanbul and meets with Bayezid; converses with Selim at Çorlu; foundation laid for Süleymaniye Mosque; Devlet Giray Han enthroned; conquest of Telemsan; Sinan Paşa's campaigns in Tripoli and Avlonya.	512b
	163.	Meeting of Turgud and Sinan Paşas at sea; conquests of Malta and Tripoli.	522a
**	164.	Mehmed Paşa, beylerbeyi of Rumelia, campaigns in Transylvania; the pope sends army to Lipva; Ulama Paşa sues for peace; Ali Paşa's battle at Eszek; the sultan arrives in Edirne; Ahmed Paşa sent to Temesvar, year 959; conquest of Temesvar, Lipva, and siege of Erlau.	524a
**	165.	Story of cam-ı cihannüma; İskender Paşa appointed beylerbeyi of Erzurum; besieges Ardanuç; writes to Tahmasp; Tahmasp disclaims right to cup; İskender Paşa captures Ardanuç; finds the cup and sends it to İstanbul.	542a
	166.	Iranians attack Erciş and Ahlat; İskender Paşa fights the Iranians; defeats them; the şah sends ambassador with offer of peace.	557b
	167.	Rüstem Paşa sent to Karaman; correspondence between the sultan and the şah; the sultan sails to Üsküdar; converses with Bayezid and Selim.	563b

***** 168.	Execution of Mustafa; the sultan moves toward Aleppo; death of Cihangir; the sultan hunts with Selim; army moves from Diyarbakır; meets with Selim's regiments; procession of the armed forces; the sultan moves to Nahçivan; conquests in Georgia; Tahmasp sends envoy with peace offering.	571b
169.	Description of winter; peace with Iran; description of spring; army discharged; the sultan arrives in İstanbul; contender Mustafa rebellion; rebel caught and hung.	600b
170.	The sultan converses with Bayezid at Çorlu.	611b
171.	Execution of Ahmed Paşa; reinstatement of Rüstem Paşa as grand vezir; praises of the grand vezir; eulogy to the sultan.	612b
	Colophon: The work was transcribed by el-Muzaffer Ali b. Emir Bey Şirvani in the middle of the month of Ramazan in 965.	617b

CAST OF CHARACTERS

I. IMPERIAL HOUSEHOLD

A. The Sultan:

Süleyman I (1494-1566; reigned 1520-1566)

*1, 6-14, 16, 17, 20, 24, 27-29, 31-33, 35, 36, 38-40, 43, 45-48, 50, 53, 57-59, 61-64

Süleyman, the main protagonist of the work, appears in two-thirds of the illustrations attired in a large white turban wrapped around a thick baton and richly patterned clothes. His ceremonial garments consist of an open-fronted outer kaftan with long sleeves that hang at the back; at the shoulders are slits, allowing the arms to pass through. Under this he wears a buttoned and belted short-sleeved inner kaftan; his arms are covered with contrasting long sleeves that either belong to his underrobe or are separate accessories, called *kolluk*, that button to the cuffs of the inner kaftan. In the first half of the manuscript he generally appears as a youthful man with a mustache while in the second half he is almost always shown with a short beard, indicating middle age. The sultan must have kept his beard after the age of thirty-eight. Whether enthroned in his otak or in a palace, he is attended by the kapıcıs, flanked by his Has Oda ağas and iç oğlans, and often accompanied by vezirs. Peyks and solaks attend him during ceremonies and hunts.

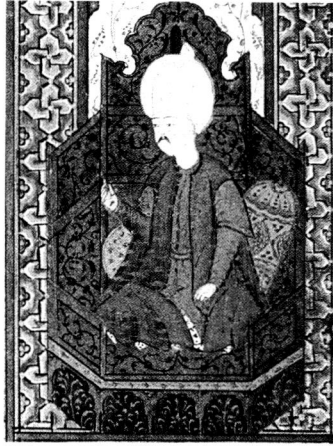

Sultan Süleyman

B. The Şehzades:

1. Bayezid (1525-1561)

   40 (?), 43 (?), 58

   The fourth son of Süleyman and Hürrem, attired in the same manner as the sultan and the other princes, has a small mustache in one scene (58). Bayezid served as sancakbeyi in Konya (1546), Kütahya (1546-1558), and Amasya (1558-1559); joined his father during the 1541 conquest of Budapest; and was appointed regent in İstanbul (1549) and Edirne (1553) when the sultan was campaigning in the east. After being defeated by his brother Selim (1559), he defected to Iran; he was later ransomed and executed with four of his sons.

2. Cihangir (1531-1553)

   40 (?)

   Cihangir, the youngest son of Süleyman and Hürrem, born a hunchback, was a sensitive youth who was very dear to his father. The prince served as sancakbeyi in Aleppo and joined his father in the Nahçivan campaign in 1553. He died in Aleppo, greatly distressed at the execution of his beloved step-brother, Mustafa.

3. Mehmed (1521-1543)

   38, 44 (?)

   Mehmed, the first-born of Süleyman and Hürrem, was the sultan's favorite son. He is most likely one of the princes with plumes in their turbans participating in a hunt (38). Mehmed took part in the Danubian campaign (1537) and served as sancakbeyi in Manisa (1542-1543), where he died. Sinan's first masterpiece, the Şehzade Mehmed Mosque and attached buildings, was constructed in his memory (1544-1548). An imposing thronelike structure covers the prince's sarcophagus in the mausoleum.

4. Mustafa (1515-1553)

   44 (?), 48

   The eldest son of Süleyman born to Gülbahar, Mustafa was the first crown prince. He served as sancakbeyi in Manisa (1533-1541) and Amasya (1541-1553), and was appointed as regent in İstanbul during his father's campaign to Iran (1534-1536). This popular and competent prince became the victim of Hürrem's ambitions for her own sons. Mustafa, accused of treason against the state, was executed in Aktepe.

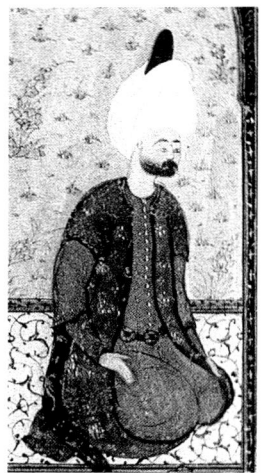

Şehzade Mustafa

*numbers identify the illustrations reproduced on pages 90-232

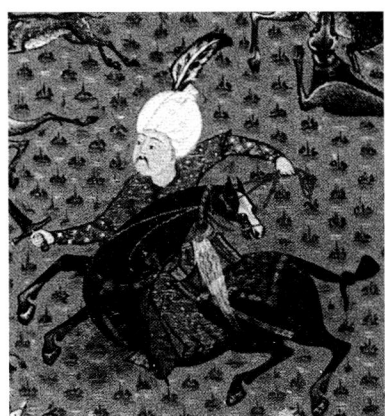

Şehzade Selim

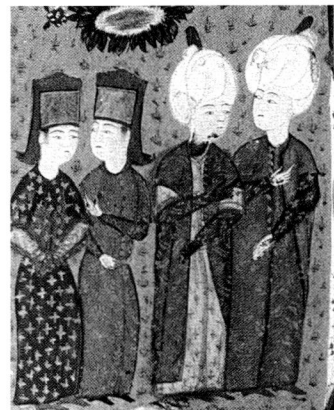

Has Oda Ağas (left) and
İç Oğlans (right)

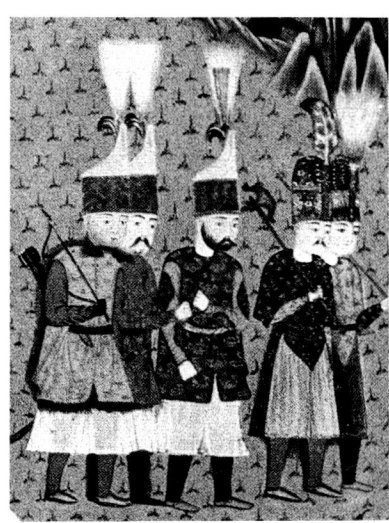

Solaks (left) and Peyks (right)

5. Selim (1524-1574)

38, 43 (?), 46 (?), 59, 60

The third son of Süleyman and Hürrem, Selim succeeded his father in 1566. He served as sancakbeyi in Manisa (1543-1558), Konya (1558-1559), and Kütahya (1559-1566); he was appointed regent in İstanbul (1548) and accompanied the sultan on many campaigns. His victory over Bayezid in 1559 secured him the Ottoman throne.

C. Attendants

1. Has Oda Ağas

4, 6-12, 14, 16, 17, 20, 24, 27, 29, 31, 32, 35, 36, 38-40, 45-48, 57-59, 61-64

These high-ranking personal attendants of the sultans in charge of the Has Oda almost always appear in pairs and wear outfits similar to those of the kapıcıs, but the flowing panel at the back of their hats is dyed red. Their duties were to carry the sultan's sword and canteen, assist him while mounting and dismounting, and serve as valets and confidential secretaries, holding the posts of silahdar, rikapdar, and çuhadar ağas, dülbend oğlanı, and sır katibi. The pair frequently depicted is most likely the Has Oda başı and the silahdar ağa.

2. İç Oğlans

1, 6, 8, 17, 24, 27, 29, 31, 33, 35, 40, 43, 47, 50, 53, 61, 63, 64

These youthful figures are always clean-shaven and are dressed in elaborate inner and outer kaftans, a style similar to that worn by the sultan and princes. They stand often in pairs behind the sultan's throne.

3. Kapıcıs

1, 3, 6, 8, 17, 24, 30-33, 35, 40, 43, 47, 49, 50, 53, 57, 58, 63, 64

They hold staffs and wear kaftans. Their distinguished hats have high gilt metal diadems and long white felt panels that flow down to the shoulders at the back. The kapıcıs guard the entrances to the imperial otak and pavilions and are always present during receptions and sessions of the Divan. Their chief, kapıcıbaşı, is at times shown with the head usher, çavuşbaşı.

4. Peyks

1, 12-16, 21, 36, 38, 39, 44-46, 51, 52, 54, 59, 62

This special corps of footmen, assigned to guard the sultan during campaigns and hunts, wear tall ovoid gilt metal hats with large plumes and tunics with hems tucked into their belts. A similar corps attend the commanders as well as the princes.

5. Solaks

3, 7, 10-16, 20, 33, 36, 38, 44, 45, 54, 59, 60, 62

Serving the same function as the peyks, members of this corps were originally made up of archers. The headdress is distinctive for its wide gilt metal diadem, tall white felt cap, and enormous white plume. They also guard the commanders and princes.

II. ADMINISTRATIVE OFFICIALS

This group includes the grand vezirs, vezirs, beylerbeyis, sancakbeyis, commanders, members of the Divan, and the ulema. For the sake of simplicity, these personages are listed alphabetically. During ceremonial functions administrative officials wear turbans with inner and outer kaftans; when participating in campaigns they might be in armor, wearing helmets with plumes, or have plumes attached to their turbans.

1. Ahmed Paşa

7 (?), 15

This vezir served as the commander during the siege of Belgrade (1521) and Rhodes campaign (1522), and was later appointed beylerbeyi of Egypt (1523). There he started an uprising against the sultan and was killed by Kadızade Mehmed Bey in 1524.

2. Ahmed Paşa (Kara)

52, 55

Vezir Kara Ahmed Paşa was active on both the eastern and western fronts, fighting in Georgia (1549) and conquering Temesvar (1552). He served as grand vezir (1553-1555) between the two terms of Rüstem Paşa and was executed in 1555.

3. Ali Efendi (Zenbilli)

1

This celebrated şeyhülislam served both Selim I and Süleyman for twenty-four years. The author of books on ethics and many fetvas, he participated in the Rhodes campaign (1522) and died in 1524.

4. Ayas Mehmed Paşa
15
Second vezir in the Divan during the 1523-1524 rebellion of Ahmed Paşa in Egypt, this official participated in the Rhodes campaign (1522) as the beylerbeyi of Rumelia, accompanied the sultan during the 1534-1536 campaign to Iran, and was appointed grand vezir after the death of İbrahim Paşa (1536). He took part in the Corfu campaign (1537) and died shortly after in 1539.

5. Bali Bey (later Paşa)
20
This distinguished commander was the eldest son of Yahya Paşa and Süleyman's paternal aunt. He took part in the conquest of Belgrade (1521) and participated in the Battle of Mohacs (1526). He fought primarily on the western frontier and was appointed beylerbeyi of Budapest (1543), losing his life the same year in the battle at Estergon.

6. Bali Bey (Küçük)
28
This officer, the commander of İzvornik, a province in Bosnia, was asked by the sultan to retrieve the Holy Crown of Hungary from Ferdinand's men and return it to its rightful owner, John Zapolya.

7. Behram Paşa
20 (?)
The beylerbeyi of Anatolia, he commanded the right wing of the army during the Battle of Mohacs (1526) and took part in the siege of Vienna (1529).

8. Canberdi Gazali
15
This Mamluk official, appointed beylerbeyi of Syria (1520), started a rebellion. He was defeated and killed outside Damascus within a year.

9. Divan-ı Hümayun Members
3, 30, 49
Members of the Imperial Council of Ministers included the grand vezir, the highest ranking three vezirs, beylerbeyis of Anatolia and Rumelia, the nişancı, two kazaskers, the reisülküttab, and the defterdars, attended by çavuşbaşı and kapıcıbaşı in addition to officers in charge of translations, petitions, messages, and a corps of secretaries. Most of these members are represented in the paintings of the Divan sessions when state affairs are discussed (3), diplomatic correspondence reviewed (30), or gifts from foreigners received (49).

10. Ferhad Paşa
1, 3
Serving as the third vezir during Süleyman's accession, he was sent to quell Canberdi Gazali's revolt in Syria (1521). He was married to Selçuk, Süleyman's paternal aunt. Ferhad Paşa was executed in 1523.

11. Hayırbay
4
This Mamluk beylerbeyi of Egypt was loyal to the sultan during Canberdi Gazali's revolt (1523-1524). He died in 1522 during the siege of Rhodes.

12. Hayreddin Paşa (Barbaros)
35
This awesome seaman and the ruler of Algiers was appointed kaptan-ı derya in 1533 and given the assignment of modernizing the navy for the defense of the Mediterranean. His fleet sailed into victory at the Battle of Preveza (1538), devastating the European armada. Barbaros Hayreddin held his post until his death in 1546 and was succeeded by such able admirals as Sinan Paşa (Rüstem Paşa's brother) and Piyale Paşa.

13. Hüseyin Paşa
21
During the Anatolian revolts of 1526, Hüseyin Paşa, the beylerbeyi of Sivas, succeeded in defeating and killing the leader of the rebels. Unfortunately, he himself died shortly after from wounds received during the battle.

14. Hüsrev Bey (later Paşa)
20
The son of Süleyman's paternal aunt, Selçuk, and Ferhad Paşa, this commander was in charge of the akıncı forces during the Battle of Mohacs (1526). He served as beylerbeyi of Bosnia several times and died at that post in 1541.

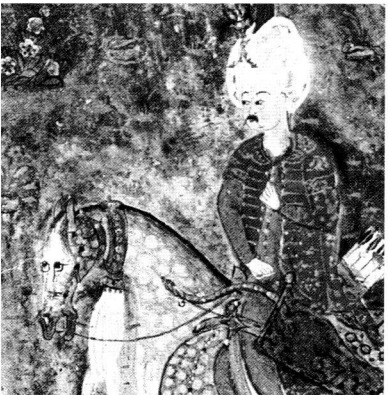

Ayas Mehmed Paşa

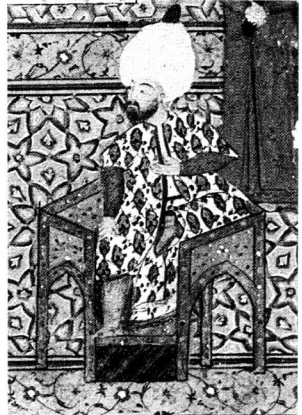

Hayırbay

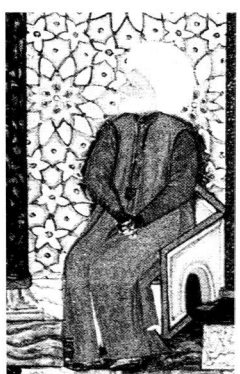

Hayreddin Paşa

15. Hüsrev Paşa

21

Not much is known of this commander who replaced Hüseyin Paşa after he died fighting against the rebels in Anatolia in 1526.

16. İbrahim Paşa

20 (?), 24, 30

Süleyman's close friend and confidant since they met in Manisa, İbrahim was a former devşirme who received an excellent education. He was made Has Oda başı after Süleyman ascended the throne; took part in the campaigns to Belgrade (1521), Rhodes (1522), Mohacs (1526), and Vienna (1529); restored order in Egypt (1523); and put down rebellions in southeastern Anatolia (1527). He was appointed grand vezir (1523) and made serasker (1529), a post reserved only for sultans. He was married to Hadice, the sultan's sister (1523). İbrahim, who was the same age as Süleyman, fell victim to his ambitions and was executed in 1536 for treason against the state.

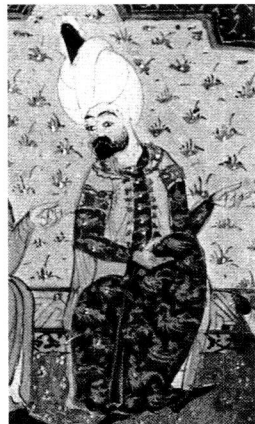
İbrahim Paşa

17. Kasım Paşa

1, 3

The tutor of Süleyman while the crown prince was in Manisa, he was made the fourth vezir when Süleyman became sultan (1520). He served as beylerbeyi of Rumelia, Anatolia, Egypt, and Morea and participated in the 1541 Hungarian campaign.

18. Kazaskers

1, 3

The kazaskers of Anatolia and Rumelia were responsible for the judicial and educational activities of the state, under the leadership of the şeyhülislam, the chief enforcer of the şeriat.

19. Mehmed Bey (later Paşa)

41, 42

The younger son of Yahya Paşa and Süleyman's paternal aunt, and the brother of Bali Bey, this distinguished commander defended Budapest against the Austrians in 1541. He replaced his brother as beylerbeyi of Budapest (1543-1548).

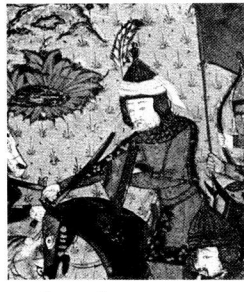
Mehmed Bey

20. Mehmed Bey (Kadızade)

15 (?)

As the grand vezir in the provincial court in Cairo, he was instrumental in stopping Ahmed Paşa's rebellion in Egypt by remaining loyal to the sultan. He succeeded in capturing and killing the rebel (1524).

21. Mehmed Paşa (Piri)

1, 3

Appointed grand vezir by Selim I, he also served Süleyman until his replacement by İbrahim Paşa (1523). He was the nephew of the şeyhülislam Zenbilli Ali Efendi.

22. Mustafa Paşa

1, 3

The second vezir during Süleyman's accession, he served as commander in the Rhodes campaign (1523), was later appointed beylerbeyi of Egypt, and died in 1529. He was married to Piri Mehmed Paşa's daughter.

23. Pervane

23

The officer who killed Kalender in 1527.

24. Rüstem Paşa

48, 49

Appointed grand vezir twice (1544-1553 and 1555-1561), Rüstem was married (1539) to Süleyman's daughter Mihrimah and was strongly supported by his mother-in-law, Hürrem. Both Mihrimah and Rüstem were patrons of the great architect Sinan and commissioned the construction of religious and charitable buildings. Their daughter married first the grand vezir Semiz Ahmed Paşa and, after his death (1580), Ahmed Feridun Paşa, the author of an illustrated history covering the Szigetvar campaign and the death of Süleyman.

25. Ulama Paşa

54

Ulama Paşa was celebrated for his bravery during the Habsburg attack on Lipva (1551) and was later appointed the beylerbeyi of Bosnia.

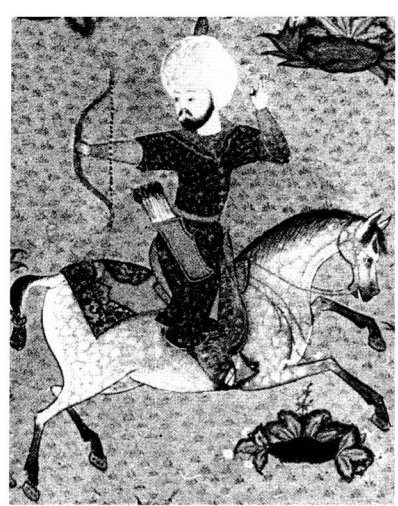
Ulama Paşa

26. Vezirs

9, 17, 24, 27, 31-33, 43, 47, 48, 50, 53, 57, 58, 63, 64

These bearded officials participate in imperial ceremonies, especially when foreign dignitaries are being received. They stand near the throne and accompany the sultan both in the palace and on campaigns.

III. MILITARY CORPS

The following groups constitute units of the armed forces, whose officers were under the command of vezirs, beylerbeyis, and sancakbeyis.

1. Janissaries

1-3, 12-14, 20, 33, 41, 54, 55, 60, 64

The janissaries constituted the fearsome infantry corps chosen from the most able-bodied of the devşirme boys. Their hats have a wide gilt metal diadem with a projecting vertical bar in the front; attached to the diadem is a white felt panel that flows in the back. The hems of their short tunics are tucked into their belts. The officers have plumes on their headdresses and wear inner and outer kaftans. The janissaries were responsible for protecting the sultan during battles and hunts, keeping order in the capital, and guarding the frontier fortresses.

2. Sipahis

5, 7, 8, 10, 12-17, 19-21, 23, 26, 28, 33, 41-43, 45, 51, 52, 54, 58, 60-63, 65

The cavalry members wear turbans or helmets and carry banners, lances, and maces. Their fighting weapons were primarily spears, swords, and bows and arrows. The officers frequently wear plumes on their headdresses.

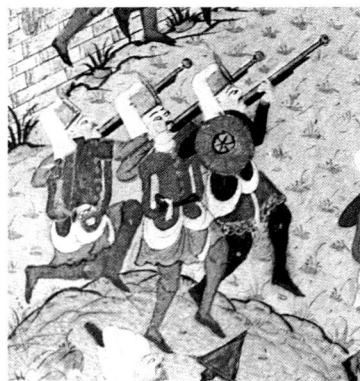
Janissaries

3. Special Units

a. Akıncıs

15, 28, 34, 41, 45

These forward attack or raiding forces wear soft furry hats. The text mentions the name of one member, Turhan Bey, who fought against the Hungarian Anton at the Battle of Güns (34). This personage has a plumed helmet instead of the usual hat of his unit.

b. Delils

19, 20, 33, 41, 55, 62

Another corps of raiders, the delils are distinguished by huge wings on their hats and leopard-skin cloaks. The text gives the names of some members, including Sinan, who defeated the Hungarian Eugene prior to the battle of Mohacs in 1526 (19); and Divane-i Rumeli, who captured an Iranian commander in 1554 (62).

c. Mehter

20, 21, 41, 44, 62

The imperial military band plays brass and percussion instruments, and accompanies sultans, princes, and commanders in battles and during parades.

d. Miners

12, 13

These men were in charge of placing explosive charges under the walls and are represented during the siege of Rhodes.

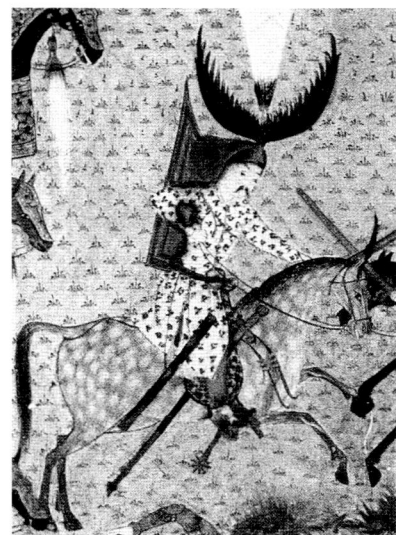
Delil

IV. OTHER PERSONAGES

A. Rebels

1. Contender Mustafa

65

The rebel from Salonica, who impersonated the executed Şehzade Mustafa, was killed by Mehmed Paşa in 1555.

2. Kalender

22 (?), 23

This rebel gathered a large following in southeastern Anatolia and was killed by the forces of İbrahim Paşa (1527). Kalender and his men wear large white turbans with flattened tops and horizontal bands.

B. Foreign Dignitaries

1. Devlet Giray Han

   53

   This ruler of the Crimean Tatars paid a visit to the palace immediately upon his accession to the throne in 1551. Devlet Giray wears the tall fur-brimmed cap of the Crimeans.

2. Elkas Mirza

   47, 51

   The adventurous brother of Şah Tahmasp and the governor of Şirvan, Elkas joined the Ottomans and fought against the Safavids (1547-1548). He was caught by his brother's forces in 1549 and imprisoned in the fortress of Alamut where he died after being held captive for thirty years.

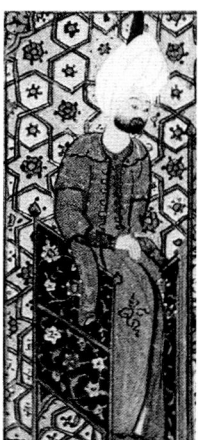

Elkas Mirza

3. Isabella

   43

   The daughter of Sigismund I, the king of Poland, Isabella was married to John Zapolya, the voyvoda of Transylvania. She paid a visit to Süleyman with her infant son in 1541. Isabella wears a long hooded cloak over a robe.

4. Louis II

   18

   The king of Hungary and the brother-in-law of Ferdinand and Charles V, Louis lost his life during the Battle of Mohacs (1526). He wears a large jeweled crown, long robe, and cloak.

5. Martinuzzi, Cardinal George

   43

   This ambitious head bishop of Varadin was appointed regent when John Zapolya died (1540) and tried to usurp the throne of Hungary. His death in 1551 was a relief both to the Ottomans and the Habsburgs. He wears inner and outer kaftans and a flat wide-brimmed hat.

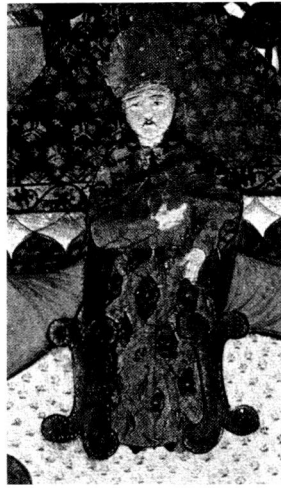

Louis II

6. Mehmed (Derviş)

   51

   Sent to Elkas Mirza as an envoy in 1549, Derviş Mehmed was the father of Arifi, the author of the *Süleymanname*. He was originally from Abadan in Iran.

7. Tahmasp

   37, 56

   Şah Tahmasp, the second Safavid ruler of Iran, was a strong shiite adversary of the Ottomans. Like the Ottoman rulers, the şah wears inner and outer kaftans; his turban is elongated, its baton long and tapered.

8. Zapolya, John (Janos Zapolyai)

   28

   The voyvoda of Transylvania, Zapolya joined the Ottomans during the Battle of Mohacs and was made king of Hungary (1529) by Süleyman. He was married to Isabella of Poland and left an infant on the throne after he died in 1540. Zapolya wears a flat hat, a robe with split seams on its sleeves, and an overrobe that closes from left to right.

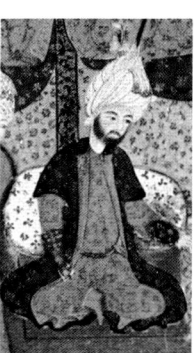

Şah Tahmasp

9. Zapolya, Stephen (Sigismund Janos)

   43

   The son of John Zapolya and Isabella, Stephen was born shortly after his father's death in 1540. Apprehensive about leaving an infant on the throne, Süleyman formally annexed Hungary and made it an Ottoman province (1541).

10. Ambassadors

    a. Austria

    30, 32

    The envoys sent by Ferdinand wear hats with upturned or narrow brims, short tunics, and leggings.

    b. France

    33

    The French envoys to the court have hats similar to those of the Austrians and wear long robes, some with split seams on the sleeves.

    c. Hijaz

    50

    The ambassador of the ruler of the Hijaz has a tall cap wrapped with a scarf and wears a long wide-sleeved robe.

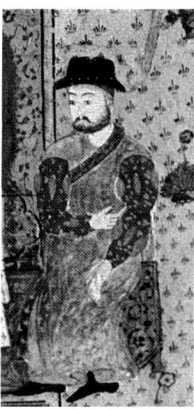

John Zapolya

d. Iran

31, 56, 63, 64

The Safavid diplomats are attired in the same manner as the Ottomans, except that they appear to wear taller, tapering turbans. The text gives the name of Sinan as one of the envoys received by Süleyman in 1554 (63) and Ferruhzade as another (64).

V. OTHER GROUPS

A. Europeans

2, 8, 9, 12-14, 19, 20, 26, 27, 34, 41, 42, 45, 54, 55

In addition to the dignitaries and ambassadors listed above, the paintings illustrate European soldiers, prisoners, and residents of cities such as Belgrade, Rhodes, Güns, and Temesvar. The soldiers wear the heavy full armor of the period, and carry swords and lances. The residents, including bearded priests with short hair and long, loose robes, are generally men, although in two scenes women are also portrayed (2 and 14).

B. Asians and Africans

4, 8, 40, 52, 53

The Africans include Egyptian or other natives, executioners, elephant riders and trainers, and a musician, most of whom are dark-skinned (4, 8, and 40). The Asians include Iranian officials (37, 51, and 56), Georgians (52), and Crimeans (53).

C. Ottomans

1, 44

The residents of İstanbul are shown attending the accession ceremonies of the sultan and watching the princes leave for their provinces.

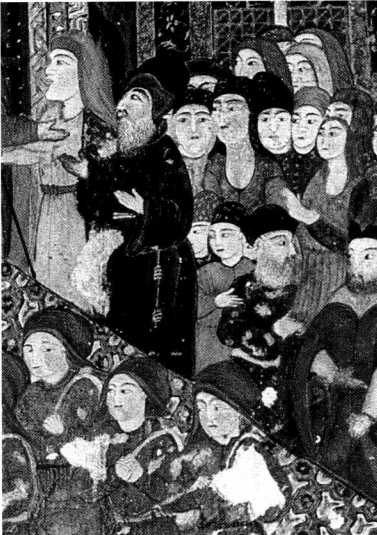

Europeans

LOCATION OF EVENTS

The majority of the scenes in the *Süleymanname* take place outdoors. Forty are devoted to foreign and domestic wars: fourteen depict battles (5, 19, 20, 23, 41, 42, 54, and 65), two show war-related events (21 and 25), four have marching armies (7, 15, 60, and 62), twelve involve episodes in or around tents (8, 17, 18, 27, 28, 33, 43, 51, 56, 58, 61, and 63), and another fourteen have architectural settings. The latter either describe specific cities or fortresses such as Belgrade (9), Güns (34), Kasr-ı Şirin (36), Tabriz (37), İstanbul (44), Temesvar (55), and a Christian town in the Balkans (2); or have formulaic buildings identifiable only through the text, such as Rhodes (12-14), Budapest (26), Estonibelgrad (45), and fortresses in southeast Anatolia (22) and Georgia (52). Seven additional outdoor scenes represent imperial hunts (10, 11, 16, 38, 39, 46, and 59).

Painter A was responsible for the depiction of specific architectural settings; Painter B executed those with generalized fortresses; Painters A, B, and C worked on the remaining outdoor scenes.

All eighteen interior scenes take place in palaces: six show the structures in the provincial capitals of Cairo (4), Edirne (6), Kayseri (48), Aleppo (49 and 50), and Amasya (64); while the rest represent buildings in the Topkapı Palace in İstanbul. A unique double folio depicts a general view of the first and second courtyards (1) of the Topkapı Palace; another double folio represents the buildings in its second courtyard (3), concentrating on the proceedings in the Kubbealtı, which seems to reappear in another scene (30). Activities in the third courtyard take place under the arcades (35), in the Arz Odası (31, 32, 47, and 53), the Has Oda (40 and 57), or other pavilions (24 and 29).

Once again it was Painter A who was responsible for the depiction of most of the provincial palaces and for almost all of the specific views and structures of the Topkapı Palace.

The following chart lists the events in chronological sequence; it gives their location, folio numbers, and painters. The numbers on the far right identify the illustrations reproduced on pages 90-232. "Outside" indicates activities, frequently sieges, taking place in front of identified fortresses; "vicinity" indicates outdoor scenes without specific settings but identified through the text.

1520	Accession Ceremonies	İstanbul: Topkapı Palace, first and second courtyards	17b-18a	A	1
	Recruitment of Tribute Children	Outside a Christian town in the Balkans	31b	A and E	2
	Meeting of the Divan	İstanbul: Topkapı Palace, second courtyard	37b-38a	A	3
	Execution of Canberdi Gazali's Envoy	Cairo: pavilion in palace	56a	A	4
1521	Death of Canberdi Gazali	Vicinity of Mastaba, near Damascus	63b	B	5
	Süleyman Entertained	Edirne: pavilion in palace	71a	A	6
	Arrival of Süleyman at Böğürdelen	Vicinity of Böğürdelen	81a	A	7
	Execution of Prisoners	Vicinity of Belgrade	98a	A	8
	Siege of Belgrade	Outside Belgrade	108b-109a	A	9
	Süleyman Hunting	Vicinity of Uzuncaabad, near Filibe	115a	B	10

1522	Süleyman Hunting	Vicinity of the Menderes River at Denizli (?)	132a	B	11
	Arrival of Süleyman at Rhodes	Outside Rhodes	143a	B	12
	Siege of Rhodes	Outside Rhodes	149a	B	13
	Fall of Rhodes	Outside Rhodes	154b	B	14
1524	Death of Ahmed Paşa	Vicinity of Cairo	170b	B	15
1525(?)	Süleyman Hunting	Vicinity of Edirne	177a	A	16
1526	Reception of the Commanders	Vicinity of Sophia	189b	A	17
	Camp of Louis II	Vicinity of Mohacs (?)	200a	A and E	18
	Battle of the Forward Attack Forces	Vicinity of Mohacs	212a	A	19
	Battle of Mohacs	Mohacs	219b-220a	A	20
	Death of Hüseyin Paşa	Vicinity of Sivas	235a	A	21
1527	Kalender Rebellion	Vicinity of Karaçayır (?), near Sivas	239a	B	22
	Death of Kalender	Vicinity of Maraş	248a	B	23
	Reception of İbrahim Paşa	İstanbul: Topkapı Palace, pavilion in third courtyard	260a	A	24
1529	Soldiers Climbing Trees During a Storm	Vicinity of Edirne	266a	B	25
	Siege of Budapest	Outside Budapest	282a	B	26
	Süleyman Inspecting Prisoners	Vicinity of Vienna	297a	B	27
	Süleyman Receiving the Crown of Hungary	Vicinity of Budapest	309a	A	28
1530	Süleyman Entertained	İstanbul: Topkapı Palace, pavilion in third courtyard	321b	C	29
	Arrival of the Austrian Ambassadors	İstanbul: Topkapı Palace, Kubbealtı in second courtyard	328a	B	30
	Reception of the Iranian Ambassador	İstanbul: Topkapı Palace, Arz Odası in third courtyard	332a	A	31
1532	Reception of the Austrian Ambassador	İstanbul: Topkapı Palace, Arz Odası in third courtyard	337a	B	32
	Reception of the French Ambassador	Vicinity of Belgrade	346a	A	33
	Battle of Güns	Outside Güns	353a	A	34
1533	Reception of Barbaros Hayreddin Paşa	İstanbul: Topkapı Palace, third courtyard	360a	A	35
1534	Arrival of Süleyman at Kasr-ı Şirin	Outside Kasr-ı Şirin	367a	A	36
1535	Tahmasp Receiving the Ottoman Ambassador	Outside Tabriz (?)	374a	A and D	37
1537	Süleyman Hunting with Mehmed and Selim	Vicinity of the Vardar River	393a	A	38
1538	Süleyman Hunting Deer	Vicinity of Babadağ	403a	C	39
1539	Circumcision Festival of Bayezid and Cihangir	İstanbul: Topkapı Palace, Has Oda in third courtyard	412a	A	40
1541	Battle of the Ottomans and Austrians	Vicinity of Budapest	422a	A	41

	Battle of İstabur	Vicinity of Budapest	433a	B	42
	Reception of Queen Isabella and Infant Stephen	Vicinity of Budapest	441a	A	43
	Princes Leaving for Their Provinces	İstanbul: outside Topkapı Palace	445a	A	44
1543	Siege of Estonibelgrad	Outside Estonibelgrad	459a	B	45
1544	Süleyman Hunting with Selim	Vicinity of Edirne	462b	B	46
1547	Reception of Elkas Mirza	İstanbul: Topkapı Palace, Arz Odası in third courtyard	471b	B	47
1548	Süleyman Conversing with Mustafa	Kayseri: pavilion in palace	477b	B	48
	Arrival of Gifts from Elkas Mirza	Aleppo: pavilion in palace (?)	498b	B	49
	Reception of the Ambassador of the Hijaz	Aleppo: pavilion in palace	503a	A	50
1549	Elkas Mirza Receiving the Sultan's Envoy	Vicinity of Aleppo (?)	506a	A and D	51
	Battle of the Ottomans and Georgians	Outside Akçakale, near Artvin	514a	B	52
1551	Reception of Devlet Giray Han	İstanbul: Topkapı Palace, Arz Odası in third courtyard	519a	A	53
	Ottomans Leaving Lipva	Vicinity of Lipva	527a	A	54
1552	Siege of Temesvar	Outside Temesvar	533a	A	55
1553	Tahmasp Receiving the Ottoman Ambassador	Vicinity of Tabriz (?)	550a	A and D	56
	Süleyman Presented with the Ruby Cup	İstanbul: Topkapı Palace, Has Oda in third courtyard	557a	A	57
	Süleyman Conversing with Bayezid	Vicinity of Yenişehir, near Bursa	570a	A	58
	Süleyman Hunting with Selim	Vicinity of Aleppo	576a	A	59
	Selim Greeted by the Commanders	Vicinity of Diyarbakır	583a	A	60
1554	Performance of the Archers	Vicinity of Pasinabad, near Erzurum	588a	A	61
	Süleyman Marching with the Army	Vicinity of Nahçivan	592a	A	62
1555	Reception of the Iranian Ambassador	Vicinity of Amasya	600a	A	63
	Reception of the Iranian Ambassador	Amasya: pavilion in palace	603a	A	64
	Death of Contender Mustafa	Vicinity of Salonica (?)	611a	B	65

PAYROLL REGISTERS OF 1557-1558

Coinciding with the completion date of the *Süleymanname* are two payroll registers that contain the names, salaries, and ranks of painters and bookbinders employed in the Ehl-i Hiref. The following is a translation of these registers. The order follows that in the original documents and the figures next to the names indicate the daily rate in akçes. It should be noted that in the original registers sometimes the names include *bin*, "son of" (abbreviated as "b."), and in other cases this word is omitted.

I. *Salaries of the Imperial Ehl-i Hiref Societies:*
   Rebiülevvel, Rebiülahir, and Cumadeyn in the year 965
   [22 December 1557 to 20 March 1558]

A. Society of the Rumiyan Painters

1. Mehmed Şah, serbölük [head of corps]	25
2. Üveys Ahmed	14
3. Bayram Derviş	17
4. Mustafa Buğdan [Moldavian]	13
5. Ali Bayram	8
6. Mehmed Melek Ahmed; deceased	10
7. Mehmed Abdürrahman	6
8. Hasan Hızır	7
9. Mustafa Yusuf	5
10. Cafer Ali	8
11. Yusuf-ı Rum [Rumelian]	11
12. Ahmed Kasım	6
13. Ferhad-ı Bosna [Bosnian]	9
14. Mehmed Hasan	5
15. Kasım-ı Arnavud [Albanian]	7
16. Mehmed Abdülevvel	2
17. Nebi Çelebi	9
18. Hüseyin Bosna [Bosnian]	6
19. Pervane Bosna [Bosnian]	2
20. Hasan Bosna [Bosnian]	5
21. Cafer-i Macar [Hungarian]	5
22. Kasım-ı Çerkes [Circassian]	6
23. Haydar-ı Arnavud [Albanian]	9
24. Pir Çelebi	5
25. Pervane Nevrekob	5
26. Ali Macar [Hungarian]	6
Apprentices of the aforementioned	
27. Ali, brother of Abdülkerim	2
28. Mustafa Divane	2
29. Mehmed Bosna [Bosnian]; resident of Edirne	1
30. Yusuf Nemçe [Austrian]	6
31. Rum, apprentice of the serbölük	6
32. Cafer Nasuh	4
33. İskender Bosna [Bosnian]	1
34. Mahmud-ı Gürci [Georgian], apprentice of Mustafa	1

B. Society of Bookbinders

1. Mehmed Ahmed	16.5
2. Hüseyin, his brother	13
3. Hasan, his brother	5
4. Mustafa, his brother	9
5. Ahmed, bookbinder of the secretaries of the Divan; normal per diem 2	9
6. Osman Bosna [Bosnian]	5
7. Hürrem-i Rum [Rumelian]	6
8. Hasan Taş	2
9. Yusuf-ı Rum [Rumelian]	5
10. Süleyman Mehmed; deceased	3

II. *Salaries of the Ehl-i Hiref Societies:*
Muharrem 965 to Muharrem 966
[24 October/22 November 1557 to 14 October/12 November 1558]

A. Society of the Rumiyan Painters

1. Kara Memi, nakkaşbaşı [head painter]	25.5
2. Üveys b. Ahmed	14
3. Bayram Derviş; died 23 Muharrem 966 [5 November 1558]	17
4. Mustafa Buğdan [Moldavian]	14
5. Ali b. Bayram	8
6. Mehmed b. Abdürrahman	6.5
7. Hasan b. Hızır	7.5
8. Mustafa b. Yusuf; four payments pending since salary not received	5.5
9. Cafer b. Ali Şerif	8.5
10. Yusuf-ı Rum [Rumelian]	11
11. Ahmed b. Kasım	6.5
12. Ferhad-ı Bosna [Bosnian]	9.5
13. Mehmed b. Hasan	5.5
14. Kasım-ı Arnavud [Albanian]	7.5
15. Mehmed b. Abdülevvel	3
16. Nebi-i Kara Memi	10
17. Hüseyin-i Bosna [Bosnian]	6
18. Pervane-i Bosna [Bosnian]	3
19. Mustafa Müzehhib [illuminator]	8
20. Ali, brother of Abdülkerim, apprentice	2
21. Mustafa Divane, apprentice	2
22. Mehmed-i Bosna [Bosnian], apprentice	1.5
23. Hürrem, apprentice	2
24. Cafer b. Nasuh, apprentice	4
25. İskender-i Bosna [Bosnian], apprentice	1.5
26. Mahmud-ı Gürci [Georgian], apprentice	1

B. Society of the Aceman Painters

1. Abdülali-i Tebrizi	20
2. Abdülhamid-i Tebrizi	16
3. Şah Mehmed-i Tebrizi	19.5
4. Ahi Bey-i Tebrizi	10
5. Alikulu Ama [blind]	4
6. Mir Ağa Tebrizi	7
7. Pervane-i Macar [Hungarian]	4
8. Kaytas-ı Freng [European], apprentice	2.5
9. Derviş Mehmed, apprentice	3

Apprentices of the aforementioned

10. Pervane, apprentice of Abdülali	2
11. Kaytas, apprentice of Abdülhamid	2
12. Hızır, apprentice of Sultan Ali	1
13. Derviş Mehmed-i Isfahan	1

C. Society of Bookbinders

1. Mehmed b. Ahmed	17
2. Hüseyin, brother of Mehmed	13.5
3. Hasan, brother of Mehmed	5.5
4. Mustafa, brother of Mehmed	9.5
5. Ahmed, bookbinder of the secretaries of the Divan	10
6. Osman Bosna [Bosnian]	5
7. Hürrem-i Rum [Rumelian]	7.5
8. Hasan b. Taş	2
9. Yusuf-ı Rum [Rumelian]	5.5
10. Süleyman b. Mehmed; started on 6 Muharrem 965 [29 October 1557]	3.5 3.5

Shortened References

Abrahamowicz 1959	Abrahamowicz, Zygmunt. *Katalog dokumentów tureckich. Dokumenty do dziejów Polski krajów ościennych w latach 1455-1652.* Warsaw, 1959.
Akalay 1969	Akalay, Zeren. "Tarihi Konularda İlk Osmanlı Minyatürleri." *Sanat Tarihi Yıllığı* 2 (1969): 102-115.
Akalay 1973	Akalay, Zeren. "Topkapı Sarayı Müzesi Kütüphanesi Hazine 753 no.lu Nizami *Hamse*si'nin Minyatürleri." *Sanat Tarihi Yıllığı* 5 (1973): 389-409.
Akalay 1978	Akalay, Zeren. "The Forerunners of Classical Turkish Miniature Painting." In *Fifth International Congress of Turkish Art*, edited by Géza Fehér, 31-47. Budapest, 1978.
Akalay 1979	Akalay, Zeren. "XVI. Yüzyıl Nakkaşlarından Hasan Paşa ve Eserleri." In *I. Milletlerarası Türkoloji Kongresi. 3: Türk Sanat Tarihi*, 607-625. İstanbul, 1979.
Akalay 1970	Akalay, Zeren. "Tarihi Konularda Türk Minyatürleri." *Sanat Tarihi Yıllığı* 3 (1970):151-166.
Alderson 1982	Alderson, A. D. *The Structure of the Ottoman Dynasty.* Westport (Conn.), 1982 (reprint).
Anafarta 1969	Anafarta, Nigar. *Hünername: Minyatürleri ve Sanatçıları.* İstanbul, 1969.
Atasoy 1970	Atasoy, Nurhan. "1558 Tarihli *Süleymanname* ve Macar Nakkaş Pervane." *Sanat Tarihi Yıllığı* 3 (1970):167-196.
Atasoy 1972	Atasoy, Nurhan. "Nakkaş Osman'ın Padişah Portreleri Albümü." *Türkiyemiz* 6 (1972):2-14.
Atasoy and Çağman 1974	Atasoy, Nurhan, and Çağman, Filiz. *Turkish Miniature Painting.* İstanbul, 1974.
Atıl 1973	Atıl, Esin. *Turkish Art of the Ottoman Period.* Washington, D.C., 1973.
Atıl 1978	Atıl, Esin. "Ahmed Nakşi: An Eclectic Painter of the Early Seventeenth Century." In *Fifth International Congress on Turkish Art*, edited by Géza Fehér, 103-121. Budapest, 1978.
Atıl 1980	Atıl, Esin. "The Art of the Book." In *Turkish Art*, edited by Esin Atıl, 137-238. Washington, D.C., and New York, 1980.
Atıl 1984	Atıl, Esin. "Mamluk Painting in the Late Fifteenth Century." *Muqarnas* 2 (1984):159-171.
Barkan 1972-1979	Barkan, Ömer Lütfi. *Süleymaniye Cami ve İmareti İnşaatı (1550-1557).* 2 vols. Ankara, 1972-1979.
Bates 1980	Bates, Ülkü. "Architecture." In *Turkish Art*, edited by Esin Atıl, 43-136. Washington, D.C., and New York, 1980.
Binney 1979	Binney, Edwin, 3rd. *Turkish Treasures from the Collection of Edwin Binney, 3rd.* Portland (Oregon), 1979.
Christie's 1976	Christie's. *Islamic and Indian Manuscripts and Miniatures. Wednesday, 17 November 1976.* London, 1976.
Çabuk 1980	Çabuk, Vahit. *Divan-ı Muhibbi (Kanuni Sultan Süleyman'ın Şiirleri).* 3 vols. İstanbul, 1980.
Çağman 1973	Çağman, Filiz. "Şahname-i Selim Han ve Minyatürleri." *Sanat Tarihi Yıllığı* 5 (1973):411-442.

Çağman 1978	Çağman, Filiz. "The Miniatures of the *Divan-ı Hüseyni* and the Influence of Their Style." In *Fifth International Congress of Turkish Art*, edited by Géza Fehér, 231-259. Budapest, 1978.
Çağman 1980	Çağman, Filiz. "Turkish Miniature Painting." In *The Art and Architecture of Turkey*, edited by Ekrem Akugal, 222-248. Oxford, 1980.
Çağman n.d.	Çağman, Filiz. "The Place of the Turkish Miniature in Islamic Art." In *Turkish Contribution to Islamic Arts*, 90-117. İstanbul, n.d.
Çağman and Tanındı 1979	Çağman, Filiz, and Tanındı, Zeren. *Topkapı Saray Museum: Islamic Miniature Painting*. İstanbul, 1979.
Çığ 1959	Çığ, Kemal. "Türk ve İslam Eserleri Müzesindeki Minyatürlü Kitapların Kataloğu." *Şarkiyat Mecmuası* 3 (1959):51-90.
Çığ 1971	Çığ, Kemal. *Türk Kitap Kapları*. İstanbul, 1971.
Danışman 1969-1971	Danışman, Zuhuri. *Evliya Çelebi Seyyahatnamesi*. 15 vols. İstanbul, 1969-1971.
Danişmend 1971	Danişmend, İsmail Hami. *İzahlı Osmanlı Tarihi Kronolojisi*. 5 vols. İstanbul, 1971.
Denny 1980	Denny, Walter B. "Ceramics." In *Turkish Art*, edited by Esin Atıl, 239-297. Washington, D.C., and New York, 1980.
Denny 1983	Denny, Walter B. "Dating Ottoman Turkish Works in the Saz Style." *Muqarnas* 1 (1983):103-121.
Derman 1970	Derman, Uğur. "Kanuni Devrinde Yazı San'atımız." In *Kanuni Armağanı*, 269-289. Ankara, 1970.
Dickson and Welch 1981	Dickson, Martin Bernard, and Welch, Stuart Cary. *The Houghton Shahnameh*. 2 vols. Cambridge (Mass.) and London, 1981.
Duda 1978-1979	Duda, Dorothea. "Ein Beispiel der Tabrizer Buchkunst am Osmanenhof." *Kunst des Orients* 12, nos. 1-2 (1978-1979):61-78.
Duda 1983	Duda, Dorothea. *Islamische Handschriften. I: Persische Handschriften*. 2 vols. Vienna, 1983.
Eldem and Akozan 1982	Eldem, Sedad H., and Akozan, Feridun. *Topkapı Sarayı: Bir Mimari Araştırma*. İstanbul, 1982.
Eyice 1970	Eyice, Semavi. "Avrupalı Bir Ressamın Gözü ile Kanuni Sultan Süleyman." In *Kanuni Armağanı*, 129-170. Ankara, 1970.
Fehér 1976	Fehér, Géza. *Turkische Miniaturen aus den Chroniken der ungarischen Feldzüge*. Budapest, 1976.
Fischer 1962	Fischer, E. *Melchior Lorch*. Copenhagen, 1962.
Forster 1968	Forster, E. S. (translator). *The Turkish Letters of Ogier Ghiselin de Busbecq*. Oxford, 1968 (reprint).
Frankfurt 1985	*Türkische Kunst und Kultur aus osmanischer Zeit*. 2 vols. Frankfurt, 1985.
Gibb 1904	Gibb, E. J. W. *History of Ottoman Poetry*. 6 vols. London, 1904.
Goodwin 1971	Goodwin, Godfrey. *A History of Ottoman Architecture*. London, 1971.
Gökbilgin 1964	Gökbilgin, M. Tayyip. "Süleyman I." *İslam Ansiklopedisi*, vol. 9, 1964, 99-155.
Grube n.d.	Grube, Ernst J. *Islamic Paintings from the Eleventh to the Eighteenth Century in the Collection of Hans P. Kraus*. New York, n.d.
Irmak and Çağlar 1973	Irmak, Sadi, and Çağlar, Behçet Kemal. *Çevdet Paşa Tarihinden Seçmeler*. İstanbul, 1973.
İnalcık 1964	İnalcık, Halil. "The Rise of Ottoman Historiography." In *Historians of the Middle East*, edited by Bernard Lewis and P. M. Holt, 152-167. London, 1964 (reprint).
İnalcık 1969	İnalcık, Halil. "Süleyman the Lawgiver and Ottoman Law." *Archivum Ottomanicum* 1 (1969):105-138.
İnalcık 1973	İnalcık, Halil. *The Ottoman Empire: The Classical Age, 1300-1600*. London, 1973.
İnan 1954	İnan, Afet. *Türk Amirali Piri Reis'in Hayatı ve Eserleri*. Ankara, 1954.
İstanbul 1983	*The Anatolian Civilisations. III: Seljuk/Ottoman*. İstanbul, 1983.
Kappert 1976	Kappert, Petra. *Die osmanischen Prinzen und ihre Residenz Amasya im 15. und 16. Jahrhundert*. Leiden, 1976.
Karatay 1961a	Karatay, Fehmi E. *Topkapı Sarayı Müzesi Kütüphanesi Farsça Yazmalar Kataloğu*. İstanbul, 1961.

Karatay 1961b	Karatay, Fehmi E. *Topkapı Sarayı Müzesi Kütüphanesi Türkçe Yazmalar Kataloğu*. 2 vols. İstanbul, 1961.
Karatay 1962-1969	Karatay, Fehmi E. *Topkapı Sarayı Müzesi Kütüphanesi Arapca Yazmalar Kataloğu*. 4 vols. İstanbul, 1962-1969.
Kuran 1978	Kuran, Aptullah. "The Mosques of Sinan." In *Fifth International Congress of Turkish Art*, edited by Géza Fehér, 559-568. Budapest, 1978.
Kürkçüoğlu 1962	Kürkçüoğlu, Kemal E. *Süleymaniye Vakfiyesi*. Ankara, 1962.
Los Angeles 1973	*Islamic Art: The Nasli M. Heeramaneck Collection*. Edited by Pratapaditya Pal. Los Angeles, 1973.
Lowry 1982	Lowry, Heath. "Calligraphy–Hüsn-i Hat." In *Tulips, Arabesques and Turbans*, edited by Yanni Petsopoulos, 169-191. London, 1982.
Mackie 1980	Mackie, Louise W. "Rugs and Textiles." In *Turkish Art*, edited by Esin Atıl, 299-393. Washington, D.C., and New York, 1980.
Meredith-Owens 1962	Meredith-Owens, Glynn M. "Turkish Miniatures in the *Selim-name*." *The British Museum Quarterly* 26, nos. 1-2 (September 1962):33-35.
Meriç 1953	Meriç, Rıfkı Melul. *Türk Nakış Sanatı Tarihi Araştırmaları. I: Vesikalar*. Ankara, 1953.
Meriç 1954	Meriç, Rıfkı Melul. *Türk Cild Sanatı Tarihi Araştırmaları. I: Vesikalar*. Ankara, 1954.
Meriç 1963	Meriç, Rıfkı Melul. "Türk Sanatı Tarihi Vesikaları: Bayramlarda Padişahlara Hediye Edilen Sanat Eserleri ve Karşılıkları." *Türk Sanatı Tarihi Araştırma ve İncelemeleri* 1 (1963):764-786.
Minorsky 1958	Minorsky, V. *The Chester Beatty Library: A Catalogue of the Turkish Manuscripts and Miniatures*. Dublin, 1958.
Oberhummer 1902	Oberhummer, Eugen. *Konstantinopel unter Sultan Suleiman dem Grossen: Aufgenommen im Jahre 1559 durch Melchior Lorichs*. Munich, 1902.
Pitcher 1972	Pitcher, Donald Edgar. *An Historical Geography of the Ottoman Empire*. Leiden, 1972.
Renda 1973	Renda, Günsel. "Topkapı Sarayı Müzesindeki H. 1321 no. lu *Silsilename*'nin Minyatürleri." *Sanat Tarihi Yıllığı* 5 (1973):443-495.
Renda 1976	Renda, Günsel. "New Light on the Painters of the *Zubdet al-Tawarikh* in the Museum of Turkish and Islamic Arts in Istanbul." In *IVème Congrès International d'Art Turc*, 183-200. Aix-en-Provence, 1976.
Rogers 1982	Rogers, J. Michael. "The Furniture and Decoration of Süleymaniye." *International Journal of Middle East Studies* 14 (1982):283-313.
Rogers 1983	Rogers, J. Michael. *Islamic Art & Design. 1500-1700*. London, 1983.
Rouillard 1938	Rouillard, Clarence Dana. *The Turk in French History, Thought and Literature (1520-1660)*. Paris, 1938.
Sohrweide 1971	Sohrweide, Hanna. "Der Verfasser der als *Sulayman-nama* bekannten İstanbuler Prachthandschrift." *Der Islam* 47 (1971):286-289.
Soucek 1973	Soucek, Svat. "A propos du livre d'instructions nautiques de Piri Reis." *Revue des Etudes Islamiques* 41, no. 2 (1973):241-255.
Sözen 1975	Sözen, Metin, et al. *Türk Mimarisinin Gelişimi ve Mimar Sinan*. İstanbul, 1975.
Stchoukine 1966	Stchoukine, Ivan. *La peinture turque d'après les manuscrits illustrés. Ire partie: de Süleyman Ier à Osman II. 1520-1622*. Paris, 1966.
Stchoukine 1972	Stchoukine, Ivan. "La *Khamseh* de Nizami, H. 753, du Topkapı Sarayı Müzesi d'İstanbul." *Syria: Revue d'Art Oriental et d'Archéologie* 49 (1972):240-246.
Titley 1981	Titley, Norah M. *Miniatures from Turkish Manuscripts: A Catalogue and Subject Index of Paintings in the British Library and British Museum*. London, 1981.
Uluçay 1956	Uluçay, Çağatay. *Haremden Mektuplar*. İstanbul, 1956.
Uluçay 1970	Uluçay, Çağatay. "Kanuni Sultan Süleyman ve Ailesi ile İlgili Bazı Notlar ve Vesikalar." In *Kanuni Armağanı*, 227-257. Ankara, 1970.
Ünver 1946	Ünver, A. Süheyl. *Ressam Nigari: Hayatı ve Eserleri*. Ankara, 1946.
Ünver 1970	Ünver, A. Süheyl. "Kanuni Sultan Süleyman'ın Son Avusturya Seferinde Hastalığı, Ölümü, Cenazesi ve Defni." In *Kanuni Armağanı*, 301-306. Ankara, 1970.

Welch and Welch 1982	Welch, Anthony, and Welch, Stuart Cary. *Arts of the Islamic Book: The Collection of Prince Sadruddin Aga Khan.* Ithaca and London, 1982.
Woodhead 1983	Woodhead, Christine. "An Experiment in Official Historiography: The Post of Şehnameci in the Ottoman Empire, c. 1555-1605." *Wiener Zeitschrift für die Kunde des Morgenlandes* 75 (1983): 157-182.
Yurdaydın 1976	Yurdaydın, Hüseyin G. *Nasuhü's-Silahi (Matrakcı), Beyan-ı Menazil-i Sefer-i Irakeyn-i Sultan Süleyman Han.* Ankara, 1976.

Select Bibliography

HISTORIES OF THE PERIOD

Adıvar, A. Adnan. *Osmanlı Türklerinde İlim.* İstanbul, 1970.

Alderson, A.D. *The Structure of the Ottoman Dynasty.* Westport (Conn.), 1982 (reprint).

Altınay, Ahmet Refik. *16. Asırda İstanbul Hayatı.* Istanbul, 1935.

Altunsu, Abdülkadir. *Osmanlı Şeyhülislamları.* Ankara, 1972.

Anderson, R.C. *Naval Wars in the Levant, 1558-1853.* Princeton, 1952.

Babinger, Franz. *Die Geschichtsschreiber der Osmanen und ihre Werke.* Leipzig, 1927.

Bayrak, M. Orhan. *Osmanlı Tarihi Yazarları.* İstanbul, 1982.

Birge, John Kingsley. *The Bektashi Order of Dervishes.* London, 1937.

Bradford, Ernle. *The Great Siege.* London, 1961.

Bradford, Ernle. *The Sultan's Admiral: Life of Barbarossa.* London, 1969.

Braudel, Fernand. *The Mediterranean and the Mediterranean World in the Age of Philip II.* 2 vols. New York, Hagerstown, San Francisco, and London, 1972-1973.

Bridge, Antony. *Suleiman the Magnificent.* New York, 1983.

Brockman, Eric. *The Two Sieges of Rhodes: 1480-1522.* London, 1969.

Cenkmen, Emin. *Osmanlı Sarayı ve Kıyafetleri.* İstanbul, n.d.

Clot, André. *Soliman le Magnifique.* Paris, 1983.

Coecke van Aelst, Pieter. *Les moeurs et fachons de faire de turcs.* Antwerp, 1553.

Coles, P. *The Ottoman Impact on Europe.* London, 1968.

Danişmend, İsmail Hami. *İzahlı Osmanlı Tarihi Kronolojisi.* 5 vols. İstanbul, 1971.

Davis, J.C. *Pursuit of Power: Venetian Ambassadors' Reports on Spain, Turkey, and France in the Age of Philip II, 1560-1600.* New York, 1970.

Downey, Fairfax. *The Grande Turke: Suleyman the Magnificent.* London, 1929.

Farooqhi, Suraiya. *Towns and Townsmen in Ottoman Anatolia: Trade, Crafts, and Food Production in an Urban Setting, 1520-1650.* Cambridge, 1984.

Fischer-Galati, S. *Ottoman Imperialism and German Protestantism, 1521-1555.* Cambridge (Mass.), 1959.

Fisher, S.N. *Foreign Relations of Turkey: 1481-1512.* Illinois, 1948.

Forrer, L. *Die osmanische Chronik des Rüstem Pascha.* Leipzig, 1923.

Forster, Edward S. (translator). *The Turkish Letters of Ogier Ghiselin de Busbecq.* Oxford, 1968.

Gibb, E.J.W. *History of Ottoman Poetry.* 6 vols. London, 1904.

Gibb, H.A.R., and Bowen, Harold. *Islamic Society and the West.* 2 vols. Oxford, 1962 (reprint).

Gökbilgin, M. Tayyıp. "Hürrem Sultan." *İslam Ansiklopedisi*, vol. 5, part 1, 1967, 593-596.

Gökbilgin, M. Tayyıp. "Süleyman I." *İslam Ansiklopedisi*, vol. 9, 1964, 99-155.

Göllner, Carl. *Turcica: die europäischen Türkendrucke des XVI. Jahrhunderts.* 2 vols. Bucharest and Baden-Baden, 1961-1968.

Gölpinarlı, Abdül Baki. *Divan Şiiri, XV-XVI Yüzyıllar.* İstanbul, 1954.

Hammer-Purgstall, Joseph von. *Geschichte des osmanischen Reiches.* 10 vols. Pest. 1827-1835.

Hammer-Purgstall, Joseph von. *Geschichte der osmanischen Dichtkunst bis auf unsere Zeit.* 4 vols. Pest, 1836-1838.

Hammer-Purgstall, Joseph von. *Des osmanischen Reichs Staatsverfassung und Staatsverwaltung.* 2 vols. Vienna, 1815.

Hasluck, F.W. *Christianity and Islam Under the Sultans.* 2 vols. Oxford, 1929.

Heyd, Uriel. *Ottoman Documents on Palestine, 1552-1615: A Study of the Firman According to the Mühimme Defteri.* Oxford, 1960.

Holt, P.M. *Egypt and the Fertile Crescent, 1516-1922.* London, 1966.

Iorga, N. *Geschichte des osmanischen Reiches.* 5 vols. Gotha, 1908-1913.

Irmak, Sadi, and Çağlar, Behçet Kemal. *Cevdet Paşa Tarihinden Seçmeler.* İstanbul, 1973.

İnal, Mahmud Kemal. *Gelibolulu Mustafa Ali. Menakıb-ı Hünerveran.* İstanbul, 1926.

İnalcık, Halil. "The Heyday and Decline of the Ottoman Empire." In *The Cambridge History of Islam. Volume I: The Central Islamic Lands,* edited by P.M. Holt, 324-353. Cambridge, 1970.

İnalcık, Halil. *The Ottoman Empire: The Classical Age 1300-1600.* London, 1973.

İnalcık, Halil. "The Rise of the Ottoman Empire." In *The Cambridge History of Islam. Volume I: The Central Islamic Lands,* edited by P.M. Holt, 295-323. Cambridge, 1970.

İnalcık, Halil. "The Rise of Ottoman Historiography." In *Historians of the Middle East,* edited by Bernard Lewis and P.M. Holt, 152-167. London, 1964.

İnalcık, Halil. "Süleyman the Lawgiver and Ottoman Law." *Archivum Ottomanicum* 1 (1969): 105-138.

İnan, Afet. *Türk Amirali Piri Reis'in Hayatı ve Eserleri.* Ankara, 1954.

Káldy-Nagy, Gyula. *Kanuni Devri Budin Tahrir Defterleri (1546-1562).* Ankara, 1971.

Káldy-Nagy, Gyula. "Rural and Urban Life in the Age of Sultan Süleyman." *Acta Orientalia Hungrica* 32 (1978): 285-319.

Kappert, Petra. *Die osmanischen Prinzen und ihre Residenz Amasya im 15. und 16. Jahrhundert.* Leiden, 1976.

Kappert, Petra. *Geschichte Sultan Süleyman Kanunis von 1520 bis 1567 (oder "Tabakat ül-Memalik ve Derecat ül-Mesalik" von Celalzade Mustafa genannt Koca Nişancı).* Wiesbaden, 1981.

Kanuni Armağanı. Ankara, 1970.

Knolles, R. *The General Historie of the Turkes.* London, 1638.

Koçu, Reşad Ekrem. *Topkapu Sarayı.* İstanbul, 1960.

Kortepeter, Carl Max. *Ottoman Imperialism During the Reformation: Europe and the Caucasus.* New York and London, 1972.

Kunt, I. Metin. *The Sultan's Servants: The Transformation of Ottoman Provincial Government, 1550-1650.* New York, 1983.

Lamb, Harold. *Suleiman the Magnificent.* New York, 1951.

Lapidus, Ira M. *Muslim Cities in the Later Middle Ages.* Cambridge (Mass.), 1967.

Lewis, Bernard, *İstanbul and the Civilization of the Ottoman Empire.* Norman (Okla.), 1963.

Lewis, Raphaela. *Everyday Life in Ottoman Turkey.* London and New York, 1971.

Lybyer, Albert Howe. *The Government of the Ottoman Empire in the Time of Suleiman the Magnificent.* Cambridge (Mass.), 1913.

Mantran, Robert. *Istanbul dans la seconde moitié du XVIIe siècle.* Paris, 1962.

Mantran, Robert. *La vie quotidienne à Constantinople au temps de Soliman le Magnifique et de ses successeurs.* Paris, 1965.

Mehmed Süreyya. *Sicill-i Osmani.* 4 vols. İstanbul, 1890-1899.

Mehmed Tahir (Bursalı). *Osmanlı Müellifleri.* 3 vols. İstanbul, 1915.

Merriman, R.B. *Suleiman the Magnificent.* Cambridge (Mass.), 1944.

Miller, Barnette. *Beyond the Sublime Porte: The Grand Seraglio of Stambul.* New Haven (Conn.), 1941.

Miller, Barnette. *The Palace School of Muhammad the Conqueror.* New York, 1973 (reprint).

Mitchell, James (translator). *Hacı Halife: The History of the Maritime Wars of the Turks.* London, 1831.

Müstakimzade. *Tuhfe-i Hattatin.* İstanbul, 1928.

Oberhummer, Eugen. *Konstantinopel unter Sultan Suleiman dem Grossen: Aufgenommen im Jahre 1559 durch Melchior Lorichs.* Munich, 1902.

d'Ohsson, Ignatius Mouradgea. *Tableau général de l'empire othoman,* 7 vols. Paris, 1788-1824.

Oransay, Gültekin (editor). *Mehmed Süreyya. Osmanlı Devletinde Kim Kimdi. I: Osmanoğulları.* Ankara, 1969.

Özergin, M. Kemal. *Sultan Kanuni Süleyman Han Çağına Ait Tarih Kayıtları.* Erzurum, 1971.

Pakalin, Mehmet Zeki. *Osmanlı Tarih Deyimleri ve Terimleri Sözlüğü.* 3 vols. İstanbul, 1971.

Parry, V.J. "The Ottoman Empire, 1481-1520." In *New Cambridge Modern History,* vol. 1, 395-410. Cambridge, 1957.

Parry, V.J. "The Ottoman Empire, 1520-1566." In *New Cambridge Modern History,* vol. 2, 510-533. Cambridge, 1958.

Pavet de Courtelle, M. *Histoire de la campagne de Mohacs par Kemal Pasha Zadeh.* Paris, 1859.

Penzer, N.M. *The Harem.* London, 1967.

Pitcher, Donald Edgar. *An Historical Geography of the Ottoman Empire.* Leiden, 1972.

Refik, Ahmed. *Kadınlar Saltanatı.* İstanbul, 1332.

Rouillard, Clarence Dana. *The Turk in French History, Thought, and Literature (1520-1660).* Paris, 1938.

Rycaut, P. *Present State of the Ottoman Empire.* London, 1670.

Schwoebel, Robert S. *The Shadow of the Crescent: The Renaissance Image of the Turk, 1453-1517.* Nieuwkoop, 1967.

Shaw, Stanford J. *The Financial and Administrative Organization and Development of Ottoman Egypt.* Princeton, 1962.

Shaw, Stanford J. *History of the Ottoman Empire and Modern Turkey.* 2 vols. Cambridge, 1976.

Sohrweide, Hanna. "Dichter und Gelehrte aus dem Osten im osmanischen Reich (1453-1600)." *Der Islam* 46, no. 3 (1970): 263-302.

Sohrweide, Hanna. "Der Verfasser der als *Sulayman-nama* bekannten İstanbuler Prachthandschrift." *Der Islam* 47 (1971): 286-289.

Stripling, G.W.F. *The Ottoman Turks and the Arabs, 1511-1574.* Urbana (Ill.), 1942 (reprint).

Stuminger, W. *Bibliographie und Ikonographie der Türkenbelagerungen Wiens 1529 und 1683.* Graz and Cologne, 1955.

Şardağ, Rüştü. *Şair Sultanlar.* Ankara, 1982.

Tansel, Şelahattin. *Yavuz Sultan Selim.* Ankara, 1969.

Tauer, Félix. *Histoire de la Campagne du Sultan Suleyman Ier contre Belgrade en 1521.* Prague, 1924.

Tindal, N. (translator). *Demetrius Cantemir. History of the Ottoman Empire.* 2 vols. London, 1734-1735.

Turan, Şerafettin. *Kanuni'nin Oğlu Şehzade Bayezid Vakası.* Ankara, 1961.

Uluçay, Çağatay. *Haremden Mektuplar.* İstanbul, 1956.

Uluçay, Çağatay. *Harem II.* Ankara, 1971.

Uluçay, Çağatay. *Padişahların Kadınları ve Kızları.* Ankara, 1980.

Unat, F. Reşid. *Osmanlı Sefirleri ve Sefaretnameleri.* Ankara, 1968.

Uraz, Murat (translator). *Peçevi Tarihi.* 2 vols. İstanbul, 1968.

Uzunçarşılı, İsmail Hakkı. *Osmanlı Devleti Teşkilatından Kapukulu Ocakları.* 2 vols. Ankara, 1943-1944.

Uzunçarşılı, İsmail Hakkı. *Osmanlı Devletinin İlmiye Teşkilati.* Ankara, 1965.

Uzunçarşılı, İsmail Hakkı. *Osmanlı Devletinin Merkez ve Bahriye Teşkilatı.* Ankara, 1948.

Uzunçarşılı, İsmail Hakkı. *Osmanlı Devletinin Saray Teşkilatı.* Ankara, 1945.

Uzunçarşılı, İsmail Hakkı. *Osmanlı Tarihi.* 4 vols. Ankara, 1982-1983 (reprint).

Vambéry, A. *Hungary in Ancient, Medieval and Modern Times.* London, 1887.

Vaughan, Dorothy. *Europe and the Turk: A Pattern of Alliances, 1350-1700.* Liverpool, 1954.

Wien 1529: Die erste Türkengelagerung. Vienna, 1979.

Woodhead, Christine. "An Experiment in Official Historiography: the Post of Şehnameci in the Ottoman Empire, c. 1555-1605." *Wiener Zeitschrift für die Kunde des Morgenlandes* 75 (1983):157-182.

Yavuz, A. Fikri, and Özen, İsmail (editors). *Bursalı Mehmed Tahir. Osmanlı Müellifleri, 1290-1915.* 2 vols. İstanbul, 1972.

Yurdaydın, Hüseyin G. *Kanuni'nin Cülusu ve İlk Seferleri.* Ankara, 1961.

ART HISTORICAL STUDIES

Akalay, Zeren. "The Forerunners of Classical Turkish Miniature Painting." In *Fifth International Congress of Turkish Art*, edited by Géza Fehér, 31-47. Budapest, 1978.

Akalay, Zeren. "Tarihi Konularda Türk Minyatürleri." *Sanat Tarihi Yıllığı* 3 (1970): 151-166.

Akurgal, Ekrem (editor). *The Art and Architecture of Turkey.* Oxford, 1980.

Aslanapa, Oktay. *Turkish Art and Architecture.* London and New York, 1971.

Atasoy, Nurhan. "1558 Tarihli *Süleymanname* ve Macar Nakkaş Pervane." *Sanat Tarihi Yıllığı* 3 (1970): 167-196.

Atasoy, Nurhan, and Çağman, Filiz. *Turkish Miniature Painting.* İstanbul, 1974.

Atıl, Esin (editor). *Turkish Art.* Washington, D.C., and New York, 1980.

Fehér, Géza. *Türkische Miniaturen aus den Chroniken der ungarischen Feldzüge.* Budapest, 1976.

Stchoukine, Ivan. *La peinture turque d'après les manuscrits illustrés. Ire partie: de Sulayman Ier à Osman II. 1520-1622.* Paris, 1966.

Glossary

Acem:	An Iranian; a non-Arab; a shiite Turk residing in Iran (especially in Azerbaijan); or a foreigner.
ağa:	Chief or master; title given to officers in charge of a special corps such as the janissaries, Enderun School, or Has Oda.
akçe:	Silver coin used in the Ottoman Empire.
akıncı:	Raider; special corps of the light cavalry sent in advance of the army to pillage the enemy countryside.
Arz Odası:	Reception Chamber in the third courtyard of the Topkapı Palace where foreign ambassadors were received and petitions submitted to the sultan.
Bab-ı Hümayun:	Imperial Gate leading into the first courtyard of the Topkapı Palace.
Babüsselam:	Gate of Salutations leading into the second courtyard of the Topkapı Palace.
Babüssaade:	Gate of Felicity leading into the third courtyard of the Topkapı Palace.
bey:	Chief or ruler; title given to governors of sancaks.
beylerbeyi:	"Bey of the beys"; governor-general of a province. Originally there were two beylerbeyis, one in charge of Rumelia and another responsible for Anatolia. As the empire grew, the number of provinces, hence beylerbeyis, increased substantially.
Birun:	Outer Service of the palace.
cloudband:	Decorative motif resembling a thin and curving cloud.
çavuş:	Usher; çavuşbaşı was the chief usher in the palace.
çintemani:	Design composed of a series of double wavy lines and triple balls, originally symbolizing tiger stripes and leopard spots.
defterdar:	Keeper of the books; treasurer of the Ottoman Empire. There were two defterdars, one in charge of the finances in Rumelia and the other responsible for those of Anatolia, both of whom were members in the Divan-ı Hümayun.
delil:	Guide; irregular corps of raiders similar to the akıncıs.
devşirme:	Tribute children recruited by the state from non-Muslim provinces and educated to fill the posts in the administrative and military ranks.
Divan:	1) Applied to both the Divan-ı Hümayun (Imperial Council of Ministers) and the sessions of the council. The English word "divan," meaning couch, derives from the upholstered benches placed along the walls of the council chamber which were used by the ministers during their meetings. 2) A collection of poems, such as the *Divan-ı Muhibbi*.
Divan-ı Hümayun:	See Divan.
Ehl-i Hiref:	"Society of the talented." A special group of artists, artisans, and craftsmen employed by the court to serve the sultan. Provincial courts and princes also had their resident Ehl-i Hiref members.
efendi:	Gentleman; title used by the ulema, religious classes, and scholars.
emir:	Lord or prince.
emirate:	Principality ruled by an emir.
Enderun:	Inner Service of the palace, the members of which were originally devşirme children trained to serve the sultan and educate new recruits.

esnaf:	Tradesmen or guilds of tradesmen and artisans.
ferman:	Imperial edict with tuğra of the sultan at the top.
fetva:	Written answer to a legal question issued by the şeyhülislam or müfti in accordance with Islamic jurisprudence.
gazi:	Warrior of the faith, or one who fights for the propagation of Islam.
grand vezir:	Chief of the vezirs and executive representative of the sultan in administrative and military affairs; the highest rank attainable in the devşirme system.
Hadis:	Traditions or the record of sayings and deeds of the Prophet Muhammed as handed down by his companions; study of the Traditions; also spelled Hadith.
han:	Sovereign or ruler; title used by the Ottoman sultans as well as other Turkish monarchs, including the Crimean Tatars.
hanate:	Domain ruled by the han.
Harem:	Sacred or protected place; name given to the quarters in the Topkapı Palace occupied by the family of the sultan.
Has Oda:	Privy Chamber, or Throne Room, in the third courtyard of the Topkapı Palace used during ceremonial activities; also called the Hırka-ı Saadet Odası (Chamber of the Holy Mantle) since it housed the sacred treasures, such as the mantle and banner of the Prophet Muhammed together with the swords of the four orthodox caliphs brought back from Egypt by Selim I after the defeat of the Mamluks in 1517.
haseki:	Favorite; highest rank in the Harem among the women of the sultan. There were four hasekis, following the Islamic tradition that allowed a man to have four wives; the one who delivered the first son was called baş haseki (head favorite).
hatayi:	Stylized lotus blossom, depicted both frontally and in profile, frequently accompanied by buds; hatayis became an integral part of scrolls used in the saz style.
Hazine:	Treasury in the third courtyard of the Topkapı Palace where sultans' valuable objects were kept.
hilat:	Robe of honor; following the Islamic tradition of presenting sumptuous robes as gifts to deserving dignitaries, the Ottoman sultans gave one or more hilats to foreign ambassadors, court officials, and esteemed artists.
hutbe:	Sermon given in the name of the ruling sultan that follows the traditional prayer on Friday, the Islamic day of rest and worship.
hümayun:	Of or pertaining to the sultan; imperial, as in sefer-i hümayun (imperial campaign) or otak-ı hümayun (imperial tent).
iç oğlan:	Page in the Inner Service who served the sultan.
janissary:	Anglicized version of *yeniçeri* meaning new recruits; this corps, recruited from the devşirme children, constituted the most highly disciplined branch of the infantry; their duties included guarding the sultan and the palace, and maintaining order and security in the capital and in the fortresses along the frontiers.
kaatı:	Découpage; calligraphy employing letters cut out of paper pasted onto a sheet; the same technique was applied in producing three-dimensional paintings.
kadı:	Judge in Ottoman courts who administered the şeriat and kanun.
kaftan:	Collarless, long- or short-sleeved robe fastened in the front, worn by both men and women. The ceremonial kaftan of the court was an open-fronted outer robe with long sleeves that hung at the back and had slits at the shoulders; the arms of the wearer would pass through these slits and expose the inner kaftan. The inner kaftan usually had short sleeves, to which separate sleeves would be buttoned. The inner kaftan was either fastened diagonally or had a straight front with a series of horizontal bands with buttons and loops; it was gathered at the waist with a jeweled belt or an embroidered sash.
kanun:	Sultanic law or secular law issued by the sultan.
kapıcı:	Imperial gatekeeper in charge of the gates of the Topkapı Palace.
kapıcıbaşı:	Head of the imperial gatekeepers who also acted as a protocol officer during ceremonial activities.
kaptan-ı derya:	"Captain of the seas"; the grand admiral of the naval forces.
kazasker:	Chief judge or chief kadı; there were two kazaskers, one in charge of Rumelia and the other responsible for Anatolia; both were members of the Divan-ı Hümayun.

kethüda:	Second in charge, deputy, or lieutenant.
Kubbealtı:	Literally "under the dome," that is, the chamber under the dome where the Divan-ı Hümayun met four times a week in the second courtyard of the Topkapı Palace.
matrak:	Game played by throwing long sticks; invented by Nasuh, who came to be called Matrakcı.
medrese:	University; frequently a part of a complex endowed by a patron.
mehter:	Military band whose members played an assortment of drums, brass, and percussion instruments; the sultan had the largest band, followed by that assigned to the grand vezir and the princes; provincial governors and commanders also had their musicians. The mehter participated in campaigns, parades, and other ceremonial activities.
millet:	Nation; used to designate the subjects of the sultan that belonged to different faiths, such as Muslims, Christians, and Jews.
musavvir:	Painter; word used to denote a painter of figures.
müfti:	Interpreter of the şeriat; the grand müfti was the şeyhülislam.
mücellid:	Bookbinder; plural: mücellidan.
müzehhib:	Illuminator.
nakkaş:	Decorator and painter; plural: nakkaşan.
nakkaşbaşı:	Head nakkaş; see also sernakkaş.
nakkaşhane:	Building or institution where the nakkaşan worked or in which they were employed.
nastalik:	An elegant type of cursive script used mainly for the transcription of literary and epic texts; also spelled nastaliq.
nesih:	The simplest form of cursive scripts; also spelled naskh.
nişancı:	Chancellor in the Divan-ı Hümayun responsible for affixing the sultan's tuğra on fermans.
otak:	Tent or tent with a canopy enclosed by a protective fabric fence; otak-ı hümayun (imperial tent of the sultan) was the most elaborately decorated one, frequently used for ceremonial receptions during campaigns.
paşa:	Title given to high-ranking officials, particularly to vezirs, governor-generals of beylerbeyliks, and military commanders.
peri:	Angel; more specifically a fairy or a beautiful spirit inhabiting paradise or a fantastic world.
peyk:	Personal guard of the sultan.
reaya:	"Flock," or the subjects of the sultan.
reis:	Naval captain.
reisülküttab:	Chief of clerks; a member of the Divan-ı Hümayun responsible for official correspondence and records.
ressam:	Painter.
Rumi:	One from Rumelia, or the European provinces of the empire. Originally the word Rum was applied to the lands of the Eastern Roman Empire, hence to Anatolia as well.
rumi:	Decorative element consisting of leaves with elongated and pointed tips, frequently employed in scrolls; at times the leaves were split and paired to create a cartouche or joined by an undulating or overlapping branch.
sancak:	"Banner" or "standard"; district governed by a bey, under the administrative jurisdiction of a beylerbeyi.
sancakbeyi:	Governor of a sancak.
saz:	An enchanted forest of hatayis and other abstract flora inhabited by peris, dragons, and jinns; applied to a genre of drawings representing this world as well as to a decorative theme with hatayi and serrate leaf scrolls in which the elements intertwine, overlap, and intersect one another.
sefer:	Campaign; the sefer-i hümayun refers to an imperial campaign.
serasker:	Commander in chief of the armed forces; title used by the sultans.
serbölük:	Head of a corps.
sernakkaş:	Head nakkaş.

shiite:	Sect of Islam which professes that Ali, the fourth caliph, and the Imams were the rightful successors of the Prophet Muhammed.
sipahi:	Cavalry.
solak:	Personal guard of the sultans.
sufi:	Mystic or mystical philosophy.
sultan:	King; title used by Muslim rulers, particularly by the Ottomans.
sülüs:	Distinctive style of cursive script; also spelled thuluth.
şah:	King; title used by muslim rulers, particularly by the Iranians.
şahname:	Book of kings; biography of the sultan.
şahnameci:	Official biographer or historiographer of the sultan.
şeyh:	Spiritual leader.
şeyhülislam:	Leader of Islam; title of the chief judge and enforcer of the Islamic laws.
şehzade:	Prince; son of the sultan.
şeriat:	Religious law of Islam.
timar:	Fief; lands assigned to individuals who were responsible for their administration and who collected taxes as revenue in return for providing the state with armed forces during campaigns.
tuğra:	Monogram of the sultan affixed to a ferman, legalizing its contents.
ulema:	Learned men, scholars, clergymen, or professors of theology.
valide sultan:	Queen mother; woman whose son was the reigning sultan.
vakıf:	Endowment or foundation trust established by the donor for the maintenance of religious, charitable, and social edifices.
vezir:	Governor-general or commander in chief in charge of a major province of the empire who had the privilege to use the title paşa.
voyvoda:	Governor or head of a vassal state, such as Transylvania, who paid a tribute and provided armed forces in return for semi-independent status.

Index

The index includes references to persons, places, and titles of manuscripts mentioned in the text; architectural monuments are listed under the cities. (Footnotes, appendices, and captions for the reference photos are excluded.)

Abadan, 55
Abdülkadir el-Gilani, 33
Abdullah (şehzade), 21
Abdullah b. İlyas, 40
Abdullah Sayrafi, 198
　Koran, 38, 41, 64
Abu Turab el-Hasani el-Hüseyni, 57
　Futuhat-ı Cemile, 56
Aden, 177
Adriatic Sea, 175
Aegean Sea, 11, 16, 117, 119, 179
Ahlat, 215
Ahmed (bookbinder), 40
Ahmed (brother of Selim I), 57
Ahmed Bey, 191
Ahmed Feridun Paşa, 32, 44
　Nüzhet el-Esrar el-Ahbar der Sefer-i Sigetvar, 48, 72
Ahmed Kamil, 41
Ahmed Karahisari, 31
　Koran, 41, 64
Ahmed Nakşi, 74
Ahmed Paşa, 16, 72, 107, 121, 124, 145
Ahmedi
　Tarih-i Al-i Osman, 44
Aka Mirak, 37
Akbar, 44
Akçakale, 205
Akşehir, 196
Aktepe, 19, 219
Alamut, 203
Albania, 11, 14, 18
Aleppo, 20, 22, 68, 72, 171, 196, 198, 201, 203, 217, 221, 223
Alexander the Great (İskender), 139, 215
Algeria, 14, 17, 18, 167
Algiers, 169
Ali (painter), 72
Ali b. Bayram, 40
Ali b. Emir Bey Şirvani, 56, 62
Ali Bey, 102, 139
Ali Çelebi
　Hümayunname, 35
Ali Efendi (Zenbilli), 90, 91, 117, 122
Ali Şir Nevai
　Divan, 42
　Hamse, 42, 70
Amasya, 19, 20, 22, 37, 41, 68, 189, 196, 217, 219, 227, 229, 231, 233
Anatolia, 11, 15, 17, 20, 29, 91, 96, 117, 134, 135, 139, 141, 143, 145, 148

Anbiyaname, 66, 69
Ankara, 60
Antioch, 198
Anton, 167
Arabian Gulf, 14, 47, 175, 177
Arabian Sea, 14
Aragon, 119
Ardanuç (Ardanuchi), 215
Arifi, 42, 44, 47, 55, 60, 62, 87, 187, 194, 198, 203, 231
　Divan, 57
　Futuhat-ı Cemile, 56, 69, 75
　Ravzat al-Uşak, 57, 70, 75
　Şahname-i Al-i Osman, 47, 55, 72
Aşık Çelebi, 32, 44
Aşıkpaşazade, 32
　Tarih-i Al-i Osman, 44
Austria, 17, 149, 153, 159
Auvergne, 119
Avlonya (Valona), 175
Ayas Mehmed Paşa, 124, 175
Azerbaijan, 14, 18, 173
Azov, Sea of, 11

Babadağ, 177
Baba Zunnun, 139
Babur, 44
Baghdad, 14, 18, 33, 37, 171, 173
Baki, 32
Bali Bey (Küçük), 155
Bali Bey (later Paşa), 109, 110, 133, 135, 191
Balkans, 11
Barbaros Hayreddin Paşa, 14, 15, 17-18, 30, 46, 47, 68, 169, 175, 177
Basra, 177
Başsaz, 143
Bayezid (şehzade), 19, 22, 66, 179, 183, 187, 191, 196, 198, 205, 219, 221, 233
Bayezid I, 60, 86
Bayezid II, 11, 32, 36, 37, 40, 41, 46, 47, 57, 74, 86
Bayram b. Derviş, 38, 40, 74
　Koran, 74
Behram Bey, 139
Behram Çavuş, 102
Behram Paşa, 134, 141
Behzad, 198
Bekir, 173
Belgrade, 11, 14, 16, 17, 20, 23, 67, 105, 107, 109, 110, 115, 127, 128, 145, 148, 153, 163, 165, 209
Beyan-ı Menazil-i Sefer-i Irakeyn, 46
Bithynia, 11

Bitlis, 18, 171
Black Sea, 14
Bodrum, 117
Böğürdelen (Sabacz), 107
Bohemia, 17, 153
Bolu, 14, 15, 90
Bosnia, 46, 134, 135, 155
Bucak, 177
Budapest, 17, 18, 22, 72, 131, 133, 134, 149, 155, 163, 183, 185, 187, 191
Bukhara, 41, 205
Bulgaria, 11, 14
Burhan-ı Ali, 196
Bursa, 11, 31, 35, 219
Busbecq, Ogier Ghiselin de, 19, 20, 231
Büyük Çekmeçe, 33

Cafer Ağa, 23
Cairo, 14, 31, 40, 42, 43, 68, 101, 124, 233
Camaspname, 44
Canberdi Gazali, 16, 72, 101, 102, 117
Cantacuzene, 60
Caspian Sea, 14
Castelnuovo, 179
Caucasus, 20, 194, 225, 227
Celaleddin Rumi, 33
Cem, 46
Cemşid (Jamshid), 59, 215, 217
Cengiz (Genghiz) Han, 201
Charles V, 14, 15, 16, 17, 19, 127, 131, 149, 167, 175, 192
Cihangir, 19, 22, 33, 179, 196, 221
Cortu, 18, 175
Coron, 17, 18, 167, 169
Crimea, 11, 14, 194
Cyprus, 115
Czechoslovakia, 14
Çanakkale, 46

Dalmatia, 179
Damascus, 14, 16, 33, 101, 102
Danişmend Reis, 105, 107
Danube River, 16, 33, 105, 107, 110, 128, 134, 191
Denizli, 117
Derviş Mehmed, 55, 203
Devlet Giray Han, 68, 207
Divane-i Rumeli, 227
Divan-ı Muhibbi, 21, 32, 38, 63, 64
Divan-ı Selimi, 42, 43
Diyarbakır, 203, 205, 223
Dnieper River, 14

Dobruja, 177
Don River, 14
Doria, Andrea, 15, 17, 18, 167, 169, 177
Drava River, 128, 133

Ebu Bekir, 59
Ebu Hanife, 33, 177
Ebussuud Efendi, 23, 32, 183, 187, 207
Edirne, 11, 20, 22, 31, 33, 34, 42, 90, 105, 107, 127, 148, 161, 177, 191, 194, 196, 219, 233
   Edirne Palace, 68
   Selimiye Mosque, 33
Eflatun, 47, 55, 194
Egypt, 11, 14, 16, 28, 101, 121, 124, 127, 145, 201
Elkas Mirza, 19, 55, 67, 72, 73, 194, 196, 198, 203
England, 119
Ereğli, 217, 219
Erlau, 56, 211
Ertuğrul, 86
Erzurum, 19, 171, 205, 215, 217, 225, 227
Eskişehir, 196
Esmahan, 24
Estergon (Esztergom), 18, 191
Estonibelgrad (Székesfehérvár), 18, 72, 191
Eszek, 128
Ethiopia, 14
Eugene, 133

Fazlı, 33
Ferdinand, 14, 15, 17, 18, 19, 131, 148, 149, 153, 155, 159, 161, 165, 167, 183, 191, 192, 207, 209, 231
Ferhad Paşa, 16, 90, 91, 102, 107
Ferruhzade Kemaleddin Bey, 231
Fethullah Arif Çelebi see Arifi
Filibe (Philippopolis, Plovdiv), 107, 115, 128, 148, 161
Firdausi, 42, 61
   Şahname, 42, 55, 62, 70
Florence, 18, 177
France, 119
Francis I, 15, 16-17, 19, 127, 165, 167, 194
Frangipani, Jean, 127
Futuhat-ı Cemile, 56, 69, 75
Fuzuli, 42, 171
   Divan, 32
   Hadikat üs-Sueda, 44
   Leyla ve Mecnun, 32

Galicia, 21
Genoa, 18, 177
Georgia, 14, 19, 173, 194, 205, 215, 223
Germany, 119, 134
Gilan, 18, 171, 173
Graz, 167
Greece, 11, 14, 17, 18
Gujerat, 18, 177
Gülbahar, 21, 90
Gülfem, 21, 90
Gülgün, 173
Güns, 17, 67, 159, 165, 167

Hacı Bektaş Veli, 141
Hadice, 22, 24, 124
Hadikat üs-Sueda, 44
Hadım Süleyman Paşa, 22, 57, 177, 192
Hadis, 30, 64
Hafiz, 42
Hafsa, 15, 21, 207
Hama, 198
Hamadan, 19, 173, 196
Hamdi Çelebi, 42
Hamse, 42, 43, 70
Hamza of Austria, 37
Hasan (bookbinder), 40

Hasan (calligrapher), 41, 74
Hasan Ağa, 23
Hasan b. Abdülcelil (Hasan Çelebi), 37, 40
Haydar Reis see Nigari
Hayırbay, 16, 101, 102, 121
Henry II, 15, 19, 194, 231
Henry VIII, 15
Herat, 42, 43, 46, 57, 198
Hijaz, 14, 201
Hoca Sadeddin, 32, 44
Homs, 198
Hormuz, 20, 47
Hümayunname, 35
Hünername, 48-49
Hungary, 14, 15, 16, 17, 18, 19, 56, 105, 110, 127, 128, 148, 149, 155, 159, 167, 183, 187, 191, 211, 215
Hürrem (wife of Süleyman), 19, 21, 22, 23, 28, 29, 33, 34, 90, 115, 124, 145, 175, 179, 187, 189, 192, 219
Hürrem Paşa, 139
Hürrem-i Rum, 41
Hüseyin (bookbinder), 40
Hüseyin Paşa, 139
Hüsrev (Khosrau), 171
Hüsrev Bey, 134, 135
Hüsrev Paşa, 139, 183
Hüsrev ve Şirin, 44

Ilok, 128
India, 32
Indian Ocean, 18, 177
Irakeyn, 173
Irak-ı Acem, 173
Irak-ı Arab, 173
Iran, 14, 19, 32, 36, 141, 171, 175, 198, 201, 203, 215
Iraq, 14, 18, 171, 173, 175
Isabella, 183, 187
Isfahan, 19, 173, 196
Ismail, 37
Ismail Mirza, 215
Italy, 18, 119, 175
İbrahim Gülşeni, 55
İbrahim Paşa, 16, 17, 18, 22, 24, 32, 33, 68, 124, 127, 128, 133, 134, 135, 143, 145, 149, 155, 156, 159, 171, 173, 175
İbrahim Peçevi, 32
İçel, 139
İskender see Alexander the Great
İskender Paşa, 196, 215
İstanbul, 11, 15, 16, 17, 18, 19, 20, 21, 22, 23, 24, 31, 33, 35, 37, 40, 41, 42, 43, 47, 55, 67, 90, 101, 115, 117, 124, 128, 139, 143, 148, 153, 155, 156, 159, 161, 163, 167, 169, 171, 173, 183, 187, 189, 191, 192, 194, 203, 205, 207, 215, 219, 221, 231, 233
   At Meydanı, 33, 124, 156, 179
   Cihangir Mosque, 221
   İbrahim Paşa Palace, 124
   Süleymaniye (mosque and complex), 20, 22, 23, 49, 207
   Şehzade Mosque, 221
   Topkapı Palace, 11, 21, 24-29, 55, 66, 68, 72, 90, 105, 145, 156, 159, 163, 189, 198, 201
      Alay Köşkü, 36
      Arz Odası, 68, 72, 161, 163, 195, 207
      Babüssaade, 27, 68, 90, 161, 207
      Babüsselam, 27, 90, 96, 159
      Harem, 21, 24, 28-29
      Has Oda, 68, 179
      Hazine, 35
      Kubbealtı, 68, 72, 96, 157
İzmit, 11
İznik, 11, 35
İzvornik, 155

Jami
   Divan, 42
Jerusalem, 14
   Dome of the Rock, 34
Jurischitz, Nicolas, 159, 167

Kadızade Mehmed Bey, 124
Kalender Çelebi, 17, 72, 141, 143
Kalila va Dimna, 35
Kanunname-i Al-i Osman, 21
Kara Ahmed Paşa, 22, 205, 211, 219, 233
Karabağ, 217, 225
Karaçayır, 141
Karahisari see Ahmed Karahisari
Karaman, 139, 205
Kara Memi (Mehmed-i Siyah or Mehmed Çelebi Siyah), 31, 36, 37-38, 40, 41, 64-65, 74
   Divan-ı Muhibbi, 38
   Koran, 41, 64
Karasu swamp, 134
Kars, 217
Kasım el-Hüseyni el-Aridi el-Kazvini
   Tarih-i Sultan Süleyman, 48
Kasım Paşa, 90, 183
Kaşan, 196
Kasr-ı Şirin, 67, 171
Kayseri, 33, 72, 139, 196
Kazvin, 19, 73, 156, 173, 177
Kefe (Kaffa), 14, 15, 21, 90
Kemal, 47
Kemalpaşazade (İbni Kemal), 32, 44
Kıyafet el-İnsaniye fi Şemail-i Osmaniye, 49
Kitab-ı Bahriye, 32, 47
Konya, 19, 22, 33, 171, 219
Koran, 20, 30, 38, 41, 64, 74
Kütahya, 22, 23, 117, 196, 217

Latifi, 33
Leyla ve Mecnun, 32
Libya, 14
Linz, 149, 153
Lipva, 56, 187, 207, 209, 211
Livana, 205
Lokman, 47, 48, 72
   Hünername, 48
   Kıyafet el-İnsaniye fi Şemail-i Osmaniye, 49
   Surname, 49
   Şahınşahname, 48
   Şahname-i Selim Han, 48
   Tarih-i Sultan Süleyman, 48
   Zübdet üt-Tevarih, 49
Louis II, 14, 16, 17, 66, 69, 102, 105, 131, 134, 155
Louise of Savoy, 16, 127
Luther, Martin, 15, 127
Lütfi, 32, 44

Macedonia, 11
Mahmud (şehzade), 22, 115
Mahmud Şah (calligrapher), 64
Malta, 16, 18, 19, 20
Manastır (Bitola), 175
Manisa, 14, 15, 21, 22, 90, 145, 189, 192
Mantık at-Tayr, 43, 72
Maraş, 102, 143, 205, 221
Marj Dabiq, 14
Marmaris, 117
Marseilles, 18
Martinuzzi, 187, 207, 209
Mastaba, 102
Mecca, 14, 34, 201
   Kaaba, 14, 34, 201
Medina, 14, 34, 201
Mediterranean Sea, 14, 18, 32, 46, 47, 101, 119, 167, 177

Mehmed (şehzade), 21, 22, 33, 47, 64, 115, 156, 175, 179, 189, 193, 221
Mehmed II, 11, 16, 24, 32, 47, 86, 115, 119
Mehmed III, 32, 211
Mehmed b. Ahmed (Mehmed Çelebi), 31, 38, 40, 83
   Koran, 41
Mehmed b. Bayram, 40, 75
Mehmed Bey, 163, 183, 185
Mehmed Paşa, 19, 183
Mehmed Sinan, 36
Mehmed Şah, 36, 37, 40
Mehmed Şerif, 38, 64
   Divan-ı Muhibbi, 38, 39, 63
Melek Ahmed, 40
Melik Ümmü
   Şahname, 44
Menderes River, 117
Mengili Giray Han, 15, 207
Meriç River, 33, 34
Messina, 167
Mihrimah, 21-22, 24, 29, 33, 179
Mirza Huy-i Şirazi, 56, 60
   Şahname-i Al-i Osman, 60, 61
Mohacs, 17, 67, 127, 128, 131, 133-135, 141-149
Moldavia, 18, 177
Morea, 17, 167
Morocco, 14
Muhammed (Prophet), 28, 57, 59
Murad I, 60, 86
Murad II, 22, 24, 32, 86, 115
Murad III, 32, 48, 49
Musa (Emir), 20
Musa Abdi, 42
   Camaspname, 44
Mustafa (bookbinder), 40
Mustafa (contender), 72, 233
Mustafa (şehzade), 19, 21, 22, 33, 47, 115, 139, 156, 171, 179, 189, 196, 219, 221, 233
Mustafa Ali (Gelibolulu), 32, 37, 44
Mustafa b. Yusuf, 37
Mustafa Dede, 41
Mustafa Paşa, 16, 90, 91, 117, 119, 121

Nadiri, 47
Nahçivan (Nakhichevan), 19, 217, 225, 227
Nasuh al-Silahi al-Matraki (Matrakcı Nasuh), 32, 44, 46-47, 156
   Beyan-ı Menazil-i Sefer-i Irakeyn, 46
   Tarih-i Feth-i Siklos, Estergon, ve Estonibelgrad (Süleymanname), 46
   Tarih-i Sultan Bayezid, 46
Nebi, 37
Nice, 18
Nigari (Haydar Reis), 31, 47
Nish, 107, 115, 161, 163
Nizami, 61
   Hamse, 42, 43
Nubia, 101
Nüzhet el-Esrar el-Ahbar der Sefer-i Sigetvar, 48, 72

Orhan, 60, 86
Osman (caliph), 28, 59
Osman (painter), 72
   Nüzhet el-Esrar el-Ahbar der Sefer-i Sigetvar, 48, 72
   Tercüme-i Şahname, 72
Osman (sultan), 11, 60, 86
Otranto, 11
Ömer, 59

Painter A, 55, 56, 57, 59, 62, 66, 67, 68, 69-70, 72, 73, 74, 75, 90, 91, 94, 96, 101, 105, 107, 109, 110, 127, 128, 131, 133, 134, 135, 139, 145, 155, 161, 165, 167, 169, 173, 175, 179, 183, 187, 189, 201, 203, 207, 209, 211, 215, 217, 219, 221, 223, 225, 227, 229, 231
Painter B, 55, 56, 60, 62, 66, 72-73, 74, 75, 115, 117, 119, 121, 122, 124, 141, 143, 148, 149, 153, 159, 163, 185, 191, 192, 194, 196, 198, 205, 233
Painter C, 66, 73, 75, 156, 177
Painter D, 66, 67, 69, 73, 75, 173, 203, 215
Painter E, 66, 67, 69, 73, 75, 94, 131
Palestine, 14, 16, 101, 117
Paris, 165
Pasinabad, 225
Pecs, 18, 56, 191
Pervane, 143
Piri Mehmed Paşa, 90, 91, 107, 109, 124
Piri Reis, 15, 47
   Kitab-ı Bahriye, 32, 47
Poland, 20, 21
Portugal, 18, 177
Preveza, 18, 177
Provence, 119

Ramazanoğlu Uzun Süleyman Paşa, 187
Ravzat al-Uşak, 57, 70, 75
Red Sea, 14, 101
Reggendorf, Wilhelm von, 149, 163, 183, 185
Reşideddin (Rashid al-Din), 44
Revan (Erivan), 19
Rhodes, 14, 16, 19, 62, 72, 117, 119, 121, 122, 127, 145, 191
   Church of Saint John, 122
Ricon, Antonio, 165
Rogatino, 21
Rumania, 11, 14
Rumelia, 29, 90, 96, 145, 183, 207, 219
Rüstem Paşa, 18, 22, 24, 32, 33, 179, 192, 198, 219, 233

Sadi, 42
Salm, Nicolas von, 149, 153
Salonica, 19, 31, 175, 233
Sam Mirza, 18, 173
Sava River, 33, 107, 110, 128, 133
Schneeberg, Joseph von, 159, 163
Selçuk, 90
Selim I, 11, 14, 15, 21, 28, 32, 33, 36, 40, 47, 57, 63, 72, 86, 90, 101, 173, 201
   Divan-ı Selimi, 42
Selim II, 19, 20, 22, 23, 24, 33, 47, 48, 67, 124, 156, 175, 179, 183, 187, 192, 196, 205, 221, 223, 225
Selimname, 44, 46
Semendria, 133, 134, 135
Seydi Ali Reis, 15, 32
Seyyid Battal Gazi, 33, 196
Sigismund I, 183
Siklos, 191
Sinai Peninsula, 101
Sinan (architect), 31, 33, 49, 192, 207, 221, 229
Sinan (delil), 133
Sivas, 139, 171, 205, 217, 227
Siyasetname, 15
Sokollu Mehmed Paşa, 20, 22-23, 24, 33, 207, 209, 211, 233
Solomon, 20, 87
Somalia, 14
Sophia, 107, 128, 148, 161
Spain, 18, 119, 134, 192
Stephen, Saint, 155
Sudan, 14
Suhrab, 173
Sultan Ali, 198
Sultaniye, 171
Surname, 49
Süleyman (bookbinder), 40

Syria, 11, 14, 16, 101, 102
Szigetvar, 19, 22, 23, 48
Şahınşahname, 48
Şahkulu (Şahkulu-ı Bağdadi), 31, 36, 37, 40, 41, 55, 64
Şahname, 42, 44, 55, 62, 70
Şahname-i Al-i Osman, 47, 55, 72
Şahname-i Selim Han, 48, 72
Şahsuvar Selimi
   Divan-ı Selimi, 43
Şehdi
   Tarih-i Al-i Osman, 47
Şeyh Hamdullah
   Koran, 41
Şeyhi, 42
   Hüsrev ve Şirin, 44
Şiraz, 40, 42, 43, 61, 198
Şirin, 171
Şirvan, 18, 47, 55, 171, 173, 194
Şükrü Bitlisi
   Selimname, 44

Tabari, 44, 47
Tabriz, 14, 16, 18, 19, 37, 40, 42, 43, 61, 67, 73, 156, 171, 173, 175, 196
Tahmasp, 14-15, 17, 18, 19, 55, 67, 73, 141, 161, 173, 194, 203, 205, 215, 225, 227, 229, 231
Taht-ı Süleyman, 227
Talikizade, 47
Tarih-i Al-i Osman, 44, 47
Tarih-i Feth-i Siklos, Estergon, ve Estonibelgrad (Süleymanname), 46
Tarih-i Sultan Bayezid, 46
Tarih-i Sultan Süleyman, 48
Taşkent, 201
Taşköprülüzade Ahmed, 32, 44
Temesvar, 56, 67, 209, 211
Tercüme-i Şahname, 42, 43, 44, 72
Timur, 44
Tortum, 205
Trabzon, 11, 15
Transoxiana, 32
Transylvania, 15, 56, 134, 148, 183, 207, 211
Tunis, 18, 169
Tunisia, 14
Turgud Reis, 19
Turhan Bey, 167

Ulama Paşa, 209
Ulvi Çelebi, 42
Uşak, 35
Uzuncaabad Valley, 115

Vakfiye, 34, 64
Van, 19, 196, 205, 215
Varadin (Petrovaradin, Peterwardein), 128, 187
Vardar River, 175
Vienna, 14, 17, 20, 148, 149, 153, 155, 167, 177, 231
Villiers de l'Isle-Adam, Philippe, 119
Visoka, 46

Yahya Bey, 33
Yahya Paşa, 109
Yakut, 198
Yemen, 177
Yenice, 175
Yenişehir, 219
Yozgat, 139
Yugoslavia, 11, 14
Yusuf el-Heravi, 56, 57

Zapolya, John, 15, 17, 18, 66, 134, 148, 149, 155, 159, 167, 183
Zapolya, Stephen, 66, 183, 187, 207
Zübdet üt-Tevarih, 49

Special Acknowledgment for Reference Photographs

The author and publishers would like to express their sincere thanks to the following persons and institutions for granting permission to reproduce the photographs used as reference in this volume.

Edwin Binney, 3rd: figs. 39-41.
Freer Gallery of Art: fig. 7.
Ernst J. Grube: figs. 29-32.
Ara Güler: fig. 5.
Reha Günay: figs. 2-4.
İstanbul Üniversite Kütüphanesi: figs. 8, 10, 15, and 17.
Los Angeles County Museum of Art: fig. 28.
Private Collection: figs. 23-27.
Topkapı Sarayı Müzesi: figs. 6, 9, 11-14, 16, 18-22, 34-38.
Türk ve İslam Eserleri Müzesi: fig. 33.